Criminal Law

in

Ireland

Sean E. Quinn
B. A. (Hons), H. Dip. in Ed.,
of King's Inns,
Barrister-at-Law,
Lecturer in Law.

Second Edition

Irish Law Publishing

Seo linn sa bhearna baoil ...

To the memory

of

my parents

Ena
(Nee McLaughlin)

and

Daniel Joseph
(Joe)

Published in 1993 by Irish Law Publishing,
15 Rathclaren, Killarney, Bray, Co. Wicklow, Ireland

First Edition   1988
Paperback Edition (with Supplement)   1991

Quinn, Sean Eugene

Criminal Law in Ireland

ISBN 1 871509 08 4 Hbk.

Printed by Colour Books Ltd., Baldoyle, Co. Dublin and
bound by Duffy Bookbinders Ltd., 106 Seville Place, Dublin.

Foreword

The purpose of this text is to make available to practitioners and students a comprehensive treatment of the criminal law that applies in Ireland, in doing this there is no great treatise on any particular item. It is hoped that the user will be able to find the material sought quickly and as quickly grasp the essentials involved.

This edition is a substantial revision of the first, new material has been added which includes: new legislation, recent case law and a greater treatment of earlier legislation. A particular addition are offences that may be committed in the business and commercial area.

The archaic and foreign nature of much of the criminal law that applies in the State is inexcusable. The criminal justice system would be more effective if it reflected the Ireland of today. The legislators should give serious consideration to their responsibilities in the area of law reform.

It is regrettable that recent changes in the criminal law are the result of media hype in an emotional response to particular events (a good example is the increase in the penalty for incest). Any reform of the criminal law ought to be based upon a comprehensive plan and not effected piecemeal. Such reform should be coordinated by a body that would not be subject to the Executive who have clearly shown a lack of commitment.

I would like to thank Anne for her patience with Ena, Niall, and myself during the writing of this book.

The law is stated as known to me on the 16th April 1993.

Any errors are my own.

Sean E. Quinn

Bray
25th April 1993

Part IV Offences of a public nature

Part V Offences against the State

Part VI The administration of justice

Statutes Revised

on

Commercial Law

(1695-1913)

by

Sean E. Quinn

Published July 1992

Statutes Revised on Commercial Law gathers together in one volume thirty four commercial law statutes, from the the year 1695 to the year 1913. It gives a revised form of the statutes at your fingertips.

The text of each statute consists of the original text with the additions and omissions rendered necessary by subsequent legislation up to and including 16th April 1992.

A table of amendments precedes the text of the statutes. The table is a detailed listing of all amendments and may be used as a quick reference to find out whether a statute has been amended.

Within the text of each statute there are references to footnotes, which elaborate upon any amendments.

To order a copy see end pages

Contents

Part I Crime

Part II Offences against the person

Part IV   Offences of a public nature

Chapter 26   Road traffic offences

Part V Offences against the State

Table of constitutional provisions

Constitution of Ireland

Statutes Revised
on
Commercial Law

(1695-1913)

* First book on statutory revision made available in the State
* All amendments up to and including 16th April 1992
* Table of Amendments for quick and easy reference
* The principle statutes on commercial law in one volume
* An essential reference to commercial law in Ireland

The text of each statute consists of the original text with the additions and omissions rendered necessary by subsequent legislation,

for example:

Statute of Frauds, 1695 as amended by:
> Wills Act, 1837
> Statute Law Revision (pre-Union Irish Statutes) Act, 1962
> Succession Act, 1965

Bills of Exchange Act, 1882 as amended by:
> Statute Law Revision Act, 1898
> Bills of Exchange (Time of Noting) Act, 1917
> Cheque Act, 1959
> Decimal Currency Act, 1970
> Central Bank Act, 1989
> ACC Bank Act, 1992

Hardback, A 5 size, set in 11 point Times (footnotes 10 point), 372+xxxxiv pages, printed on 90 gms. matt paper, sewn and case-bound in red rexine cloth, with gold block on spine, PRINTED and BOUND in IRELAND.

Table of Statutes

Table of Statutes

Table of Statutes

Table of Statutes

Table of Statutes

Table of Statutes

Trace

your

Irish Ancestors

by

Sean E. Quinn

Published June 1989

A guide to the basic records for genealogical research:

> **Census Returns**
> **Civil Registers**
> **Parish Registers**
> **Primary Valuation**
> **Tithe Books**

and the genealogical repositories that hold such records:

> **National Library of Ireland**
> **National Archives**
> **Public Records Office, Belfast**
> **Registrar-Generals Office's**
> **Registry of Deeds**
> also
> **Other important repositories**

together with:

> **Distribution of Surnames for each County**

£8.50 Hbk or £4.95 Pbk (64 pp)

ISBN 1 871509 02 5 Hardback
ISBN 1 871509 03 3 Paperback

Available from: Sean E. Quinn, 15 Rathclaren, Bray, Co. Wicklow

Table of Cases

The abbreviations
> *"R V"*
> *"A. G. V"*
> *"D. P. P. V"*
> *"The People V" and*
> *"The State V"*

are omitted in the following table

Abbreviations:

IR	Irish Reports
ILRM	Irish Law Reports Monthly
ILTR	Irish Law Times Reports
ILT	Irish Law Times
AER	All England Law Reports
KB / QB	Kings Bench / Queens Bench
WLR	Weekly Law Reports

Table of Cases

xlv

Table of Cases

Chapter 1

Introduction

Criminal law is concerned with the interaction of the criminal justice system and those acts or omissions which are known as crimes. It is not possible to construct a scientific definition of criminal law, for there is no logical test as to whether an act is or is not a crime. The only means of determining this question is by reference to precedents or Acts of Parliament.

Public law

Criminal law is a branch of "public law", i.e. that law which is concerned with the relationship of members of the community with the State, other examples of public law are constitutional law and administrative law. Private Law is concerned with the relationship of members of the community with each other, it includes: the law of contract; law of tort; law of real property and family law.

Public wrong

The difference between a crime and a tort is that while they are both wrongs, a crime is a public wrong and a tort is a private wrong. In the case of a private wrong, it is for the injured party to initiate legal proceedings on his own behalf for the purpose of compensating him or restoring him to the position in which, but for the injury, he would have been. He may at any time after the institution of legal proceedings abandon or compromise his claim.

Whenever a public wrong has been committed, then whether or not it involves a civil wrong, the offender becomes liable to punishment by the State, not for the purpose of compensation to anyone who may have been injured but as a penalty for the crime and in order to deter the offender and others.

Definition

A crime may be defined as an act or omission forbidden by the State, which is punishable after due process of law. There are thus three essentials of a crime; firstly that it is a harm, brought about by human act or omission, which the State desires to prevent; secondly that punishment is a method of prevention which may involve imprisonment, fine, community service, and compensation order; thirdly that legal proceedings are employed to decide whether the accused did cause the harm, and is according to law to be punished for doing so.

What makes an act criminal ?

The criminal law has evolved over many centuries (see below). The reason why certain acts are crimes and other acts are deemed not to be so is something which is beyond the scope of this book. It would not be

1

easy to identify definite principles that make acts or omissions crimes. Certain acts which were criminal in the past are no longer so, certain acts which are now crimes were not so in the past and no doubt many acts which are not crimes at present will be deemed to be so in the future.

The established offences against the person, property and the State appear to fit easily into the notion of what are crimes, many criminal law books in the past have concentrated solely on the those type of offences. Road traffic and misuse of drugs offences are now finding their way into criminal law books, they are dealt with here as they were in the first edition and are added to with a consideration of offences under the Companies Acts.

Those acts (or omissions) that are deemed to be criminal are evolving with society itself. A developing society strives for order and regulation, which regulates persons in their public lives. The private lives of persons, being subject to public order and morality (as per the Constitution) are matters for themselves and the imposition of a moral behaviour on persons by society has not proven itself successful. In the future the protection of person (singly and collectively) may dictate which acts become criminal.

Punishment

As noted punishment is a method for the prevention of crime. Punishment may take a number of forms: imprisonment, fine; forfeiture, or community service. In the case of imprisonment a person when convicted may be sentenced to penal servitude (which was introduced as a substitute for transportation by the Penal Servitude Act, 1857, section 2), imprisonment, or imprisonment with or without hard labour. There is now no practical distinction in the treatment of prisoners based on the type of imprisonment that they have received. A sentence of penal servitude may only be imposed by statutory authority (see *State (Jones) V O'Donovan (1973)*), a sentence of penal servitude may only be imposed for a term of not less than 3 years nor more than 7 years. It has been held that no one should be required to suffer imprisonment with hard labour, which can only be imposed by statutory authority, and should be specified in the sentence, for a continuous period exceeding 2 years (see *A. G. V Duffy (1931)*). There is no limit at common law to the term of simple imprisonment that might be imposed.

The Prevention of Crimes Act, 1908 makes provision that juvenile offenders (those between 17 and 20 years of age) may be given detention in St. Patricks Institution in lieu of imprisonment; a young person (those between 15 and 17 years of age) may be given detention in exceptional circumstance. A child (between 7 and 15 years of age) may be sent to a reformatory or an industrial school.

The Courts (No. 2) Act, 1986 at section 2 provides:

(1) Where on summary conviction a fine is imposed a court may order that, in default of due payment of the fine, the person liable to pay the fine shall be imprisoned for a term not exceeding the appropriate period

specified in the following scale:

not exceeding £50	5 days
exceeding £50 but not exceeding £250	15 days
exceeding £250 but not exceeding £500	15 days
exceeding £500	90 days

Approach to punishment

Factors which influence the imposition of imprisonment:

(a) the imprisonment of an offender restricts him in repeating an offence and protects the public (incapacitation).

(b) an offender and potential offenders may be less likely to offend for fear of imprisonment (deterrent).

(c) after a term of imprisonment an offender might become a reformed person (rehabilitation).

(d) a desire on the part of society and the victims of crime for vengeance (retribution).

The Supreme Court has stressed the importance of rehabilitation:

People (A. G.) V O'Driscoll (1972)

It was held by the Supreme Court that the object of imposing sentence is not merely to deter but also to induce the criminal to turn to an honest life.

People (D. P. P.) V Conroy (1989)

It was held by the Supreme Court as one of the objects of the court in passing sentence must be the inducement of an accused to turn to an honest life, the possibility of his rehabilitation can be taken into account.

There is at the present time much talk of victim support. The programme of government (referred to below) stresses the need for a requirement that the impact on the victim be taken into account before sentencing.

The Criminal Justice Act, 1993, at section 5 provides that in determining sentence a court shall take into account any effect on the victim and by section 6(1) gives courts a general power to require offenders to pay compensation to the victim for any resulting personal injury or loss. The power is to be exercised unless the court sees reason to the contrary.

Law Reform Commission

The Law Reform Commission in a consultation paper published in March 1993 has made a number of provisional recommendations in this area. The commission recommends that the legislature formulate in statutory form a coherent policy governing sentencing and set out by way of statute a clear statement that the sentence to be imposed on an offender be determined by reference to the "just deserts" principle of distribution; whereby the severity of the sentence be measured in proportion to the seriousness of the offending behaviour and that the sentence be no more severe than the sentence for more serious offending behaviour nor less severe than the sentence for less serious offending behaviour.

Sources of law

The sources of criminal law in Ireland are:

      (a) Common law as it developed in England,

      (b) Statutes of various parliaments, and

      (b) Statutes of the Oireachtas.

Common law

Blackstone writing in 1765 stated "the chief cornerstone of the laws of England which is general and immemorial custom, or common law, from time to time declared in the decisions of the courts of justice; which decisions are preserved among our public records, explained in our reports, and digested for general use in the authoritative writings of the venerable sages of the law".

The common law as it came to be applied in Ireland, was largely unaffected by the establishment of the Irish Free State, as the pace of legislative change is slower in Ireland than in England, the common law is today more intact in Ireland than in England.

Parliaments of Ireland

In 1210 King John came to Ireland, before his departure he compelled the Cambro-Norman lords in Ireland to swear that they would observe the laws and customs of England in Ireland, the Parliament of Ireland dates from this period. From earliest times the parliament had difficulties exercising its powers, it was restricted by "Poynings' Law" of 1494 and later the "Sixth of George I" passed in 1720 by the British parliament.

The legislative curbs on the Parliament of Ireland gave rise to opposition amongst the ascendancy classes throughout the eighteenth century. The establishment of the Volunteers following the American War of Independence eventually led to the successful assertion by Grattan of the independence of the Irish Parliament on the 16th April 1782.

The independent Irish Parliament did not last long after the French Revolution and the United Irishmen. The Government bought itself a majority in the Parliament and on the 28th March 1800, an Act of Union between Great Britain and Ireland was finally accepted. On 2nd August 1800, the Parliament of Ireland met for the last time.

The Parliaments of the United Kingdom of Great Britain and Ireland sitting from 1801 to 1922, sought to reform and codify much of the criminal law. Today in Ireland a large proportion of the offence against the person and property date from that period of change.

The following statutes still have application in Ireland:

      Dublin Police Act, 1842

      Town Improvement (Ireland) Act, 1854

      Accessories and Abettors Act, 1861

      Larceny Act, 1861

      Malicious Damage Act, 1861

      Forgery Act, 1861

Introduction

Offences Against the Person Act, 1861
False Personation Act, 1874
Explosive Substances Act, 1875
Falsification of Accounts Act, 1875
Customs Consolidation Act, 1876
Criminal Law Amendment Act, 1885
Punishment of Incest Act, 1908
Post Office Act, 1908
Forgery Act, 1913
Prevention of Corruption Act, 1916
Larceny Act, 1916

They have been replaced and updated in England.

The Oireachtas

The Constitution of Saorstát Éireann was enacted by Dáil Éireann on 25th October 1922 sitting as a Constituent Assembly. It provided that the laws in force at the date of the coming into operation of the Constitution would continue to be in force and effect until the same, be repealed or amended by the Oireachtas.

The Constitution of Ireland came into effect on 29th December 1937. Article 50.1 states "Subject to this Constitution and to the extent to which they are not inconsistent therewith, the laws in force in Saorstát Éireann ... shall continue to be of full force and effect until the same or any of them shall have been repealed or amended by enactment of the Oireachtas." The Oireachtas where it has introduced legislative changes, has tended to copy that which has taken place in the current United Kingdom parliaments, there are many examples of this to be found in the text. In addition and because of similar statutory provision, English case law is very persuasive despite the existence of the Constitution.

Hence the criminal law that applies in Ireland (twenty-six counties) may not be described as Irish criminal law, for it consists in large measure of the common law of England together with the many statutes passed prior to the establishment of the Irish Free State. The criminal justice system that applies in Ireland is not Irish, its origins are to be found in a system which was imposed over the centuries.

Future developments

The introduction of the Code napoleon in 1804 and its later spread throughout continental Europe, encouraged the codification of criminal law. The codification of criminal law, was seriously considered in England later in the century. In 1878 a Criminal Code Bill was introduced in parliament; it was reintroduced in 1879 after it had been recast by a committee of judges, and again in 1880, with a few further alterations. Had the Bill been passed it would have recast the law in a briefer and more precise shape. Many reforms have been effected piecemeal in England since. In 1985 in England the Law Commission issued a report which contained a draft of the projected criminal code.

Introduction

The Government of Ireland appointed in July 1989 had in its programme for government declared itself in favour of the codification of the criminal law, yet no moves were ever made in this direction.

The Government of Ireland appointed in January 1993 has committed itself to law reform and in its Programme for Government stated:

"We will also bring forward a comprehensive programme of criminal law reform".

As part of the programme it is proposed to:

Bring forward legislation providing for the review of unduly lenient sentences, ...

Revise and strengthen the law on serious fraud and on offences of dishonesty generally, ...

Introduce a modern juvenile justice bill;

Introduce legislation to deal with street crime;

Update the legislation on offences against the person, including more appropriate sentencing for the use of weapons;

Revise the law relating to fines and provide for their indexation;

Clarify the law on powers of arrest and abolish the out-dated division of crimes into felonies and misdemeanours.

Reform the outdated law on insanity as a defence, and introduce a new defence of diminished responsibility; and

Legislation will be introduced in 1993 to bring our law into conformity with the European Convention on Human Rights.

On the 3rd March 1993 the Minister for Justice stated in the Dail that: "I have a substantial programme of criminal law reform under way in the Department".

Future developments in the area of criminal law in Ireland will be influenced by moves towards European integration. In 1989 the Court of Justice of the European Communities in the *Greek Maize* case ruled that the Treaties impose duties on the Member States in the area of criminal law.

The level of fraud against the funds of the European Communities has led to an examination of the criminal law of Member States to see whether a contribution could be made in combating such fraud by revising the criminal law.

The European Convention on Human Rights will be fundamental to the development of a European criminal law, in addition within the civil law system that applies on the continent the concept of codification is paramount.

The proposed Treaty on European Union of 1991 at Title I further enhances the European Convention on Human Rights; Title V deals with security policy and Title VI deals with cooperation in the fields of justice and home affairs. This treaty if it is proceeded with will see the development of a European criminal law applicable in Ireland. The strong influence of E. E. C. Directives in the Companies Acts will be noted later in the text.

6

Chapter 2

Criminal responsibility

Actus non facit reum nisi mens sit rea
This maxim in translation means "an act does not make a man guilty of a crime, unless his mind be also guilty." It draws attention to, the two essential elements of a criminal offence and means that a criminal act must be accompanied by a criminal state of mind. The mental element of a crime is described as the *mens rea* and the other elements as the *actus reus*. If there was no *actus reus* or if an accused had no *mens rea* at the time of the *actus reus* then he must be acquitted, unless *mens rea* is expressly or impliedly excluded by the definition of the offence. It is convenient to consider the mental and physical elements of a crime separately.

Actus reus
The *actus reus* is the necessary act which must have been committed for the crime to be proved. The act includes conduct, its result and the surrounding circumstances. It is this conduct which together with the *mens rea* makes the crime.
Examples of such conduct would be:
(a) a physical act, as in moving the body e.g. assault;
(b) words, as in incitement, conspiracy, or blackmail;
(c) an omission, as can result in manslaughter, or misprision of felony;
(d) possession, as in the case of articles for housebreaking, explosives, controlled drugs, firearms, offensive weapons, or of seditious documents;
(e) a state of affairs;
(f) conduct of others as in vicarious liability, see below.

Actus reus of various offences
Consider what the *actus reus* is in a number of offences:

Assault of a peace officer in due execution of his duty (Offences against the Person Act, 1861, section 38)
The *actus reus* is:
      (i) assault,
      (ii) upon a peace officer,
      (iii) in the execution of his duty.
Thus to assault your next door neighbour, whom you dislike intensely who happens to be a member of an Garda Siochana as he arrives home from work is not this offence. Ingredient (iii) is missing.

Bigamy (Offences against the Person Act, 1861, section 57)
The *actus reus* is:
      (i) accused must 'marry' another,
      (ii) while married.

If the wife of an accused had died unbeknown to him the day before the ceremony, he will not have committed bigamy. Ingredient (ii) is missing.

Defilement of a girl under seventeen years (Criminal Law Amendment Act, 1935, section 2)

The *actus reus* is
        (i) carnal knowledge
        (ii) girl under 17 years of age

If a man has carnal knowledge of a girl, whom he believes to be 16 years, though she was in fact 17, he does not commit this offence. Ingredient (ii) is missing.

There are various offences which may require other ingredients:
        (i) committed by a particular class of persons (clerk or servant)
        (ii) against property of a certain kind (postal packets)
        (iii) without a person's consent (rape, stealing)
        (iv) in a dwelling-house (Larceny Act, 1916, section 13))
        (v) certain relationship (incest)

Causation

Where a criminal offence requires specific consequences of certain conduct it must be established that such consequences have been caused by the accused person.

Consider the following cases:

R V Michael (1840)

The accused intending to murder a child, gave laudanum to the child's nurse so that it would be administered as a medicine. The nurse decided not to administer it, later however her five year old daughter did administer it and the child died. The accused was convicted of murder.

R V White (1910)

The accused put cyanide into his mother's drink intending to kill her. She was found dead later having sipped from the glass, but medical evidence showed that she died from a heart attack and not the poison. The accused was found guilty of attempted murder.

See oblique intention below and also Chapter 6 on Homicide.

Mens rea

Mens rea is the essential mental element of a criminal offence, without it anyone who caused the *actus reus* would be guilty of the offence. *Mens rea* originated in the idea that a person should not be liable to be punished for a crime unless he was morally blameworthy. At common law *mens rea* is always required for an offence (though see below), in the case of an offence created by statute, unless the statute specifically rules out *mens rea*, the courts will hold that *mens rea* is required, because of the principle that, the interpretation of the statute which is most favourable to the accused must be adopted.

As an example consider again the offence of bigamy (at page 293): it is an offence for a person being married to marry another during the lifetime of their husband or wife. The *actus reus* of bigamy is complete if a person marries another while married, however an accused will be acquitted for lack of *mens rea* if the accused taught that a spouse was dead.

As a general rule a person will not be held criminally liable for one crime, even though he may have committed another.

In practicality a person will not be liable for an act or omission unless:

(i) his conduct was voluntary,
(ii) he knew what he was doing,
(iii) he foresaw the particular consequences of certain offences

It is possible to distinguish between a number of different mental attitudes which an accused may have in respect of the offence charged:

Motive

Any motive that a person may have for the commission of a crime is not relevant, be it good or bad. It may however be relevant, as circumstantial evidence, or in deciding punishment on conviction.

R V Hicklin (1868)

The defendant was convicted of having in his possession copies of an obscene book. On appeal his conviction was quashed on the ground that the books were not kept by the defendant for gain nor to prejudice good morals. By way of case stated it was held, that although the motive of the defendant was an honest one nevertheless he had the intention which constituted the criminality of the act.

Intention

Intention as it has been interpreted by the courts may be considered of two types.

(a) direct Intention where a person desires to bring about a certain objective and subsequently tries to bring about that objective.

(b) oblique Intention where a person desires to bring about a certain objective and in order to bring about that objective, he must do something else which he does not desire to do.

Recklessness

Reckless as to whether or not a result is to be caused is sufficient. A person who does not intend to cause a particular result may take an unjustifiable risk of causing it and if he does so, he may be held to be reckless, however not all risk-taking constitutes recklessness.

Negligence

Negligence has a narrow application in the area of criminal law. In this case the test is objective; would a reasonable man have realised that there was some risk involved.

Blameless inadvertence

A person may reasonably fail to foresee the harm that would follow from his actions.

In general, in order to establish the criminal responsibility of an accused for an offence at common law. It must be shown; that the conduct contributed to the *actus reus*; and that the accused foresaw at the time of that conduct that it would result in consequences, including those which did occur.

Exclusion of *mens rea*

There are two categories of cases from which the requirement of *mens rea* is excluded:

(a) statutory offences involving what is called strict liability; and

(b) statutory offences committed by a servant (employee) in the course of carrying out his master's (employer's) duties, which were not authorised and where vicarious liability (see below) attaches to the master.

Strict liability

If *mens rea* need not be proved in respect of one or more elements of the *actus reus* of an offence, that offence is one of strict liability. In the case of an offence of strict liability it must be proved that the *actus reus* was the result of voluntary conduct on the part of an accused.

Offences of strict liability are strict, but they are not absolute and the general defences that there are available to a person charged with any other criminal offence are available equally on a charge of an offence of strict liability. If an offence is one of absolute liability involuntary conduct on the part of an accused will not be a defence.

There is a presumption that *mens rea*, is an essential element in every offence. The presumption of *mens rea* is liable to be displaced by the words of a statute creating an offence, or by the subject matter with which the offence deals. A statute may contain words, such as "knowingly", "maliciously" or "wilfully", which suggest *mens rea*. Where a statute is silent as to *mens rea*, the presumption that it is required may be rebutted.

The following cases illustrate the position:

Woodrow (1846)

The accused was found guilty of having in his possession adulterated tobacco, although he did not know that it was adulterated. The statute was for the protection of the revenue and there was absent from it "knowingly" or any similar words.

R V Prince (1875)

Prince took an unmarried girl under sixteen years out of the possession and against the will of her father and mother (section 55 of the Offences against the Persons Act, 1861 at page 84). The girl looked much older and the jury found that she had told Prince that she was eighteen, that he *bona fide* believed her, and that his belief was reasonable. It was held on appeal that a reasonable belief that a girl was over sixteen was no defence to the charge.

To be contrasted with:

R V Hibbert (1869)

The accused took a fourteen year old girl off the street to another place and had sexual intercourse with her. He was acquitted of the offence under section 55 as it was not proved that he knew the girl to be in the custody of her father; *mens rea* was required as to this element.

R V Bishop (1880)

The accused advertised in the newspapers for patients suffering from "hysteria, nervousness and perverseness" and received into her house several young women so described, who were in fact lunatics. She was convicted of receiving lunatics into her house, it not being an asylum or hospital registered under the Act (Lunatics Act, 1845). An honest belief on the part of the accused that the women were no lunatics was not material.

Cundy V LeCocq (1884)

A licensed victualler, had sold liquor to a drunken person, in contravention of the Licensing Act, 1872, section 13. He was convicted despite a *bona fide* mistake as to the condition of the person served.

The instances where offences of strict liability can arise are:

(a) acts which may not be considered criminal in any real sense, but are acts which in the public interest are prohibited under a penalty;

(b) public nuisances;

(c) case in which although the proceedings are criminal in form, it is really only a summary mode of enforcing a civil right;

(d) where the courts in their construction of a statute have regard to what can be seen as a danger to society in the offence charged, the greater the degree of danger the more likely is the offence to be interpreted as one of strict liability.

Apart from the examples of strict liability at common law above, many offences of strict liability are created by statute. The Misuse of Drugs Acts, the Road Traffic Acts and the Offences against the State Acts, contain examples of such offences. The drastic effects of a statute imposing strict liability is often offset by, the same statutes providing statutory defences, i.e. section 29 of the Misuse of Drugs Act 1977, at page 253.

Vicarious liability

Vicarious liability arises where a person is held legally responsible for the wrongful acts of another. A person may be held liable for the acts of another, where he has delegated to him the performance of certain duties imposed on himself by statute; or in an employment situation a master may be held liable because acts which are done by a servant, may in law be deemed the acts of the master.

Where there has been a general delegation of authority by a master to

his servant, the master will generally be liable for the servant's infringements of a statute which concerns the running of a business.
Allen V Whitehead (1930)

The respondent was the occupier and licensee of a refreshment house which was open day and night. He employed a manager on eight consecutive nights, women known by the manager to be prostitutes, had been to the refreshment house and had remained there contrary to the respondent's instructions, given after a previous warning by the police. The respondent though he rarely visited the refreshment house and was unaware of what had taken place was convicted under the Metropolitan Police Act, 1839, with knowingly permitting or suffering prostitutes in a place where refreshments are sold and consumed.

Where there has been a delegation of authority it must be complete:
O'Reilly V Keatinge (1971)

A motor vehicle belonging to the accused was stationary in Meath Street, Dublin and his brother who was in charge of the vehicle, sold ice-cream to passers-by. The accused was charged with engaging in a form of stall trading, without holding a street traders licence, contrary to the Street Trading Act, 1926. It was held that the defendant as the seller in law contravened the statute.

At common law there is no general principle that a master is vicariously liable for a crime committed by his servant:
R V Huggins (1730)

A prison warden had been charged with the murder of a prisoner. The death had been caused by his servant without his knowledge. He was acquitted
Devlin V Nugent (1942)

The accused was charged with permitting intoxicating liquor to be consumed at his hotel premises at a time prohibited by the Intoxicating Liquor Act, 1927. The drink had been supplied and served by the hall porter, without knowledge or permission of the accused. The drink that was supplied was from a receptacle used by the night porter, and the hall porter had no authority or permission, except when acting as the night porter, to take drink from the receptacle. The accused was not convicted.

An exception to this general rule is the offence of public nuisance, the objection of the law being to prevent the nuisance from being continued:
R V Stephens (1866)

An accused was held liable for the obstruction by his servants of the navigation of a public river by depositing rubbish therein.
Evening Standard Case (1954)

An inaccurate report of the evidence of a criminal trial was telephoned in by a reporter and the defendant newspaper published it. It was held that the newspaper was liable for contempt.

It may also be that vicarious liability extends at common law to charge of criminal libel against the proprietor of newspaper in respect of libels published by his servants, section 7 of the Libel Act, 1843 provided a defence where such a publication was made without authority.

There is no vicarious liability for attempting to commit an offence, or for the aiding or abetting of an offence.

Innocence of an accused

It is a cardinal principle of the criminal law that a person is presumed innocent until proven guilty. It follows from this principle that in a criminal trial the burden of proof is on the prosecution to prove their case beyond a reasonable doubt.

Woolmington V Director of Public Prosecutions (1935)

Viscount Sankey L.J. ". Throughout the web of the English criminal law one golden thread is always to be seen, that it is the duty of the prosecution to prove the prisoner's guilt, subject to matters as to the defence of insanity and subject also to any statutory exceptions. If, at the end of, and on the whole of, the case there is a reasonable doubt, created by the evidence given by either prosecution or the prisoner, whether the prisoner killed the deceased with malicious intention, the prosecution has not made out the case, and the prisoner is entitled to an acquittal. ..."

People V McMahon (1946)

In the Court of Criminal Appeal, Maguire P. in reference to the Woolmington case stated; " The court is of opinion that this principle is a true one, and as applicable as to the facts of this case, imposes on the prosecution the necessity of negativing every supposition consistent with the innocence of the accused."

The principle is subject to modification during the course of a criminal trial, whenever the defence is one of insanity (See: *People V Hayes (1967)* above), or because the definition of the crime so enacts, or one of the matters to be proved lies peculiarly within the knowledge of the defendant.

The onus of proof has been shifted by statute in a number of instances; the Road Traffic Act, 1961, section 38 (at page 227) which prohibits driving without a driving licence, presumes until the contrary is proven by the defendant, that he did not hold a driving licence.

Facts peculiarly within the knowledge of a party:

People (A. G.) V Shribman and Samuels (1946)

The accused were charged with conspiring to export certain articles without a licence such as was required by the Emergency Powers (Control of Export) Order, 1940. The Court of Criminal Appeal held that the existence of a licence was a matter peculiarly within the knowledge of the accused.

Where a plea of self-defence is raised the onus is still the prosecution to prove guilt beyond reasonable doubt, there is no question of an accused having to establish his defence in such a way to raise a doubt as to his guilt.

People (A. G.) V Quinn (1965)

Walsh J. stated in the Supreme Court "..the only question the jury has to consider is whether they are satisfied beyond reasonable doubt that the accused killed the deceased (if it be a case of homicide) and whether the jury is satisfied beyond reasonable doubt that the prosecution has negatived the issue of self-defence. If the jury is not satisfied beyond reasonable doubt on both of these matters the accused may be acquitted."

People (A. G.) V Byrne (1974)

It was held by the Court of Criminal Appeal that, it is essential that the jury should be told that the accused is entitled to the benefit of any doubt and that where two views on a matter are justified, they should adopt the view which is favourable to the accused, unless the prosecution has established the conflicting view beyond reasonable doubt

Chapter 3

Classification of crimes

At common law crimes are classified as the major offences of felonies or misdemeanours, to which are added minor offences which may be tried summarily. Most offences are the creation of statute and it was the practise that they be classified according to their degree of importance.

In the early days of the common law the word "crime" applied generally to any illegal act which entailed criminal punishment, but was usually applied in the narrower sense to an act that was punishable on indictment.

The word "offence" also meant an illegal action, but was usually confined to an act punishable on summary conviction. As will be noted below the indictable and the non-indictable overlap to some extent and are no longer exclusive of each other. In view of the drafting practise referred to in the following paragraph, the words "crime" and "offence" are used interchangeably.

The distinction between those crimes that are classed as either felonies or misdemeanours has become unclear, the modern practise in the creation of offences, is to refer simply to an "offence" and a distinction is made as between punishment on conviction on indictment, and punishment on summary conviction. It is also the practice that where an older statute is being amended, the crime that was previously classified as either a felony or a misdemeanour is declared to be an "offence", e.g. Explosive Substances Act, 1883, section 3, at page 326.

In the past all felonies and most misdemeanours? were triable only on indictment, now by the Criminal Justice Act, 1951, section 2 (at page 346) many lesser felonies and misdemeanours may be dealt with summarily in the District Court.

The procedural classification into indictable offences and summary offences is a useful measure of the gravity with which an offence is viewed by society.

Felonies
In the early days of the common law all crimes were felonies (treason the most serious of felonies was in a separate category, see chapter 34), for which the punishment was death and forfeiture of all property. Thus the convicted felon and his family both suffered.

The felonies at common law were added to by statute. Examples of felonies are: murder, manslaughter, burglary, larceny, bigamy and rape. There is a wider power of arrest without warrant in respect of felonies. As time passed the punishment in respect of felonies became less severe.

Misdemeanours
The common law judges, in order to avoid the harshness of the death penalty in the case of felonies, created a lesser class of offence known as

15

a misdemeanour. The penalty for a misdemeanour at common law has been either fine or imprisonment without limitation of period or amount.

In addition to offences having evolved as misdemeanours at common law, offences have been declared to be so by statute. "assault" is a misdemeanour at common law, while "malicious wounding" is declared to be a misdemeanour in section 20 of the Offences against the Person Act, 1861. There is no maximum punishment for a misdemeanour, and there are felonies which are subject to a lessor penalty than some misdemeanours, there are many examples in the Larceny Act, 1916.

Distinction between felonies and misdemeanours

A felony differed from a misdemeanour in that:

(1) In the past, all felonies produced a forfeiture; whilst no misdemeanours did. All forfeiture for felony and treason were abolished by the section 1 of the Forfeiture Act, 1870, which provided: No confession, verdict, inquest, conviction,or judgment of or for any treason or felony or *felo de se* shall cause any attainder or corruption of blood, or any forfeiture or escheat, provided that nothing in this Act shall affect the law of forfeiture consequent upon outlawry.

(2) In the past all felonies except "petty" larceny, (see page 110) were punished with death; whilst no misdemeanour was.

(3) Where a felony has been committed any person, who reasonably suspects any other of being the felon may arrest him.

(4) A person seeing a felony being committed, is required to arrest the felon. If a person makes no attempt to arrest a felon it is misprision of felony (see page 22)

(5) Where a person is convicted of a felony, he loses his public office, or pension, cannot vote in an election, or sit in the Oireachtas, until he is pardoned or worked out his sentence.

(6) Civil proceedings may not be instituted for loss or damage arising out of the commission of a felony, until the criminal proceedings are completed.

(7) Where a felon is killed as a felon the excuse of justification is available.

(8) In the case of felonies only, the distinction is drawn between the four classes of participation in a crime.

Minor offence

The Constitution at Article 38.2 provides that:

Minor offences may be tried by courts of summary jurisdiction. The Constitution does not go on to define a minor offence, nor has the Oireachtas legislated as to the meaning of a minor offence, however, it is clearly an offence to be dealt with otherwise than by a court sitting with a jury.

It follows then that minor offences may be sought amongst those many offences which are triable summarily before the District Court.

The courts have considered the question: what are minor offences and how they are to be distinguished from the non-minor offences.

Melling V O'Mathghamhna (1962)

The Supreme Court was of the view that the punishment an offence might attract was a criterion for deciding whether or not an offence is minor.

Conroy V Attorney General (1965)

It was held that the making of a disqualification order under the section 26 of the Road Traffic Act, 1961, was not a punishment.

Kostan V Ireland (1978)

It was held that the forfeiture of fish and gear, which might be worth up to £100,000 was not minor.

L'Henryenat V Attorney General (1983)

It was held by the High Court that the existence of a penalty involving a forfeiture of property does not, *per se*, remove the corresponding offence from the category of minor offences.

State (Rollinson) V James (1984)

It was held by the Supreme Court that, a penalty of £500 as laid down by the Finance Act, 1926 did not make an offence non-minor.

In both the Melling and the Conroy case the Supreme Court have been prepared to accept imprisonment of up to six months as being a minor punishment. The other Melling criteria for considering whether or not an offence is minor are; the moral guilt involved, the state of the law when the Constitution was enacted, and public opinion at the time of that enactment.

Cartmill V Ireland (1988)

It was held by Murphy J. in the High Court:

(1) In determining whether an offence is of a minor or major nature, the only punishment which must be examined is that which must be referred to as "primary punishment", i.e., punishment in the ordinary sense, be it a custodial sentence or the intentional penal deprivation of property whether by means of fine or other direct method of deprivation. Other punitive and unpleasant consequences flowing from a conviction, such as the loss of a licence to carry on business or the forfeiture of equipment in connection with that business, however drastic the effect, even on the very livelihood of the convicted person, are too remote in character to be considered in weighing the seriousness of an offence by the punishment it may attract.

(2) The test whether the particular offence is major or minor will normally depend on the effective penalty validly imposed.

(3) It is not necessary in all cases to await the decision of the District Justice before forming an opinion of the seriousness or otherwise of the offence concerned. For example, a mandatory or maximum penalty laid down by the legislature will constitute a reliable guide as to the minor or major nature of that offence.

Chapter 4

Criminal participation and association

Participation in a crime

At common law four degrees of participation in a felony exist:
- (a) a principal in the first degree;
- (b) a principal in the second degree;
- (c) an accessory before the fact;
- (d) an accessory after the fact.

Participants of any degree may be termed "accomplices". There is now little practical importance to the distinctions between the first three of these four classes of accomplices. The punishment for any particular offence is the same in the case of all three classes, the older common law rules that distinguished between them have been removed by statute.

The only important surviving difference between the various degrees of participation in a crime is in the case of an accessory after the fact. It will be seen in subsequent chapters, that in respect of particular offences, there is often particular provision in relation to accessories.

The Accessories and Abettors Act, 1861, was the statute that swept away the old common law rules in respect of accomplices:

Accessories before the fact indictable as principals s. 1
Whosoever shall become an accessory before the fact to any felony, whether the same be a felony at common law or by virtue of any act passed or to be passed, may be indicted, tried, convicted, and punished in all respects as if he were a principal felon.

Accessories before the fact s. 2
Whosoever shall, counsel, procure, or command any other person to commit any felony, whether the same be a felony at common law or by virtue of any act passed or to be passed, shall be guilty of felony, and may be indicted and convicted either as an accessory before the fact to the principal felony, together with the principal felon, or after the conviction of the principal felon, or may be indicted and convicted of a substantive felony whether the principal felon shall or shall not have been previously convicted, or shall or shall not be amenable to justice, and thereupon be punished in the same manner as any accessory before the fact to the same felony, if convicted as an accessory, may be punished.

Accessory after the fact s. 3
Whosoever shall become an accessory after the fact to any felony, whether the same be a felony at common law or by virtue of any act passed or to be passed, may be indicted and convicted either as an

18

accessory after the fact to the principal felony, together with the principal felon, or after the conviction of the principal felon, or may be indicted and convicted of a substantive felony whether the principal felon shall or shall not have been previously convicted or shall or shall not be amenable to justice, and may thereupon punished in like manner as any accessory after the fact to the same felony, if convicted as an accessory, may be punished.

Punishment of Accessories after the fact s. 4

Every accessory after the fact to any felony (except where it is otherwise specially enacted), whether the same be a felony at common law or by virtue of any act passed or to be passed, shall be liable, at the discretion of the court, to be imprisoned ...for any term not exceeding two years ..

Prosecution of Accessory after Principal has been convicted s. 5

If any principal offender shall be in anywise convicted of any felony, it shall be lawful to proceed against any accessory, either before or after the fact, in the same manner as if such principal felon had been attained thereof, ...

Abettors in Misdemeanours s. 8

Whosoever shall aid, abet, counsel, or procure the commission of any misdemeanour, whether the same be a misdemeanour at common law or by virtue of any act passed or to be passed, shall be liable to be tried, indicted and punished as a principal offender.

Principal in the first degree

A principal in the first degree is the actual perpetrator of the offence. It is not necessary that a principal in the first degree be present when the offence takes place, nor is it necessary that the act be carried out by his own hand, the felony may be committed by the hand of an innocent agent.
R V Manley

If a person sends a six year old child into a shop to steal something for him, that person and not the child is the principal in the first degree in this theft.

An animal may be employed as an innocent agent, anyone who sets a dog on people is himself guilty of assaulting them, so a person who sends a trained dog to purloin meat from a butcher's stall, might be convicted of the larceny of the meat, as a principal in the first degree; even though he were out of sight when the dog took it.
R V Butt (1884)

The accused made a false statement to his employer's book-keeper, knowing that such statement would be recorded in the accounts. He was convicted as principal for falsifying his employer's accounts.

See also *R V Michael* at page 8.

19

There may be more than one principal in the first degree, a person may have been simultaneously assaulted by two or more people. Or both parents may have sent their child into a shop to steal for them.

Principal in the second degree

A principal in the second degree is one by whom the perpetrator of the offence is aided and abetted at the time of its commission. "aiding and abetting" involves giving help or encouragement during the commission of the offence. Some actual encouragement must be given, mere presence is not sufficient. Presence may be actual presence at the scene of the crime such as to be an eye-witness or it may be an constructive presence, as where the aider and abettor is some distance away, but near enough to give whatever help is required.

For example, if A is inside a house, committing a burglary, B and C may be waiting outside it, ready to help him in carrying off the stolen property or to protect him by giving warning of the approach of the police.

A person cannot be guilty of aiding and abetting in the commission of an offence, if the facts which constitute such offence is unknown to him.

Accessory before the fact

An accessory before the fact is a person, who though absent at the time that the offence was committed, procures, counsels, commands another to commit a felony.

The procurement may be personal, or through the intervention of a third party. It may also be direct, by hire, counsel, command, or conspiracy; or indirect, by showing an express liking, approval, or assent to another's design of committing a felony. Where the procurement is through an agent, it is not necessary that the accessory should name the person to be procured to do the act. If the agent is innocent, the person procuring his act is a principal and not an accessory. The procurement must be continuing; for if the procurer repents, and before commission, expressly countermands his orders, and the principal notwithstanding commits the felony, the original proposer will not be an accessory.

The bare concealment of a felony contemplated by another will not make the party concealing it an accessory before the fact; nor will a silent acquiescence, or words which amount to a bare permission, be sufficient to constitute this offence.

Where one felony is counselled but another is committed, the accessory before the fact is only liable where the felony counselled was likely to lead to the offence that was committed. For example; if A hires B to kill C by stabbing him and B then kills C by administering poison, A is an accessory before the fact to the murder. On the other hand if A instigates B to steal C's car and in order to do so B kills C, A is not an accessory before the fact to that murder. An exception, however, arises where the crime counselled was one which itself was likely to cause this other crime that actually was committed; for if, when A has hired B to murder C, B by mistake kills C's twin brother D instead, A may be convicted as an accessory to D's murder.

People (D. P. P.) V Egan (1989)

It was held by the Court of Criminal Appeal that:

(1) A person could aid and abet the commission of a crime without being present when the crime was committed, and accordingly be liable to be dealt with as a principal offender.

(2) In order to be convicted of the principal offence, it was not necessary for the prosecution to establish that a person who had aided and abetted the principal offender before the crime was committed had knowledge of the actual crime intended. It is sufficient that a person who gave assistance knew the nature of the intended crime.

(3) The applicant in this case was an accessory before the fact of the crime committed by the principal offender because he knew that a crime was to be committed, that it involved the theft of goods and with this knowledge he assisted the principal offender when he agreed before the crime took place to make his workshop available to hide stolen goods.

The aided and abettor is liable with the principal for such crimes as were done in execution of their common purpose, which need not necessarily be arranged beforehand, between the principals but which must exist at the time of the commission of the offence.

Accessory after the fact

An accessory after the fact is one who has no prior connection with the felony, but who knowing that the felony has been committed, subsequently shelters one of the felons (including an accessory) in any way to secure their escape from justice.

It is necessary that the felony be completed at the time the assistance is given and that the accessory, at the time when he assists or comforts the felon, should have notice, direct or implied that he had committed the felony.

There must be an intention to help the felon to escape justice, active assistance to the felon is required, mere failure to report the felons presence will not suffice. A wife who aides, assists, or hides her husband knowing him to have committed a felon is not an accessory, however no other relationship of persons is excused.

Abstaining from arresting a known felon, and so allowing him to escape, is not enough to make a person guilty as an accessory of the felony itself (but it does make him guilty of misprision of felony).

In the case of a misdemeanour an accessory after the fact does not involve criminal responsibility.

Liability of secondary parties

R V Anderson & Morris (1966)

Parker C.J. stated "Where two persons embark on a joint enterprise each is liable for the acts done in pursuance of that joint enterprise and that includes liability for unusual consequences if they arise from the execution of the joint enterprise but (and this is the crux of the matter) that, if one of the adventurers goes beyond what has been tacitly agreed as part of the common enterprise his co-adventurer is not liable for the consequences of that unauthorised act."

People (D. P. P.) V Pringle and Others (1981)

It was held by the Court of Criminal Appeal:

The existence of a common design may be clearly inferred from the facts and the evidence adduced at a trial. Criminal responsibility for the acts of others done in pursuance of a common enterprise still exists in law.

Criminal association

Those not guilty of participation in a criminal offence, may find themselves otherwise associated with a crime. Misprision or compounding of a felony are the lesser degrees in which a person may become connected with a felony subsequent to its actual commission.

Misprision of felony

Misprision of felony occurs where a person, knowing that a felony has taken place does not give information to the authorities that might lead to the felon's arrest, or does himself make an attempt to arrest the felon, or where a person during the commission of a felony fails to act or stands passively.

Accordingly the ingredients of the offence are:

(i) knowledge that a felony has been committed; and

(ii) concealment of such knowledge.

A person is bound to disclose to the proper authorities all material facts relating to a felony the commission of which he has definite knowledge, such as name of felon if known; the place felony committed, etc. If he fails to perform this duty as soon as is reasonable, he is guilty of the offence. The duty may be preformed by reporting to the police. There is no duty of disclosure in the case of a legal adviser, doctor, clergyman or servant, where the commission of a felony has been disclosed to them in a professional capacity. Also an employer is entitled to give an employee a second chance.

Misprision of felony is a misdemeanour at common law punishable by fine and imprisonment. Active concealment or personal gain is not essential for this offence. Misprision of felony is a passive offence, if a person were to render active assistance he would be an accessory after the fact. In the case of a misdemeanour there is no offence of misprision.

Compounding a felony

Compounding a felony occurs where a person for valuable consideration, enters into agreement with a felon not to prosecute him. It occurs where a person who has been stolen from, enters into an agreement with the thief that in return for not prosecuting him, the stolen goods shall be returned. It is committed by the bare act of agreement, whether it is performed or not. Compounding a felony is a misdemeanour at common law.

This is a more serious offence than misprision of felony, for it includes that offence and goes further. All other members of the community are permitted by law to prosecute for this crime, even though a person may have suffered no injury and indeed has no concern with the crime.

There is statutory provision for similar offences:

The Larceny Act, 1861, at section 102 (at page 125) makes it an offence to advertise a reward for the return of any property lost or stolen, on the basis that no questions will be asked.

The Larceny Act, 1916, at section 5(3) (at page 114) makes it an offence for any person; to corruptly take any money or reward, under pretence of aiding any person to recover any stolen dog. This is punishable by eighteen months imprisonment and it is an offence by section 34 (at page 126) to corruptly take a reward under pretence to recover any stolen property under circumstances which amount to a felony or a misdemeanour, for which the penalty is seven years imprisonment.

Compounding a misdemeanour

There is no offence of compounding a misdemeanour, or stifling a prosecution for a misdemeanour. Any attempt by two or more persons to defeat or pervert the course of justice by stifling a prosecution for a misdemeanour could amount to a conspiracy, as would an agreement between an accused person and his bail whereby the latter is to be indemnified, if the accused was to abscond.

Chapter 5

Exemptions from criminal responsibility

It has been seen that *mens rea*, is a necessary element in every criminal offence, if it is absent the commission of an *actus reus* produces no criminal responsibility. There are certain defences having general application which exempt a person from criminal responsibility, in addition there are special defences available in the case of particular crimes. In the chapters that follow dealing with particular types of offences any special defences that may be availed of will be considered.

The circumstances when the presence of *mens rea* may be negated will now be considered. Blackstone in his *Commentaries on the Laws of England* published in 1765 classified the various conditions which in point of law negative the presence of a guilty mind as follows :

I Where there is no will -

        Infancy,

        Insanity,

        Intoxication,

        Corporations.

II Where the will is not directed to the deed -

        Mistake

III Where the will is overborne by compulsion -

        Public civil subjection,

        Private civil subjection,

        Duress per minas,

        Necessity.

It is convenient to use this classification when considering the many circumstances in a criminal trial where the presence of *mens rea* may be negated.

To which may be added:

        Self-defence,

        Diplomatic immunity

These various exemptions from criminal responsibility will be raised by an accused at his trial as a defence to a criminal charge, see also provocation at page 54.

Where there is no will

Infancy

Seven years and under

When a child reaches eight years of age the criminal law assumes that he has reached the age of discretion. There is an irrebuttable presumption that an child under eight years is *doli incapax* (incapable of knowing right from wrong and incapable of forming a wrongful or felonious intent). A child of seven years and under therefore cannot be

guilty of any crime.
Walters V Lunt (1951)

A seven year old child helped himself to certain goods and took them home. His parents, were charged with receiving stolen goods from him, knowing them to be stolen. It was held that they could not be convicted since the child, being under age, could not have been guilty of stealing and therefore the goods were not stolen.

Over seven and under fourteen years

There is a presumption that a child between eight years and fourteen years of age has not reached the age of discretion and is *doli incapax*. This presumption may be rebutted by proof of "mischievous discretion", expressed in the *maxim malitia supplet aetatem*; that is the child was able to distinguish between right and wrong and that he knew that what he was doing was morally wrong.

Before there can be a conviction of such an child, it must be shown by evidence, independent of the evidence of the offence that at the time he had formed a malicious intent. The measure is not of the child's age, but of his understanding and judgment.

The evidence of mischievous discretion to rebut the *prima facie* presumption of law should be clear and strong and beyond all doubt. Where such a child is indicted, two question must be decided by the jury: first, whether he committed the offence; and secondly, whether at the time he had a guilty knowledge that he was doing wrong. The fact that the child did the acts constituting the offence is not in itself any evidence whatever of the guilty state of mind which is necessary for conviction, nor is the mere knowledge by the child that the act was against the law sufficient.

Proof of the "mischievous discretion" required to rebut the presumption has been considered in the following cases:
Green V Cavan County Council C. C. (1959)

The applicant sought damages for malicious injury to sluice gates, around which oil had collected, and which had been set on fire and destroyed by two children, one of twelve years and the other of seven years. It was held that the applicant was entitled to compensation for malicious injuries.
Monagle V Donegal County Council (1961)

The applicant brought proceeding for the loss of property destroyed as a result of fire caused it was alleged, by the malicious act of a boy of about eight years and six months. The respondent appealed against a judgment in favour of the applicant. It was held by the High Court that the onus is on the applicant to satisfy the court by evidence that if a fire was caused by children, such children were not *doli incapax* either because they were over fourteen years or, if between seven and fourteen years, that they appreciated the consequences of what they were doing.

Thus it is necessary to prove that the child committed the act and knew that what he was doing was wrong.

Over fourteen years

Any incapacity of children to commit crime ceases upon their reaching fourteen years of age. A child in this age group has full criminal responsibility, they are presumed at law to be *doli incapaces*, and capable of distinguishing right from wrong and subject to the same rule as adults.

The only limitation on this is in the area of punishment; formerly a child under seventeen years could not suffer the death penalty. Children between fifteen years and seventeen years of age are known as young persons and those over seventeen years of age are known as juvenile adults.

Insanity

All persons who have reached the age of discretion are presumed by law to be sane, and to be accountable for their actions. This presumption of sanity may be rebutted by evidence which satisfies a jury (on the balance of probabilities) that the accused was insane at the time of the commission of the offence. Insanity gives rise to an incapacity, or defect of understanding, such that there can be no consent of the will and an action otherwise criminal is not punishable.

McNaughten rules

Since 1843, the McNaughten rules have been recognised as the main authoritative statement of the law on insanity.

R V McNaughton (1843)

The accused Daniel McNaughton had been indicted at the Central Criminal Court for the murder of Edward Drummond (private secretary to the Prime Minister of England, Sir Robert Peel). He had shot his victim in the back, as he was walking up Whitehall on 20th January 1843. The accused pleaded not guilty. After evidence of the shooting, witnesses were called for the accused, to prove that, at the time of committing the act, he was not in a sound state of mind. Some of the medical witnesses had previously examined the accused; others had not seen him until he appeared in court. Tindal C.J., told the jury that the question to be determined was whether at the time of the act in question was committed the accused had or had not the use of his understanding, so as to know that he was doing a wrong or wicked act. The verdict was "not guilty on the ground of insanity".

In consequences of his acquittal a debate took place in the House of Lords and a series of questions was put to the Law Lords, in relation to the law respecting alleged crimes committed by persons afflicted with insane delusions.

The answers given by the judges have been accepted as laying down the law as to insanity with reference to criminal responsibility and are known as the McNaughten Rules.

The questions and the answers are given below:

Exemptions from criminal responsibility

Question 1. "What is the law respecting alleged crimes committed by persons afflicted with insane delusions in respect of one or more particular subjects or persons: as, for instance, where at the time of the commission of the alleged crime the accused knew he was acting contrary to law, but did the act complained of with a view, under the influence of insane delusions, of redressing or revenging some supposed grievance or injury, or of producing some public benefit?"

Answer - "..., we are of opinion, that, notwithstanding the party did the act complained of with a view, under the influence of insane delusions, of redressing or revenging some supposed grievance or injury, or of producing some public benefit, he is nevertheless punishable, according to the nature of the crime committed, if he knew, at the time of committing such crime, that he was acting contrary to law, ..."

Question 2 "What are the proper questions to be submitted to the jury when a person alleged to be afflicted with insane delusions respecting one or more particular subjects or persons, is charged is charged with the commission of a crime (murder, for example), and insanity is set up as a defence?"

Question 3 "In what terms ought the question to be left to the jury as to the prisoner's state of mind at the time when the act was committed?"

Answers - to the second and third questions:

The rules may be summarised as follows : "That the jury ought to be told in all cases that every man is presumed to be sane, and to possess a sufficient degree of reason to be responsible for his crimes until the contrary is proved to their satisfaction; and that, to establish a defence on the ground of insanity, it must be clearly proved that, at the time of the committing of the act, the party accused was labouring under such a defect of reason, from disease of mind, as not to know the nature and quality of the act he was doing, or, if he did know it, that he did not know he was doing what was wrong. ... If the accused was conscious that the act was one which he ought not to do, and if that act was at the same time contrary to the law of the land, he is punishable; ...."

Question 4 "If a person under an insane delusion as to the existing facts commits an offence in consequence thereof, is he thereby excused?"

Answer - "The answer must, of course depend on the nature of the delusion; but making the same assumption as we did before, that he labours under such partial delusion only, and is not in other respects insane, we think he must be considered in the same situation as to responsibility as if the facts with respect to which the delusion exists were real. For example, if, under the influence of his delusion, he supposes another man to be in the act of attempting to take away his life, and he kills that man, as he supposes in self-defence, he would be exempted from punishment. If his delusion was that the deceased had inflicted a serious injury to his character and fortune, and he killed him in revenge

27

for such supposed injury, he would be liable for punishment."

Question 5 "Can a medical man, conversant with the disease of insanity, who never saw the prisoner previously to the trial, but who was present during the whole trial, and the examination of all the witnesses, be asked his opinion as to the state of the prisoner's mind at the time of the commission of the alleged crime, or his opinion whether the prisoner was conscious, at the time of doing the act, that he was acting contrary to law, or whether he was labouring under any and what delusion at the time?"

Answer - "We think the medical man, under the circumstances supposed, cannot in strictness be asked his opinion in the terms above stated, because each of those questions involves the determination of the truth of the facts deposed to, which it is for the jury to decide: and the questions are not mere questions upon a matter of science, in which case such evidence is admissible. But where the facts are admitted or not disputed, and the question becomes substantially one of science only, it may be convenient to allow the question to be put in that general form, though the same cannot be insisted on as a matter of right."

Summary of rules

The rules may be summarised as follows:

Rule 1. Every person is presumed to be sane, and to possess a sufficient degree of reason to be responsible for his crimes until the contrary is proved to the satisfaction of a jury.

Rule 2. To establish a defence on the ground of insanity, it must be clearly proved that at the time of the committing of the act, the party accused was labouring under such a defect of reason, from disease of mind, as not to know the nature and quality of the act he was doing; or if he did know it, that he did not know what he was doing was wrong.

Rule 3. If the accused was conscious that the act was one which he ought not to do and if that act was at the same time contrary to the law of the land, he is punishable.

Rule 4. Where a person under an insane delusion as to existing facts commits an offence in consequence thereof, and making the assumption that he labours under such partial delusion only, and is not in other respects insane, he must be considered in the same situation as to responsibility as if the facts with respect to which the delusion exists were real.

Attorney General V Boylan (1937)

It was contended on behalf of the accused that the judge should have told the jury that if the result of the evidence was to leave them in doubt as to the sanity of the accused they should give him the benefit of the doubt and find him to be insane. It was held by the Court of Criminal Appeal, that the contention was unsustainable.

People (A. G.) V Fennell 1 (1940)

It was held by the Court of Criminal Appeal that insanity must be

established on behalf of an accused to the satisfaction of the jury.
Attorney General V O'Brien (1936)
   It was pointed out that the McNaughten Rules were framed in answer
to questions asked specifically with regard to "persons afflicted with
insane delusions".

Not sole and exclusive test

   The above rules do not have wide and general application as to what
constitutes insanity, they define the law as to insane delusions. Irresistible
impulse is an addition; that may be pleaded as a ground of insanity. A
person is said to act under an irresistible impulse to do an act when from
disease of the mind he is incapable of restraining himself from doing it,
although he may know at the time of committing it that the act was
wrong.
People (A. G.) V Hayes (1967)
   Henchy J. said "In the normal case, tried in accordance with the
McNaughten rules, the test is solely one of knowledge: did he know the
nature and quality of his act or did he know that the act was wrong? The
rules do not take into account the capacity of a man on the basis of his
knowledge to act or refrain from acting, and I believe it to be correct
psychiatric science to accept that certain mental diseases, such as
paranoia or schizophrenia, in certain cases enable a man to understand
the morality or immorality of his act or the legality or illegality of it, or
the nature and quality of it, but nevertheless prevent him from exercising
a free volition as to whether he should or should not do that act. ....,
but if it is open to the jury to say, as say they must, on the evidence that
this man understands the nature and quality of his act, and understands
its wrongfulness, morally and legally, but that nevertheless he was
debarred from refraining from assaulting his wife fatally because of a
defect of reason, due to mental illness, it seem to me that it would be
unjust, in the circumstances of this case, not to allow the jury to consider
the case on those grounds."
Doyle V Wicklow County Council (1974)
   A youth had set fire to an abattoir. It was established that he had
caused the damage deliberately, there was also evidence that he was
suffering from a mental disorder which prompted him to set fire as a
means of protest against the slaughter of animals in the belief that he was
justified in doing so, although he knew his act to be contrary to law.
   It was held by the Supreme Court; Griffin J. "In my opinion, the
McNaughten rules do not provide the sole and exclusive test for
determining the sanity or insanity of an accused". He made reference to
the *Hayes* case in his judgment and adopted it as a correct statement of
the law on insanity.
People V O'Mahoney (1986)
   It was held by the Supreme Court that the defence of diminished
responsibility (in England) does not form part of Irish law and could not

exist side by side with the present law on Insanity.

Detention of insane persons

Those who successfully plead insanity do not walk free. An accused found not guilty by reason of insanity will be kept in custody during the pleasure of the Government. The place of detention is not a prison, but the Central Mental Hospital, Dundrum, Co. Dublin.

The Trial of Lunatics Act, 1883 at section 2 provides:

(1) Where in any indictment or information any act or omission is charged against any person as an offence, and it is given in evidence on the trial of such person for that offence that he was insane, so as not to be responsible, according to law, for his actions at the time when the act was done or omission made, then, if it appears to the jury before whom such person is tried that he did the act or made the omission charged, but was insane as aforesaid at the time when he did or made the same, the jury shall return a special verdict to the effect that the accused was guilty of the act or omission charged against him, but was insane as aforesaid at the time when he did the act or made the omission.

(2) Where such special verdict is found, the Court shall order the accused to be kept in custody as a criminal lunatic, in such place and in such manner as the Court shall direct till the pleasure of the (Government) shall be known; and it shall be lawful for the (Government) thereupon, and from time to time, to give such order for the safe custody of the said person during (its) pleasure in such place and in such manner as (the Government) may seem fit.

Director of Public Prosecutions V Gallagher (1991)

Where a person detained under section 2(2) of the Trial of Lunatics Act, 1883 seeks to secure release from detention, he may apply to the executive for his release on the grounds that he is not suffering from any mental disorder. Where such an application is made, the executive, must inquire into all the relevant circumstances of the case and in so doing must use fair and constitutional procedures and such an inquiry and its result may be the subject of judicial review so as to ensure compliance with such procedures.

McCarthy J. in the course of his judgment noted that at the Central Criminal Court, a jury had returned a special verdict as provided for in the Act. He said that the overriding consideration is that this special verdict is a verdict of acquittal. In his view the making of an order did not involve the administration of justice, but rather constituted the carrying out of the role of the executive in caring for society and protecting the common good.

Automatism

Where a defence of insanity has been raised unsuccessfully, or where it has not been pleaded, automatism may be raises as a defence to criminal responsibility, this is where a person is not able to physically control their actions, notwithstanding that their body may have committed the external element of an offence. If such a case arose then the actions of an accused would not be voluntary.

Intoxication

The excess of alcohol abuse has long been given consideration by the courts. In the early years of the nineteenth century, self-induced drunkenness was regarded as a factor aggravating guilt. Intoxication may arise by alcohol or by drugs or by a combination of both. The principals governing intoxication by alcohol and by drugs are the same. Drunkenness caused by the voluntary act of an accused does not of itself excuse him from criminal responsibility. Where the primary cause of the drunkenness is involuntary, he will not, while under its influence, be accountable for his actions. Involuntary drunkenness could arise by mistake or by negligence or malice of others or through a weakened physical condition following lack of sleep or food or deprivation of blood, in which circumstances a person would be more affected by a small quantity of drink. Accordingly drunkenness may be successfully pleaded where it is claimed to have negated the *mens rea* necessary for the offence charged.

Director of Public Prosecutions V Beard (1920)

The accused placed his hand over the mouth of a girl in furtherance of a rape. He unintentionally killed her by pressing his thumb on her throat when trying to prevent her from screaming. He was drunk at the time of the offence.

The law relating to drunkenness was reviewed in this case and the following are the principal points made in the course of the judgment:

1. If the accused was actually insane within the meaning of the McNaghten rules when he committed the alleged crime, then although his insanity was the result of alcoholic excess, he has as complete a defence as he would have had if it had been induced by any other means; but, where insanity is not pleaded, the jury should not be told to consider whether the accused knew that what he was doing was wrong.

2. Evidence of drunkenness rendering the accused incapable of forming the specific intent essential to constitute the crime charged should be taken into consideration with the other facts proved in order to determine whether or not he had this intent.

3. Evidence of drunkenness falling short of a proved incapacity in the accused to form the intent necessary to constitute the crime in question, and merely establishing that his mind was affected by drink so that readily gave way to some violent passion, affords no defence.

Attorney General (N. I.) V Gallagher (1963)

Gallagher was charged with the murder of his wife. Having decided to kill her, he bought a knife and a bottle of whiskey. After drinking the whiskey he killed her. His defence was that he was either insane or so drunk as to be incapable of forming the intent necessary for murder.

In the House of Lords it was stated that: "If a man while sane and sober forms an intention to kill and makes preparation for it, knowing it is the wrong thing to do, and them gets himself drunk as to give himself dutch courage to do the killing, and whilst drunk carries out his intention, he cannot rely on this self-induced drunkenness as a defence to a charge of murder, nor even as reducing it to manslaughter. "

Director of Public Prosecutions V Majeskie (1976)

A number of charges were brought against the accused. of assaults occasioning actual bodily harm (section 47, Offence against the Person Act, 1861). The accused claimed that he had been acting under the influence of a combination of drugs and alcohol. The jury were directed that self-induced intoxication was no defence to assault.

The House of Lords reaffirmed the rules laid down in the *Beard* and *Gallagher* cases, and held that in crimes of basic intent, as distinct from crimes of specific intent, self-induced intoxication provided no defence; it was irrelevant to offences of basic intent such as assault.

The question with regard to intent is not whether an accused had an intent, but whether he had a specific intent.

A crime of "basic intent" or "general intent" is, a crime whose definition expresses, or more often implies, a *mens rea* which does not go beyond the *actus reus*. It is a reckless course of conduct and recklessness is enough to constitute the necessary *mens rea* in crimes of basic intent. Examples of such crimes include rape, manslaughter, assault occasioning actual bodily harm and malicious wounding.

A crime of "special intent" or "specific intent", is a crime where the prosecution has to prove that the purpose for the commission of the act extends to the intent expressed or implied in the definition of that crime. Crimes of "specific intent" include larceny, murder and wounding with intent. Self induced intoxication could be a defence to such a charge.

Corporations

A corporation is an artificial person created by law and as such would not be capable of forming a human intent. In so far as is possible corporations are placed in the same position as individuals in regard to the commission of offences by their servants or agents. Where a *mens rea* can be imputed to a company through its servants or agents, it can be convicted. Where no *mens rea* is necessary to make a principal liable for an offence, a corporation may be made liable for an offence.

The Interpretation Act, 1889 at section 2(1) provides: In the construction of every enactment relating to an offence punishable on indictment or on summary conviction, whether contained in an act passed before or after ...(1st January 1890) the expression 'Person' shall, unless the contrary intention appears, include a body corporate.

A corporation cannot be found guilty of an offence where imprisonment is the only punishment, their being no provision for a fine. There are in addition a number of personal offences for which a corporation could not be indicted e. g. perjury, bigamy, murder, or offences involving personal violence. The Offences against the State Act, 1939 and the Road Traffic Act, 1961 are amongst those statutes that provide for corporate liability.

Where the will is not directed to the deed

Mistake

The maxim is: *ignorantia facti excusat; ignorantia jurit non excusat* (ignorance of the fact excuses; ignorance of the law does not excuse).

Ignorance of law

Ignorance of the law will not excuse any person who has capacity to understand the law. A knowledge of the law of the land is not essential to lead to a conviction. The law is administered upon the principle that all persons must be taken to know it conclusively without any proof that he does know it.

It is no defence on behalf of an alien that he did not know he was doing wrong, the act not being an offence in his own country.

It has long been established that ignorance of the law is no excuse:
R V Bailey (1800)
The accused a sea captain was charged and convicted under a statute passed when he was at sea, at a time when he could not have known that the law in question existed.

Mistake of fact

Mistake of fact is a defence because it prevents an accused from having the necessary *mens rea*, which the law requires for the offence with which he is charged. It is allowed as an excuse, where the accused acted under an honest and reasonable belief in a state of affairs which if true would have justified the act done. The law looks at the circumstances from the point of view of the accused, and does not punish him if, assuming the facts to be as they seemed to him, that he committed no wrong. The supposed circumstances must have been such that had they been real no *mens rea* could have possibly arisen.

An old case where a mistake of fact negatived criminal liability was:
R V Levett (1638)
Levett under the impression that thieves were in his house, thrust his rapier into the decease (who was hiding behind a curtain), believing that she was one of them. He was charged with unlawful homicide, however it was resolved that it was not manslaughter; for he did it ignorantly, without the intention to hurt the deceased.

Where threats of physical violence are used to obtain possession of what is *bona fide* believed to be one's own property or property to which one is entitled, even in these circumstances no offence is committed.

In general the mistake of fact must be a reasonable one, which itself will be a question of fact. A jury may be assisted by the Judge as to what might be a reasonable mistake and what might be an unreasonable mistake.

Kenny in his *Outlines of Criminal law* gives an illustration:

"A man, before going to church, fired off his gun, and left it empty. But during his absence some person went out shooting with the gun; and, on returning, left it loaded. The owner, late in the same day, took up the gun again; and in doing this touched the trigger. the gun went off and killed his wife, who was in the room. Foster held that in these circumstances the man had reasonable grounds to believe the weapon was not loaded.

Thus in 1880, at Clonmel, a woman who had placed a child naked on a hot shovel, in the honest belief that it was a deformed fairy sent as a substitute for the real child, (who would be restored if the changeling were thus imperilled), was convicted and was sentenced to imprisonment. So, in 1895, again at Clonmel, were men who had caused the death of the wife of one of them by holding her over a fire and searing her with a red hot poker, in the honest expectation of thereby exorcising a demon that was supposed to possess her.

In regard to reasonableness note the English case of *D. P. P. V Morgan (1975)*, at page 73.

Mistake of fact is no defence in circumstances where strict liability is imposed by the law in relation to an offence. A strict liability offence (see chapter 2) does not require *mens rea* and a mistake no matter how reasonable will not excuse. These type of offence have been considered earlier and are also found amongst the road traffic offences.

The position as to mistake may be summarised as follows:

(1) The mistake must relate to matters of fact not to matters of law.

(2) The mistake must be of such a character that, had the supposed circumstances been real, they would have prevented any guilt from attaching to the person in doing what he did.

(3) The mistake must be a reasonable one.

(4) The offence involved must not be one of strict liability.

Where the will is overborne by compulsion

Public civil subjection

A mistake even of law may afford a defence to a public servant who has obeyed unlawful orders under a reasonable (though mistaken) belief that they were lawful. Thus when violence is exercised by a prison officer in carrying out an invalid sentence then, though the violence is criminal, the person's public civil subjection grants him immunity.

There is no clear authority extending any such exemption from criminal responsibility to the military.

Keighley V Bell (1866)

Willes J. stated "an officer or soldiers acting under the orders of his superior not being necessarily or manifestly illegal would be justified by his orders."

Accordingly this "defence" is much more likely to be upheld where the accused is an innocent agent.

In certain circumstances obedience to orders of a superior may negative *mens rea*

R V James (1837)

The accused was charged with having unlawfully and maliciously obstructed an airway in a mine. He had done so in accordance with his masters instructions and believed that he was acting lawfully. He was deemed to be an innocent agent and found not guilty.

Private civil subjection

It was only in the case of conjugal subjection that this ever amounted to an exemption from criminal responsibility. At common law it was presumed that a married woman acted under the coercion of her husband, in the commission by her of a crime, when the offence was committed in the presence of her husband. The converse did not apply in the case of a husband committing a crime in the presence of his wife. In the *People V Murray and Murray (1977)*, at page 52; it was held that there is no presumption of marital coercion, where a wife is charged with murder.

State (D. P. P.) V Walsh and Conneely (1981)

It was held by the Supreme Court that the respondent Conneely could not avail of the former presumption of law that the act of a wife committed in the presence of her husband was caused by his coercion, since that presumption had not survived the enactment of Article 40 of the Constitution which declared that all citizens shall be held equal before the law.

Duress per minas (by threats)

A person compelled by physical force and against his will to do an act which if voluntarily done would be a crime, is free from criminal responsibility; the person compelling is liable. Moral coercion as distinct from physical coercion would not afford a defence for the commission of a criminal act.

Attorney General V Whelan (1934)

"Threats of immediate death or serious personal violence so great as to overbear the ordinary powers of human resistance should be accepted as a justification for acts which would otherwise be criminal."

It must be shown that the overpowering of the will was operative at the time of the crime and that the accused had no opportunity to escape from the threat. Duress could not be a defence in cases of murder, however note:

Director of Public Prosecution V Lynch (1975)

It was held that on a charge of murder it is open to a accused as a principal in the second degree to plead duress. Any threat must be to a person; threats to property no matter how grave will not suffice.

Where duress is raised as a defence, it is for the prosecution to negative it. A jury should be directed to consider whether the will of the accused, subjectively considered was overborne and whether his action under duress were reasonable.

Duress may be more often raised, as a mitigation not of the offence, but of the punishment.

Attorney General V Farnan & Others (1933)

The Central Criminal Court held, that, when by special verdict a jury finds that an offence has been committed under duress the verdict is not a verdict of "not guilty", but is merely to be taken into account in mitigation of punishment.

Duress per neccessitatem (coercion of necessity)

The fact that a person who has inflicted harm upon another, did so for the greater good is recognised in the civil area. To commit an offence in order to save human life may be excusable. Mere personal necessity would not be an acceptable excuse.

R V Dudley and Stephens (1884)

Two men who had been shipwrecked after eighteen days without food killed a boy who was with them and ate him. The defence of necessity failed, however their sentence of death was commuted to six months imprisonment.

R V Bourne (1939)

The defendant was a gynaecologist who had performed an abortion on a young girl who had become pregnant as a result of being raped. He had done so after obtaining the consent of her parents and having consulted a medical colleague. He was charged under section 58 of the Offences against the Person Act, 1861. He claimed that he had formed the opinion that without the operation the girl would have become a physical wreck. The jury was directed that the word "unlawfully" in the section meant that no person could be guilty of the offence unless it was proved that the act was not done in good faith for the purpose of preserving the life of the mother. The word "life" was to be interpreted reasonably widely and did not mean life as opposed to death. The defendant was found not guilty.

Having regard to the recent *X Case (1992)*; a case similar to the above in Ireland could have the same result.

As yet there is no definitive Irish authority in the area of coercion of necessity.

The use of force is lawful for the necessary defence of self or others or property; but the justification is limited by the necessity of the occasion and the use of unnecessary force is an assault. "If one man strikes another a blow, or does that which amounts to an assault on him, that other has a right to defend himself, and to strike a blow in his defence without waiting until he is struck, but he has no right to revenge himself; and if when all danger is past he strikes a blow not necessary for his defence, he commits an assault and battery. "

R V Rose (1884)

The accused, heard his mother scream "murder" and saw his father, a powerful and aggressive man pressing his mother against the bannisters at the top of the stairs in such a way that it seemed that the father was about to cut her throat with a knife, although no knife was ever found. He shot his father and was charged with murder. He was acquitted, the jury having been directed that the law of self-defence extended to the defence of parents and children and if the accused had acted in the honest belief, held on reasonable grounds, that shooting his father was the only way of saving his mother's life, he should be acquitted.

Devlin V Armstrong (1971)

The accused incited a crowd who had been stoning the police to build a barricade to keep the police out of the Bogside, to defend the barricade and throw petrol bombs. She claimed to have done this in the honest and reasonable belief that the police were going to enter the Bogside and assault people and damage property. It was held that she had no defence on the basis of self-defence because there was no sufficiently close relationship between herself and the people of the Bogside, whom she claimed to be defending.

Attorney General V Keatley (1954)

"A man has a right to defend any man by reasonable force against unlawful force" ... "There is of course, implicit in this statement the requirements to be deduced from the passage already quoted (above) that the use of force is necessary and that no more force than is necessary is used. These two matters are eminently questions of fact to be decided, in a criminal trial, by the jury".

Attorney General V Dwyer (1972)

This was a point of law stated for the opinion of the Supreme Court; "Where a person, subject to a violent and felonious attack, endeavours by way of self defence, to prevent the consummation of that attack by force, but, in doing so, exercises more force than is necessary but no more than he honestly believes to be necessary in the circumstances whether such person is guilty of manslaughter and not murder." This question was answered by the court in the affirmative. In their consideration of the question the Supreme Court distinguished between the above type of self defence and what it called a full self defence. "A homicide is not unlawful if it is committed in the execution or advancement of justice or in reasonable self defence of person or property, or in order to prevent the commission of an atrocious crime, or by misadventure. In the case of such self defence, the homicide is justifiable and is therefore not unlawful."

"In such a case where the evidence in the trial discloses a possible defence of self-defence, the onus remains throughout on the prosecution to establish that the accused is guilty of the offence charged......the homicide is not unlawful if the accused believed on reasonable grounds that his life was in danger and that the force used by him was reasonably necessary for his protection. In such a case he is entitled to a complete acquittal."

See self-defence and assault at page 62, and also see *D. P. P. V Kelso* at page 323.

Diplomatic immunity

The Diplomatic Relations and Immunities Act, 1967 gives force of law to the provisions of the Vienna Conventions on Diplomatic Relations signed on 18th April 1961 and 24th April 1963.

Total inviolability

Total inviolability is extended to the person of a diplomatic agent his private residence, papers and property. He is not liable to any form of arrest, detention or prosecution, and his persons at all times must be treated with respect.

Diplomatic agent means the head of a diplomatic mission and members of the diplomatic staff of the mission. The members of the family of a diplomatic agent, forming part of his household, if they are not Irish citizens enjoy the same privileges and immunities.

Diplomats are specially privileged against prosecution for any breach of the criminal law. Such diplomatic immunity may be expressly waived by the diplomat's own Government. The immunity extended to any kind of offence.

Chapter 6

Inchoate offences

Inchoate crimes are crimes that are not fully developed, the *mens rea* of the complete crime is present, the intention is to carry out the complete crime, though the act done is only a step towards the execution of the complete crime.

The inchoate offences are:

    Attempt;
    Conspiracy;
    Incitement/Soliciting

Attempt

An attempt is a proximate act towards the carrying out of an indictable offence. It is a misdemeanour at common law to attempt to commit an offence, whether such offence was a crime at common law or by statute.

The *mens rea* of attempt is the intent to carry out the complete offence, so that the *mens rea* of attempt is essentially that of the complete crime.

(a) it must be shown that the person accused of an attempt to commit a crime intended or foresaw those consequences of conduct contained expressly or implicitly in the definition of the crime.

(b) it must be proved that the person accused of attempt intended those consequences referred to in (a), even though a lesser degree of *mens rea* might be sufficient if he were charged with the completed crime.

R V Whybrow (1951)

The accused, by a device which he had constructed, administered an electric shock to his wife while she was in a bath. The trial judge directed the jury that, if he did so with intent to kill his wife or to do her grievous bodily harm, he would be guilty of attempted murder. The Court of Criminal Appeal held that this was a wrong direction. An intent to kill had to be proved. "But if the charge is one of attempted murder, the intent becomes the principal ingredient of the crime."

An attempt to commit either a felony or a misdemeanour is a misdemeanour, however, there are case where attempted felonies have been made felony by statute, e.g. attempts to murder under the Offences against the Person Act, 1861 (at page 52); attempted obstruction of Government under the Offences against the State Act, 1939 (page 308).

The *actus reus* of attempt is when some act is carried out; which may be regarded as a movement towards the commission of the offence and such act cannot be regarded as having any other purpose.

Eagleton (1855)

Parke, B. "The mere intention to commit a misdemeanour is not criminal. Some act is required, and we do not think that all acts towards committing a misdemeanour are indictable. Acts remotely leading towards the commission of the offence are not to be considered as attempts to commit it, but acts immediately connected with it are ..."

How are these acts to be distinguished ?

R V Taylor (1859)

The accused approached a haystack and lit a match. On noticing that he was being watched, he extinguished the match. The jury were told that the facts warranted their finding the accused guilty of an attempt to burn the haystack if they thought that he intended to set fire to it.

R V Button (1900)

The accused, a very good runner, entered for two races in the name of Sims, stating, untruthfully, that he had never run a race. He was given a start in each of the races and won, but did not claim the prize money when questions were raised as to who he really was. He was convicted of attempting to obtain money by false pretences. On appeal; Mathew, J. stated "The pretences which the prisoner made were not too remote, and the conviction was good."

People (A. G.) V Thornton (1952)

On a charge of an attempt to procure the miscarriage of a girl. It was held by the Court of Criminal Appeal that on a charge based on an alleged attempt to commit a crime, the jury should be informed by the trial judge that a mere desire to commit the crime, or a desire followed by an intention to do so, is not sufficient to constitute an attempt.

Also see *R V Robinson (1915)* at page 138.

It appears therefore that the *actus reus* of an attempt to commit an offence exists when an accused performs an act which may be regarded as a movement towards the commission of the offence, and the performance of that act cannot reasonably be interpreted as having any other objective than the commission of the offence.

The fact that an accused was attempting to do something that was, not possible in the circumstances, does not prevent a conviction for attempt. It is not material that an accused, due to his lack of knowledge of the surrounding circumstances, was aware of the impossibility of carrying out his intention. A person is guilty of an attempt to steal by taking money from a cash register, although not possible because there was no money in it. There are a number of crimes which it is impossible to attempt to commit. Such crimes would include the following:

(a) crimes of omission where the *actus reus* does not include any consequences of the omission, e.g. misprision of treason (at page 299).

(b) crimes which, by definition may be committed negligently or recklessly, but not intentionally, e.g. involuntary manslaughter (at page 55).

If on the trial of a person charged with either a felony or a misdemeanour the jury feel that the offence was incomplete, but are of the opinion that an attempt was made, they may deliver a verdict of attempt.

At common law the penalty for an attempt is a matter for the court, which would have due regard to the gravity of the offence attempted, however, there is often statutory provision for the punishment of an attempt, e.g. the Misuse of Drugs Act, 1977 at section 21 provides for punishment as if the convicted person were guilty of the substantive offence.

Conspiracy

Conspiracy is an agreement between two or more persons to do an unlawful act, or to do a lawful act by unlawful means. It is a misdemeanour at common law. All conspiracies are misdemeanours, even conspiracy to murder, however a conspiracy to cause explosions by section 3 of the Explosive Substances Act, 1883, is a substantive offence.
People (A. G.) V Keane (1975)
It was held by the Court of Criminal Appeal that charges of conspiracy ought not, in practice, to be laid when the substantive offence can be proved.
The following points arise:
> (a) an agreement;
> (b) two or more persons;
> (c) the act agreed upon.

an agreement
An agreement means a decision having been made to carry out the unlawful act. A mere intention is not sufficient, it is necessary that there be an actual agreement between parties. Once agreement has been reached, the offence is complete even though no further act is done in pursuance of the agreement or where the parties had not settled the means to be employed. Such an agreement can be inferred from the subsequent conduct of the persons involved.

Anything said, done or written by any one of the accused in execution of their common purpose is admissible in evidence against all of them. Proof of the conspiracy in most cases depends on inferences to be drawn from the conduct of the parties. Only rarely will direct evidence of the agreement be available.
People (A. G.) V O'Connor and O'Reilly (1943)
It was held by the Court of Criminal Appeal that while there was no evidence of express agreement, the evidence adduced afforded ample grounds to justify the inference of a conspiracy.

two or more persons
The name of the crime indicates that it is one of combination, a person cannot by himself con-spire. Persons married to each other cannot be guilty of conspiring together, however, a husband and wife and a third party can be convicted of conspiring together.
R V McDonnell (1966)
McDonnell was charged with his own limited company, for the conduct of whose affairs he was solely responsible. On a motion to quash the indictment it was held that as a matter of law the one man responsible for the affairs of a limited company cannot be convicted of conspiring with

that company.

One person alone may be convicted of conspiracy with persons who are unknown, or not in custody, or dead, or whose trial has been postponed. But if two persons are jointly indicted for conspiring together both must be convicted or both acquitted; so also if three persons are jointly indicted for conspiring together and two are acquitted.

There does not have to be direct communication between the alleged conspirators. The existence of the conspiracy may be shown by the detached acts of the several conspirators.

an unlawful act

To do an unlawful act, or to do a lawful act by unlawful means ? "unlawful" as used in conspiracy has never been clearly defined, it includes civil as well as criminal wrongs.

An agreement to commit any indictable or summary offence is a conspiracy. Examples of conspiracies are :

(1) Agreement to commit any criminal offence
(2) Agreement to commit any fraudulent or malicious tort,
(3) Agreement to prevent the course of justice,
(4) Agreement to effect a lawful purpose with a corrupt intent, or by improper means.

Shaw V Director of Public Prosecutions (1962)

Shaw and others published a "Ladies Directory" containing details of prostitutes and was charged with conspiring with the prostitutes to corrupt public morals. The House of Lords held that there was such an offence at common law and upheld the conviction.

Scott V Commissioner of Police (1974)

Scott agreed with others to copy certain films without permission and without paying fees, so as to enable him to make "pirate" copies and to distribute them commercially. He was convicted with conspiracy to defraud and appealed unsuccessfully to the Court of Appeal. He had submitted that since the count did not include an element of deceit, it was bad in law. In the House of Lords; Viscount Dilhorne stated: "... it is clearly the law that an agreement by two or more by dishonesty to deprive a person of something which is his or to which he is or would be or might be entitled and an agreement by two or more by dishonesty to injure some proprietary right of his, suffices to constitute the offence of conspiracy to defraud."

Ellis v O'Dea & Governor of Portlaoise Prison (1991)

Finlay C.J. stated that it is a fundamental principle of the Irish common law that a person joining in a conspiracy or a joint venture outside the State, in furtherance of which an overt criminal act is committed within the State, will be amenable to the jurisdiction of the Irish courts even where he has not committed an overt act within the State.

Inchoate offences

The punishment for conspiracy is a matter for the court, it has been held that a higher sentence should not be passed for conspiracy than could be passed for the substantive offence except in very exceptional cases. In the case of conspiracy to murder the Offences against the Person Act, 1861 at section 4 (see page 53) provides for a maximum punishment of ten years.

People (A. G.) V Giles (1973)

It was held by the Supreme Court that conspiracy to rob was an indictable misdemeanour at common law and that, subject to the selection of the appropriate sentence in a particular case, there was no limit on the period of imprisonment which might be imposed for the offence.

Incitement/Soliciting

To incite or solicit any other person to commit an indictable offence, even though it is not committed is a misdemeanour at common law.

There are no Irish authorities to suggest that the incitement of a summary offence is itself indictable.

There are three aspect to the crime of incitement:

        (a) a definite act of solicitation;
        (b) the incitement must be communicated;
        (c) impossibility is not relevant.

act of solicitation

A definite act of solicitation is essential.

R V Higgins (1801)

The defendant was convicted of soliciting and inciting another to steal from his master, although there was no evidence that anything had been stolen. On appeal it was held that the mere act of solicitation was a sufficient act to constitute the *actus reus* of a crime.

Lord Kenyon said "But it is argued, that a mere intent to commit evil is not indictable, without an act done; but is there not an act done, when it is charged that the defendant solicited another to a commit felony. The solicitation is an act ..."

People (A. G.) V Capaldi (1949)

The applicant was convicted in the Circuit Court of unlawfully inciting a doctor to commit a felony contrary to section 58 (at page 94) of the Offences Against the Person Act, 1861. He had brought a pregnant girl to a doctor and asked the doctor to do something for her. The defence claimed that the words and conduct of the accused amounted only to an expression of desire that something be done for the girl, and not an incitement to commit a crime.

It was held by the Court of Criminal Appeal that the words and conduct of the accused were not expression of mere desire, but constituted an effort to employ the doctor to perform an illegal operation.

43

communication

The incitement must be communicated. The offence may not only be committed by an individual personally, but also by an incitement in a newspaper.

Wilson V Danny Quastel Ltd. (1966)

Parker C.J. stated "There can be no incitement of anyone unless the incitement, whether by words or written matter, reaches the man whom it is said is being incited"

inciting the impossible

It is not relevant that the crime incited is impossible to commit:

R V McDonough (1963)

The defendant mistakenly believed that there were some stolen lamb carcasses in cold storage at a meat market. He offered them for sale to butchers, acknowledging that they were stolen. The Court of Appeal upheld his conviction for soliciting (inciting) the butchers to handle stolen property.

R V Fitzmaurice (1983)

The defendant's father had asked him to recruit people to commit a robbery. He recruited one person who recruited two others and put them in touch with his father. Unknown to the defendant, no crime was to be committed. His father planned to claim reward money for preventing a robbery. He was convicted of incitement to rob. The person he recruited had already been acquitted of conspiracy on the grounds of impossibility.

The Court of Appeal declared that the fact that the conspiracy had been impossible did not necessarily mean that the incitement would be. The offence he had incited had not itself been impossible to commit at the time he incited it, and therefore he was liable. He would not have been liable had it been physically impossible at any time.

Attempts

An attempt at incitement is also an offence. If the crime is committed the person is liable as an accessory before the fact in the case of a felony or as a principal in the case of a misdemeanour. It is not an offence to incite someone to be an accessory before the fact to a crime.

Statutory offences of inciting

Incitement of particular crimes are contained in the relevant statutes:

Offences against the Person Act, 1861, section 4, incitement to murder;

Misuse of Drugs Act, 1977, section 21(1); soliciting or inciting any other person to commit an offence under that Act, which is punishable in the same way as the substantive offence;

Prohibition of Incitement to Hatred Act, 1989 deals specifically with incitement in a particular area (at page 277).

Chapter 7

Homicide

Homicide is the killing of a human being by a human being. Not all homicides are a breach of the criminal law. A number of circumstances variously described as either excusable or justifiable are considered to be lawful. A homicide that is not justifiable at law, or excusable by the law is an unlawful or felonious homicide. Such crimes are as follows: murder, manslaughter, suicide, infanticide and genocide. Infanticide is considered in chapter 11 and genocide is considered in chapter 37.

The common law position on homicide has been supplemented by the Criminal Justice Act, 1964 and the Criminal Justice Act, 1990.

Excusable or justifiable
Death may be caused where force is used in carrying out a lawful arrest or in the suppression of a riot. However any force used must have been reasonable in the circumstances. Formerly where death was caused in the lawful sentence of a competent court

Death may be caused where a person is engaged in a lawful act without negligence (misadventure). This excuse applies in the case of sports such as boxing or football, however the force used must not be excessive. Another instance of this would be a patient dying in surgery, where there had been no negligence. Where in any chance-medley (i.e. sudden combat) one person stops fighting, but the other continues his assault, and the former one having having no other means of escape, kills his assailant, the necessity of self-defence prevents the homicide from being a felony.

The Offences against the Person Act, 1861 at section 7 provides that: No punishment shall be incurred by any person who shall kill another by misfortune or in his own defence, or in any other manner without felony (see also self defence at pages 36, 62).

Murder

Common law definition
Murder has been described by Coke in 1797 as "..when any man of sound memory, and of the age of discretion, unlawfully killeth within any county of the realm, any reasonable creature in *rerum natura* under the King's peace, with malice aforethought, either expressed by the party or implied by law, so as the party wounded, or hurt, ... die of the wound or hurt, ... within a year and a day after the same."

These ingredients of murder must be examined, they apply not only to murder but to the other unlawful homicides as well.

any man
This means a person to whom criminal responsibility may be attached.

unlawfully killeth

This is to distinguish murder from the non-felonious homicides referred to above. The killing must be unlawful and not excusable or justifiable.

within any county

The Offences against the Person Act, 1861 at section 9 provides that; in relation to murder or manslaughter a person may be tried in Ireland, where the offence has been committed abroad. See also jurisdiction.

any reasonable creature

This means a human being, at common law this did not include an unborn child. The Constitution at Article 40.3.3 provides that the State shall acknowledge the right to life of the unborn, having regard to this provision it is unlikely that the courts could uphold the common law position. A child was considered to be "in being" when it has an existence independent of its mother, it was not necessary for the umbilical cord to be cut for this to be so. Injuries inflicted before birth, or during birth which cause death before birth were not murder, however an injury inflicted before birth, which causes death after birth may be murder.

the king's peace

All persons are free to live their lives peacefully. The only exclusion from this would be the killing of an enemy alien during the actual course of war.

malice aforethought

This was the *mens rea* of murder at common law, it has now been altered by statute (see Criminal Justice Act, 1964, section 4 below).

At common law malice had been categorised as follows:

(a) express malice: which consisted of an intention to kill, the particular person who was killed, or a person other than the one who was killed.

(b) universal or general malice: which consisted of an intention to kill some person but not caring who is killed, as where a gun would be fired into a crowd of people.

(c) implied malice: which consisted of an intention to cause grievous bodily harm which resulted in a killing.

(d) constructive malice: which consisted of the intention to either commit a felony, or oppose a police officer, which results in a killing.

within a year and a day

The prosecution must prove that the death of the victim occurred within a year and a day of the injuries inflicted by the accused. This reflected the undeveloped state of medicine in the distant past. It is doubtful that this would be upheld by the courts if it came to be considered (what if there had been a deliberate infliction of the AIDS virus and death occurring after a year and a day)

Mens rea of murder

The mental element now required of murder is to be found in the Criminal Justice Act, 1964 at section 4 which provides:

(1) Where a person kills another unlawfully the killing shall not be murder unless the accused person intended to kill, or cause serious injury to, some person, whether the person actually killed or not.

(2) The accused person shall be presumed to have intended the natural and probable consequences of his conduct; but this presumption may be rebutted.

The emphasis in the section is on two concepts:

Intention

An accused may admit to having killed the victim, but will plead innocence on the basis of not having had such an intention. It can be seen that the intent required is much broader than a simple intention to kill the person who was actually killed. The other intents included are: an intention to kill some other person; an intention to cause serious injury to the person killed and an intention to cause serious injury to some other person.

If any one of these intents can be established then an accused is guilty. It is not possible to look into the mind of an accused. The intent must be inferred beyond reasonable doubt, from the surrounding circumstances. Subsection 2 assists in the establishment of what was in the mind of an accused person. (see also intention, at page 9)

Presumption

The accused person shall be presumed to have intended the natural and probable consequences of his conduct; but this presumption may be rebutted. The effect of this presumption is to shift the onus of proof on to an accused in respect of his conduct. The forseeability of the consequences (result of the conduct) of an accused is what is in question. The greater the likehood of a particular result occurring the more likely an accused foresaw such a result and thus intended it. The more likely that death or serious injury could be a consequence of his conduct, the less believable that such was the intent of his conduct.

Question of causation

The killing may be by any cause whatsoever. If a person does any act, of which the probable consequences may be and eventually is death, such a killing may be murder, although the deceased was not struck by such person. Thus in murder (as in the case of manslaughter) a person will be held liable not only in cases of direct violence, but also where an act on their part led through a chain of events to a death.

The principles as to causation are illustrated by case law:

Where an actual killing is not caused solely by the accused this will not necessarily exempt him from liability, see *R V Lowe* below.

R V Wall (1802)

Governor Wall was tried and executed in 1802 for the murder of Sergeant Armstrong nearly twenty years earlier for sentencing him to an illegal flogging; though death might not have resulted but for the deceased having drank alcohol whilst he was ill.

Where death is caused partly by an accused and partly by the conduct of others, a court may hold that the death is too remote.

R V Jordan (1956)

The accused had stabbed the deceased who had died in hospital not having received normal treatment. His conviction was quashed because at the time of his death, the original wound caused by the stabbing had nearly healed.

R V Blaue (1975)

The accused stabbed the victim who was taken to hospital. The victim, a Jehovah's Witness, was informed that without a blood transfusion she would probably die. She refused and died. The accused appealed against his conviction for manslaughter on the grounds that the victim's refusal to accept a blood transfusion broke the chain of causation. The court dismissed the appeal, the refusal to accept the blood transfusion did not break the chain of causation.

If a person under an apprehension of personal violence does an act which causes his death, as for example jumps out a window or into a river, the person who threatened is answerable for the consequences, see *R V Halliday* at page 64.

A killing may be caused by mental suffering or shock.

R V Tower (1874)

The accused violently assaulted a young girl who was holding a four and half months old child in her arms. The screams of the girl so frightened the child that it cried till it was black in the face. From that day it had convulsions and died a month later. It was held that there was evidence to go to the jury of manslaughter.

Absence of body

The absence of a body, will not stand in the way of a conviction.

Attorney General V E. & R. Edwards (1935)

This was a trial for the murder of an infant whose parents were not married to each other. The trial judge certified that it was a fit case for appeal on the grounds that the body had not been found and that no medical evidence had, or could have been tendered that the infant had died a violent death, and whether the jury, in the absence of direct evidence of a killing, and on the facts before them, were entitled to infer that the infant had been murdered. It was held by the Court of Criminal Appeal, that the verdict could not be set aside.

Attorney General V Ball (1936)

The accused was indicted for matricide. He made a statement to the effect that his mother had committed suicide and that he had put her body into the sea. A bloodstained hatchet was found in the house and a very large amount of blood was splashed about. It was held that there was evidence sufficient to go to the jury that the deceased met her death at the hands of the accused.

See also *People (A. G.) V Thomas (1954)* at page 354.

People (Attorney General) V Cadden (1956)

It was held by the Court of Criminal Appeal, that a jury may convict on purely circumstantial evidence but to do this they must be satisfied that not only the circumstances were consistent with the prisoner having committed the act but also that the facts were such as to be inconsistent with any other rational conclusion than that he was the guilty person.

Penalty

By section 1 of the Criminal Justice Act, 1990; No person shall suffer death for any offence. "any" would cover every offence.

By section 2 of the same Act: A person convicted of treason or murder shall be sentenced to imprisonment for life.

People V Murtagh (1966)

It was held that in ... the case of murder where the penalty is penal servitude for life, no lesser penalty may be pronounced.

Murder and the Criminal Justice Act, 1990

The Criminal Justice Act, 1990, as already noted abolished the death penalty and substituted imprisonment for life and provided that minimum periods of imprisonment shall be served by persons convicted of treason or of certain categories of murder. References immediately following are to the 1990 Act.

Special provisions s. 3(1)

The Act applies to:

(i) murder of a member of the Garda Siochana acting in the course of his duty, or

(ii) murder of a prison officer acting in the course of his duty, or

(iii) murder done in the course or furtherance of an offence under section 6, 7, 8 or 9 of the Offences against the State Act, 1939, or in the course or furtherance of the activities of an unlawful organisation within the meaning of section 18 (other than paragraph (f)) of that Act, and

(iv) murder, committed within the State for a political motive, of the head of a foreign state or of a member of the government of, or a diplomatic officer of, a foreign state; and an attempt to commit any such murder.

The Offences against the State Act, 1939 provides:

Section 6: usurpation of the functions of government,

Section 7: obstruction of government,

Section 8 : obstruction of the President,

Section 9 : interference with certain public servants,

Section 18(f) : relates to organisations which advocate the non-payment of monies to the public purse.

Distinct offence s. 2(a)

2 (a) ..murder to which this section applies, and an attempt to commit such a murder, shall be a distinct offence from murder an from an attempt to commit murder and....

Murder to which section 3 applies is a new offence replacing the offence of capital murder. See *People (D. P. P.) V Murray (1977)*, below.

Minimum period of imprisonment s. 4

Where a person (other than a child or young person) is convicted of treason or murder or attempt to murder to which section 3 applies, the court -

(a) in the case of treason or murder, shall in passing sentence specify as a minimum period of imprisonment to be served by that person a period of not less than forty years,

(b) in the case of an attempt to commit murder, shall pass a sentence of imprisonment of not less than twenty years as the minimum period of imprisonment to be served by that person.

Restriction on power to commute s. 5(1)

The power conferred by section 23 of the Criminal Justice Act, 1951, to commute or remit a punishment shall not, in respect of a person convicted under section 3, be exercisable before the minimum period specified above, less any reduction under section 5(2) below.

Presidential pardon

The Constitution at Article 13 provides:

6. The right of pardon and the power to commute or remit punishment imposed by any court exercising criminal jurisdiction are hereby vested in the President, but such power of commutation or remission may, except in capital cases, also be conferred by law on other authorities.

9. The powers and functions conferred on the President, ... shall be exercisable and performable by him only on the advise of the Government, ...

A Presidential pardon is unaffected by the provisions of the Act.

Remission by good conduct s. 5(2)

The rule of practice whereby prisoners generally may earn remission of sentence by industry and good conduct shall apply in the case of a person convicted under section 3. It is the practice to grant one-quarter remission of sentences of penal servitude for good conduct

Temporary release s. 5(3)

Any power conferred by rules made under section 2 of the Criminal Justice Act, 1960, to release temporarily a person serving a sentence of imprisonment shall not, in the case of a person convicted under section 3, be exercisable during the period for which the commutation or remission of his punishment is prohibited by section 5(1) unless for grave reasons of a humanitarian nature, and any release so granted shall be only of such limited duration as is justified by those reasons.

Procedure s. 6

(1) Where a person is accused of murder to which section 3 applies or of any attempt to commit such a murder, he shall be charged in the indictment with murder to which that section applies or, as the case may be, with an attempt to commit such a murder.

(2) A person indicted for murder to which section 3 applies may-

(a) if the evidence does not warrant a conviction for such murder but warrants a conviction for murder be found guilty of murder,

(b) if the evidence does not warrant a conviction murder but warrants a conviction for manslaughter be found guilty of manslaughter.

(3) A person indicted for an attempt to commit a murder to which section 3 applies may, if the evidence does not warrant a conviction for such an attempt but warrants a conviction for an attempt to commit murder, be found guilty of an attempt to commit murder.

It follows from the provisions of this section that where a person is charged with murder, he may not afterwards be convicted of murder to which section 3 applies.

Consequential amendments

By section 7 of the Act there are a number of consequential amendments to the effect that the sentence of "death" is replaced by "imprisonment for life". The Acts affected are: the Piracy Act, 1837, Treason Act, 1939 and the Defence Act, 1954.

Mens rea

Section 3(2)(a) goes on to provides that: a person shall not be convicted of murder to which this section applies or of an attempt to commit such a murder unless it is proved that he knew of the existence of each ingredient of the offence specified in the relevant paragraph of subsection (1) or was reckless as to whether or not that ingredient existed.

Sub-section 2(b) provides that the law relating to murder shall apply to this offence; which means section 4 of the Criminal Justice Act, 1964 (see above).

It must be shown in respect of an accused:

1. he knew of the existence of each ingredient of the offence specified in the relevant paragraph of subsection (1) or

2. was reckless as to whether or not that ingredient existed.

In respect of section 3(1)(i) this could require proof that:

(a) the accused intended to kill or cause serious injury to the victim,

(b) the victim was a member of the Garda Síochána,

(c) the victim was acting in the course of his duty,

(d) the accused knew the victim to be a member of the Garda Síochána,

(e) the accused knew that the victim was acting as a member of the Garda Síochána in the course of his duty.

Note the following case in respect of the former offence of capital murder:

People (D. P. P.) V Marie and Noel Murray (1977)

The accused who were husband and wife, escaped in a car after an armed robbery. The driver of a private car, who was passing at the time, pursed the robbers in his car until eventually the robbers' car stopped and the accused ran away from it. The pursuer stopped his car and ran after and overtook the husband. When he was about to seize the husband, the wife shot and killed him. The pursuer was a member of the Garda Siochana who was not in uniform and who was not on duty. The accused were convicted in the Special Criminal Court of capital murder and sentenced to death. On a final appeal from the Court of Criminal Appeal it was held by the Supreme Court:

1 The offence of capital murder is a new statutory offence which requires proof of *mens rea* in relation to each of its constituent elements.

2 That the requisite *mens rea* to support a conviction for capital murder may be established by proof of the specific intention mentioned in section 4 of the 1964 Act as applied to a victim known by the accused at the time of the killing to be a policeman acting in the course of his duty.

Attempts to murder

Attempted murder

It is not possible to attempt murder without intending to kill. In the case of murder itself an intent to cause serious injury is sufficient, however in the case of an attempt to murder an intent to kill is required. See *People V Douglas and Hayes* below.

The Offence against the Person Act, 1861 creates a number of ancillary offence:

Conspiracy s. 4

All person who shall conspire, confederate, and agree to murder any person, whether he be (an Irish citizen) or not, and whether he be within (Ireland) or not, and whosoever shall solicit, encourage, persuade, or endeavour to persuade, or shall purpose to any person, to murder any other person, shall be liable to ten years imprisonment.

Administration of poison s. 11

Whosoever shall administer to or cause to be administered to or to be taken by any person any poison or other destructive thing or shall by any means whatsoever wound or cause grievous bodily harm to any person, with intent to commit murder, shall be liable to life imprisonment

Destruction of buildings s. 12

Whosoever, by explosion shall destroy or damage any building with intent to commit murder, shall be liable to life imprisonment.

Setting fire to a ship s. 13

Whosoever shall set fire to any ship or vessel with intent to commit murder shall be liable to life imprisonment.

Attempt to poison etc. s. 14

Whosoever shall attempt to administer to, any person any poison or other destructive thing, or shall shoot at any person, or shall attempt to drown, suffocate, or strangle any person, with intent to commit murder, shall be liable to life imprisonment.

People (D. P. P.) V Douglas & Hayes (1985)

It was held by the Court of Criminal Appeal that; While it was anomalous that where a person shoots at another intending to cause serious injury and that person dies, the offence of murder has been committed, while if he does not die the offence of shooting with intent to murder has not been committed, section 14 of the 1861 Act specifically required proof of an intent to kill and it was irrelevant that the court of trial was satisfied that those who fired the shots would have been guilty of murder had any person been killed. In order to determine whether an intent to kill existed, a court may take into account that a reasonable man would have foreseen that the natural and probable consequence of the acts was to cause death and that the accused acted in reckless disregard of that likely outcome of the acts, but such factors of themselves would not constitute proof of such intent.

Attempt by any other means s. 15

Whosoever shall, by any means other than those specified above, attempt to commit murder, shall be liable to life imprisonment.

Sending letters s. 16

Whosoever shall maliciously send, any letter or writing threatening to kill or murder any person, shall be liable to ten years imprisonment.

These offences would not have been created if the common law as to assault had been sufficient to deal with circumstances that might have arisen. All of the above except the offence under section 4 are felonies, see also the offence of attempting to choke under section 21, at page 64.

Manslaughter

Manslaughter is the unlawful and felonious killing of another person without any malice either express or implied. It is a diverse crime, covering all unlawful homicides which are not murder. At common law murder and manslaughter were the one offence of homicide, a jury may return an alternative verdict of manslaughter where an accused in indicted for murder. It is usual to divide manslaughter into two forms; voluntary and involuntary.

Voluntary manslaughter

Voluntary manslaughter is an unlawful killing which is reduced from murder to manslaughter because of provocation.

Provocation

Provocation is a defence to a charge of murder, the effect of which is to reduce to manslaughter what would otherwise be murder. Such a killing may occur where as the result of a quarrel two persons fight and as excessive and unreasonable force is used there is a death.

Where a person used force in defence of his own life and its use was such as was necessary in the circumstances, he having no means of escape and no other means of resistance, then it is excusable homicide.

Provocation may consist of violent assault accompanied by gross insults. It would also arise where one spouse finds another in the act of adultery and kills immediately. An unlawful imprisonment or an unlawful arrest may be a sufficient provocation to reduce to manslaughter a killing inflicted by the actual person imprisoned or arrested.

The provocation must be so recent and so strong, that the accused person at the time of the killing was not the master of himself. If there is time between the provocation and the killing for the blood to cool, the offence will be murder.

The distinction between the objective and the subjective condition of the accused has been considered by the courts: Did the accused lose his self-control ? Were the circumstances such that a reasonable person would have lost his self-control ?

People V MacEoin (1978)

The Court of Criminal Appeal ruled that the subjective test is to be applied in relation to provocation, was the accused actually provoked ? Before the plea of provocation fails, the prosecution must prove beyond reasonable doubt:

(a) That the accused was not provoked to such an extent that having regard to his temperament, character and circumstances he lost his self-control at the time of the wrongful act, and

(b) That the force used was unreasonable and excessive having regard to the provocation.

Whether there was sufficient provocation or not is a matter of fact for the jury, but as to whether there is enough evidence of this to be submitted to the jury is for the judge.

People (D. P. P.) V Kehoe (1992)

It was held by the Court of Criminal Appeal: Whereas it is accepted law that when a defence of provocation is put forward the onus is on the prosecution to establish beyond reasonable doubt that the accused was not provoked to such an extent that having regard to his temperament, character and circumstances he lost control of himself at the time of the wrongful act, it is clear that a psychiatrist could not give any relevant, admissible evidence in relation to the state of mind, temperament etc. of the accused, which the accused could not give himself. ... as far as criminal cases are concerned such evidence is properly to be confined to matters such as insanity.

Involuntary manslaughter

Involuntary manslaughter is committed where a person brings about the death of another by acting in some unlawful manner, without the intention of killing or doing an act likely to kill.

It may arise in the following ways:

> (a) by an unlawful and dangerous act; or
> (b) by the omission to perform a legal duty; or
> (c) by a lawful act performed with criminal negligence.

an unlawful act

The unlawful act must be done with the intention of causing physical harm, or alarm to another, but not with the intention of causing death or grievous bodily harm (sometimes called constructive manslaughter).

The accused is not guilty of murder because he lacks the necessary malice aforethought, however the unlawful act must be in the nature of an assault which does require *mens rea*.

The following cases illustrate this mode of involuntary manslaughter:

R V Wild (1837)

The accused gave a guest who would not go a kick which resulted in his death. There was no intention of his intending to cause any serious harm, but he was convicted of manslaughter because "a kick is not a justifiable mode of turning a man out of your house, though he be a trespasser".

R V Connor (1885)

A mother threw a piece of iron at a child with the intention of frightening him, it struck and killed another child. She was convicted of manslaughter.

R V Larkin (1943)

The accused flourished an open razor, intending only to frighten a man who had been associating with his mistress. The mistress who had been drinking, swayed against the accused and her throat was cut by the razor. He was convicted of manslaughter.

People (A. G.) V Crosbie and Meehan (1966)

The English case of Larkin was upheld and Kenny J. stated "the act causing death must be unlawful and dangerous to constitute the offence of manslaughter. The dangerous quality of the act must be judged by objective standards."

omission to perform a duty

The intentional or grossly negligent omission to perform a legal duty, in which neither death nor grievous bodily harm was intended or known to be a likely consequence; can result in a manslaughter.

Unless it is provided for specifically by statute, the common law imposes no duty upon a person to act in a particular way towards another. In certain cases a person owes a legal duty to others and where his failure to perform that legal duty is coupled with criminal negligence as distinct from negligence generally and results in death, he is guilty of manslaughter. The legal duty must be owed by the accused person because of his custody of, or control over, the deceased person, who must have been helpless. The death that resulted must have been unintentional.

Such a legal duty would exist where there is:
(a) a special relationship;
(b) a voluntary assumption of responsibility;
(c) a contractual duty;
(d) a statutory duty;
(e) a duty arising because of previous conduct.

Accordingly a person would have no legal duty to protect a stranger.

The following cases may be noted:

R V Lowe (1850)

The accused a colliery engineer left his post, leaving in charge of the engine a boy who to his knowledge was unable to control it. As a result of which another was killed. The accused was convicted of manslaughter.

R V Instan (1893)

The accused, lived with her aunt, who was seventy-three years of age and a helpless invalid. During the final ten days of the aunt's life, the accused failed to supply her with food or medical attendance, thus accelerating her death. She was convicted of manslaughter.

R V Senior (1899)

A member of a sect which believed that the acceptance of medical aid was tantamount to a lack of faith in God, omitted to obtain aid for his eight month old child who had pneumonia and died. Evidence was given which showed that the child's life would have been saved by medical treatment. The father was convicted of manslaughter.

act performed with criminal negligence

Manslaughter by negligence does not lend itself to precise and concise definition. A person may be doing some act lawful in its nature, but doing it recklessly and therefore unlawfully. The degree of negligence

must be much higher than that which might ground liability in tort.
Attorney General V Dunleavy (1948)

It was stated that the trial judge should instruct the jury that manslaughter is a serious crime and that before convicting of manslaughter they must be satisfied that the fatal negligence was of a very high degree and was such as to involve a high degree of risk of substantial personal injury to others.

Because of the very high degree of negligence required for manslaughter in relation to motor accidents, the offence of dangerous driving causing death (at page 218) was created.

It was held by the Court of Criminal Appeal, that the trial judge should see that the jury is given clearly to understand as follows:

(a) that negligence in this connection means failure to observe such a course of conduct as experience shows to be necessary if, in the circumstances, the risk of injury to others is to be avoided, i.e., failure to behave as a reasonable driver would;

(b) that the jury must be satisfied that negligence upon the part of the accused was responsible for the death in question;

(c) that there are different degrees of negligence, fraught with different legal consequences;

(d) that manslaughter is a felony and a very serious crime, and that before convicting of same the jury must be satisfied that the fatal negligence was of a very high degree, and was such as to involve, in a high degree, the risk or likelihood of substantial personal injury to others.

The following case was approved of:
Andrew V D. P. P. (1937)

It was held by the House of Lords that to kill a person while driving recklessly or at a speed or in a manner which was dangerous to the public was not manslaughter in the absence of "criminal negligence".
R V Dant (1865)

The accused turned out a very vicious and dangerous horse to graze. It kicked a child on the head and killed her, he was convicted of manslaughter.

Where a person kills another accidentally while doing what is an unlawful act of a minor nature, not amounting to felony or misdemeanour, it is not manslaughter
Attorney General V Maher (1936)

Accused drove a motor car without a licence and in the course of doing so killed a man. There was no evidence of culpable negligence. It was held that the evidence was not sufficient to uphold a charge of manslaughter.

The consideration of "recklessness" in a number of English cases, points towards a category of "killing recklessly".

Killing recklessly may arise where the accused either:

(a) recognises an obvious and serious risk of causing physical injury and nevertheless takes it, or

Homicide

(b) gives no thought to the possibility of there being a serious risk of causing physical injury which would be obvious to a reasonable man.
See *Kong Cheuk Kwan V The Queen (1985)*

Manslaughter is a felony at common law, by section 5 of the Offences against the Person Act, 1861 the punishment is penal servitude for life. Whereas the penalty for murder is mandatory, the punishment for manslaughter is at the discretion of the court, such punishment may reflect the circumstances giving rise to the offence.

Suicide

Suicide is the taking of ones own life with malice aforethought and it is a felony. At common law no suicide could be buried in consecrated ground, a person who took their own life was buried on the highway, with a stake through his body and his goods were forfeited. In later times a suicide was buried between the hours of nine and twelve at night, without any service. The confiscation of goods of suicides was put to an end with the general abolition of forfeiture for felony by the Forfeiture Act, 1870 (at page 15).

Attempted suicide

An attempt at suicide is a misdemeanour and by the Summary Jurisdiction (Ireland) Amendment Act, 1871, section 9 as amended by section 85 of the Court of Justice Act, 1936, such a charge may be tried summarily by a Judge of the District Court if the person charged shall confess and consent to be so tried.

Any person who instigates another to commit suicide is guilty of murder.

Suicide pacts

R V Abbot (1903)

It was held that if two parties mutually agree to commit suicide, and only one accomplishes that object, the survivor is guilty of murder. This is known as a suicide pact.

Suicide Bill

A suicide bill was introduced in the Senate in March 1993:

s. 3. The rule of law whereby it is a crime for a person to commit suicide is hereby abrogated.

s. 4. (1) A person who aids, abets, counsels or procures the suicide of another, or an attempt to commit suicide, shall be liable on conviction on indictment to imprisonment for a term not exceeding ten years.

(2) If on the trial of an indictment for murder or manslaughter it is proved that the accused aided, abetted, counselled or procured the suicide of the person in question, the jury may find him guilty of that offence.

Chapter 8

Assault and battery

The principal non-fatal offences against the person, other than sexual assault offences are common law assault and battery and the aggravated assault offences contained in the Offences against the Person Act, 1861.

At common law assault and battery are distinct offences. Usually both offences are committed together and the entire transaction is described in law as "an assault and battery". This has been shortened in lay terms as "an assault" and even lawyers use "an assault" as synonymous with "battery". Hence it is common for the term "assault" to cover both.

Assault

An assault is an act by which any person, intentionally, or possibly, recklessly, causes another person to fear the immediate application to himself of unlawful physical force. The *mens rea* of assault is the intention to create in the person's mind a belief in the immediate application of unlawful physical force. The *actus reus* is the creation in the mind of a person the belief that unlawful physical force is to be used immediately against him.

Words on their own are insufficient to constitute an assault and words may mitigate a physical act as in the *Tuberville* case below. Words uttered after a victim has been placed in an apprehensive state would not mitigate an assault as it has already taken place. If in the *St. George* case below, it was stated afterwards "the gun is not loaded". Words such as "your money or your life" accompanied by the physical means to carry out such a threat would constitute an assault.

Alarm is essential to an assault. Hence if a person is so far away, that he cannot possibly touch him, it is no assault, furthermore to constitute an assault there must be the means of carrying the threat into effect. If a person is unaware of a threat to themselves such as waving a knife over them whilst they are asleep there is no assault. There must be an intention or recklessness as to the creation of an apprehension of unlawful physical force in the mind of the potential victim.

Tuberville V Savage (1669)

The plaintiff was alleged to have put his hand upon his sword and said "if it were not assize time, I would not take such language from you". It was held by the Court that this was not an assault.

Stephens V Meyers (1830)

It was not held to be an assault, where the defendant had advanced upon another with threats and clenched fists and, at the last moment, was prevented from striking him.

R V St. George (1840)

It was held that it was an assault to point an unloaded gun at someone who believed it to be loaded and was put in fear.

Battery

A battery is the actual intended use of unlawful force on another person without his consent. The *mens rea* of battery is the intention to apply unlawful physical force. The *actus reus* is the actual application of unlawful physical force. The force applied need not be violent, no actual harm need be done or threatened. The slightest force will suffice as long as it was exercised in a hostile manner. The force applied or threatened need not involve immediate contact, it is sufficient if harm is done or threatened to a person's clothes without touching his skin, similarly the hostile force may be exercised directly or even indirectly, as by striking a horse thus making it throw its rider.

Defences to assault

The exercise of force against the person of another is not always unlawful. It may be shown by an accused that he was justified or excused in law by what he did.

Misadventure

It is a good defence that the alleged assault happened by misadventure. There are many cases of accidents which cannot be set up as a defence in an action for trespass to the person, but which would certainly be a good defence upon an indictment. In general the same circumstances that would excuse a homicide (see chapter 7), would also be a good defence in relation to assault.

Consent

As a general rule it is a good defence that the person complaining of assault or battery consented to the acts complained of, if such consent is freely given by a rational and sober person, knowing the nature of the act, unless the consent is to bodily injury or to acts likely or intended to do bodily harm or to an injury constituting a breach of the public peace.

Further exceptions to this general rule would be:

Blows given in the course of athletic contests. As in the case of a lawful sport, it is good defence that the alleged assault occurred during a friendly contest; or that it happened by accident whilst the accused was engaged in some sport or game, which was not dangerous.

Blows given during innocent horseplay amongst friends or acquaintances.

It is unlawful to strike another person with such a degree of violence that bodily harm is a probable consequence, and consent cannot be a defence in such circumstances.

In the case of a surgical operation, carried out by a competent surgeon, however great the risk, the consent of the patient will be a full justification for what would otherwise be an aggravated assault.

Chastisement

It was a good defence at common law that the alleged battery was the correcting of a child by its parents, but such punishment must be of a moderate and reasonable nature. A schoolteacher was similarly entitled, but with the abolition of corporal punishment in schools, this is now most unlikely.

Self-defence

It is a good defence, in justification even of a wounding, that the accused was attacked first and committed the alleged assault in his own defence. It is not necessary that a person should wait to be actually struck before striking in self-defence. There is in such circumstances a duty to retreat, if possible.

Spouses may justify an assault in defence of one another, as may a parent in defence of his child, and a master in defence of his servant any force used in such circumstances, must be reasonable, for if it were excessive, or greater than was necessary for mere defence, or if it were after all danger was past and was by way of revenge, then there can be no justification.

The right of self defence extends to the defence of property. It is a good defence that the assault was committed, by the accused in defence of his property or possessions, but again any force used must be reasonable in the circumstances. Only after he has been requested to leave and on refusing to do so, may a trespasser be removed by force. However in the case of a burglar force may be used to expel such a person immediately. Also force may be used to resist anyone who attempts to take possession of a persons goods. See also the consideration of self defence at page 37.

Execution of process

It is good defence that the accused was an officer of justice implementing a process. However no greater of force can be used than was necessary to secure the prisoner. A person may justify laying his hands upon another to prevent him from fighting, or committing a breach of the peace.

Particular offences

At common law both assault and battery are misdemeanours, assault at common law is more often referred to as "common assault" the remainder of the law with regard to "assaults" is principally contained in the Offences against the Person Act, 1861. All references below are to the 1861 Act unless otherwise stated. By this Act the more serious offences are made felonies, while the lesser offences are ranked as misdemeanours.

Common assault

By section 42 of the Act; where any person shall unlawfully assault or beat any other person they may be tried summarily.

The Criminal Justice Act, 1951, section 11 provides that a person convicted of either common assault or battery shall be liable to a fine of £50 and or six months imprisonment.

By section 47 of the Act, whosoever shall be convicted on indictment for a common assault is liable to one years imprisonment.

State (Clancy) V Wine (1980)

It was held by the High Court, that where a person is charged with common assault, he may be prosecuted either summarily or upon indictment and that the mode of prosecution to be employed, is the choice of the prosecuting authority, and the person charged has no right to be consulted on the matter.

Wounding with intent s. 18

Whosoever shall unlawfully and maliciously by any means whatsoever wound or cause any grievous bodily harm to any person, or shoot at any person, or, by drawing a trigger or in any, other manner, attempt to discharge any kind of loaded arms at any person, with intent, in any of the cases aforesaid, to maim, disfigure, or disable any person, or with intent to resist or prevent the lawful apprehension or detainer of any person, shall be guilty of felony... and liable to life imprisonment.

This section creates four types of assault offences:
1. To "wound" any person,
2. To "cause grievous bodily harm" to any person,
3. To "shoot at" any person,
4. To attempt, "by drawing a trigger, or in any other manner", to discharge any kind of loaded arms at any person.

Each of these offences may be done with any of the following intents:
> (a) to maim,
> (b) to disfigure,
> (c) to disable,
> (d) to do some other grievous bodily harm,
> (e) to resist or prevent the lawful apprehension or
> (f) detainer of any person.

Accordingly there are 24 separate offences in section 18 of the Act.

To <u>maim</u> is to injure any part of a person's body, such as to render him less able to defend himself.

Foley V Corporation of Dublin (1939)

A violent attack was made on a Garda, while he was seeking to bring disturbers of the public peace to justice. He sustained a fracture of his right jaw and his left jaw was broken. He lost five teeth and others were loosened. It was held by the High Court that the injuries suffered amounted to maiming under section 106 of the Grand Jury (Ireland) Act, 1836 (since repealed).

To <u>disfigure</u> is to do some external injury, which takes from a person's appearance.

To <u>disable</u> is to do something which creates a permanent disability and not just a temporary injury.

<u>grievous bodily harm</u> means serious harm, but it need not be either permanent or dangerous.
People (A. G.) V Goulding (1964)
The applicant was charged under the Offences against the Person Act, 1861 sections 18 and 20 Per O'Dalaigh, C.J. : "It should be noted that in defining wounding with intent to do grievous bodily harm the trial Judge inadvertently said it was something that interfered with the health or comfort of another. This sets too low an onus upon the prosecution. 'grievous bodily harm' requires that the interference be a 'serious' one."
Harm may be caused without personal contact, for example: if A breaks his leg from jumping out of a window to avoid an attack by B, then B will be liable. Whether in any particular case, the harm done was grievous is for a jury to decide.

To constitute a <u>wound</u> there must be a breaking of the whole skin, hence a mere scratch is not a wound, nor will it be sufficient that bones have been broken, if the skin is not also broken.
People (A. G.) V Messit (1974)
It was held by the Supreme Court that a wound, for the purposes of section 18 and 20, must include a severance of the entire skin. To constitute a maiming, disfiguring or disabling or other grievous bodily harm within section 18, the injury must be a serious one though not necessarily a permanent one.
The intent is important in these offence and it is the above "intents" that distinguish between a charge under this section and what is to follow. The unlawful infliction of grievous bodily harm without "malice" is not an offence under this section, but would perhaps be a "common assault". In order for there to be a conviction it is necessary for the appropriate intent to be proved. It is not necessary that the person whom it was intended to harm should be the one who was actually harmed.

Unlawful wounding s. 20
Whosoever shall unlawfully and maliciously wound or inflict any grievous bodily harm upon any other person, either with or without any weapon or instrument, shall be guilty of a misdemeanour... and liable to five years imprisonment.
The term "wound" and "grievous bodily harm" as used in this section have the same meaning as above, in section 18. With regard to "inflict" any injury which is held to constitute an assault, need not

necessarily be inflicted directly. The absence of the word "assault" has the effect of giving this offence a wider construction than the above.

R V Martin (1881)

Shortly before the end of a performance in a theatre, the accused who intended to cause terror in the minds of the audience, turned off the lights on a staircase and placed an iron bar across one of the doorways. In the panic that followed a number of persons suffered injury. The accused was charged under section 20; he was convicted.

R V Halliday (1889)

The accused terrified his wife with threats of personal violence and in order to escape began to climb out the window, with the result that she fell and broke her leg. The conviction of the accused was upheld on appeal.

R V Cunningham (1957)

The meaning of "maliciously" was considered in this case; it involves an actual intention to do the particular kind of harm which, in fact, was done, or recklessness as to whether such harm might occur or not.

Attempting to choke s. 21

Whosoever shall, by any means whatsoever, attempt to, choke, suffocate, or strangle any other person, or shall, by any means calculated to, choke, suffocate, or strangle, attempt to render any other person insensible, unconscious, or incapable of resistance, with intent in any of such cases thereby to enable himself or any other person to commit, or with intent in any of such cases thereby to assist any other person in committing any indictable offence, shall be guilty of felony and shall be liable to life imprisonment.

Administering drugs s. 22

Whosoever shall unlawfully apply or administer to or cause to be taken by, or attempt to apply or administer to or attempt to cause to be administered to or taken by, any person, any chloroform, laudanum, or other stupefying or overpowering drug, matter or thing, with intent in any of such cases thereby to enable himself or any other person to commit, or with intent in any such cases thereby to assist any other person in committing, any indictable offence, shall be guilty of felony and be liable to life imprisonment.

Administering poison to endanger life s. 23

Whosoever shall unlawfully and maliciously administer to or cause to be administered to or taken by any other person poison or other destructive or noxious thing so as thereby to endanger the life of such person, or so as thereby to inflict upon such person any grievous bodily harm, shall be guilty of felony... and liable to ten years imprisonment.

It must be shown that; whatever was administered did endanger life or cause grievous bodily harm. Whether the thing administered is a "noxious thing" or not may depend on the quantity administered, some drugs being harmless in small quantities, and dangerous only in large quantities. It has been held that heroin is a "noxious thing".

Administering poison with intent to injure s. 24

Whosoever shall unlawfully and maliciously administer to or cause to be administered to or taken by any other person any poison or other destructive or noxious thing, with intent to injure, aggrieve, or annoy such person, shall be guilty of misdemeanour... and shall be liable to five years imprisonment.

R V Dones (1897)

The defendant squirted a solution of household ammonia during a fight. It was held that this was not "administering".

It need not be shown that "harm" has been caused in relation to, this offence. In respect of both offences it is necessary that "intent" be shown.

By section 25 of the Act upon an indictment for section 23, the jury may convict of the lesser offence under section 24.

Assault with intent s. 38

Whosoever shall assault any person with intent to commit felony, or shall assault, resist, or wilfully obstruct a peace officer in the due execution of his duty, or any person acting in aid of such officer, or shall assault any person with intent to resist or prevent the lawful apprehension or detainer of himself or of any other person for any offence, shall be guilty of a misdemeanour,.. and shall be liable to two years imprisonment.

This section creates a number of offences:

1. Assault with intent to commit a felony,
2. Assaulting, resisting, or wilfully obstructing:
(a) a peace officer in due execution of his duty,
(b) a person, acting in aid of a peace officer in due execution of his duty,
3. Assaulting any person with intent, to resist, or prevent, the lawful apprehension or detainer of:
(a) himself, or
(b) any other person.

An offence under this section may with the consent of the Director of Public Prosecutions be dealt with in the District Court.

The Prevention of Crimes Act, 1871, provides:

Assault on a constable s. 12

Where any person is convicted of an assault on any constable when in the execution of his duty, such person shall be guilty of an offence against this Act.

This is a summary offence for which the penalty is a £20 fine and or six months imprisonment, or in the case of a similar offence within two years nine months imprisonment.

R V Forbes and Webb (1865)

An accused was convicted of assaulting plain clothes policemen in the execution of their duty. His claim that he did not know that they were policemen was held irrelevant. "The offence was, not assaulting them knowing them to be in execution of their duty, but assaulting them being in the execution of their duty".

Assault occasioning actual bodily harm s. 47

Whosoever shall be convicted upon an indictment of any assault occasioning actual bodily harm shall be liable,... to five years imprisonment. The Criminal Justice Act, 1951, section 2 provides that this offence may be tried summarily.

Actual bodily harm need not be an injury of a permanent nature; nor need it amount to grievous bodily harm, as mentioned above. The absence of any reference to "wound" or "inflict" in this section, gives the offence a narrower construction than the other offences above.

R V Miller (1954)

In relation to a charge under this section the Judge directed the jury that actual bodily harm meant "any hurt or injury calculated to interfere with the health and comfort" of the victim.

For this offence it is not necessary to prove, that the risk of injury was foreseen, the intent is the same as in the case of a common assault.

Assault with intent to rob

The Larceny Act, 1916, section 23 (as amended by the Criminal Law (Jurisdiction) Act, 1976) provides that the penalty for an assault with intent to rob is life imprisonment (see page 136).

Other non-fatal offences upon the person

Kidnapping

This is an offence at common law committed, where any person of any age or either sex is stolen or carried away by force or fraud against the persons will. It has been held that the offence is committed if there is a carrying away of the person even for a short distance.

The Criminal Law Act, 1976, section 11 declares that kidnapping is a felony and is punishable by life imprisonment. See also the offence of child stealing at page 90.

False imprisonment

False imprisonment is the unlawful and total restraint of the personal liberty of another, whether by constraining him or compelling him to go to a particular place or by confining him in a prison or police station or private place, or by detaining him against his will in a public place.

People V Edge (1943)

The Supreme Court held that a boy under fourteen years or a girl under sixteen years has not got the legal capacity to consent and such apparent consent would not be a valid defence to a charge of false imprisonment or kidnapping.

The Criminal Law Act, 1976, section 11 declares that false imprisonment is a felony and punishable by life imprisonment.

It is not essential that a person be aware of his imprisonment, he may be either asleep or drunk. The offence may or may not involve an assault.

"false" means unlawful, where it is clear that no charges are to be levelled against an arrested person, he should be released at once. Any restraint must be completed in every direction, there is no false imprisonment, where a person is free to move in a particular direction.

Walters V W. H. Smith & Son (1914)

A private detective arrested the plaintiff on suspicion that he had stolen from one of the defendant's shops. He had not done so. It was held that in the case of a private citizen, an arrest for an already committed offence was lawful only if it could be proved that the offence had been committed, and that the person carrying out the arrest had reasonable and probable cause for his suspicion.

The plaintiff was awarded damages for false imprisonment.

Chapter 9

Sexual offences

The law as to sexual offences is contained in the following:
>Offences against the Person Act, 1861;
>Criminal Law Amendment Act, 1885;
>Criminal Law Amendment Act 1935;
>Criminal Law (Rape) Act 1981 and the
>Criminal Law (Rape) (Amendment) Act, 1990.

The 1981 Act is the principal Act and it was amended considerably by the 1990 Act. All references below are to the 1981 Act as amended unless otherwise stated.

The Criminal Justice Act, 1993, at section 5 requires courts, when determining the sentence to be imposed for a sexual offence or an offence involving violence or the threat of violence, to take into account any effect (including any long term effect) of the offence on the victim.

A sexual assault offence s. 1

A sexual assault offence means a rape offence and any of the following, namely, aggravated sexual assault, attempted aggravated sexual assault, sexual assault, attempted sexual assault, aiding, abetting, counselling and procuring aggravated sexual assault, attempted aggravated sexual assault, sexual assault or attempted sexual assault, incitement to aggravated sexual assault or sexual assault and conspiracy to commit any of the foregoing offences.

There are accordingly three types of sexual assault offences:
>Rape offences,
>Aggravated sexual assault and
>Sexual assault

A rape offence s. 1

A rape offence means any of the following, namely rape, attempted rape, burglary with intent to commit rape, aiding, abetting, counselling and procuring rape, attempted rape or burglary with intent to commit rape, and incitement to rape, and, rape under section 4 (of the 1990 Act), attempted rape under section 4, aiding, abetting, counselling and procuring rape under section 4, or attempted rape under section 4, and incitement to rape under section 4.

There are thus three types of rape offence:
>Rape,
>Burglary with intent to commit rape, and
>Rape under section 4 of the 1990 Act.

In addition there are ancillary offences in relation to:
attempt: this is to make an effort to accomplish something.
aiding: this is to help another in doing something

abetting: this is to encourage or assist in something.
counselling: this is to advise or suggest something.
procuring: this is to obtain or acquire, and
incitement: this is to urge on or stir up.

Rape s 2(1)

A man commits rape if,

(a) he has sexual intercourse with a woman who at the time of the intercourse does not consent to it, and

(b) at the time he knows that she does not consent to the intercourse or he is reckless as to whether she does or does not consent to it,

and references to rape in this Act and any other enactment shall be construed accordingly.

Sexual intercourse

Sexual intercourse means penetration of the vagina by the penis.

The Act at section 1(2) provides that references to sexual intercourse shall be construed as references to carnal knowledge as defined in section 63 of the Offences against the Person Act, 1861, so far as it relates to natural intercourse (under which such intercourse is deemed complete on proof of penetration only).

By section 63 of the 1861 Act whenever, it may be necessary to prove carnal knowledge, it shall not be necessary to prove the actual emission of seed in order to constitute a carnal knowledge, but the carnal knowledge shall be deemed complete upon proof of penetration only.

The slightest penetration shall suffice and it is not necessary to prove that the hymen was ruptured. Accordingly "sexual intercourse" includes sexual intercourse as is commonly understood, yet also includes acts which would not ordinarily amount to sexual intercourse

People (A. G.) V Dermody (1956)

The appellant was charged with unlawful carnal knowledge, of a girl under fourteen years of age. In evidence she said that the man had put his private part "a wee bit" into hers, but the evidence showed that the hymen had not been ruptured.

It was held by the Court of Criminal Appeal, that the offence of rape, or unlawful carnal knowledge contrary to the Criminal Law Amendment Act, 1935, could be sufficiently proved by proof of penetration, even though emission could not be proved.

A jury that had a reasonable doubt as to whether penetration occurred in a rape case could bring in a verdict of attempted rape where the verdict so permitted. See *People (D. P. P.) V Riordan* below.

Capacity to commit

The expression "man" as used in section 2(1) of the 1981 Act includes a male person of any age. Thus any male person of eight years of age and over (see infancy chapter 5) may be convicted of a rape offence.

There were two exceptions to this at common law: husbands and boys under fourteen years. At common law a husband could not, (this marital exemption has now been abolished, see below) as principal in the first degree commit rape on his wife, a wife was irrebuttably presumed to consent to sexual intercourse with her husband by virtue of the marriage contract. The exception for the husband could be found in the use of the words "<u>unlawful</u> sexual intercourse" in the statutory definition of rape prior to amendment by the 1990 Act.

There were circumstances however, in which the wife's consent to sexual intercourse at common law was considered as having been revoked.

(a) Where a decree of nullity has been granted.

(b) Where a divorce *a mensa et thora* (later a Judicial Separation) had been granted.

(c) Where there was a separation agreement and, in particular where such an agreement contained a non-molestation clause.

(d) Where the husband was subject to an injunction forbidding him to interfere with his wife. See *R V Clarke (1949)*.

(e) Where a husband had given an undertaking to the court in order to avoid the issue of such an injunction referred to in (d).

A husband was never entitled to use physical violence or fear in order to have sexual intercourse with his wife, if he did this amounted to an assault. See *R V Miller (1949)*.

Abolition of marital exemption in relation to rape s. 5 (1990 Act)

(1) Any rule of law by virtue of which a husband cannot be guilty of rape of his wife is hereby abolished.

(2) Criminal proceedings against a man in respect of the rape by him of his wife shall not be instituted except by or with the consent of the Director of Public Prosecutions.

Capacity to commit offences of a sexual nature s. 6 (1990 Act)

Any rule of law by virtue of which a male person is treated by reason of his age as being physically incapable of committing an offence of a sexual nature is hereby abolished.

At common law a boy under the age of fourteen years, was irrebuttably presumed physically incapable of rape, attempted rape, or of sodomy, whether he was or was not fully developed and actually did commit the offence.

Consent

The absence of consent of the victim is an essential feature of the *actus reus* of rape, and it is for the prosecution to prove the absence of such consent. The question to be asked is, not was the act against the will, but was it without consent.

Where consent is obtained by personal violence or by threats of personal violence there is no real consent.

Consent obtained by fraud is no real consent:

R V Flattery (1877)

The defendant professed to give surgical and medical advice. On the pretence that he was performing a surgical operation he had intercourse with a young girl, she offered no resistance. It was held that he was guilty of rape.

R V Williams (1923)

The defendant had sexual intercourse with one of his pupils to whom he was giving singing lessons, by the pretence that it was a method of training her voice. The girl offered no resistance. It was held that he was guilty of rape.

It is rape to have sexual intercourse with a woman, who is asleep or otherwise unconscious, as she is therefore unable to give or withhold consent. See *R V Mayers (1872)*

It is rape to have sexual intercourse with a woman due to plying her with drink. See *Camplin (1845)*. However if the drunkenness is due to her own excesses, the offence may be sexual assault and not rape.

The Criminal Law Amendment Act, 1885, section 4 provides: Whereas doubts have been entertained whether a man who induces a married woman to permit him to have connection with her by personating her husband is or is not guilty of rape, it is hereby enacted and declared that every such offender shall be deemed to be guilty of rape.

The question of consent does not arise in relation to defilement of girls under seventeen years, see the Criminal Law Amendment Act, 1935 considered below.

By section 2(2) of the Act: It is hereby declared that if at a trial for a rape offence the jury has to consider whether a man believed the a woman was consenting to sexual intercourse, the presence or absence of reasonable grounds for such belief is a matter to which the jury is to have regard, in conjunction with any other relevant matters, in considering whether he so believed.

By section 9 of the 1990 Act: It is hereby declared that in relation to an offence that consists of or includes the doing of an act to a person without the consent of that person any failure or omission by that person to offer resistance to the act does not of itself constitute consent to the act.

Mens rea of rape

The mental element of rape is contained in section 2(1)(b) of the Act: a man commits rape if at the time he knows that she does not consent to the intercourse or he is reckless as to whether she does or does not consent to it.

Three questions arise as to consent: time; knowledge and recklessness.

The time factor is important both before and during the act, a New Zealand case illustrates:

Kaitamaki v The Queen (1984)

This case was referred to the Judicial Committee of the Privy Council.

The evidence of the accused was that after he had penetrated the woman he became aware that she was not consenting; he did not however desist from intercourse. The trial judge directed the jury that if, having realised the woman was not willing, the defendant continued with the act of intercourse, it then became rape. On appeal to the Privy Council, the defence sought to establish the proposition that rape is penetration without consent: once penetration is complete the act of rape is concluded. Intercourse if it continues, is not rape, it was argued, because for the purposes of (section 63) it is complete upon penetration.

The appeal was dismissed, their Lordships agreed with the Court of Appeal of New Zealand. The Court, had expressed the opinion that the purpose of the section was to remove any doubts as to the minimum conduct needed to prove the fact of sexual intercourse. "complete" is used in the sense of having come into existence, but not in the sense of being at an end. Sexual intercourse is a continuing act which only ends with withdrawal. Accordingly a man is guilty of rape if he continued intercourse after he realised that the woman was no longer consenting.

A man must know that a woman does not consent to the intercourse, a mistaken belief as to consent would lack the necessary knowledge. The leading English case is:

Director of Public Prosecutions V Morgan (1976)

Morgan spent the evening with three friends and then invited them to his home to have sexual intercourse with his wife which, against her will each did. At their trial the accused claimed that even if she did not consent, nevertheless they had believed that she was consenting. The trial judge directed the jury that such a mistaken belief was a good defence provided that there had been reasonable grounds for such a belief. Subsequently the House of Lords held that the *mens rea* of rape was an intention to commit non-consensus intercourse and that therefore a mistaken belief, even if unreasonably held that the victim was consenting meant that the accused did not commit the offence.

The amendment to the law on rape brought about by section 2 of the 1981 Act above, occurred after this case.

The meaning of "reckless" has been considered by the English courts. The test of recklessness is a subjective one.

R V Satnam S. and Kewal S. (1984)

Bristow J. for the Court of Appeal stated that the word "reckless" in relation to rape involves a different concept to its use in relation to other crimes. In relation to offences against the person the forseeability, or possible forseeability, is as to the consequences of the criminal act. In the case of rape the forseeability is as to the state of mind of the victim.

In summing-up a case to a jury and to give a proper direction as to the issue of consent ".. the judge should, in dealing with the state of mind of the defendant, first of all direct the jury that before they could convict of rape the Crown had to prove either that the defendant knew that the woman did not want to have sexual intercourse, or was reckless as to whether she wanted to or not. If they were sure he knew she did not want to they should find him guilty of rape knowing there to be no consent. If they were not sure about that, then they would find him not guilty of such rape and should go on and consider reckless rape. If they thought he might genuinely have believed that she did want to, even though he was mistaken in his belief, they would find him not guilty if they were sure he had no genuine belief that she wanted to, they would find him guilty. If they came to the conclusion that he could not care less whether she wanted to or not, but pressed on regardless, then he would have been reckless and could not have believed that she wanted to, and they would find him guilty of reckless rape"

Nature of rape

In the *D. P. P. V Tiernan* case considered below, the Chief Justice considered the nature of the crime of rape. "The crime of rape must always be viewed as one of the most serious offences contained in our criminal law even when committed without violence beyond that constituting the act of rape itself. In *A. G. V Conroy (1965)*, this court stated that the nature of the offence was such as to render unconstitutional any statutory provision which could permit it ever to be regarded as a minor offence.

The act of forcible rape not only causes bodily harm but is also inevitably followed by emotional, psychological and psychiatric damage to the victim which can often be long term, and sometimes of lifelong duration.

In addition to those damaging consequences, rape can distort the victim's approach to her own sexuality. In many instances, rape can also impose upon the victim a deeply distressing fear of sexually transmitted disease and the possibility of a pregnancy and of a birth whose innocent issue could inspire a distress and even a loathing utterly alien to motherhood.

Rape is a gross attack upon the human dignity and the bodily integrity of a woman and a violation of her human and constitutional rights. As such it must attract very severe legal sanctions.

All these features which I mention in summary and not as an attempted comprehensive account of the character of rape apply even when it is committed without any aggravating circumstances. They are of such a nature as to make the appropriate sentence for any such rape a substantial immediate period of detention or imprisonment."

Sexual assault s. 2 (1990 Act)

(1) The offence of indecent assault upon any male person and the offence of indecent assault upon any female person shall be known as sexual assault.

(2) A person guilty of sexual assault shall be liable on conviction on indictment to imprisonment for a term not exceeding five years.

(3) Sexual assault shall be a felony.

Sexual assault may be defined as an assault accompanied by

circumstances of indecency. Assault as used here may mean an assault or a battery. Indecency could refer to a touching or threatened touching by, or of the sexual parts of the body.
People (A. G.) V O'Connor (1949)
It is not open to a jury to convict on a charge of indecent assault upon a female where the evidence proved shows that the person assaulted consented to the act committed upon her.

The 1935 Act at section 14, provides that: It shall not be a defence to a charge of indecent assault upon a person under the age of fifteen years to prove that such person consented to the act alleged to constitute such indecent assault.

Indecent assault

Indecent assault is an offence that exists alongside sexual assault.
Doolan V Director of Public Prosecutions (1992)
It was held by O'Hanlon J. in the High Court that assault is a common law misdemeanour which is capable of being committed in different ways. Indecent assault is a common law misdemeanour: being an assault committed in a particular way.

Aggravated sexual assault s. 3 (1990 Act)

(1) In this Act "aggravated sexual assault" means a sexual assault that involves serious violence or the threat of serious violence or is such as to cause injury, humiliation or degradation of a grave nature to the person assaulted.

(2) A person guilty of aggravated sexual assault shall be liable on conviction on indictment to imprisonment for life.

(3) Aggravated sexual assault shall be a felony.

This offence may be committed by either a man or a woman and against either a man or woman.

Aggravated sexual assault involves either:

(a) serious violence, or

(b) the threat of serious violence, or

(c) is such as to cause injury of a grave nature to the person assaulted, "injury" may be either damage or harm,

(d) is such as to cause humiliation of a grave nature to the person assaulted, "humiliation" would cause a person to feel disgraced, or

(e) is such as to cause degradation of a grave nature to the person assaulted "degradation" would bring disgrace on a person or reduce them to a lower status.

Rape under section 4 s. 4 (1990 Act)

(1) In this Act "rape under section 4" means a sexual assault that includes -

(a) penetration (however slight) of the anus or mouth by the penis, or

(b) penetration (however slight) of the vagina by any object held or manipulated by another person.

(2) A person guilty of rape under section 4 shall be liable on conviction on indictment to imprisonment for life.

(3) Rape under section 4 shall be a felony.

This offence may be committed by either a man or a woman. While (b) may only be committed against a woman, (a) may be committed against either a man or woman.

(a) is confined to a penetration by the penis only.

(b) is confined to a penetration of the vagina only. An "object" is something solid that can be seen or touched, examples might be a banana, bottle, knife or stick.

Buggery as it relates to mankind (see below) and which is an offence under section 61 of the Offences against the Person Act, 1861 and which consists of a penetration of the anus by the penis, is now included as a type of "rape under section 4".

Restriction on evidence s. 3(1)

If at a trial any person is for the time being charged with a sexual assault offence to which he pleads not guilty, then, except with the leave of the judge, no evidence shall be adduced and no question shall be asked in cross-examination at the trial, by or on behalf of any accused person at the trial, about any sexual experience (other than that to which the charge relates) of a complainant with any person.

People (D. P. P.) V McDonagh & Cawlly (1990)
While it was desirable that an application under section 3 of the 1981 Act be made as early as possible in a trial, it would not always be possible to make a single ruling on such an application; and it was not inconsistent with the section for a further or different application to be made at a later stage, the trial judge being required to exercise a discretion by reference to the factors clearly laid down in section 3.

Corroboration of evidence in offences of a sexual nature s. 7(1990)

(1) Subject to any enactment relating to the corroboration of evidence in criminal proceedings, where at the trial on indictment of a person charged with an offence of a sexual nature evidence is given by the person in relation to whom the offence is alleged to have been committed and, by reason only of the nature of the charge, there would, but for this section, be a requirement that that the jury be given a warning about the danger of convicting on the uncorroborated evidence of that other person, it shall be for the judge to decide in his discretion, having regard to all the evidence given, whether the jury should be given a warning; and accordingly any rule or practice by virtue of which there is such a requirement as aforesaid is hereby abolished.

(2) If a judge decides, in his discretion, to give such a warning as aforesaid, it shall not be necessary to use any particular form of words to do so.

Alternative verdicts s. 8 (1990 Act)

(1) A person indicted for rape may, if the evidence does not warrant a conviction for rape but warrants a conviction for rape under section 4 or aggravated sexual assault or sexual assault, be found guilty of rape under section 4 or of aggravated sexual assault or of sexual assault, as may be appropriate.

(2) A person indicted for rape may, if the evidence does not warrant a conviction for rape but warrants a conviction for an offence under section 1 (Defilement of girl under fifteen years of age) or 2 (Defilement of a girl under seventeen years) of the Criminal Law amendment Act, 1935 or under section 3 of the Criminal Law Amendment Act 1885 (Procurement), be found guilty of an offence under the said section 1, 2 or 3, as may be appropriate.

(3) A person indicted for rape under section 4 may, if the evidence does not warrant a conviction for rape under section 4 but warrants a conviction for aggravated sexual assault or for sexual assault, be found guilty of aggravated sexual assault or of sexual assault, as may be appropriate.

(4) A person indicted for aggravated sexual assault may, if the evidence does not warrant a conviction for aggravated sexual assault but warrants a conviction for sexual assault, be found guilty of sexual assault.

(5) A person indicted for an offence made felony by section 1 of the Criminal Law Amendment Act, 1935, may, if the evidence does not warrant a conviction for the felony or an attempt to commit the felony but warrants a conviction for an offence under section 2 of the Criminal Law Amendment Act, 1935 or section 3 of the Criminal Law Amendment Act, 1885, or rape under section 4 or aggravated sexual assault or sexual assault, be found guilty of an offence under the said section 2 or 3 or of rape under section 4, or of aggravated sexual assault or of sexual assault, as may be appropriate.

Complainant

A complainant means a person in relation to whom a sexual assault offence is alleged to have been committed. Throughout the 1981 Act the term "person" has been substituted (by section 17(2)(a) of the 1990 Act) for the term "woman" by the 1990 Act. The legislation in this area is gender neutral where possible.
People (D. P. P.) V Brophy (1992)
It was held by the Court of Criminal Appeal that where a complainant in a case involving a sexual offence does not make a complaint at the first reasonably available opportunity then evidence of the fact of the complaint as well as the terms thereof are inadmissible.

Trial by Central Criminal Court s. 10 (1990 Act)

A person indicted for a rape offence or the offence of aggravated sexual assault or attempted aggravated sexual assault or of aiding, abetting, counselling or procuring the offence of aggravated sexual assault or attempted aggravated sexual assault or of incitement to the offence of aggravated sexual assault or conspiracy to commit any of the foregoing offences shall be tried by the Central Criminal Court.

The offence of sexual assault continues to be tried in the Circuit Criminal Court.

Exclusion of the public s. 6

(1) Subject to subsections (2), (3) and (4), in any proceedings for a rape offence or the offence of aggravated sexual assault, or attempted aggravated sexual assault or of aiding, abetting, counselling or procuring the offence of aggravated sexual assault or attempted aggravated sexual assault or of incitement to the offence of aggravated sexual assault or conspiracy to commit any of the foregoing offences, the judge shall exclude from the court during the hearing all persons except officers of the court, persons directly concerned in the proceedings, *bona fide* representatives of the press and such other persons as the judge, may in his discretion permit to remain.

(2) Subject to subsection (3), during the hearing of an application under section 3 (including that section as applied by section 5) or under section 4(2), the judge, shall exclude from the court all persons except officers of the court and persons directly concerned in the proceedings.

(3) Subsections (1) and (2) are without prejudice to the right of a parent, relative or friend of the complainant or, where the accused is not of full age, of the accused to remain in court.

(4) In any proceedings to which subsection (1) applies the verdict or decision and the sentence (if any) shall be announced in public.

This provision does not apply to proceedings for the offence of sexual assault.

Anonymity of accused s. 8(1)

After a person is charged with a sexual assault offence no matter likely to lead members of the public to identify him, as the person against whom the charge is made shall be published in a written publication available to the public or be broadcast except -

(a) as authorised, or

(b) after he has been convicted of the offence.

This may be dispensed with, but not where it might enable members of the public to identify a person as a complainant.

The previous provision was confined to the offence of rape only, the provision now is much wider.

Sentencing

The 1861 Act at section 48 provides: Whosoever shall be convicted of the crime of rape shall be guilty of felony, and being convicted thereof shall be liable, to be kept in penal servitude for life.

The actual sentence to be passed is at the discretion of the court,

however see the proposals under the Criminal Justice Bill, 1993.
Director of Public Prosecutions V Tiernan (1988)

Finlay C.J. "This is an appeal to the Supreme Court by the appellant against the decision of the Court of Criminal Appeal, ...dismissing his application for leave to appeal against a sentence of 21 years' penal servitude imposed on him for rape. It is brought pursuant to a certificate issued by the Attorney General pursuant to section 29 of the Courts of Justice Act, 1924 ... The grounds upon which the Attorney General certified that the decision of the Court of Criminal Appeal involved a point of law of exceptional public importance, and that it was desirable in the public interest that an appeal should be taken to the Supreme Court was that it involved the guidelines which the court should apply in relation to sentences for the crime of rape. ... Whilst in every criminal case a judge must impose a sentence which in his opinion meets the particular circumstances of the case and of the accused person before him, it is not easy to imagine the circumstances which would justify departure from a substantial immediate custodial sentence for rape and I can only express the view that they would probably be wholly exceptional.

The facts of this case

Unfortunately, the facts of the rape to which this appellant pleaded guilty contain very many aggravating circumstances. They are:

(1) It was a gang rape, having been carried out by three men.

(2) The victim was raped on more than one occasion.

(3) The rape was accompanied by acts of sexual perversion.

(4) Violence was used on the victim in addition to the sexual acts committed against her.

(5) The rape was performed by an act of abduction in that the victim was forcibly removed from a car where she was in company with her boyfriend, and her boyfriend was imprisoned by being forcibly detained in the boot of the car so as to prevent him assisting her in defending herself.

(6) It was established that as a consequence of the psychiatric trauma involved in the rape the victim suffered from a serious nervous disorder which lasted for at least six months and rendered her for that period unfit for work.

(7) The appellant had four previous convictions, being (a) for assault occasioning actual bodily harm, (b) for aggravated burglary associated with a wounding, (c) for gross indecency, and (d) for burglary. Of this criminal record, particularly relevant as an aggravating circumstance to a conviction for rape are the crimes involving violence and the crime involving indecency.

The above summary of the facts surrounding the crime in this case reveals that very many thought not all of the most serious aggravating circumstances which can be attached to the crime of rape were present. ..

I would doubt that it is appropriate for an appellate court to appear to be laying down any standardisation or tariff of penalty for cases. ...

The mitigating circumstances in rape are indeed limited. ...

I have no doubt, however, that in the case of rape, an admission of guilt made at an early stage in the investigation of the crime which is followed by a subsequent plea of guilty can be a significant mitigating factor. I emphasise the admission of guilt at an early stage because if that is followed with a plea of guilty it necessarily makes it possible for the unfortunate victim to have early assurance that she will not be put through the additional suffering of having to describe in detail her rape and face the ordeal of cross-examination.:"

In England the judiciary are not given the independence in sentencing that their Irish counterparts have:

R V Roberts and Roberts (1982)

Lane C.J. delivering the judgment of the Court of Appeal, stressed the seriousness of this particular crime which, other than in wholly exceptional circumstances, called for an immediate custodial sentence to mark the gravity of the offence, emphasize public disapproval, serve as a warning to others, punish the offender and, last but by no means least, to protect women.

R V Billam and Others (1986)

The Court of Appeal laid down the following guide-lines on appropriate sentences for rape and attempted rape:

1. At the top of the scale comes the defendant who has carried out a campaign of rape, committing the crime upon a number of different women or girls. A sentence of fifteen years or more may be appropriate. Where a defendant has perverted tendencies, a life sentence will not be inappropriate.

2. For rape committed by an adult without any aggravating or mitigating features, five years should be taken as the starting point in a contested case.

3. Where rape is committed by two or more men acting together, or by a man who has broken into or otherwise gained access to a place where the victim is living, or by a person who abducts the victim and holds her captive, the starting point should be eight years.

4. In the case of young offenders, there should be some reduction to reflect their youth.

5. The starting point for attempted rape should normally be less than for the completed offence.

6. Aggravating or mitigating factors.

(i) Aggravating factors -

(a) violence is used, over and above the force necessary to commit the rape, or

(b) a weapon is used to frighten or wound the victim, or

(c) the rape is repeated, or

(d) the rape has been carefully planned, or

(e) the defendant has previous convictions, or

(f) the victim is subjected to further sexual indignities or perversions, or

(g) the victim is either very old or very young, or

(h) the effect upon the victim, whether physical or mental, is of special seriousness.

(ii) Mitigating factors -

(a) a plea of guilty, or

(b) the victim behaved in a manner calculated to lead the defendant to believe that she would consent to sexual intercourse.

Attempted rape

If there is not sufficient evidence for a conviction for rape, an accused may be convicted of attempted rape. The penalty for attempted rape is seven years imprisonment, however note the provisions of the Criminal Law Amendment Act, 1935, section 1 below with regard to a second or subsequent conviction of attempted rape of a girl under fifteen years. *People (D. P. P.) V Riordan (1992)*

A ground of appeal to the Court of Criminal Appeal was that the verdict of the jury that the applicant was guilty of attempted rape, suggested a rejection of the evidence of the prosecutrix and that according to her evidence, it was rape or nothing.

The court took into account that the girl was screaming, was thrown to the floor and stated that it was quite possible that she could not be certain if there was penetration. The trial judge had told the jury that if there was no penetration, they could bring in a verdict of attempted rape.

Egan J. on behalf of the court said that the jury were entitled to have a reasonable doubt as to whether there was penetration within the meaning of the act and that accepting the rest of the girl's story, they were clearly entitled to bring in a verdict of attempted rape.

Other offences involving sexual intercourse

It can be seen from the above that, in order to constitute the offence of rape, it is always necessary that sexual intercourse should take place without the consent of the woman, however by the Criminal Law Amendment Act, 1935, such an act when committed with a young girl is criminal, even though it may be done with her consent. Reference immediately following are to the 1935 Act.

Defilement of girl under fifteen years of age s. 1

Any person who unlawfully and carnally knows any girl under the age of fifteen years shall be guilty of a felony, for which the penalty is life imprisonment. An attempt at this offence is a misdemeanour, for which the penalty on first conviction is five years imprisonment or on a second or subsequent conviction is ten years imprisonment.

Defilement of a girl under seventeen years s. 2

Any person who unlawfully and carnally knows any girl who is over the age of fifteen years and under the age of seventeen years shall be guilty of a misdemeanour, for which the penalty on first conviction is five years imprisonment or on a second or subsequent conviction is ten years imprisonment. An attempt at this offence is also a misdemeanour, for which the penalty on first conviction is two years imprisonment or on a second or subsequent conviction is five years imprisonment.

The above offences are of the same character as rape and the same principles of proof apply, with the exception that consent is no defence. See *A. G. (Shaughnessy) V Ryan (1960)* below. Moreover if consent is missing in the above circumstances, then the accused is liable to the more serious charge of rape.

Consider the following cases:

People (A. G.) V O'Connor (1949)

On a charge of unlawful carnal knowledge of a girl under the age of fifteen years or, under the age of seventeen years, there must be precise evidence of age.

People (A. G.) V Kearns (1949)

The accused was charged with the unlawful carnal knowledge of a girl under the age of fifteen years of age, he pleaded guilty. On his plea in mitigation of sentence the trial judge refused to admit evidence that the appearance of the girl led the accused to believe that the girl was over seventeen years of age. It was held by the Court of Criminal Appeal that such evidence should have been admitted.

A. G. (Shaughnessy) V Ryan (1960)

It was held by the Supreme Court that consent is no defence to a charge of attempting to have carnal knowledge of a girl over the age of fifteen years and under the age of seventeen years.

Defilement of Idiots etc. s. 4

Any person who, in circumstances which do not amount to rape, unlawfully has carnal connection of any woman or girl who is an idiot, or an imbecile, or is feebleminded shall if the accused knew of the women's state of mind, be guilty of a misdemeanour, for which the penalty is two years imprisonment.

An idiot is a person born without a mind; an imbecile is a person deprived of the mind by disease or injury; and a feebleminded person is a person, so born or, who through disease or injury, is of impaired mental faculties.

There is an offence under the Lunacy Act, 1890, section 324, which relates specifically to persons having the care or charge of any female lunatic and has the same penalty.

The Mental Treatment Act, 1945, section 254 provides that where a person has been convicted of an offence under section 4 and such person had the charge of the woman or girl the penalty shall be five years imprisonment.

Sexual offences

The Criminal Law Amendment Act, 1885, provides:

Householder Permitting Defilement of Young Girl s. 6

Any person who being the owner or occupier of any premises induces or knowingly suffers any girl to be in such premises for the purposes of being unlawfully and carnally known by any man, shall be liable where the girl is under fifteen years to five years imprisonment, or where the girl is under seventeen years to two years imprisonment.

Unlawful Detention with Intent s. 8

Any person who detains any woman -

(1) In or upon any premises with intent that she may be unlawfully and carnally known by any man, or

(2) In any brothel,

shall be liable to two years imprisonment.

Incest

This offence involving sexual intercourse does not involve the consent of the woman but is dependent upon specified degrees of consanguinity between the parties.

Incest was not a crime at common law although it was punishable by the ecclesiastical courts and became a statutory crime by the Punishment of Incest Act, 1908.

Where there is no consent on the part of the female the offence committed is rape. The 1935 Act at section 12 made a number of amendments to sections 1, 2 and 4, references immediately following are to the 1908 Act as amended.

The Criminal Justice Act, 1993 at section 12 increased the penalty for incest. The Law Reform Commission had previously recommended that there should be no increase in such penalty

Incest by males s. 1

(1) Any male person who has carnal knowledge of a female person, who is to his knowledge his grand daughter, daughter, sister, or mother commits an offence and shall be liable on conviction to imprisonment for a term not exceeding twenty years.

Provided that if, on indictment for this offence, it is proved that the female person is under fifteen years of age then the male will be subject to section 1 of the Criminal Law Amendment Act, 1935 above.

(2) Consent of the female is no defence, in the absence of consent the male will be guilty of the more serious charge of rape.

(3) If any male person attempts to commit this offence, he shall be guilty of a misdemeanour, the penalty on conviction of this is two years imprisonment.

(4) On conviction of a male offender where female is under twenty-one years of age, the court may divest the offender of all authority over

such female and remove the offender from such guardianship.

Incest by females s. 2
Any female above the age of seventeen years who with consent permits her grandfather, father, brother, or son to have carnal knowledge of her knowing of the relationship is guilty of a misdemeanour and commits a like offence.

The knowledge of the accused person of the relationship is essential to the offence of incest. The relationship of the parties may be proved by oral evidence or by certificates of marriage and birth, together with identification. An admission as to the relationship would be sufficient evidence of such.

Additional provisions of the Act ss. 3, 4, 5 & 6
3. The expression "brother" and "sister" respectively, include half-brother and half-sister legitimate or illegitimate.

4.(3) If on the trial of any indictment for rape, the jury are satisfied that the defendant is guilty of this offence, but are not satisfied that the defendant is guilty of rape, the defendant may be found guilty of this offence.

5. All proceedings under the Act are to be held in camera.

6. No prosecutions may be commenced without the sanction of the Director of Public Prosecutions.

Abduction of females

The Offences against the Persons Act, 1861, created most of the offences in this area. References immediately following are to the 1861 Act, unless otherwise indicated.

Abduction of a girl under sixteen years of age s. 55
Whosoever shall unlawfully take or cause to be taken any unmarried girl, being under the age of sixteen years, out of the possession and against the will of her father or mother shall be liable on conviction to two years imprisonment. This offence does not involve carnal knowledge. See *R V Prince (1875)* at page 10.

Abduction of a girl under eighteen years of age
The Criminal Law Amendment Act, 1885, section 7 as amended by the Criminal Law Amendment Act, 1935 provided that: Any person who, with intent that any unmarried girl under the age of eighteen years should be unlawfully and carnally known, takes or causes to be taken such girl out of the possession and against the will of her father or mother shall be liable to two years imprisonment.

The former position as to a reasonable belief as to the age of the girl was a good defence, has been removed by the 1935 Act. The consent of the girl herself is no defence, not even where the proposal to go away comes from the girl and not from the man. But where the initiative and the active arrangements for the going away were taken and made by the girl this is a defence.

Abduction of heiress s. 53

Whosoever shall take away or detain any woman who is a heiress with intent that she be married or carnally known where it is against her will or the will of her mother or father where she is under twenty-one years of age shall be liable on conviction to fourteen years imprisonment.

An "heiress" as subsequently defined in England is; any female, who has property, or the expectation of property.

Abduction of any woman with intent to marry her s. 54

Whosoever shall, by force take away or detain against her will any woman of any age, with intent to marry or carnally know her shall be liable on conviction to fourteen years imprisonment.

Prostitution and brothel keeping

Prostitution

Prostitution itself is not a criminal offence. However the offences dealt with below arise out of activities connected with prostitution.

R V deMunck (1918)

Darling J. stated ...prostitution is proved if it is shown that a woman offers her body for purposes amounting to common lewdness for payment in return.

Procurement

The Criminal Law Amendment Act, 1885 at section's 2 and 3 as amended by the Criminal Law Amendment Act, 1935 makes the following provisions :

Section 2, Any person who, procures or attempts to procure any girl or woman-

(1) not being a common prostitute, or of known immoral character, to have unlawful carnal connection, within or without this country, with any other person or persons, or

(2) to become, either within or without this this country a common prostitute;

(3) to leave this country with intent that she may become an inmate of or frequent a brothel elsewhere, or

(4) to leave her usual place of abode in this country (such place not being a brothel) with the intent that she may, for the purposes of prostitution, become an inmate or frequent a brothel, within or without this country.

shall be guilty of a misdemeanour for which the penalty is two years imprisonment.

Section 3, Any person who;

(1) by threats or intimidation procures or attempts to procure any woman or girl to have unlawful carnal connection either within or without this country; or

(2) by false pretence or false representation procures any woman or girl not being a common prostitute or of known immoral character, to have an unlawful carnal connection within or without this country; or

(3) applies, administers to, or causes to be taken by any woman or girl any alcoholic or other intoxicant, or any drug matter, or thing, with intent to stupefy or overpower so as thereby to enable any person to have unlawful carnal connection with any woman or girl.

shall be guilty of a misdemeanour, for which the penalty is two years imprisonment.

It is to be noted that the above offence may be committed by any person be they male or female and that there is no age limit in respect of the girl or woman victim, most of the offences are of an extra-territorial nature. In respect of section 3, sub-sections (1) and (3) it is not necessary that sexual intercourse should have taken place, sub-section 2 could apply to a man who procures a woman to have sexual intercourse with himself.

The Criminal Law Amendment Act, 1935 provides:

Keeping a brothel s. 13(1)

any person who-

(a) keeps or manages or acts or assists in the management of a brothel, or

(b) being the tenant, lessee, occupier, or person in charge of any premises, knowingly permits such premises or any part thereof to be used as a brothel or for the purposes of habitual prostitution, or

(c) being the lessor or landlord of any premises or the agent of such lessor or landlord, lets such premises or any part thereof with the knowledge that such premises or some part thereof are to be used as a brothel, or is wilfully a party to the continued use of such premises or any part thereof as a brothel,

shall be guilty of a misdemeanour and liable on first conviction is a £100 fine and or six months imprisonment and, in the case of a second or subsequent conviction to a £250 fine and or five years imprisonment.

Also see Licensing Act, 1872 at page 266.

Suppression of prostitution s. 16(1)

Every common prostitute who is found loitering in any street, thoroughfare, or other place and importuning or soliciting passers-by for purposes of prostitution or being otherwise offensive to passers-by shall be guilty of an offence and shall on summary conviction be liable on a first offence to a £2 fine or, in the case of a second or subsequent offence to six months imprisonment.

Sexual offences
See also the Dublin Police Act, 1842, section 14(11) at page 259.

The Vagrancy Act, 1898, as amended by the Criminal Law Amendment Act, 1912 (which also extended the Act to Ireland) provides:

Persons trading in prostitution s. 1
(1) Every male person who
(a) knowingly lives wholly or in part on the earnings of prostitution; or
(b) in any public place persistently solicits or importunes for immoral purposes,
shall be guilty of an offence.
(2) If it is made to appear to a court of summary jurisdiction by information on oath that there is reason to suspect that any house or any part of a house is used by a female for the purposes of prostitution, and that any male person residing in or frequenting the house is living wholly or in part on the earnings of the prostitute, the court may issue a warrant authorising any Garda to enter and search the house and to arrest that male person.
(3) Where a male person is proved to live with or be habitually in the company of a prostitute, or is proved to have exercised control, direction or influence over the movements of a prostitute in such a manner as to show that he is aiding, abetting, or compelling her prostitution with any other person or generally, he shall be deemed to be living on the earnings of prostitution.
By section 7(5) of the 1912 Act this offence may be tried on indictment. The penalty on summary conviction is six months imprisonment, or on indictment is two years imprisonment.

The Offences against the Persons Act, 1861, provides:

Buggery and Sodomy s. 61
Whosoever shall be convicted of the abominable crime of buggery, committed either with mankind or with any animal, shall be liable to penal servitude for life.
Buggery consists of having carnal knowledge as follows:
(a) by a man with a man *per anum,*
(b) by a man with a woman *per anum,*
(c) by a man with an animal *per anum* or *per vaginam,*
(d) by a woman with an animal *per anum* or *per vaginam.*
All the above are known as sodomy, (c) and (d) are also known as bestiality. Consent is no defence, the consenting party may be guilty as a principal.
A husband and wife can be convicted of this offence. At common law a girl under twelve years is deemed incapable of committing this offence or any attempt thereto. As in the case of rape, carnal knowledge shall be deemed complete upon proof of penetration only no emission of seed is

required, corroboration of evidence is required in these cases.

Attorney General V Troy (1950)

Troy was convicted of buggery and appealed on the ground that the medical evidence was the only evidence that the boy had been interfered with but that it was not corroboration that he had interfered with the boy and that the trial judge had failed to make this clear. It was held by the Court of Criminal Appeal that the medical evidence did not corroborate the evidence of the boy.

Attempt to commit an infamous crime s. 62

Whosoever shall attempt to commit the said abominable crime, or shall be guilty of any assault with intent to commit the same, or of any indecent assault upon any male person, shall be guilty of a misdemeanour, and being convicted thereof shall be liable, to be kept in penal servitude for any term not exceeding ten years.

The Criminal Law Amendment Act, 1885, provides:

Gross indecency s. 11

Any male person who, in public or in private, commits or is party to the commission of, or procures or attempts to procure the commission by any male person of, any act of gross indecency with another male person, shall be liable on conviction of such offence to two years imprisonment.

Gross indecency is not defined in the Act. It means any sexual act between male persons other than buggery and there is no need for physical contact. Consent is no defence to this offence and both parties involved may be guilty.

People (A. G.) V McClure (1945)

The accused had pleaded guilty to a charge of gross indecency. He was thirty-three years old and this was his first offence. It was held by the Court of Criminal Appeal that given the good character of the accused, and the fact that it was a first offence, the sentence would be reduced.

Norris V Attorney General (1984)

The plaintiff claimed that the above provisions infringed Article 40 of the Constitution. It was held by the High Court; that neither section 61 or 62 made any distinction between men and women or between homosexuals and heterosexuals and that accordingly, neither contravened Article 40. The Supreme Court in upholding the decision of the High Court further declared, that neither the omission from the 1861 Act and the 1885 Act of offences relating to acts of gross indecency by females, nor, the omission of offences relating to the sexual activities of heterosexuals outside marriage was contrary to Article 40.

This decision was appealed to the European Court of Human Rights which found Ireland to be in breach of the Convention on Human Rights.

Chapter 10

Offences concerning children and young persons

There are a number of offences that are specific to children, when considering these regard should be had to offence covered elsewhere, in particular those in the chapters on Homicide, Assault and Battery, Sexual Offences and Childbirth.

The following statutes treat of this area:

> Offences against the Person Act, 1861;
> Children's Dangerous Performance Act, 1879;
> Children Act, 1908;
> Gaming and Lotteries Act, 1956;
> Intoxicating Liquor Act, 1962;
> Pawnbrokers Act, 1964;
> Intoxicating Liquor Act, 1988;
> Tobacco (Health, Promotion and Protection) Act, 1988;
> Child Care Act, 1991.

The Offences against the Persons Act, 1861 provides:

Wilful neglect s. 26

Whosoever, being legally liable, either as a master or mistress, to provide for any apprentice or servant necessary food, clothing or lodging, shall wilfully and without lawful excuse refuse or neglect to provide the same, or shall unlawfully and maliciously do or cause to be done any bodily harm to such, such that life shall be endangered or life injured, shall be guilty of a misdemeanour and liable to three years imprisonment.

Exposing children whereby life endangered s. 27

Whosoever shall unlawfully abandon or expose any child being under the age of two years, whereby the life of such child shall be endangered, or the health of such child shall have been or shall be likely to be permanently injured, shall be guilty of a misdemeanour and shall be liable to three years imprisonment.

Child stealing s. 56

Whosoever shall unlawfully, either by force or fraud, lead or take away, or decoy or entice away or detain, any child under the age of fourteen years, with intent to deprive any parent, guardian, or other person, having the lawful care or charge of such child of the possession of such child, or with intent to steal any article upon or about the person of such child, shall be guilty of felony, and liable to seven years imprisonment.

Children's Dangerous Performance Act, 1879

Section 3, as amended provides: any person who shall cause any male young person under the age of sixteen years and any female young person under the age of eighteen years to take part in any public exhibition or performance whereby, in the opinion of a Court of summary jurisdiction, the life or limbs of such child shall be endangered, and the parent or guardian, or any person having the custody of such child, who shall aid or abet the same, shall severally be guilty of an offence £10

and where in the course of a dangerous public exhibition or performance any accident causing actual bodily harm occurs to any such child the employer of such child may be charged with assault.

Section 4 provides: Whenever any person is charged with an offence against this Act it shall lie on the person charged to prove that the child is not of the age as alleged.

The Dangerous Performance Act, 1897 at section 2 provides:

Except where an accident causing actual bodily harm occurs to any child or young person, no prosecution or other proceeding shall be instituted for an offence against the Children's Dangerous Performance Act, 1879, as amended by this Act, without the consent in writing of the superintendent of the district or, in the case of the Dublin Metropolitan Area, of the Commissioner.

The Children Act 1908, provides:

Cruelty s. 12
If any person over the age of seventeen years, who has the custody, charge, or care of any child or young person, wilfully assaults, ill-treats, neglects, abandons, or exposes such child or young person, or causes or procures such young person to be assaulted, ill-treated, neglected abandoned, or exposed, in a manner likely to cause such child or young person unnecessary suffering or injury to his health (including injury to or loss of sight, or hearing, or limb, or organ of the body, and any mental derangement) that person shall be guilty of a misdemeanour, for which the penalty on indictment is £100 and or two years imprisonment and summarily is £25 and or six months imprisonment.

"seventeen years" was substitutes for "sixteen years" by section 4 of the Children (Amendment) Act, 1957.

A person shall be deemed to have neglected a child if he fails to provide adequate food, clothing, medical aid, or lodging or fails to take steps to procure the same.

A person may be convicted, notwithstanding that actual suffering or injury to health, or the likelihood of such suffering or injury to health, was obviated by the action of another person, or that the child or young person has died.

Upon the trial for the manslaughter of a child or young person of whom the accused had the custody, charge or care, the court may find an accused guilty of this offence.

Being knowingly interested, directly or indirectly, in any sum of money that is to accrue or to be paid in the event of the death of a child or young person is an aggravation of this offence.

Suffocation of infant s. 13

Where it is proved that the death of an infant under the age of three years of age was caused by suffocation (not being suffocation caused by disease or the presence of any foreign body in the throat or air-passage of the infant) whilst the infant was in bed with some other person over sixteen years of age, and that other person was at the time of going to bed under the influence of drink, that other person shall be deemed to have neglected the infant in a manner likely to cause injury to its health within the meaning of the Act.

Begging s. 14

If any person causes or procures any child or young person, or having the custody, charge or care of a child or young person, allows that child or young person to be in any street, premises, or place for the purpose of begging or receiving alms, or of inducing the giving of alms, whether or not there is any pretence of singing, playing, performing, offering anything for sale or otherwise, this is an offence for which the penalty is £25 and or six months imprisonment.

Exposure to burning s. 15

If any person over the age of sixteen years, who has the custody, charge, or care of any child under the age of seven years, allows that child to be in any room containing an open fire grate not sufficiently protected to guard against the risk of the child being burnt or scalded, without taking reasonable precautions against that risk, and by reason thereof the child is killed or suffers serious injury, this is an offence for which the penalty is a £10 fine.

This does not however affect any liability for any indictable offence.

Frequenting brothels s. 16

If any person having the custody, charge, or care of a child or young person between the ages of four and seventeen years allows that child or young person to reside in or frequent a brothel, this is an offence for which the penalty is £25 and or six months imprisonment.

Where a person is charged with an offence under section 6 of the Criminal Law Amendment Act, 1885, it may be reduced to this offence.

Seduction and prostitution s. 17

If any person having the custody, charge or care of a girl under the age of seventeen years causes or encourages the seduction or prostitution or unlawful carnal knowledge of that girl, this is a misdemeanour for which the penalty is two years imprisonment.

A person shall be deemed guilty of this offence, if he has knowingly allowed the girl to consort with, or to enter or continue in the employment of, any prostitute or person of known immoral character. See also sexual offences, chapter 9.

The Gaming and Lotteries Act, 1956 provides:

Unlawful gaming s. 14(c)
Any gaming carried on at an amusement hall or funfair is unlawful if a person under the age of sixteen years is permitted to play. See also the consideration of gaming later.

The Intoxicating Liquor Act, 1962 provides:

Intoxicating liquor in confectionery s. 27(2)
Intoxicating liquor in confectionery shall not be sold to a person who is under the age of sixteen years. A person who knowingly contravenes this section is liable to a £50 fine.

The Pawnbrokers Act, 1964, provides:

Pawning s. 19(1)(a)
A pawnbroker shall not knowingly take anything in pawn from a person under the age of sixteen years whether offered for pawning by that person on his own behalf or on behalf of another. The penalty is a £50 fine and or six months imprisonment. It shall be a good defence for a pawnbroker to show that he did not know and had no reason to suspect that the person was under the age of sixteen years.

The Intoxicating Liquor Act, 1988, provides:

Sale of intoxicating liquor s. 31
(1) The holder of any licence shall not-
(a) sell or deliver or permit any person to sell or deliver intoxicating liquor to a person under the age of eighteen years,
(b) sell or deliver or permit any person to sell or deliver intoxicating liquor to any person for consumption on his licensed premises by a person under the age of eighteen years,
(c) permit a person under the age of eighteen years to consume intoxicating liquor on his licensed premises, or
(d) permit any person to supply a person under the age of 18 years with intoxicating liquor on his licensed premises.
(2) The holder of a licence of any licensed premises shall not sell or deliver or permit any person to sell or deliver intoxicating liquor to any person for consumption off his licensed premises by a person under the age of eighteen years in any place other than a private residence.
(3) A person who contravenes subsection (1) or (2) of this section shall be guilty of an offence and shall be liable on summary conviction to a fine not exceeding-

(a) £300, in case of a first offence, or

(b) in the case of a second or any subsequent offence,

and the offence shall be deemed for the purposes of Part III (which relates to the endorsement of licences) of the Act of 1927 to be an offence to which that Part of that Act applies.

(4) In any proceedings against a person for a contravention of subsection (1) or (2) of this section, it shall be a defence for such person to prove that the person in respect of whom the charge is brought produced to him an age card relating to such person or that he had other reasonable grounds for believing that such person was over the age of 18 years, or, if the person is charged with permitting another person to sell or deliver intoxicating liquor contrary to the said subsection (1) or (2), to prove that an age card was produced by the person concerned to that other person or that that other person had other reasonable grounds for believing as aforesaid.

It is to be noted that the word "knowingly" is absent in respect of offences under subsection (1) and (2), thus the reason for the statutory defence.

The Tobacco (Health, Promotion and Protection) Act, 1988 provides:

Restriction on sale of tobacco products s. 3

(1) Any person who sells, offers to sell, or makes available in relation to the sale of any other product, any tobacco product to a person under the age of 16 years, whether for his own use or otherwise, or who sells to any person, acting on behalf of a person under the age of 16 years, any tobacco products, shall be guilty of an offence and shall be liable, on summary conviction, to a fine not exceeding £500.

(3) Whenever a person is prosecuted for an offence under this section, it shall be a defence for him to establish that he had taken all reasonable steps to assure himself that the person to whom the tobacco products were sold, offered for sale or made available had attained the age of 16 years.

Restriction on sale of cigarettes s. 4

Any person who sells, offers to sell or makes available in relation to the sale of any other products, cigarettes to a person otherwise than in packets of ten or more cigarettes shall be guilty of an offence and shall be liable on summary conviction to a fine not exceeding £500.

Sale of cigarettes s. 39

If a person sells to a person under the age of sixteen years any cigarettes, whether for his own use or not, it is an offence for which the penalty is a £2 fine and on a second offence a £5 fine.

Offences concerning children and young persons

The Child Care Act, 1991 provides:

Sale etc. of solvents s. 74

(1) It shall be an offence for a person to sell, offer or make available a substance to a person under the age of eighteen years or to a person acting on behalf of that person if he knows or has reasonable cause to believe that the substance is, or its fumes are, likely to be inhaled by the person under the age of eighteen years for the purpose of causing intoxication.

(2) In proceedings against any person for an offence under subsection (1), it shall be a defence for him to prove that at the time he sold, offered or made available the substance he was under the age of eighteen years and was acting otherwise than in the course of or furtherance of a business.

(3) In proceedings against any person for an offence under subsection (1), it shall be a defence for him to prove that he took reasonable steps to assure himself that the person to whom the substance was sold, offered or made available, or any person on whose behalf that person was acting, was not under the age of eighteen years.

On summary conviction the penalty is a £1,000 fine and or twelve months imprisonment.

Chapter 11

Offences concerning childbirth

Infanticide

Infanticide is the murder of a young child by its mother. In order that such women would not be liable for sentence of death the Infanticide Act, 1949 was passed

Infanticide s. 1

(1) On the preliminary investigation by the District Court of a charge against a woman for the murder of her child, being a child under the age of twelve months, the Justice may, if he thinks proper, alter the charge to one of infanticide and send her forward for trial on that charge.

(2) Where upon the trial of a woman for the murder of her child, being a child under the age of twelve months, the jury are satisfied that she is guilty of infanticide, they shall return a verdict of infanticide.

(3) A woman shall be guilty of infanticide if -

(a) by any wilful act or omission she causes the death of her child, being under the age of twelve months, and

(b) the circumstances are such but for this section, the act it would have amounted to murder, and

(c) at the time of the act or omission the balance of her mind was disturbed by reason of her not having fully recovered from the effect of giving birth to the child or by reason of the effect of lactation consequent upon the birth of the child

and may for that offence be tried and punished as for manslaughter (penal servitude for life).

(4) Section 60 of the Offences Against the Person Act, 1861, shall have effect as if the reference therein to the murder of any child included a reference to infanticide.

Abortion

At common law it was not murder to kill a child in the womb or while in the process of being born, this was because the unborn child was deemed to have no separate existence apart from its mother. The destruction of an unborn child by means of an unlawful miscarriage is criminal and a statutory offence is contained in the Offences against the Person Act, 1861. Also note Article 40.3.3 of the Constitution below. All references are to the 1861 Act unless otherwise stated.

Procuring abortion s. 58

(A) Every woman, being with child, who, with intent to procure her own miscarriage, shall unlawfully administer to herself any poison or other noxious thing, or shall unlawfully use any instrument or other

94

means whatsoever with the like intent,.... shall be guilty of a felony and on conviction liable to penal servitude for life,

(B) .... whosoever with intent to procure the miscarriage of any woman, whether she be or be not with child, shall unlawfully administer to her or cause to be taken by her any poison or other noxious thing, or shall unlawfully use any instrument or other means whatsoever with the like intent, shall be guilty of felony and on conviction liable to penal servitude for life.

"Poison or other noxious thing". The administering of a recognised poison, even in a small harmless quantity, is an offence. Where something other than a recognised poison is used, it must be shown to be harmful.

"other means'". This has been held to include the fingers of the hand.

"intent" If the substance administered is a poison or other noxious thing or if any instrument or other means is used to procure an abortion, then, provided that there was an intent to procure a miscarriage, the fact that no miscarriage was or could be produced is not relevant.

These sections of the Offences against the Person Act, 1861 are entitled "attempts to procure Abortion".

In the English *R V Bourne (1939)* case at page 36 the word "unlawfully" allowed a limited defence in the case of abortion.

Conspiracy and aiding and abetting

If a woman is not pregnant and administers to herself any poison, etc., she is unable to commit the principle offence and therefore cannot be convicted of the crime of attempt. It should be noted that in (A) it is essential that the woman be pregnant, whereas this is not the case in (B). It has been held that a woman, even though she is not pregnant, may be convicted of conspiring with others, or of aiding and abetting others to administer any poison, etc. to her contrary to (B)

Procuring drugs, &c. to cause abortion s. 59

Whosoever shall unlawfully supply or procure any poison or other noxious thing, or any instrument or thing whatsoever, knowing that the same is intended to be unlawfully or employed with intent to procure the miscarriage of any woman, whether she be be or be not with child, shall be guilty of misdemeanour and on conviction liable to three years imprisonment.

"procure" As used firstly in section 59 means getting possession from another.

Article 40.3.3 of the Constitution

The State acknowledges the right to life of the unborn and, with due regard to the equal right to life of the mother, guarantees in its laws to respect, and, as far as practicable, by its laws to defend and vindicate that right.

This subsection shall not limit freedom to travel between the State and another state.

This subsection shall not limit freedom to obtain or make available, in the State, subject to such conditions as may be laid down by law, information relating to services lawfully available in another state.

The first paragraph of the article has been judicially considered in the *Dublin Well Women* and *X* cases (see below). The second paragraph was put by the Government to the People with the intention of ensuring that the article could not be used to prevent a woman from exercising her freedom to travel abroad for an abortion (see *X case* below). The last paragraph was put by the Government to the People with the intention of ensuring the freedom to receive and impart information, subject to such conditions as may be laid down by law, it is not the intention that it will be permitted to promote abortion, or to encourage the woman to select it in preference to the other options, or to provide an abortion referral service.

Abortion referral
A. G. / S.P.U.C. V Open Door Counselling/Dublin Well Women (1988)

The defendants carried on a service to pregnant women which included non-directive counselling. Abortion might be one of the options discussed during such counselling, and where the client wished to consider such option further, the defendants arranged to refer her to a medical clinic in Britain where abortions are performed. The plaintiff claimed that the activities of the defendants were unlawful having regard to the provisions of the Constitution and an order prohibiting the defendants from carrying on the said activities.

In the High Court; Hamilton P. stated "I am satisfied that the activities of both defendants, through their servants and agents amount to counselling and assisting pregnant women to travel abroad to obtain further advice on abortion and to secure an abortion." He went on to state that such activities were unlawful having regard to Article 40.3.3 .

On appeal to the Supreme Court; Finlay C.J. varied the order of Hamilton P. as follows "and it is ordered that the defendants ..... be perpetually restrained from assisting pregnant women within the jurisdiction to travel abroad to obtain abortions by referral to a clinic, by the making for them of travel arrangements, or by informing them of the identity and location of and the method of communication with a specified clinic or clinics or otherwise."

This judgment must now be seen in the light of the two additional paragraphs (accepted by the People in November 1992) to article 40.3.3 above.

Legal abortion
Where there is a real and substantial risk to the life of a mother which can only be avoided by the termination of a pregnancy then such termination is permissible.

Attorney General V X and Others (1992)
It was held by Costello J. in the High Court
if the court is appraised of the situation in which the life of the unborn is
threatened then the court would be failing in its constitutional duty to
protect it ..
(3) The court may order the curtailment of the exercise of the
constitutional right to liberty where it has been abused by the exercise of
it to commit a wrong such as the procurement of an abortion.
(8) The prevention of a woman travelling abroad to procure an abortion
by means of an injunction is a measure proportionate to the aim of
Article 40.3.3
It was held by the Supreme Court on appeal:
(2)   the absence of legislative action does not relieve the courts of their
duty to implement the constitutional guarantee.
(3) if a conflict of rights cannot be avoided, a hierarchy of rights was
envisaged.
(4) On the true interpretation of Article 40.3.3 of the Constitution where
it is established as a matter of probability that there is a real and
substantial risk to the life of the mother which can only be avoided by
the termination of the pregnancy then such termination is permissible.
The test of inevitable or immediate risk to the life of the mother
insufficiently vindicates the mother's right to life.
(5)   The right to life takes precedence over the right to travel.
With regard to the meaning of the word "life" see *R V Bourne* p.36.

The Censorship of Publications Act, 1929, as amended provides:

Advocating the procurement of abortion s. 16
(1) it shall not be lawful for any person, otherwise and under and in
accordance with a permit in writing granted to him under this section-
(a) to print or publish or cause or procure to be printed or published,
or
(b) to sell or expose, offer, or keep for sale, or
(c) to distribute, offer or keep for distribution,
any book or periodical publication which advocates or which might
reasonably be supposed to advocate the procurement of abortion or
miscarriage or any method, treatment, or appliance to be used for the
purpose of such procurement.
The penalty on summary conviction is a £50 fine and or 6 months
imprisonment.

Concealment of birth

Concealing the birth of a child s. 60
If any woman shall be delivered of a child, every person who shall, by
any secret disposition of the dead body of the said child, whether such
child died before, at, or after its birth, endeavour to conceal the birth

thereof, shall be guilty of a misdemeanour and be liable of two years imprisonment.

Provided that if any person tried for the murder of any child (note infanticide above) shall be acquitted thereof, it shall be lawful for the jury by whose verdict such person shall be acquitted to find, in case it shall so appear in evidence, that the child had recently been born, and that such person did, by some secret disposition of the dead body of such child, endeavour to conceal the birth thereof, and thereupon the court may pass such sentence as if such person had been convicted upon an indictment for the concealment of the birth.

The offence may be committed by any person; and any person who assists in concealing the body is a principal in the first degree.

R V Berriman (1854)

There is no offence of concealment unless a child "had arrived at that stage of maturity at the time of birth that it might have been a living child"; per Earle J. Thus the concealment of a few months old foetus would be no offence.

If a person is acquitted of Infanticide and there is sufficient evidence, such person may be convicted of this offence.

Secret disposition

Mere denial of the birth is not sufficient without some actual and secret disposition of the body. What is a secret disposition must depend on the circumstances of each particular case. A mere abandonment of the body will not sufficient, there must have been an attempt to prevent the body being found. The concealment must be from the world at large and not from any particular individual. A mere concealment of the fact of birth would not suffice.

Body of child

In order to convict a woman of endeavouring to conceal the birth of her child a dead body must, as a rule, be found and identified as that of the child of which she is alleged to have been delivered.

Chapter 12

What is stealing ?

The law relating to stealing and related offences is contained in the:

Larceny Act, 1861;

Larceny Act, 1916 and

Larceny Act, 1990.

The purpose of the 1861 Act was described as "to consolidate and amend the statute law relating to larceny and other similar offences." and the purpose of the 1916 Act (which is the principal Act) was described as "to consolidate and simplify the law relating to larceny triable on indictment and kindred offences.", in doing this it partly replaced and repealed the earlier Act. The 1990 Act altered certain penalties and replaced parts of the 1916 Act.

Kenny in his "*Outlines of Criminal Law*" says of the English law of Larceny: "The rules relating to it can be traced back through a history of several centuries; and they have now become so complex as to be scarcely intelligible without a knowledge of their historical development."

The term "larceny" was used at common law, the various Acts are so entitled and marginal notes in the 1916 Act apply the term to various (thirteen) species of stealing. No definition of the term is given in the Acts. The term "steals" is used throughout the Acts and it is "stealing" that is defined in the Principal Act. This definition of stealing sweeps away many of the restriction that there were at common law, by which action by certain parties and certain kinds of property could not be the subject of larceny.

This chapter is primarily concerned with the various points that arise out of the definition of stealing contained in section 1 of the Larceny Act, 1916. There is in addition a consideration of some general matters in relation to offences under the Acts. It is to the 1916 Act that all references in this and the following chapters are too unless otherwise stated.

Definition s. 1

For the purpose of the Act-

(1) A person steals who, without the consent of the owner, fraudulently and without a claim of right made in good faith, takes and carries away anything capable of being stolen with intent, at the time of such taking, permanently to deprive the owner thereof:

Provided that a person may be guilty of stealing any such thing notwithstanding that he has lawful possession thereof, if, being a bailee or part owner thereof, he fraudulently converts the same to his own use or the use of any person other than the owner;

(2) (i) the expression "takes" includes obtaining possession -

    (a) by any trick;

99

(b) by intimidation;

(c) under a mistake on the part of the owner with knowledge on the part of the taker that possession has been so obtained;

(d) by finding, were at the time of the finding the finder believes that the owner can be discovered by taking reasonable steps;

(ii) the expression "carries away" includes any removal of anything from the place which it occupies, but in the case of a thing attached, only if it has been completely detached;

(iii) the expression "owner" includes any part owner, or person having possession or control of, or a special property in, anything capable of being stolen;

(3) Everything which has value and is the property of any person, and if adhering to the reality then after severance therefrom, shall be capable of being stolen:

Provided that-

(a) save as hereinafter expressly provided with respect to fixtures, growing things, and ore from mines, anything attached to or forming part of the realty shall not be capable of being stolen by the person who severs the same from the realty, unless after severance he has abandoned possession thereof; and

(b) the carcase of a creature wild by nature and not reduced into possession while living shall not be capable of being stolen by the person who has killed such creature, unless after killing it he has abandoned possession of the carcase.

Analysis of definition

The definition of stealing uses various phrases such as:

(a) without the consent of the owner;

(b) fraudulently;

(c) without a claim of right made in good faith;

(d) with intent at the time of such taking;

(e) carries away;

(f) everything which has value;

(g) property of any person;

(h) adhering to the realty;

(i) creatures wild by nature;

(j) abandoned possession.

It also identifies many kinds of larceny; such as:

Larceny by a bailee;

Larceny by a trick;

Larceny by intimidation;

Larceny by a mistake;

Larceny by finding;

Larceny by a part owner;

Larceny by an owner.

These will now be examined.

Consent of the owner

If a person takes with the consent of the owner, then there can be no stealing. As stated in section 1 the expression "owner" includes any part owner, or person having possession or control of, or a special property in, anything capable of being stolen. Given this definition regard must be had not only to an owner but to a person having possession of goods as well.

If a person in possession has consented to goods being taken out of his possession, it is not larceny The fact that the legal owner did not or would not have consented is not relevant Any consent on the part of the owner, must be given freely. An apparent consent may be vitiated, as can be seen below, by either a trick or intimidation or mistake.

An owner may be convicted of stealing: see *Rose V Matt (1951)* below. See also *D. P. P. V Keating* below.

Fraudulently

The meaning of "fraudulently" has been considered by the English Court of Criminal Appeal.
R V Williams (1953)
Goddard C.J. said: "The court thinks that the word 'fraudulently' does add and is intended to add, something to the words 'without a claim of right' and that it means that the taking must be intentional and deliberate, that is to say, without mistake. The person who takes the property must know when he takes it that it is the property of another person, and he must take it deliberately, not by mistake, and with an intention to deprive the person from whom it is taken, of the property in it."

Claim of right

There can be no stealing where a person takes something, believing that he has a right to do so. Where there is a mistake of fact or of law, or even if a person uses violence to recover what he believes to be his own property, there can be no crime. Any claim of right must be made in good faith, an open taking may be evidence of good faith
People (A. G.) V Grey (1944)
The appellant, an officer of a public company was charged with taking property contrary to section 20.1(ii) (see page 149). It was held by the Court of Criminal Appeal that a claim by the appellant that, he honestly believed that he was entitled to take the property should have been left to the jury with the direction that if when he took the property, he honestly believed that he was entitled to do so, he ought to be acquitted, even though his claim to be so entitled was not well founded in law or in fact.
People (D. P. P.) V O'Loughlin (1979)
The police found stolen machinery on the land of the accused, he was convicted of larceny. During the course of the trial the judge had refused to allow evidence in support of a claim of right based on an alleged belief by the accused that he had been entitled to take the

machinery from its owner because the latter owed him money. It was held by the Court of Criminal Appeal that the accused should have been allowed to introduce evidence in support of his alleged claim of right, because such, although not well founded in law or in fact may be established.

Director of Public Prosecutions V Morrissey (1982)

The defendant was charged with feloniously stealing meat contrary to section 2 of the Act (see below). He had ordered the meat at the meat counter of a supermarket. He admitted taking the meat but explained that he did not know why he had done so as he had not got the money to pay for it. The District Justice stated a case as to whether such facts sufficed to sustain a charge. It was held by the High Court that in the absence of evidence to the contrary the only necessary inference from the giving of the meat to the defendant was that he was required to show the meat and pay the price of it before leaving and that he had accepted it with this knowledge. It follows in the absence of evidence to the contrary the only necessary inference was that on leaving the shop without his disclosing his possession of the meat and without paying for it, the defendant at the time of leaving if not at the time of receiving the meat, had the intention of depriving the owner of it and that he had obtained it fraudulently and without the consent of the owner.

With intent at the time of such taking

There must be an intention at the time of the taking, to permanently deprive the owner of his property. A person must have at the time of the time of the taking made up his mind that he was going to permanently deprive the owner of his property, this is the intention of stealing known as the *animus furandi*, it is the *mens rea* of larceny.

To constitute larceny it is unnecessary that an accused should take the goods for his own benefit. It was held to be larceny where an employee took food to supply his employers horses with a greater quantity than that allowed (*R V Privett (1846)*).

Where an accused intended only to temporarily deprive an owner of his property then he cannot be convicted of stealing. However a person who takes money will not be entitled to be acquitted merely because he had a hope or expectation that he would repay it.

If a person receives goods innocently and subsequently appropriates them, he cannot be guilty of larceny.

R V Hehir (1895)

Hehir was given a £10 note in mistake for a £1 note. When Hehir discovered its true value, he fraudulently appropriated it to his own use. On this evidence he was convicted of larceny. It was held on appeal that the subsequent fraudulent misappropriation of the £10 note, innocently acquired was not larceny.

Director of Public Prosecutions V Keating (1989)

It was held by Lynch J. in the High Court that:

(1) Where the offence of larceny depends upon the fraudulent

intention of an accused, which intention is to be ascertained from his conduct at the time of the alleged offence.

(2) Where, on the evidence, the conduct of a person accused of the larceny of goods in a shop is such as to indicate, in the absence of a plausible explanation, that he intended to fraudulently deprive the shipowner thereof, the offence of larceny has been committed even before such person has left the premises.

Carries away

In order to constitute larceny, there must not only be a taking, but also asportation, or carrying away. A bare removal from the place in which the goods are found, though they are not made off with is a sufficient asportation. By definition the expression "carries away" includes any removal of anything from the place which it occupies, but in the case of a thing attached, only if it has been completely detached.

R V Simon (1664)

The accused intending to steal a plate, took it out of a chest in which it was and laid it on the floor. He was discovered before he could make away with it. There was held to be sufficient asportation.

R V Taylor (1911)

The accused put his hand into a pocket, seized a purse and drew it to the edge of the pocket, but was unable to remove it completely. This was held a sufficient asportation.

Anon

Where an accused was not able to carry off the goods on account of their being attached by a string to the counter. There was held to be no asportation.

Everything which has value / Property of any person

"Everything which has value and is the property of any person, and if adhering to the reality then after severance therefrom, shall be capable of being stolen".

If a thing has no value then it cannot be the subject of a larceny. It is economic value that is taken into account, sentimental value does not count. However the measure of such value has not been fixed. The test to be applied is whether the thing in question has value of any kind and is the property of any person.

Adhering to the realty

"save as hereinafter expressly provided with respect to fixtures, growing things, and ore from mines, anything attached to or forming part of the realty shall not be capable of being stolen by the person who severs the same from the realty, unless after severance he has abandoned possession thereof"

Land and things attached thereto (such as a house) cannot be the subject of a larceny

R V Clinton (1869)
It was held not to be larceny to appropriate seaweed lying between high and low water mark on the shore exclusively owned by another.
A corpse is not capable of being stolen at common law.

Creatures wild by nature

At common law larceny cannot be committed with respect to animals *ferae naturae* (unless they are dead, tamed, or in confinement) such as deer or hares in a forest; fish in an open river; or wild fowl.
The definition at section 1 provides: "the carcase of a creature wild by nature and not reduced into possession while living shall not be capable of being stolen by the person who has killed such creature, unless after killing it he has abandoned possession of the carcase."
Animals *ferae naturae* when killed by a person become the property of the owner of the land where killed. If the person kills an animal and leaves it, intending to abandon possession, but afterwards returns and takes it away, such a taking is larceny. But if the person after killing, conceals the animal on the land, intending to return and take it away, such a taking away is not larceny.
There is particular statutory provision in respect of wild animals in certain circumstances, where their taking amounts to a criminal offence.
Animals *mansuetae naturae*: those reduced into possession, have a value and being the property of persons are capable of being stolen. Also see sections 3, 4, and 5 of the 1916 Act below.

Abandonment of possession

With respect to things forming part of the realty which have been severed therefrom and to creatures wild by nature (animals *ferae naturae*) that have been killed, the abandonment of possession dictates whether such are capable of being stolen.
If a person came into possession of things this established ownership, however if there was an abandonment of possession by one person, then ownership in such things would be transferred to another person. In the case of things severed from the realty, or creatures wild by nature that have been killed, on abandonment the ownership vest in the landlord.
Larceny is an offence against possession, it is a trespass against the goods of another. At common law a change of possession was essential to larceny, where there was no such an infringement there could be no larceny. It was for this reason that a distinction came to be drawn between "legal" possession and "physical" possession. The person (servant or employee) who had physical possession was deemed to have a mere custody of goods and thus could become liable for stealing such goods

Larceny by a bailee

A bailee is a person who has the lawful, but not the legal possession of goods belonging to another. The goods are entrusted to a bailee for a specific purpose without any intention to transfer the ownership. The intention of the bailee at the time of obtaining possession of the goods is not relevant, as the question of intention arises when the actual appropriation or conversion is made. The provisio to section 1(1) states: a person may be guilty of stealing any such thing notwithstanding that he has lawful possession thereof, if, being a bailee ... thereof, he fraudulently converts the same to his own use or the use of any person other than the owner.

R V Wainwright (1960)

The accused was a company representative and was given goods on the instruction to sell them on the company's behalf at fixed retail prices. He sold the goods on his own behalf at lower prices and there was no dispute that it was his intention to keep the money received for himself. It was held that he was properly convicted of larceny as bailee of the goods.

R V Richmond

The accused was a commercial traveller and was entrusted with silk for sale, and it was his duty at the end of six months to send in an account for the entire six months and to return the unsold silk. Before the end of the six months he appropriated the silk to his own use. It was held that he was rightly convicted of larceny as a bailee.

Larceny by a trick

This may arise where the physical possession as distinct from the legal possession of goods is given. The owner does not intend to part with his entire right to the goods, but with the temporary possession of them only.

R V Edmundson

The accused went to a tailor and order a suit of clothes. When he saw the clothes completed he asked the tailor to send them on to him as he had no money with him, and promised to pay on delivery. When he received the clothes with the bill, he shut the door on the person delivering them, and never paid. It was held that this was larceny by a trick.

R V Brown

The accused overheard an employer telling his employee to go to S. and pay him some money. He falsely stated that he lived a few doors from S. and offered to deliver the money. He was given the money which he appropriated to his own use. This was held to be larceny by a trick.

R V Russett (1892)

The accused agreed to sell a horse for £23, of which £8 was to be paid at once, and the remainder upon delivery of the horse. The £8 was handed over and a receipt given by which it was stated that the balance would be given upon delivery of the horse. The accused never delivered the horse. It was held to be larceny by a trick on the ground that the prosecutor never intended to part with his property in the £8 until the accused had fulfilled his part of the bargain, which he never intended to do.

R V Hands

The accused put a metal disc instead of a coin into a cigarette vending machine, and so obtained a cigarette, it was held that he was guilty of larceny.

See also *obtaining by false pretences* at page 137.

Larceny by intimidation

Where a person obtains possession of goods by frightening the owner, as by threatening him with temporary imprisonment unless he delivers up his goods, and the owner does deliver under the influence of the fear inspired by his threat this is considered a taking such as to constitute larceny. In circumstances such as these there is a delivery by the owner, however having regard to the provisions of subsection 2(i) this "delivery" is a "taking".

R V McGrath (1870)

The accused acted as auctioneer at a mock auction, knocked down some cloth to a woman, she not having bid, as he knew. The woman denied that she had bid; the accused asserted that she had, and must pay before she could leave the auction room. The woman tried to leave, when an accomplice prevented her. She then in fear paid over money and took away the cloth which was given to her. This was held to be larceny of the money handed over.

Larceny by mistake

It is also a constructive taking, where the possession is obtained under a mistake on the part of the owner, with knowledge on the part of the taker that possession has been so obtained.

R V Middleton (1873)

The accused had a Post Office savings account in which he had 55p, he wished to withdraw 50p. He went to a post office and handed in his deposit book and a warrant of withdrawal for the 50p. The clerk by mistake gave him an amount in excess of £8, which the accused took away. He was convicted of larceny.

Larceny by finding

Where goods are found and at the time of finding the finder believes that the owner can be discovered by taking reasonable steps and he does not take such steps then this constitutes a larceny. If the finder really believes that the owner cannot be found and appropriates the goods to himself, in such a case there is no larceny. It must be put to a jury whether or not they are satisfied that an accused believed that he could find the owner.

R V Moore

A person dropped a banknote in a shop. The shopkeeper found the note, at the time he picked it up he did not know, nor had he reasonable

means of knowing who the owner was. When the shopkeeper heard who the owner was, he afterwards converted it to his own use. The jury found that it was his intention when he found the note, to take it to his own use whomsoever the owner was and that he believed the owner could be found. It was held that the shopkeeper was rightly convicted of larceny.
Cartwright V Green

A bureau was given to a carpenter to repair, and he found money hidden in it, which he kept and converted to his own use. It was held to be larceny.

Larceny by a part owner

At common law a part owner could not commit larceny of property of which he had possession jointly with a co-owner. Now, however the provisio to section 1(1) states: a person may be guilty of stealing any such thing notwithstanding that he has lawful possession thereof, if, being a .. part owner thereof, he fraudulently converts the same to his own use or the use of any person other than the owner.

By section 40(4) of the 1916 Act: If any person, who is a member of any co-partnership or is one of two or more beneficial owners of property, steals or embezzles any such property of or belonging to such co-partnership or to such beneficial owners he shall be liable to be dealt with, tried, and punished as if he had not been or was not a member of such co-partnership or one of such beneficial owners. (see the position re: Husband and Wife below)

Larceny by owner

An owner may be convicted of stealing his own goods. this is so having regard to the definition of owner which includes any part owner, or person having possession or control of, or a special property in, anything capable of being stolen.
Rose V Matt (1951)

The accused left a clock as security for goods sold to and taken away by him on the condition that if the price of the goods was not paid within a month, the clock could be sold. Five days later the accused without the knowledge and consent of the prosecutor took away the clock and subsequently admitted that he had done so because he was afraid it would be sold before he could pay for the goods. He was convicted of larceny of his own clock.

Additional provisions

Simple larceny s. 2

Stealing for which no special punishment is provided shall be simple larceny, punishable with ten years imprisonment.
State (Foley) V Carroll (1980)

It was held by the High Court, that the offence of simple larceny in section 2, is not the creation of statute but is an offence at common law

for which a statutory penalty is provided by that section.
Director of Public Prosecutions V Cassidy (1990)
The accused took goods the property of his employer without his
authority or consent. At the time of taking the goods, the accused had
the intention of permanently depriving his employer thereof. The
accused was charged and convicted under section 2. The District Justice
stated a case for the High Court, as to whether the accused could be
convicted of an offence under section 2 notwithstanding that he might
on the same facts be charged with and punished for an offence under
section 17(1)(a) (see page 144).

It was held by Gannon J. that section 2 provides for the punishment of
larceny where it is not provided for by any other section of the Act or
any other statute. Punishment under section 2 is not precluded merely
because an accused person may also be penalised under another section.

Attempt to steal
Re Michael Woods (1970)
It was held by the Supreme Court, that an attempt to steal is an offence
at common law and the punishment is either fine or imprisonment.

Accessories and abettors s. 35
Every person who knowingly and wilfully aids, abets, counsels,
procures or commands the commission of an offence punishable under
this Act shall be liable to be dealt with, indicted, tried and punished as a
principal offender.
Director of Public Prosecutions V O'Reilly (1990)
A question arose as to whether the prosecution was required to establish
in an aggravated burglary that an accused was physically present on or
about the premises at which the burglary occurred. A was case stated as
to whether such physical presence was required.
It was held in the High Court by Egan J. that by virtue of section 35 of
the 1916 Act physical presence of the accused was not required in order
for him to be treated as a principal offender; and the case should be
remitted to the District Court.

Husband or wife
At common law the possession of husband and wife was one and the
same, so that neither could be convicted of stealing the other's goods,
this has been changed by statute.
The Married Women's Status Act, 1957, at section 9 provides:
(1) Subject to subsection (3), every married woman shall have in her
own name against all persons whomsoever, including her husband, the
same remedies and redress by way of criminal proceedings for the
protection and security of her property as if she were unmarried.
(2) Subject to subsection (3), a husband shall have against his wife the
same remedies and redress by way of criminal proceedings for the
protection and security of his property as if she were not his wife.

(3) No criminal proceedings concerning any property claimed by one spouse (in this section referred to as the claimant) shall, by virtue of subsection (1) or subsection (2), be taken by the claimant against the other spouse while they are living together, nor, while they are living apart, concerning any act done while living together by the other spouse, unless such property was wrongfully taken by the other spouse when leaving or deserting or about to leave or desert the claimant.

Arrest without warrant s. 41

(1) Any person found committing any offence punishable under this Act except an offence under section 31 (Threatening to publish, with intent to extort) may be immediately apprehended without a warrant by any person ...

(2) Any person to whom any property is offered to be sold, pawned, or delivered, if he has reasonable cause to suspect that any offence has been committed against this Act with respect to such property, shall, if in his power, apprehend .. the person offering the same, together with such property, to be dealt with according to law.

(3) Any (Garda) may take into custody without warrant any person whom he finds lying or loitering in any highway, yard, or other place during the night (9pm to 6am), and whom he has good cause to suspect of having committed or being about to commit any felony against this Act, and shall take such person .. to be dealt with according to law.

Penalties under the 1916 Act

The most common penalty for an offence under the 1916 Act is ten years imprisonment except in the case of: Possession of articles (s. 28 five years); Corruptly taking a reward (s. 34 seven years); Handling stolen property (s. 33 fourteen years); Burglary (s. 23A fourteen years) and life imprisonment in respect of Robbery or assault with intent to rob (s. 23) and Aggravated Burglary (s. 23B)

Law reform

The offences with which the Larceny Acts deal with are better understood than they were at common law, however the Law Reform Commission has made 71 recommendations for change in respect of larceny and related offences. In September 1992 it published a report on "The law relating to dishonesty" (LRC 43-1992).

Chapter 13

Subjects of larceny

Through the period of the development of the common law, distinctions were made as to different kinds of larceny. A distinction was made according to the value of the thing stolen. If it were worth only 12d. (5P) or less, the offence was a "petty" larceny. If the thing were worth more than 12d. the offence was "grand" larceny. This distinction ceased to apply after 1827.

Thereafter larceny was still considered to be either "simple" or "aggravated". Aggravated larceny was of various kinds. The circumstances by which larceny could be aggravated were:
   (a) place where it was committed, i.e. a dwelling-house.
   (b) manner in which it was committed, i.e. robbery.
   (c) person by whom it was committed, i.e. embezzlement.
   (d) nature of the thing stolen, i.e. wills, postal packets.

The purpose of the following provisions of the Acts, was to make larcenable things which were not so at common law and make larcenable things notwithstanding they are in the possession of the taker. A number of other important statutory larcenies are dealt with in the chapters that follow.

Larceny Act, 1861

Stealing dogs s. 18
Whosoever shall steal any dog, shall on summary conviction be liable to six months imprisonment or a fine of up to £20 over and above the value of the dog.

Possession of stolen dogs s. 19
Whosoever shall unlawfully have in his possession or on his premises any stolen dog, or the skin of any stolen dog, knowing such dog to have been stolen or such skin to be the skin of a stolen dog, shall, on summary conviction be liable to a £20 fine.

Stealing birds or beasts ordinarily kept in confinement s. 21
Whosoever shall steal any bird, beast, or other animal ordinarily kept in a state of confinement or for any domestic purpose, not being the subject of larceny at common law, or shall wilfully kill any such bird, beast, or animal, with intent to steal the same or any part thereof shall on summary conviction be liable to six months imprisonment and or £20 fine over and above the value and in the case of a second or subsequent offence be liable to twelve months imprisonment.

Persons found in possession of stolen birds, &c. s. 22

If any such bird, or any plumage thereof, or any dog, or any such beast, or the skin thereof, or any such animal, or any part thereof, shall be found in the possession or on the premises of any person .. then such person knowing shall be liable on summary conviction to forfeiture and for every subsequent offence liable to the same penalties as in section 21.

Killing pigeons s. 23

Whosoever shall unlawfully and wilfully kill, wound, or take any house dove or pigeon under such circumstances as shall not amount to larceny at common law, shall, on summary conviction be liable to a £2 fine over and above the value.

Wills or codicils s. 29

Whosoever shall, either during the life of the testator or after his death, ... for any fraudulent purpose destroy, cancel, obliterate, or conceal, the whole or any part of any will, codicil, or other testamentary instrument, whether the same shall relate to real or personal estate, or to both, shall be guilty of felony and liable to life imprisonment

Stealing records or other legal documents s. 30

Whosoever shall for any fraudulent purpose take from its place of deposit for the time being, or from any person having the lawful custody thereof, or shall unlawfully and maliciously cancel, obliterate, injure, or destroy the whole or any part of any record, writ, return, panel, process, interrogatory, affidavit, rule, order, or warrant of attorney, or of any original document whatsoever of or belonging to any court of record, or relating to any matter, civil or criminal, begun, depending, or terminated in any such court, .. shall be guilty of felony and liable to five years imprisonment.

Miners removing ore with intent to defraud s. 39

Whosoever, being employed in or about any mine, shall take, remove or conceal any ore of any metal, ... with intent to defraud any proprietor .., shall be guilty of felony and liable to two years imprisonment.

Larceny Act, 1916

The Larceny Act, 1990 at section 9 provides that a person convicted on indictment of an offence under the following sections of the Larceny Act, 1916: 3, 4, 5, 6, 7, 8, 9, 10, 11, shall be liable to a term of imprisonment not exceeding ten years or a fine or both.

Cattle etc. s. 3

Every person who steals any horse, cattle, or sheep shall be guilty of a felony, and on conviction liable to ten year imprisonment.

Killing animals s. 4

Every person who wilfully kills any animal with intent to steal the carcase, skin, or any part of the animal killed, shall be guilty of felony, and on conviction liable as if he had stolen such animal.

Dogs s. 5

Every person who -

(1) steals any dog after a previous summary conviction of any such offence, or

(2) unlawfully has in his possession or on his premises any stolen dog, or the skin thereof, knowing such dog or skins to have been stolen, after a previous summary conviction of any such offence, or

(3) corruptly takes any money or reward, directly or indirectly, under pretences or upon account of aiding any person to recover any stolen dog, or any dog which is in the possession of any person not being the owner thereof;

shall be guilty of a misdemeanour, and on conviction liable to eighteen months imprisonment.

Wills s. 6

Every person who steals any will, codicil, or other testamentary instrument, either of a dead or of a living person, shall be guilty of felony.

Documents s. 7

Every person who steals the whole or any part of -

(1) any document of title to lands; or

(2) any record, writ, return, panel, petition, process, interrogatory, deposition, affidavit, rule, order, warrant of attorney, or any original document of or belonging to any court of record, or relating to any cause or matter, civil or criminal, begun, depending, or terminated in any such court; or

(3) any original document relating to the business of any office of employment under the State ....

shall be guilty of felony,

By section 46 of the Act the expression "document of title to lands" includes any deed., map, roll, register, paper, or parchment, written of printed, or partly written and partly printed, being or containing evidence of the title, or any part of the title, to any real estate or to any interest in or out of any real estate.

Fixtures, trees, etc. s. 8

Every person who

(1) Steals, or, with intent to steal, rips cuts severs or breaks -

(a) any glass or woodwork belonging to any building; or

(b) any metal or utensil or fixture, fixed in or to any building; or

(c) anything made of metal fixed in any land being private property, or in any place dedicated to public use or ornament, or in any burial-ground:

(2) Steals, or, with intent to steal, cuts, breaks, roots up, or otherwise destroys or damages the whole or any part of any tree, sapling, shrub, or underwood growing -

(a) in any place whatsoever, the value of the article stolen or the injury done being to the amount of one shilling at the least, after two previous summary convictions of any such offence; or

(b) in any park, pleasure ground, garden, orchard, or avenue, or in any ground adjoining or belonging to any dwelling-house, the value of the article stolen or the injury done exceeding the amount of one pound;or

(c) in any place whatsoever, the value of the article stolen or the injury done exceeding the amount of five pounds:

(3) Steals, with intent to steal, destroys or damages any plant, root, fruit, or vegetable production growing in any garden, orchard, pleasure ground, nursery-ground, hothouse, greenhouse, or conservatory, after a previous summary conviction of any such offence;

shall be guilty of a felony.

Goods in process of manufacture s. 9

Every person who steals to the value of ten shillings (50p), any woollen, linen, hempen, or cotton yarn or any goods or article of silk, woollen, linen, cotton, alpaca or mohair, or of any one or more of those materials mixed with each other, or mixed with any other material, whilst laid, placed or exposed, during any stage, process of manufacture, in any building, field or other place, shall be guilty of felony.

Abstracting of electricity s. 10

Every person who maliciously or fraudulently abstracts, causes to be wasted or diverted, consumes or uses any electricity shall be guilty of felony.

Ore from mines s. 11

Every person who steals, or severs with intent to steal, the ore of any metal, or any *lapis calaminaris*, manganese, mundick, wad, black cawke, black lead, coal, or canned coal from any mine bed or vein thereof, shall be guilty of felony.

Poaching by night

The Night Poaching Act, 1828 provides:

Persons taking or destroying game or rabbits by night ... s. 1
If any person shall by night:

unlawfully take or destroys any game or rabbits in any land, whether open or enclosed, or upon any road, highway, or path; or

unlawfully enters or is on any land, whether open or enclosed, with any gun, net, engine or other instrument for the purpose of taking or destroying game

then such person shall be guilty of an offence for which the penalty on summary conviction in the case of a first offence is three months imprisonment and in the case of a second offence is six months imprisonment and on indictment in the case of a third offence it being a misdemeanour is seven years imprisonment.

Persons to number of three or more   s. 9
Where three or more persons by night unlawfully enter or be upon any land, open or enclosed, or any road etc. for the purpose of taking or destroying game or rabbits, and if any such person is armed with any gun, stick, club or other offensive weapon they shall be guilty of a misdemeanour for which the penalty is ten years imprisonment.

Meaning of "night" s. 12
"night" means from first hour after sunset to last hour before sunrise. It is the actual time of sunset at the particular place and not Greenwich mean time.

What shall be deemed "game" s. 13
"game" shall be deemed to include hares, pheasants, partridges, grouse, heath or moor game, black game and bustards.

The Night Poaching Act, 1844, section 1 provides:

Punishments and forfeitures imposed by 1828 Act
All the pains, punishments and forfeitures imposed by (above Act), upon persons by night unlawfully taking or destroying any game or rabbits in any land open or enclosed, as therein set forth, shall be applicable to and imposed upon any person by night unlawfully taking or destroying any game or rabbits on any public road, highway, or path, or the sides thereof, or at the openings, outlets, or gates, from any such land into any such public road, highway or path, open or enclosed; ...

Chapter 14

Handling stolen property

The Larceny Act, 1990 at section 3 substitutes section 33 of the 1916 Act which dealt with "receiving" with a new section on "handling stolen property", at section 7 it elaborates on the scope of offences relating to stolen property and in addition at section 12(5) provides: "The common law offence of receiving stolen property is hereby abolished." There is no case law on the new offence that has been created by the 1990 Act, therefore reference is made to case law in respect of the former offence of "receiving" and to English cases in respect of section 22 (handling stolen goods;a similar offence) of the Theft Act, 1968.

Handling stolen property s. 33

(1) A person who handles stolen property knowing or believing it to be stolen property shall be guilty of felony and shall be liable on conviction on indictment to imprisonment for a term not exceeding 14 years or to a fine or both.

(2) For the purposes of this Act-

(a) a person handles stolen property if (otherwise than in the course of the stealing), knowing or believing it to be stolen property, he dishonestly-

(i) receives the property, or

(ii) undertakes or assists in its retention, removal disposal or realisation by or for the benefit of another person, or

(iii) arranges to do any of the things specified in sub-paragraph (i) or (ii) of this paragraph;

in such circumstances that it is reasonable to conclude that he knew or believed the property to be stolen property, he shall be taken to have so known or believed unless the court or the jury, as the case may be, is satisfied having regard to all the evidence and that there is a reasonable doubt as to whether he so knew or believed; and

(c) believing property to be stolen property includes thinking that such property was probably stolen property.

(3) A person to whom this section applies may be indicted and convicted whether the principal offender has or has not been previously convicted or is or is not amendable to justice.

The ingredients of the offence are :

    (a) person must handle property;

    (b) property must be stolen;

    (c) handling must be otherwise than in the course of stealing;

    (d) person must known or believed it to be stolen property;

    (e) person must have acted dishonestly.

Handling

Handling is the conduct which constitutes the *actus reus* of the offence. Section 33(2)(a) clarifies what is meant by "handling" :
A person handles stolen property if ... he dishonestly-
(i) receives the property, or
(ii) undertakes or assists in its

>   retention,
>   removal
>   disposal or
>   realisation

by or for the benefit of another person, or
(iii) arranges to do any of the things specified in sub-paragraph (i) or (ii) of this paragraph;

Using the above format the many ways that "handling" arises can be listed and the meaning of the terms used may be considered:

Receives

A person handles stolen property if, he dishonestly:
(a) receiving the property; or
(b) arranges to receive the property.

All forms of handling other than receiving are subject to the qualification that it must be proved that an accused was acting "by or for the benefit of another person,".
Possession

In order to establish receiving, it must be proved, that an accused took possession of the stolen property or joined with others to share possession or control of it at some stage. It is not necessary that he should have the goods in his hands, It will be sufficient, if the goods are in the hands of an associate, or on the accused's premises, or in the hands of a servant.

Actual possession is not necessary, constructive possession is sufficient.
People (A. G.) V Kelly & Robinson (1953)

The applicant Kelly was convicted under section 26(1) of the Larceny Act, 1916, while Robinson was convicted under section 33(1) of the same Act. Certain articles were stolen from a shop. Robinson was seen in the vicinity with others, and his car was used in committing the offence. The following night a house was raided by the Gardai. Kelly was seen through a window with three others, sorting the stolen goods. By the time the Gardai were admitted the stolen goods were hidden. Two of the four pleaded not guilty, claiming that they had been visiting the house at the time it was raided.

The trial judge stated in explaining the nature of the offence of receiving goods knowing them to have been stolen "A person may have joint possession of the property with one person or others, though the property may be in the physical custody of another person. If you were satisfied that Hand had in his house this stolen property and that all the people that were there had some control over this property, or that he was holding it for them, they would have what is called constructive possession of it -- if that was the position, they would have received the property knowing it to be stolen. If they knew it was stolen, they of course must know it was stolen property at that particular time .."

It was held by the Court of Criminal Appeal that the trial judge had correctly and adequately instructed the jury on the nature of "constructive possession".

Minister for Posts and Telegraphs V Campbell (1966)

In the High Court it was stated by Davitt P. "A person cannot in the context of a criminal case, be properly said to keep or have possession of an article unless he has control of it either personally or by someone else. He cannot be said to have actual possession of it unless he personally can exercise physical control over it; and he cannot be said to have constructive possession of it unless it is in the actual possession of some other person over whom he has control so that it would be available to him if and when he wanted it. ... He cannot properly be said to be in control or possession of something of whose existence and presence he has no knowledge."

People (A. G.) V Nugent and Byrne (1964)

The applicants were convicted of receiving stolen monies contrary to section 33(1). Monies stolen in a shop were found in Nugent's car. The car had been under observation by the Gardai, but there was a period of five minutes after its arrival when the car was not under observation. Byrne was a passenger in the car. Both denied all knowledge of the stolen monies.

It was held by the Court of Criminal Appeal that there was no evidence that Byrne was aware, or should have been aware, that there were stolen monies in the car. The only evidence connecting him with the car was his own evidence that he had been merely a passenger in the car.

Davitt P. stated "If Nugent was aware that the money was in his car then he was in control of it, and it could properly be said to be in his possession. ... If he was not aware that the money was in his car then it must have been put there by somebody else without his knowledge. ... A person is not necessarily aware at all times of what is in the back of his car."

People (A. G.) V Lawless (1968)

The Court of Criminal Appeal approved of the following passage from Archbold, 36th ed. par. 2096: "The actual manual possession or touch of the goods by the prisoner, however, is not necessary to the completion of the offence of receiving; it is sufficient if they are in the actual possession of a person over whom the prisoner has a control, so that they would be forthcoming if he ordered it."

If the "thief" (person other than the receiver) retains exclusive control there is no receiving. It is not necessary that the receiver should receive any advantage, or profit in any way from the possession of the goods.

Where it is not possible to prove an actual receipt of the stolen property, the evidence may show that an accused has arranged to receive them.. Where an accused had made preparations to receive and has not yet reached the stage of an attempt to do so, any preparation may constitute a sufficient arrangement.

Where there is an innocent receipt, a subsequent intention to appropriate the property does not constitute the necessary intention for the offence.

Undertakes

A person handles stolen property if, he dishonestly:
undertakes in its retention by another person, or
undertakes in its retention for the benefit of another person, or
undertakes in its removal by another person, or
undertakes in its removal for the benefit of another person, or
undertakes in its disposal by another person, or
undertakes in its disposal for the benefit of another person, or
undertakes in its realisation by another person, or
undertakes in its realisation for the benefit of another person,

Assists

A person handles stolen property if, he dishonestly:
assists in its retention by another person, or
assists in its retention for the benefit of another person, or
assists in its removal by another person, or
assists in its removal for the benefit of another person, or
assists in its disposal by another person, or
assists in its disposal for the benefit of another person, or
assists in its realisation by another person, or
assists in its realisation for the benefit of another person,

Arranges

A person handles stolen property if, he dishonestly:
arranges to do any of the above undertaking or assisting.

Thus handling may arise in thirty four different ways

Retention: This involves keeping or continuing to have possession of.
R V Pitchley (1972)
The accused lodged £150 in an account on behalf of his son, being unaware that it was stolen. When he became aware that the money was stolen, he did nothing about it until he was questioned by the police. It was held that the accused retained the money because he continued to keep possession of it.
R V Brown (1969)
It was held that permitting stolen goods to remain in one's house and thereby providing accommodation for them amounted to assisting in

their retention.

Removal: To move the stolen property from one place to another.

Disposal: To get rid of (could include destruction).

Realisation: To turn stolen property into money or some other property.
R V Deakin (1972)
Deakin bought a quantity of liquor knowing it to have been stolen. His conviction for handling by undertaking in the realisation of stolen goods was upheld.

It seems clear that an accused can be convicted of the offence of handling, without having had physical contact with the stolen property.

All forms of handling other than receiving or arranging to receive are subject to the qualification that an accused was acting "by or for the benefit of another person". If this were not the case almost all thieves would be handlers as well. However the thief may be guilty of handling if he himself retains etc. for the benefit of another person. In other cases this other person would normally be the thief.

Property must be stolen
The property must be stolen. To ascertain the meaning of the word "stolen" reference should be made to the definition of stealing in chapter 12, in addition it is given a wider meaning by virtue of:

Scope of offences relating to stolen property s. 7 (1990 Act)
(1) The provisions of the Principal Act and of this Act relating to handling property which has been stolen shall apply whether the property was stolen in the State or elsewhere, and whether the stealing occurred before or after the commencement of this Act, provided that the stealing amounted to an offence where and at the time when the property was stolen; and references to stolen property shall for the purposes of those provisions be construed accordingly.
Attorney General V Finegan (1933)
The applicant was convicted of having in County Louth, receiving a bicycle lamp knowing it to have been stolen. At the trial it appeared that the lamp had been taken from a bicycle just outside the boundary of the State. It was held by the Court of Criminal Appeal that the evidence that the lamp had been stolen outside the State, did not oust the jurisdiction of the court.
(2) For the purposes specified in subsection (1) of this section references to stolen property shall include, in addition to the property originally stolen and parts of it (whether in its original state or not)-
(a) any property which directly or indirectly represents, or has at any time represented, the stolen property in the hands of the thief as being the proceeds of any disposal or realisation of the whole or part of the

stolen property or of property so representing the stolen property; and

(b) any other property which directly or indirectly represents, or has at any time represented, the stolen property in the hands of a handler of the stolen property or any part of it as being the proceeds of any disposal or realisation of the whole or part of the stolen property handled by him or of property so representing it.

(3) For the purposes specified in subsection (1) of this section, no property shall be regarded as having continued to be stolen property after it has been restored to the person from whom it was stolen or to other lawful possession or custody, or after that person and any other person claiming through him to have otherwise ceased, as regards that property, to have any right to restitution in respect of the theft.

R V Schmidt (1866)

A. stole goods from a railway company and sent them to B. by the same railway company. The theft was discovered by an employee of the company, who stopped the goods and gave them to a porter to keep, but then subsequently ordered the porter to take the goods to B. It was held that, as the company had resumed possession, the goods were no longer stolen goods and that B. could not be convicted of receiving.

(4) For the purposes specified in subsection (1) of this section, property shall be regarded as stolen property whether it has been stolen, embezzled, fraudulently converted or obtained by false pretences or by the commission of any offence under section 29, (demanding with menaces), 30, (demanding with menaces with intent to steal), or 31, (threatening to publish with intent to exhort), of the Principal Act (Larceny Act 1916); and "steal", "theft" and "thief" shall be construed accordingly. (see *Walters V Lunt* at page 25).

Property is defined in section 46(1) of the Principal Act which now provides: The expression "property". subject to section 7 of the Larceny Act, 1990, includes any description of real and personal property, money, debts, and legacies, and all deeds and instruments relating to evidencing the title or right to any property, or giving a right to recover or receive any money or goods.

(5) In section 46(1) of the Principal Act, the definition of "property" is hereby amended by the insertion, after "The expression 'property', of 'subject to section 7 of the Larceny Act, 1990,'.

It is not necessary, to prove from whom or by whom the property was stolen, see section 33(3) above.

The circumstances under which the accused received the property may of themselves prove that it was stolen property.

otherwise than in the course of the stealing

The handling required for the offence must be "otherwise than in the course of the stealing" If an accused received the property in the course of stealing, it followed that he was a principal in the theft and this necessarily meant that he could not be convicted of receiving.

Handling stolen property

People (A. G.) V Carney and Mulcahy (1953)

It was held by the Supreme Court that: If the time when the goods are proved to be in possession of the accused is so closely related to the time when the goods are proved to have been stolen as reasonably to exclude the possibility of some other person having been involved, there is no evidence on which a jury could properly convict the accused of receiving and the case should go to the jury merely on a charge of larceny.

O'Leary V Cunningham (1980)

It was held by the Supreme Court that, as the evidence established that the accused was guilty of robbery of money on the occasion mentioned in the charges, the accused could not be convicted of having received that money on the same occasion, knowing it to have been stolen.

It has been held in England that the words "the stealing" refer to the stealing by which the property had become stolen before the handler handled it.?

Knowing or believing to have been stolen

Section 33(2) of the Act clarifies in some detail what is meant by "knowing or believing the property to be stolen", see above.

"knowing or believing" together with "dishonestly" (see below) constitute the *mens rea* of the offence of handling.

This belief that the property was stolen, may be proved by direct evidence or circumstantially by evidence of facts from which knowledge may be inferred. There is a presumption that an accused will, if innocent, explain his possession on oath at the earliest possible time.

People (A. G.) V Shaw (1960)

It was held by the Court of Criminal Appeal that, the evidence of a third party that the goods were sold to him by the accused shortly after the theft can, in the absence of any explanation given by the accused of the manner in which the goods came into his possession, properly be treated by the jury as corroborative of the thief's evidence that the goods were stolen by him and received by the accused.

The prosecution may be assisted in their task of proving knowledge or belief by the common law "doctrine of recent possession"

People (A. G.) V Oglesby (1966)

The accused was convicted in the Circuit Court on the charge of receiving a tape recorder the property of *C. I. E.* knowing it to have been stolen. The accused had told the guards that he had bought the tape recorder from a man in a pub. It was held by the Court of Criminal Appeal, that the so called doctrine of recent possession does not exist, but that it is a convenient way of referring to inferences of fact which, in the absence of any satisfactory explanation, may be drawn as a matter of common sense from other facts. It is the duty of a trial Judge to state any explanation to the jury; he may then comment on it.

The onus of proving guilty knowledge, however always remains on the prosecution.

People (A. G.) V Lillis (1958)

It was held by the Court of Criminal appeal that, in a case of receiving stolen goods, a direction that the jury should convict if they were satisfied that the explanation given by the accused of how the goods came into his possession was a fabrication could not convey to the jury that the burden of proof had shifted in any degree from the prosecution and is a proper direction.

Dishonestly

"dishonestly" is not defined in the Act and it is unclear whether or not it adds anything to the *mens rea*. The term "dishonesty" (note the difference) was introduced in the English Theft Act, 1968, section 2 of that act gives some explanation of what is involved in "dishonesty" and it has also been considered by the courts:

Feely (1973)

It was held by the Court of Appeal that dishonesty was a question of fact for the jury to decide on the standards of the ordinary decent person.

Ghosh (1982)

A two stage test was set for dishonesty:

1. The jury must decide if the behaviour was dishonest by the standards of the ordinary decent person. If he was not, he is not guilty.

2. If the defendant was dishonest by those ordinary decent standards he is only guilty if he realised that people would so regard his behaviour.

The test is subjective but does not allow the defendant to claim he is honest when he knows that by the ordinary standards of society people would regard him as dishonest.

The Law Reform Commission Report on Dishonesty takes issue with juries having to decide the meaning of dishonesty and at par. 15.32 states "To by-pass the judge and leave the definition of fundamental legal concepts to the jury would be an unwarranted exercise in misguided populism." Accordingly, the Commission recommended that dishonesty should be defined in terms of the absence of a claim of legal right.

It seems reasonable to assume that a good defence to a charge of handling would be a claim of right.

Additional provisions

Joint Indictment s. 44(5)

On the trial of two or more persons indicted for jointly handling any stolen property, the court or jury, as the case may be, may find any of the accused guilty if satisfied that he handled all or any part of such property whether he did so jointly with the other accused or with any of them.

Alternative verdicts s. 8 (1990 Act)

(1) If, on the trial of a person for an offence, consisting of or including the stealing, embezzlement or fraudulent conversion of any property, or the obtaining of any property by false pretences, or for an offence under section 29, (demanding with menaces), 30, (demanding with menaces with intent to steal), or 31, (threatening to publish with intent to exhort), of the Principal Act (Larceny Act 1916), it is proved that the person handled the property the subject of the charge in such circumstances as to constitute an offence under section 33, he may be convicted of that offence, but shall not be sentenced to a term of imprisonment exceeding 10 years.

(2) If, on the trial of a person for an offence, under section 33 of handling property alleged to have been stolen or alleged to have been embezzled, fraudulently converted or obtained by false pretences or by the commission of an offence under section 29, (demanding with menaces), 30, (demanding with menaces with intent to steal), or 31, (threatening to publish with intent to exhort), of the Principal Act (Larceny Act, 1916), it is proved that the person stole, embezzled or fraudulently converted the property or obtained it by false pretences or by the commission of an offence under section 29, (demanding with menaces), 30, (demanding with menaces with intent to steal), or 31, (threatening to publish with intent to exhort), of the Principal Act (Larceny Act, 1916), as the case may be, he may be convicted of the offence which he is proved to have committed as aforesaid.

Restitution s. 45

If any person guilty of any such felony or misdemeanour as is mentioned in this Act, in stealing, taking, obtaining, extorting, embezzling, converting, or disposing of, or in knowingly receiving any property, is prosecuted to conviction by or on behalf of the owner of such property, the property shall be restored to the owner or his representative.

The general rule is that the property rights in stolen goods always remain in the original owner, no matter how many times they may change hands for good consideration, whether by sale in market overt or otherwise.

This is done by means of a restitution order.

Related offences

Advertising a reward for the return of stolen property s. 102 (1861)

Whosoever shall publicly advertise a reward for the return of any property whatsoever which shall have been stolen or lost, and shall in such advertisement use any words purporting that no questions will be asked, or shall make use of any words purporting that no questions will be asked, or shall make use of any words in any public advertisement purporting that a reward will be given or paid for any property which shall have been stolen or lost, without seizing or making any inquiry after the person producing such property, or shall promise or offer in any such public advertisement to return to any pawnbroker or other person who may have bought or advanced money by way of loan upon any property stolen or lost the money so paid or advanced, or any other sum of money or reward for the return of such property, or shall print or publish any such advertisement, shall forfeit the sum of fifty pounds for every such offence

Corruptly taking a reward s. 34

Every person who corruptly takes any money or reward, directly or indirectly, under pretence or upon account of helping any person to recover any property which has, under circumstances which amount to felony or misdemeanour, been stolen or obtained in any way whatsoever, or received, shall (unless he has used all due diligence to cause the offender to be brought to trial for the same) shall be guilty of felony and on conviction liable to seven years imprisonment.

The Criminal Justice Act, 1951, provides:

Unlawful possession s. 13

(1) A member of the Garda Siochana may arrest without warrant a person whom he reasonably suspects of having or conveying in any manner anything stolen or unlawfully obtained.

(2) A person who is charged before the District Court with having in his possession or on his premises with his knowledge or conveying in any manner anything which may be reasonably suspected of being stolen or unlawfully obtained and who does not give an account to the satisfaction of the Court how he came by it shall be guilty of an offence, for which the penalty is £5 and or two months imprisonment.

Attorney General V Brodigan

An accused who was suspected of being concerned in a housebreaking either as principal or receiver, was charged in the District Court with unlawful possession of a sum of money contrary to section 13 of the Criminal Justice Act, 1951. The evidence against him was that he had spent a considerable sum of money of which he gave no satisfactory account but no sum of money had been found on his person or on his premises, and none of the money spent by him was identifiable as the subject-matter of the housebreaking. It was held that the possession necessary to support such a charge, must be referable to the time when such charge was preferred, and that in the absence of evidence of possession at such time, such charge must be dismissed.

The Criminal Justice Act, 1984, provides:

Withholding information regarding stolen property s. 16(1)

Where a member of the Garda Siochana -

(a) has reasonable grounds for believing that an offence consisting of the stealing, fraudulent conversion, embezzlement or unlawful obtaining or receiving of money

or other property has been committed,

(b) finds any person in possession of any property,

(c) has reasonable grounds for believing that the property includes, or may include the property referred to in (a) and

(d) informs that person of his belief, he may require that person to give him an account of how he came by the property.

Failure to give an account is an offence, for which the penalty on summary conviction is £1,000 fine and or twelve months imprisonment.

Note that this provision applies whether or not a person has been arrested.

Chapter 15

Burglary and related offences

At common law burglary was the breaking and entering of a dwelling house by night with the intent to commit a felony therein, whether the felony was committed or not. The 1916 Act at section 25 (since repealed) similarly had requirements in respect of "breaking", "entering", "dwelling house" "felony" and "night". The interpretation of the section was beset with technical difficulties and was repealed and replaced by the Criminal Law (Jurisdiction) Act, 1976. The current offence is contained in sections 23A and 23B of the 1916 Act.

Burglary s. 23A
(1) A person is guilty of burglary if-

(a) he enters any building or part of a building as a trespasser and with intent to commit any such offence as is mentioned in subsection (2), or

(b) having entered any building or part of a building as a trespasser, he steals or attempts to steal anything in the building or that part of it, or inflicts or attempts to inflict on any person therein any grievous bodily harm.

(2) The offences referred to in subsection (1)(a) are offences of stealing anything in the building or part of a building in question, of inflicting on any person therein any grievous bodily harm or raping any woman therein and of doing unlawful damage to the building or anything therein.

(3) References in subsections (1) and (2) to a building shall apply also to an inhabited vehicle or vessel, and shall apply to any such vehicle or vessel at times when the person having a habitation in it is not there as well as at times when he is there.

(4) A person guilty of burglary shall be liable to fourteen years imprisonment.

enter

The term "enter" is not defined in the Act. What is required is an effective and substantial entry in the circumstances of the case.

At common law there was a sufficient entry when any part of the body of the accused went over the threshold, for example a finger. If an instrument was inserted into the building for the purpose of committing an ulterior offence, there was an entry even though no part of the body was introduced into the building. On the other hand, the insertion of an instrument for the purpose of gaining entry and not for the purpose of committing the ulterior offence, was not an entry if no part of the body had entered.

R V Collins (1972)

Collins had climbed a ladder to an open window through which he saw a sleeping girl, with whom he had some slight acquaintance. The girl awoke and believing that Collins was her boyfriend, welcomed him to her bed, where intercourse took place. On discovering her mistake the girl struck Collins. Collins was convicted of burglary in that he had entered a building as a trespasser with intent to commit rape.

The Court of Appeal allowed an appeal on the basis that the jury were never invited to consider the question whether Collins did enter the premises as a trespasser, that is to say knowing perfectly well that he had no invitation to enter or reckless of whether or not his entry was with permission.

R V Brown (1985)

Brown had been seen partially inside a broken shop window, his feet still on the ground outside, rummaging through the goods. He was convicted of burglary and appealed on the basis that entry meant a complete entry. His appeal was dismissed, it being held that the entry had to be "effective". Whether it is so depends on the circumstances of the case, and it was obviously effective here.

trespass

"Trespass" which is a civil concept; involves an entry on land without an invitation of any sort and without lawful justification. A trespass is not criminal unless an intent to commit a criminal act was there at the time of the trespass. It would not be trespass where a person stumbled into a building or where a person was dragged involuntarily into a building. Where consent to entry is obtained by fraud, then the entry is a trespass.

In the case of mistake, a defendant ought not to be guilty of burglary if he honestly believes that the owner has consented, or honestly believes that he has a right of entry even though his mistake in the circumstances is an unreasonable one. Note *R V Collins* above.

The questions that arise are:

1. did the person entering have permission to enter ?
2. had a person with permission to enter exceeded the limits of such permission ?

R V Jones (1976); R V Smith (1976)

Smith and Jones had entered a bungalow belonging to the father of one of them and had taken two televisions. They were convicted of burglary. They appealed on the basis that a person who had a general permission to enter, such as a son, could not be a trespasser for the purposes of the offence. The Court of Appeal dismissed the appeal. James L.J. stated "it is our view that a person is a trespasser....if he enters premises of another knowing that he is entering in excess of the permission that has been given to him, or being reckless that he is acting in excess of the permission given or that he is acting recklessly as to whether he exceeds that permission, then, that is sufficient for the jury to decide that he is in fact a trespasser. "

intent

The "intent" must have existed at the time of the entry, the subsequent formation of an intention to steal after an entry will not suffice. It is not relevant that the stealing was or was not possible; it is sufficient that an accused had an intent to steal.

The intent required is to commit any of the following:
(a) stealing anything in the building or part of a building in question;
(b) inflicting on any person therein any grievous bodily harm; or
(c) raping any woman therein; or
(d) doing unlawful damage to the building or anything therein.

building

"building" itself is not defined, presumably it covers not only houses, but shops and offices, however subsection 3 states that references to a building shall apply also to an inhabited vehicle or vessel at times when the the person having a habitation in it is not there as well as well as at times when he is there. Outbuildings of a house seem to be a building. To be a building, the structure must have some degree of permanence and it seems clear that it would not include a tent even though some person lived in the tent.

Aggravated burglary s. 23B

(1) A person is guilty of aggravated burglary if he commits any burglary and at the time has with him any firearm or imitation firearm, any weapon of offence or any explosive; and for this purpose-

(a) firearm includes an airgun or airpistol, and imitation firearm means anything that has the appearance of being a firearm, whether capable of being discharged or not;

(b) weapon of offence means any article made or adopted for use for causing injury to or incapacitating a person or intended by the person having it with him for such use; and

(c) explosive means any article manufactured for the purpose of producing a practical effect by explosion, or intended by the person having it with him for that purpose.

(2) A person guilty of aggravated burglary shall be liable on conviction on indictment to imprisonment for life.

at the time

"at the time" for a person to be convicted, it is necessary to show that he had the firearm etc. with him at the time he committed the burglary.
R V Francis (1982)

The accused gained entry to a house, armed with sticks. After throwing away the sticks he stole property. The Court of Appeal substituted a conviction for burglary for one of aggravated burglary. Unless the accused intended to steal when he entered the house, he was only guilty of aggravated burglary if he had a weapon with him at the time when he stole.
R V O'Leary (1986)

The accused armed himself after entering a house. It was held by the

Court of Appeal that the material time for the possession of a weapon is
the point at which the accused actually stole.

The Larceny Act, 1990 at section 9 provides that a person convicted
on indictment of an offence under sections: 13, 15 and 16 of the 1916
Act shall be liable to a term of imprisonment not exceeding ten years or
a fine or both. These sections deal with burglary type offences, which do
not have a trespassing requirement, so that a person who is not
trespassing on a property can be convicted of an offence.

Larceny in dwelling-houses s. 13

Every person who steals in any dwelling house any chattel, money, or
valuable security shall-

(a) if the value of the property stolen amounts to five pounds; ..

be guilty of felony

No breaking or entry with intent to commit an offence need be
proved, but the building must be a dwelling-house, and the goods must
be under the protection of the house.

An owner of a house may be convicted of stealing property belonging
to another under this section. A visitor to a house may also be convicted
under this section. The property stolen may belong to any other person.

"valuable security"

By section 46(1) of the 1916 Act: The expression "valuable security"
includes any writing entitling or evidencing the title of any person to
any share or interest in any public stock, annuity, fund, or debt of any
part (of the State), or in any stock, annuity, fund, or debt of any body
corporate, company, or society, whether within or without (the State), or
to any deposit in any Bank, and also includes any script, debenture, bill,
note warrant, order, or other security for payment of money, or any
accountable receipt, release or discharge, or any receipt or other
instrument evidencing the payment of money, or the delivery of any
chattel personal, and any document of title to lands or goods as
hereinbefore defined.

"dwelling house"

By section 46(2) of the 1916 Act: The expression "dwelling house"
does not include a building although within the same curtilage with any
dwelling-house and occupied therewith unless there is a communication
between such building and dwelling-house, either immediate or by
means of a covered and enclosed passage leading from one to the other.

Larceny from ships, docks, etc. s. 15

Every person who steals-

(1) any goods in any vessel, barge or boat of any description in any
haven or any port of entry or discharge or upon any navigable river or
canal or in any creek or basin belonging to or communicating with any
such haven, port, river, or canal; or

Burglary and related offences

(2) any goods from any dock, wharf or quay adjacent to any such haven, port, river, canal, creek, or basin; or

(3) any part of any vessel in distress, wrecked, stranded, or cast on shoe, or any goods, merchandise, or articles of any kind belonging to such vessel;

shall be guilty of felony

Larceny by tenants or lodgers s. 16

Every person who, being a tenant or lodger, or the husband or wife of any tenant or lodger, steals any chattel or fixture let to be used by such person in or with any house or lodging shall be guilty of felony

Possession of articles

The Larceny Act, 1990 amended the Larceny Act, 1916. The Principal Act at section 28 dealt with possession of housebreaking implements, a new section 28 deals with possession of articles. The section as it now stands creates two offences. Unlike the older offence the new offences are not confined to "night", in addition they are both felonies whereas the older offence was a misdemeanour. See, possession in chapter 14.

Possession of articles s. 28

(1) A person who is, when not at his place of abode, in possession of any article with the intention that it be used in the course of or in connection with-

(a) larceny or burglary, or

(b) an offence under section 29, 30, 31 or 32 of this Act, or

(c) an offence under section 112 (which deals with taking a vehicle without lawful authority) of the Road Traffic Act, 1961,

shall be guilty of felony and be liable on conviction on indictment to imprisonment for a term not exceeding 5 years or to a fine or to both.

(2) A person who is, without lawful authority or reasonable excuse, in possession of any article made or adapted for use in the course of or in connection with-

(a) larceny or burglary, or

(b) an offence under section 29, 30, 31 or 32 of this Act, or

(c) an offence under section 112 (which deals with taking a vehicle without lawful authority) of the Road Traffic Act, 1961,

shall be guilty of felony and be liable on conviction on indictment to imprisonment for a term not exceeding 5 years or to a fine or to both.

(3) Where a person is convicted of an offence under this section, the court may order that any article for the possession of which he was so convicted shall be forfeited and either destroyed or disposed of in such manner as the court may determine.

(4) An order under subsection (3) of this section shall not take effect until the ordinary time for instituting an appeal against the conviction or order concerned has expired or, where such an appeal is instituted, until

it or any further appeal is finally decided or abandoned or the ordinary time for instituting any further appeal has expired.

The constituent parts of the section may be considered:

Possession of articles with intent

(1) A person who is, when not at his place of abode, in possession of any article with the intention that it be used in the course of or in connection with-

(a) larceny or burglary, or

(b) an offence under section 29, 30, 31 or 32 of this Act, or

(c) an offence under section 112 (which deals with taking a vehicle without lawful authority) of the Road Traffic Act, 1961,

shall be guilty of felony and be liable on conviction on indictment to imprisonment for a term not exceeding 5 years or to a fine or to both.

For this offence a person must not be at his place of abode, and must have an intention to use any article that he is in possession of, in the commission of any of the seven specified offences.

place of abode
R V Bundy (1977)

It was held that by the English Court of Appeal that a "place of abode" comprised two elements: the element of a site at which the occupier intended to abide and the element of intention to abide at that site. A "place of abode" means a fixed place, so that a car out on the road is not a place of abode, when a person was in transit in a car moving from one site to another the car was not his place of abode.

It follows that a car at a fixed place could be a "place of abode"

any article

This is very broad especially when compared with the older offence, which was confined to implements of housebreaking. Amongst the items covered could be bankcards, coathangers, keys and screwdrivers. It would be for the jury to decide whether the article could be used in the commission of the specified offences.

intention

It must be shown that there was an intention on the part of the accused, to use the article in the commission of one of the specified offence. The offence under section 1(b) above, in addition to larceny, burglary and taking a vehicle without lawful authority are the blackmail offences of:

Section 29, demanding with menaces,

Section 30, demanding with menaces with intent to steal,

Section 31, threatening to publish with intent to exhort, and

Section 32, obtaining by false pretence.

Possession of articles made or adopted for use

(2) A person who is, without lawful authority or reasonable excuse, in possession of any article made or adapted for use in the course of or in connection with-

(a) larceny or burglary, or

(b) an offence under section 29, 30, 31 or 32 of this Act, or

(c) an offence under section 112 (which deals with taking a vehicle without lawful authority) of the Road Traffic Act, 1961,

shall be guilty of felony and be liable on conviction on indictment to imprisonment for a term not exceeding 5 years or to a fine or to both.

any article made or adapted for use

The reference in subsection (1) to "any article" is added to in subsection (2) by the addition of "made or adapted for use". A made article is produced for some or a variety of purposes, an adapted article is an article which has undergone some alteration.

R V Simpson (1983)

A court is entitled to take judicial notice of the fact that something is made for a particular use and the fact that it can be used for a particular purpose does not take it out of that category.

See section 10 of the Firearms and Offensive Weapons Act, 1990, regarding a "weapon of offence" at page 329 which is similar to section 23B(1)(b) of the Larceny Act, 1916 in relation to aggravated burglary.

lawful authority or reasonable excuse

For this offence there is no requirement as to intention as above, and a person may be at his place of abode. It would be open to a person to show that he was in possession of the articles with lawful authority or reasonable excuse. Many a person particularly tradesmen would have in their possession articles that could be used in the commission of the specified offences

Forfeiture

(3) Where a person is convicted of an offence under this section, the court may order that any article for the possession of which he was so convicted shall be forfeited and either destroyed or disposed of in such manner as the court may determine.

(4) An order under subsection (3) of this section shall not take effect until the ordinary time for instituting an appeal against the conviction or order concerned has expired or, where such an appeal is instituted, until it or any further appeal is finally decided or abandoned or the ordinary time for instituting any further appeal has expired.

The use of "may" is an indication that a court may use its discretion when it comes to forfeiture.

Chapter 16

Robbery and related offences

The section 23 of the 1916 Act was substituted by the Criminal Law (Jurisdiction) Act, 1976, it is practically the same as section 8 of the English Theft Act, 1968. In subsection (2) the same penalty is provided for in respect of "robbery" and of "an assault with intent to rob" (see assault, chapter 8). All reference below are to the Larceny Act, 1916, unless otherwise stated.

Robbery s. 23

(1) A person is guilty of robbery if he steals, and immediately before or at the time of doing so, and in order to do so, he uses force on any person or puts or seeks to put any person in fear of being then and there subjected to force.

(2) A person guilty of robbery, or of an assault with intent to rob shall be liable on conviction on indictment to imprisonment for life.

The elements of the definition of robbery are:
  (a) steals;
  (b) time;
  (c) force or fear; and
  (d) any person

Steals

Robbery is essentially an aggravated form of stealing; and if there is no stealing, or attempt to steal, there can be no robbery or attempted robbery. Robbery is complete when the theft is complete.

The force, or threat of force, if it is to amount to robbery, must be used in order that the accused might steal; therefore, where a person does not steal, he cannot be convicted of robbery.

Any defence that may be raised for stealing could defeat a conviction:
R V Robinson (1977)

The accused ran a club which was owed money by V. He attacked V at night in the street brandishing a knife an took £5 which fell from V's wallet.

It was held on appeal that the accused story that he believed he had a right to take the £5 was, if believed a good defence, even if he did not believe that he had a right to take it by force. The conviction was quashed (see claim of right, at page 101).

Time

Where force is used in order to steal, it will constitute the offence only where it is used at the very time of stealing, or immediately before.

The whole course of the conduct of an accused may be regarded as stealing, rather than the act which satisfies the minimum requirement for

133

appropriation.
R V Hale (1978)

The defendant entered the house of a woman. He put his hand over her mouth to stop her screaming, went upstairs, took her jewellry and then tied her up and gagged her before making off. He was convicted of robbery.

The Court of Appeal dismissed his appeal and held that the jury were entitled to convict, relying on the force used at the start when the accused put his hand over the woman's mouth; further the force used in tying her up also occurred "immediately before or at the time of stealing" as is required since the act of appropriation was a continuing one and the stealing was not over when she was tied up.

Force or fear

Any actual or threatened use of force against a person will suffice.

(a) The force may be minimal but must be more than a slight physical contact. A mere accidental use of force will not suffice.

(b) The force or threat of force must be against a person, a threat to damage property will not suffice.

(c) A threat of future force will not suffice (but this may constitute blackmail, see below)

(d) The question of whether or not force, has been used in an alleged robbery is for the jury.
R V Dawson (1976)

The Court of Appeal held in upholding a conviction, that it was open to a jury to decide that nudging the victim so as to cause him to lose his balance (thereby enabling an accomplice to steal his wallet) was sufficient "force" to justify a conviction for robbery.

Any person

The actual or threatened force can be against any person and need not be against the person whose property is stolen, it does not matter that such person has no interest whatever in the property.

The Larceny Act, 1990 at section 9 provides that a person convicted on indictment of an offence under the following sections (considered immediately below) shall be liable to a term of imprisonment not exceeding ten years or a fine or both.

In dwelling-houses s. 13

Every person who steals in any dwelling-house any chattel, money, or valuable security shall-

(b) if he by any menace or threat puts any person being in such dwelling-

shall be guilty of felony.

Note the meaning of the expressions "dwelling-house" and "valuable security" at page 129.

From the person s. 14

Every person who steals any chattel, money or valuable security from the person of another shall be guilty of felony

People (A. G.) V Mills (1953)

A Miss Williams was going in one of the entrances to Clerys in Lower O'Connell Street, Dublin. She had her handbag, which contained her purse on her left arm. In the entrance at the same time were the accused and Mrs. Whelan, she saw Miss Williams bag open and the accused left hand withdrawing her purse right out from the bag. She tapped Miss Williams on the shoulder saying "That man has taken your purse" whereupon Miss Williams, looking at her bag, found that it was open but that the purse was in it.

Davitt P. in the Court of Criminal Appeal stated that if the evidence of Mrs. Whelan was accepted in its entirety, it clearly established the offence under section 14.

Blackmail

There is no offence of "blackmail", the term is colloquial. The word was used originally to describe the tribute paid to Scottish chieftains by English landowners in the border counties in order to secure immunity from raids on their property. Sections 29, 30 and 31 of the 1916 Act prescribe the offences commonly referred to as "blackmail". See also possession of articles in chapter 15.

Demanding with menaces s. 29

(1) Every person who -

(i) utters, knowing the contents thereof, any letter or writing demanding of any person with menaces, and without any reasonable or probable cause, any property or valuable thing;

(ii) utters, knowing the contents thereof, any letter or writing accusing or threatening to accuse any other person (whether living or dead) of any crime to which this section applies, with intent to extort or gain thereby any property or valuable thing from any person;

(iii) with intent to extort or gain any property or valuable thing from any person accuses or threatens to accuse either that person or any other person (whether living or dead) of any such crime;

shall be guilty of felony

(2) Every person who with intent to defraud or injure any other person-

(a) by any unlawful violence to or restraint of the person of another, or

(b) by accusing or threatening to accuse any person (whether living or dead) of any crime.

compels any person to execute, make, accept, endorse, alter, or destroy any valuable security

shall be guilty of felony

(3) This section applies to any crime punishable with death or imprisonment for not less than seven years, or any assault with intent to

commit any rape, or any attempt to commit any rape, or any solicitation, persuasion, promise or threat offered or made to any person, whereby to move or induce such person to commit or permit the crime of buggery.

(4) It is immaterial whether any menaces or threats be of violence, injury, or accusation to be caused or made by the offender or by any other person.

Demanding with menaces with intent to steal s. 30

Every person who with menaces or by force demands of any person anything capable of being stolen with intent to steal the same shall be guilty of felony.

Menaces

Thorne V Motor Trade Association (1937)

Lord Wright said "I think the word 'menace' is to be liberally construed and not as limited to threats of violence but as including threats of any action detrimental to or unpleasant to the person addressed."

R V Bernhard (1938)

It was held that if the person making the demand honestly thought that she was entitled to be acquitted even though the threat (in this case publicity) was not the kind of threat that she was entitled to use to enforce her claim.

Threatening to publish with intent to exhort s. 31

Every person who with intent -

(a) to extort any valuable thing from any person, or

(b) to induce any person to confer or procure for any person any appointment or office of profit or trust,

(1) publishes or threatens to publish any libel upon any other person (whether living or dead); or

(2) directly or indirectly threatens to print or publish, or directly or indirectly proposes to abstain from or offers to prevent the printing or publishing of any matter or thing touching any other person (whether living or dead).

Chapter 17

Obtaining by false pretences

At common law dishonesty was only a crime when it took the form of a wrong to the possession of the owner. A statutory provision for the punishment of a mere private cheating was made in England in 1757, and was later followed in the 1916 Act. The earlier Acts dealing with this offence are repealed, but the phrases in them are in substance the same as in the 1916 Act, and consequently most of the decisions upon the repealed statutes are applicable.

The statutory provisions are contained in:

> Larceny Act, 1916 (section 32);
> Criminal Justice Act, 1951 (section 10);
> Forgery Act, 1861;
> False Personation Act, 1874.

False pretences s. 32

Every person who, by any false pretence, -

(1) with intent to defraud, obtains from any other person any chattel, money, or valuable security, or causes or procures any money to be paid, or any chattel or valuable security to be delivered to himself or to any other person for the use or benefit or on account of himself or any other person; or

(2) with intent to defraud or injure any other person, fraudulently causes or induces any other person-

(a) to execute, make accept, endorse, or destroy the whole or any part of any valuable security; or

(b) to write, impress, or affix his name or the name of any other person, or the seal of any body corporate or society, upon any paper or parchment in order that the same may be afterwards made or converted into, or used or dealt with as a valuable security;

shall be guilty of a misdemeanour and be liable (1990 Act, section 9) to a term of imprisonment not exceeding ten years or a fine or both.

Obtaining by false pretences

Obtaining by false pretences is the offence created in subsection (1). To constitute this offence, it is necessary that:

(1) A pretence or representation must be made.
(2) The pretence must be made to the person from whom the property was obtained or his agent.
(3) The pretence must be to a matter of fact and not opinion.
(4) The pretence must have relation to past or present facts.
(5) The pretence must be false to the knowledge of the accused.
(6) The pretence must be the cause of the obtaining.
(7) The obtaining must be with intent to defraud.
(8) The intent must be to deprive the owner wholly of his property.

These points now arise for consideration.

A pretence or representation must be made.

The pretence or representation may be made by words or conduct. It is a matter for a jury to say whether the words or conduct are reasonably capable of supporting the pretence charged and that they were so meant by the accused and understood as such.

R V Murphy (1876)

A person who obtained goods by sending by post half notes in payment, but sent the corresponding halves to another person in payment for other gods was held to have been properly convicted of obtaining the first mentioned goods by false pretences.

R V Jones (1898)

An accused went into a restaurant and ordered a meal, he had no money and no intention of paying. No question was put to him, nor inquiry made as to his means. No statement was made by him as to whether he could pay for the meal.

It was held that he could not be convicted of obtaining by false pretences. (He was convicted of Obtaining credit under false pretences, see section 13, Debtors (Ireland) Act, 1872 at page 151).

R V Barnard (1837)

The accused went into a shop in Oxford wearing a cap and gown. This was held to be a pretence that he was a member of the University.

Finkel V Levine (1951)

The accused had been involved in a transaction whereby counterfeit dollar bills were given by one of them to a third party in exchange for sterling at a price above the normal exchange rate.

In the Court of Criminal Appeal Maguire C.J. said: "It is quite true that there was no evidence of any statement being made by either accused that the dollar bills were genuine .... there was quite sufficient evidence from which the jury could conclude that the accused by there conduct, if not in so many words, represented that the bills were genuine

Must be made to the person from whom the property was obtained

The pretence must be made to the person from whom the property was obtained or his agent. A false pretence made to a third party will not suffice, though it may have been intended to be reported to the person from whom the property was to be obtained.

R V Robinson (1915)

The accused was a jeweller who, after insuring his stock against theft, tied himself up and called for assistance, telling the police that he had been attacked and his safe robbed. He had hoped that the police would report the supposed loss to his insurers. Subsequently he admitted that he had hoped to make a claim on the insurers. He was convicted on a charge of attempting to obtain money by false pretences. On appeal Reading C.J. stated "... we think that the appellant's act was only remotely connected with the commission of the full offence, and not immediately connected with it...We think the conviction must be quashed."

Pretence must be to a matter of fact and not opinion.

The pretence made must be a definite fact not expressions of opinion, mere praise or puffing.
R V Bryan (1857)

The accused stated that certain spoons produced by himself were of the best quality and that they were equal to Elkington's A. The misrepresentations were made to pawnbrokers, for the purpose of obtaining advances of money on the spoons. The spoons were of inferior quality and not worth the money advanced.

Pollock C.B. on behalf of the Court for the Consideration of Crown Cases said: "I think it may be fairly laid down that any exaggeration or depreciation in the ordinary course of dealings between buyer and seller during the progress of a bargain is not the subject of a criminal prosecution."

It would have been a misrepresentation of fact in the above case if the accused had stated that the spoons were Elkington's. A misstatement as to some specific fact within the knowledge of the accused will suffice.
R V Ardley (1871)

The accused went into the shop of a watchmaker and jeweller. He stated that he was a draper, and was £5 short of the money required to pay a bill. He asked the shopkeeper to buy a chain he was then wearing. The accused stated "It is 15-carat fine gold, and you will see it stamped on every link", he claimed that he had paid over £9 for it. The chain was bought and later found to be of a quality not much better than 6 carat gold. A jury found that the accused had knowingly made a false representation and he was convicted.

On appeal Bovill C.J. said: "The case differs from *R V Bryan*, because here there was a statement as to a specific fact within the actual knowledge of the prisoner, namely, the proportion of pure gold in the chain."

Pretence must have relation to past or present facts.

The pretence must have relation to past or present facts. A promise as to future conduct or a representation relating solely to intention will not suffice. It has been held that a false promise should not involve the promisor in liability for obtaining money by false pretences. A promise is regarded as being different to an ordinary representation of fact.
R V Dent (1955)

The appellant had been convicted on seven counts of obtaining cheques by false pretences. He carried on business as a pest destroyer, and had entered into contracts with farmers to destroy vermin on their land for a year. He had done no work under the contracts. The false pretence alleged were that he had falsely represented that he was *bona fide* entering into contracts for a year and that he had falsely pretended that he intended to perform them.

Devlin J. said: "we are satisfied that a long course of authorities in criminal cases has laid it down that a statement of intention about future conduct, whether or not it be a statement of existing fact, is not such a statement as will amount to a false pretence in criminal law. "

Where a false promise is coupled with a false statement as to existing fact, it will be different.

R V Jennison (1862)

The accused, a married man obtained £8 from a woman by representing that he was unmarried, that he would furnish a house and would marry her.

It was held that while the false promise of marriage could not be the subject of an indictment, the false pretence that he was an unmarried man could be.

Must be false to the knowledge of the accused

The pretence must be false to the knowledge of the accused. This guilty knowledge must be proved beyond reasonable doubt. The falsity may be inferred from the circumstances of the case and need not be proved by direct evidence. It is not necessary to prove that every detail of the pretence was untrue if the falsity of the substance of the pretence is shown.

Pretence must be the cause of the obtaining.

The false pretence must be the cause of the obtaining. If the victim was not deceived, there cannot be a conviction for the obtaining but only for the attempt. The victim may have known of the falsity and parted with the goods in order to entrap the accused, or he may have believed that he would be paid.

R V Light (1915)

Rowlatt J in the Court of Criminal Appeal said: "It is abundantly clear that a person cannot be convicted of the offence of obtaining goods or money by false pretences unless the mind of the prosecutor has been misled by the false pretence, and he has been induced to part with the property thereby. But in our judgment it is a complete fallacy to suppose that the same principle has any application in the case of attempt only. "

Obtaining must be with intent to defraud

The obtaining must be with intent to defraud. It is not enough that the pretence did obtain the property, it must have been made with the purpose of defrauding.

R V Williams (1836)

The accused a servant, obtained goods from another by a misrepresentation, intending that his master should retain them in part payment of a debt for which he could not get payment.

It was held that as the accused did not intend to defraud but merely to secure payment of a debt he could not be convicted.

Intent must be to deprive the owner wholly of his property

The intent must be to deprive the owner wholly of his property. It has already been seen (chapter 15, on stealing) that it cannot be stealing if the accused obtained the legal ownership of property. This offence fills the gap and it has often been held that if the legal ownership is not obtained, then the offence of obtaining by false pretences is not committed.

It is essential that the owner should have intended to pass ownership in the thing alleged to have been obtained by false pretences.

R V Harvey (1787)

The accused was indicted for stealing a horse. He had agreed to buy the horse for £8. He mounted the horse saying that he would return immediately and pay for it. He rode away and never returned.

Gould J. stated that it was impossible to make this case a felony. It was a sale; and the possession as well as the property was parted with. The accused had defrauded the owner of the price of the horse, but not of the horse itself.

False pretences and valuable securities s. 32(2)

Section 32(2) of the 1916 Act would appear to create a number of offences. There has been little judicial consideration of the subsection.

R V Thornton (1964)

The offence is not committed if the document to which the signature of another person was obtained by false pretences imposed no liability upon anyone other than the accused, e.g. the person upon whom the false pretence was practised was only a witness.

The Criminal Justice Act, 1951 provides:

Obtaining by false pretences s. 10

Every person who, by any false pretence, with intent to defraud, obtains anything capable of being stolen or causes it to be delivered to himself or to any other person for the use or benefit or on account of himself or any other person is guilty of a misdemeanour and liable to five years imprisonment.

This offence may be tried summarily.

This is a like offence, the substitution of the words "anything capable of being stolen", has the effect of broadening the offence. There may under this section a conviction of obtaining a dog by false pretences.

Attempt at obtaining by false pretences

Every attempt to commit a crime is itself an indictable misdemeanour at common law. Accordingly whenever the intention to obtain money or goods by false pretences is clear by an overt act, this may be an attempt to commit the statutory misdemeanour.

Attorney General V Sullivan (1964)

S. a registered midwife was charged with unlawfully attempting to obtain money by false pretences with intent to defraud. It was alleged that she had prepared certain prescribed forms which, if genuine, would have signified her professional attendance on the patients named on the said forms, and had them signed by the said patients S. did not attend any of these patients and the forms submitted by her were fictitious and, it was alleged were presented with fraudulent intent.

It was held by the Supreme Court that each false "claim" was an act sufficiently proximate to constitute an attempt to commit the offence of obtaining by false pretences. It was held further that the offences in question are quiet clearly common law offences.

See also *R V Light (1915)* above.

False pretences and fraudulent conversion
People (A. G.) V Heald (1954)

The applicant was the matron of a convalescent home run by an order of nuns and had authority to collect and expend fees and charges from patients in her discretion. She received into the home two elderly ladies on their paying her £2,000, which she placed in her own personal bank account, concealing this from the nuns. The nuns had discontinued their practice of receiving patients on a lump sum basis.

The applicant was charged with 1, larceny and 2, fraudulent conversion contrary to section 20.1(IV)(b) of the Larceny Act 1916, she was acquitted of larceny and acquitted of fraudulent conversion.

It was held by the Court of Criminal Appeal, that, in order to sustain the conviction it must be shown that the applicant had authority to receive the sum of money on behalf of the nuns and the onus of proving such authority lay on the prosecution.

It was also held that, as there was a count of larceny in the indictment the jury could have been told that they could convict of obtaining money by false pretences on that count, the applicant had been in peril on a charge of false pretences and her acquittal of larceny precluded her from being now tried upon a charge of false pretences. The court accordingly ordered that the conviction should be quashed.

People (A. G.) V Singer (1961)

It was held by the Court of Criminal Appeal that false pretences contrary to section 32 and fraudulent conversion contrary to section 20 are mutually exclusive.

False pretences and larceny by a trick

It is sometimes difficult to distinguish between larceny by a trick (see chapter 12) and obtaining by false pretences. In the case of obtaining by false pretences the owner intends to part with his property in the goods whereas in the case of a larceny by a trick he does not so intend. In the case of obtaining by false pretences, the property in the goods (as well as the possession) is obtained by fraud.

The Forgery Act, 1861, provides:

Personating owners of stock transferable at the bank or of shares in companies s. 3

Whosoever shall falsely and deceitfully personate any owner of any share or interest of or in any stock, annuity, or other public fund which now is or hereafter may be transferable ...., or any owner of any share or interest of or in the capital stock of any body corporate, company, or society ..., or any owner of any dividend or money payable in respect of any such share or interest as aforesaid, and shall thereby transfer or endeavour to transfer any share or interest belonging to any such owner, or thereby receive or endeavour to receive any money due to any such owner, as if such offender were the true and lawful owner, shall be guilty of felony and liable to imprisonment for life.

Personation of owners of stock s. 4

If any person falsely and deceitfully personates any owner of any share or interest of or in any such stock (as defined in the National Stock Act, 1870) ... or of any such stock certificate or coupon as aforesaid .. and thereby obtains or endeavours to obtain any such stock certificate or coupon, or receives or endeavours to receive any money due to any such owner, as if such person were the true and lawful owner, he shall be guilty of felony and liable to imprisonment for life.

The False Personation Act, 1874, provides:

Personation in order to obtain property s. 1

If any person shall falsely and deceitfully personate any person, or the heir, executor, or administrator, wife, widow, next of kin, or relation of any person, with intent fraudulently to obtain any land, estate, chattel, money, valuable security, or property he shall be guilty of felony for which the penalty is penal servitude for life or two years imprisonment.

Cheating

Cheating is a misdemeanour at common law for which the penalty is imprisonment, it has been defined as "...deceitful practices, in defrauding or endeavouring to defraud another of his own right by means of some artful device, contrary to the plain rules of common honesty. "

Chapter 18

Embezzlement and Fraudulent Conversion

Embezzlement

Persons in employment where they appropriate the property of their employer may be guilty of the statutory offence of embezzlement. At common law a servant could not be convicted of larceny, as he had properly acquired the legal possession of the goods of his master.

R V Bazeley (1799)

The accused was tried for feloniously stealing a £100 bank note. He was a cashier in a bank. A customer paid £137 to his own account, including a hundred-pound note, the accused put this note into his own pocket.

It was held not to be a felony as the thing was not taken by the accused out of the possession of the owner and had been delivered into his possession.

Accordingly it was necessary that an offence of embezzlement be created by statute and the Embezzlement (Ireland) Act, 1811 was passed.

The distinction between embezzlement and larceny as regards clerks and servants is: in larceny the thing stolen is taken out of the possession of the master, whereas in embezzlement the thing is appropriated before it has come into the possession of the master in breach of the duty to hand over that thing to the master.

The doctrine of possession is very technical and it is not always clear whether it is larceny or embezzlement that a person may be guilty of. The absolute necessity for accuracy as far as the indictment is concerned is removed by section 44(2), see below.

Embezzlement by clerks or servants s. 17(1)

Every person who -

(1) being a clerk or servant or person employed in the capacity of a clerk or servant -

(a) steals any chattel, money or valuable security belonging to or in the possession or power of his master or employer; or

(b) fraudulently embezzles the whole or any part of any chattel, money or valuable security delivered to or received or taken into possession by him for or in the name or on the account of his master or employer :

shall be guilty of felony

The essentials in this offence are:
> (a) person in employment;
> (b) the appropriation;
> (b) property of employer.

Person in employment

The person to whom the subsection relates must be a clerk or servant or person employed in such a capacity. The relationship between master and servant involves a greater degree of control by the master of the servant's work than does a contract for services with an independent contractor. Whether such relationship exists is a question of fact for the jury.

The courts have had regard to the following:

(a) the master's power of selection of his servant;
(b) the payment of wages or other remuneration;
(c) the master's right of control of the method of doing the work; and
(d) the master's right of suspension or dismissal.

Section 17(1) does not apply where a person is an agent, but only where the relationship of master and servant exists. An agent is a person employed to act and contract as the representative of another person, who is his principal. A servant is a person who, as an instrument for the performance of work, gives his time and labour to and under the control and bound to obey the orders of his master.

People (A. G.) V Warren (1945)

A rate collector appointed by Dublin Corporation was convicted in the Circuit Court of embezzlement contrary to Section 17(1) of the Larceny Act, 1916. It was held by the Court of Criminal Appeal that the appellant, was not a servant of the Corporation and the conviction was set aside.

The appropriation

The appropriation may consist of stealing or of fraudulent embezzlement. As to the meaning of "steals" and "fraudulently" see chapter 12. Embezzlement may be proved by showing that an accused failed to account for or denied the receipt of money or chattel involved. It is not sufficient to prove a general deficiency in account, some specific sum must be proved to be embezzled.

Attorney General V Gleeson (1929)

A clerk was indicted under Section 17(1)(b) of the Larceny Act, 1916. It was held by the Court of Criminal Appeal, that the case of false entries and general deficiencies in tots made by the prosecution, if proved to the satisfaction of the jury, exhibited all the essential ingredients of the crime of embezzlement.

Property of employer

The chattel (or any part thereof), money or valuable security must belong to, or be in the possession or power of the employer, or have been delivered to or received or taken into possession for or in the name or on the account of the employer.

Such a requirement will be satisfied where:

(a) a third party delivers something to the servant so that upon receipt of it by him the master becomes the owner of it and the servant misappropriates it.

(b) a third party delivers something to the servant intending thereby to deliver possession of that thing to the master, and the servant misappropriates it.

(c) a servant steals or embezzles things belonging to his master and sells them to a third party from whom he receives money.

If money has been received in some other way that is not embezzlement.

Embezzlement by public servants or police s. 17(2)

Every person who

(2) being employed in the public service or in the police -

(a) steals any chattel, money or valuable security belonging to or in the possession the State or entrusted to or received or taken into possession by such person by virtue of his employment; or

(b) embezzles or in any manner fraudulently applies or disposes of for any purpose whatsoever except for the public service any chattel, money or valuable security entrusted to or received or taken into possession by him by virtue of his employment:

shall be guilty of felony

The "pubic service" would include those employed in the civil service, by a State authority, a public authority and probably those whose salaries come from central funds.

Embezzlement by officers of Bank of Ireland s. 19

Every person who being an officer or servant of the Bank of Ireland, secretes, embezzles, or runs away with any bond, deed, note, bill, dividend warrant, warrant for the payment of any annuity, interest or money, security, money or other effects of or belonging to the Bank of Ireland and entrusted to him or lodged or deposited with the Bank of Ireland, or with him as such officer or servant, shall be guilty of felony

Verdict s. 44(2)

If on the trial of any indictment for any offence against section 17, it is proved that the defendant stole the property in question, the jury may find him guilty of stealing; and on the trial of any indictment for stealing the jury may in like manner find the defendant guilty of embezzlement.

Fraudulent conversion

Fraudulent conversion has to do with the person who has obtained ownership on behalf of someone else. Although fraudulent conversion, unlike larceny and embezzlement, catches a person who is the owner of the goods, the definition of the offence is phrased widely enough to catch a person who has possession or, even only custody of the goods. Agents and independent contractors not being subject to absolute direction from an employer could not be convicted of embezzlement

146

and were also exempt under the common law. A trustee, since he has possession and even legal ownership of the things he holds for his *cestui que trust*, could not by appropriating them commit any offence against the common law.

Conversion s. 20

(1) Every person who -

(i) being entrusted either solely or jointly with any other person with any power of attorney for the sale or transfer of any property, fraudulently sells, transfers, or otherwise converts the property or any part thereof to his own use or benefit, or the use or benefit of any person other than the person by whom he was so entrusted; or

(ii) being a director, member or officer of any body corporate or public company, fraudulently takes or applies for his own use or benefit, or for any use or purpose other than the use or purpose of such body corporate or public company, any of the property of such body corporate or public company: or

(iii) being authorised to receive money to arise from the sale of annuities or securities ….; or

(iv)(a) being entrusted either solely or jointly with any other person with any property in order that he may retain in safe custody or apply, pay, or deliver, for any purpose or to any person, the property or any part thereof or any proceeds thereof; or

(b) having either solely or jointly with any other person received any property for or on account of any other person; fraudulently converts to his own use or benefit, or the use or benefit of any other person, the property or any part thereof or any proceeds thereof;

shall be guilty of a misdemeanour

(2) Nothing in (1)(iv) above shall apply to or affect any trustee under any express trust created by a deed or will, or any mortgagee of any property, real or personal, in respect of any act done by the trustee or mortgagee in relation to the property comprised in or affected by any such trust or mortgage.

The essential in this offence are:

(a) the money, property, etc. was entrusted to the accused for a particular purpose;

(b) it was used it for some other purpose;

(c) the misuse was fraudulent and dishonest.

It is for a jury to decide the question whether a person has been "entrusted" with property or has received it "for or on account of" another person.

Attorney General V Lawless (1930)

It was held by the Court of Criminal Appeal that on a charge of fraudulent conversion under section 20(1)(iv)(b), the question of whether money has been received by the accused "for on account of" other persons is in fact to be decided by the jury, and they must be expressly directed to find on the point.

People (Attorney General) V Cowan (1958)

The appellant a solicitor, was convicted of having fraudulently converted to his own use a sum of money received by him for and on behalf of a client who had instructed him to obtain a grant of administration on his behalf to the estate of his infant son, to which he was entitled. A bank draft of the proceeds of the estate, made out to the client was at the applicants requests signed by him. The applicant lodged the bank draft to his own account. The client was not informed nor was he aware of the nature of the document he signed. Despite several demands he did not receive the money due to him. It was held by the Court of Criminal Appeal that the appellant when he received the money did so on his client's account. The appeal was dismissed and dismissed again by the Supreme Court.

See also *People (A. G.) V Grey (1944)*, at page 101.

Conversion by trustee s. 21

Every person who, being a trustee, of any property for the use or benefit either wholly or partially of some other person, or for any public or charitable purpose, with intent to defraud converts or appropriates the same or any part thereof to or for his own use or benefit, or the use or benefit of any person other than such person as aforesaid, or for any purpose other than such public or charitable purpose as aforesaid, or otherwise disposes of or destroys such property or any part thereof, shall be guilty of a misdemeanour

No prosecution shall be commenced -

(a) by any person without the sanction of the Director of Public Prosecutions;

(b) by any person who has taken any civil proceedings against such trustee, without the sanction also of the court or judge before whom such civil proceedings have been had or are pending.

Trustee s. 46

The expression "trustee" means a trustee on some express trust created by some deed, will, or instrument in writing, and includes the heir or personal representative of any such trustee, and any other person upon or to whom the duty of such trust shall have devolved or come, and also an executor and administrator, and an official receiver, assignee, liquidator or other like officer acting under any present or future Act relating to joint stock companies or bankruptcy.

See section 22 of the 1916 Act which deals with factors at page 151.

Evidence s. 43

(2) No person shall be liable to be convicted of any offence against sections 6, 7(1), 20, 21, and 22 upon any evidence whatsoever in respect of any act done by him, if at any time previously to his being charged with such offence he has first disclosed such act on oath, in consequence of any compulsory process of any court of law or equity in any action suit, or proceeding which has been *bona fide* instituted by any person aggrieved.

(3) In any proceeding in respect of any offence against sections 6, 7(1), 20, 21 and 22, a statement or admission made by any person in any compulsory examination or deposition before any court on the hearing of any matter in bankruptcy shall not be admissible in evidence against that person.

Penalties

The 1990 Act at section 9 provides that a person convicted on indictment of an offence under sections 17, 19, 20, and 21, shall be liable to a term of imprisonment not exceeding ten years or a fine or both.

Chapter 19

Offences of a commercial nature

In addition to offences considered elsewhere; there are a number of other statutes that create additional offences in the business and commercial area:

Larceny Act, 1861 and 1916;
Debtors (Ireland) Act, 1872
Falsification of Accounts Act, 1875;
Moneylenders Act, 1900 and 1933;
Bankruptcy Act, 1988;

See also: Forgey Act, 1861 in chapter 17 on obtaining by false pretences and Merchandise Marks Act, 1887 in chapter 25 on forgery.

Larceny Act, 1861

Keeping fraudulent accounts s. 82

Whosoever, being a director, public officer, or manager of any body corporate or public company, shall as such receive or possess himself of any property of such body corporate or public company otherwise than in payment of a just debt or demand, and shall, with intent to defraud, omit to make or to cause or direct to be made a full and true entry thereof in the books and accounts of such body corporate or public company, shall be guilty of a misdemeanour and liable to seven years penal servitude.

Wilfully destroying books, etc. s. 83

Whosoever, being a director, manager, or public officer, of any body corporate or public company, shall, with intent to defraud, destroy, alter, mutilate, or falsify any book, paper, writing or valuable security belonging to the body corporate or public company, or make or concur in the making of any false entry, or omit or concur in omitting any material particular, in any book of account or other document, shall be guilty of a misdemeanour and liable to seven years penal servitude.

Publishing fraudulent statements s. 84

Whosoever, being a director, manager, or public officer, of any body corporate or public company, shall make circulate, or publish, or concur in making, circulating, or publishing, any written statement or account which he shall know to be false in any additional particular, with intent to deceive or defraud any member, shareholder, or creditor of such body corporate or public company, or with intent to induce any person to become a shareholder or partner therein, or to intrust or advance any property to such body corporate or public company, or to enter into any security for the benefit thereof, shall be guilty of a misdemeanour and liable to seven years penal servitude.

Factors obtaining advances s. 22

(1) Every person who, being a factor or agent entrusted either solely or jointly with any other person for the purpose of sale or otherwise, with the possession of any goods or of any documents of title to goods contrary to or without the authority of his principal in that behalf for his own use or benefit, or for the use or benefit of any person other than the person by whom he was so entrusted, and in violation of good faith-.

(i) Consigns, deposits, transfers, or delivers any goods or documents of title so entrusted to him as and by way of a pledge, lien, or security for any money or valuable security borrowed or received, or intended to be borrowed or received by him; or

(ii) Accepts any advances of any money or valuable security on the faith of any contract or agreement to consign, deposit, transfer, or deliver any such goods or documents of title;

shall be guilty of a misdemeanour

Provided that no such factor or agent shall be liable to prosecution, for consigning, depositing, transferring or delivering any such goods or documents of title, in case the same shall not be made a security for or subject to the payment of any greater sum of money than, the amount which at the time of such consignment, deposit, transfer, or delivery, was justly due and owing to such agent from his principal, together with the amount of any bill of exchange drawn by or on account of such principal and accepted by such factor or agent.

See also conversion at section 20 of the 1916 Act at page 147.

Debtors (Ireland) Act, 1872

Obtaining credit under false pretences etc. s. 13

Any person shall in each of the cases following be deemed guilty of a misdemeanour and liable to one years imprisonment:

(1) If in incurring any debt or liability he has obtained credit under false pretences, or by means of any other fraud;

(2) If he has with intent to defraud his creditors, or any of them, made or caused to be made any gift, delivery, or transfer of or any charge on his property;

(3) If he has with intent to defraud his creditors, concealed or removed any part of his property since or within two months before the date of any unsatisfied judgment or order for payment of money obtained against him.

The ingredients necessary in respect of section 13(1) are:

(a) there must be the incurring of a debt or liability;

The meaning of credit has been considered in the English legislation, which is similar:

Fisher V Raven (1963)

Dilhorne L.C. said: "To commit an offence against the section credit has to be obtained and in its ordinary significance, in my view, the expression 'obtained credit' connotes the obtaining of credit in respect of the payment of money and no more."

(b) there must be an obtaining of credit; and

(c) there must be fraud.

A person may be convicted of the offence under section 13(1) even though his fraudulent conduct falls short of false pretences. A person without means who orders a meal in a restaurant (though he makes no verbal representation at the time as to his ability to pay for the same), is liable to be convicted of "obtaining credit by means of fraud other than false pretences" under the latter part of section 13(1) (see *R V Jones (1898)*, page 138); but not obtaining goods by means of false pretences. The court considered that he had been rightly convicted, since he knew that the goods had been supplied, not on personal knowledge, but on the understanding that the "ordinary custom" to pay directly after the goods had been consumed would be observed.

R V Ingram (1956)

It was held that an electrician who had obtained contracts from shopkeepers for electric signs at an agreed price and had obtained payment of part of the price in advance, but had not done any work, save for matters of a preparatory nature, and had not returned any of the advance payments, was properly convicted under section 13(1).

Future intentions included

It has been seen in chapter 17 that to establish the offence of obtaining either money or credit by false pretence (Larceny Act, 1916, section 32), there must be a misstatement of an existing fact, either by stating that a fact exists which does not exist, or by stating that a fact does not exist which does exist. It must be a statement of existing fact as distinguished from mere promise or statements about the future, expectations, and things of that sort. An offence under section 13 is not limited to past or present fact

See *R V Dent (1955)* at page 139.

It is unnecessary in respect of offences under section 13 that the accused be a bankrupt.

Falsification of Accounts Act, 1875

Punishment for falsification of accounts, &c. s. 1

That if any clerk, officer, or servant, or any person employed or acting in the capacity of a clerk, officer, or servant, shall wilfully and with intent to defraud, to destroy, alter, mutilate, or falsify any book, paper, writing, valuable security, or account which belongs to or is in possession of his employer, or has been received by him for or on behalf of his employer, or shall wilfully and with intent to defraud, make or concur in making any false entry in, or omit or alter, or concur in omitting or altering, any material particular from or in any such book, or any document or account, then and in every such case the person so offending shall be guilty of a misdemeanour the penalty for which is seven years penal servitude, or two years imprisonment.

Intention to defraud sufficient indictment s. 2

It shall be sufficient in any indictment under this Act to allege a general intent to defraud without naming any particular person intended to be defrauded.

Act to be read with Larceny Act, 1861 s. 3

This Act shall be read as one with the Larceny Act, 1861.

R V Butt (1884)

A person may be guilty even though he procures an entry in books by an innocent agent.

R V Solomons (1909)

A taxi was entrusted to a driver on the terms that he should comply with certain regulations and receive, a proportion of his takings as indicated by the meter, in lieu of wages. He put the meter out of action and appropriated the fares to himself. He made a false return of his takings when signing a sheet which was filled up from the automatic record of the meter.

It was held that he was a servant within the Act, and that the sheet was an account within the meaning of the Act.

R V Wines (1954)

The accused, who was the manager of a radio department of a co-operative society, admitted that he had made the false eateries in respect of which he was charged. He denied that he had done so, with the object of covering up thefts by him, he claimed that he had done so with the intention of making the gross profit of his department appear higher than it actually was, in order to retain his employment. The jury were directed that there was an intent to defraud and convicted the accused.

It was held by the Court of Criminal Appeal that the jury were directed properly as, on the accused's own version, he intended by the false eateries to induce the society to retain him in their service and pay him wages and thereby act to their financial detriment.

Moneylenders Acts 1900 and 1933

The 1900 Act provides as follows:

Penalties for false statements and representations s. 4

If any money-lender, or any manager, agent, or clerk of a money-lender, or if any person being a director, manager, or other officer of any corporation carrying on the business of a money-lender, by any false, misleading, or deceptive statement, representation, or promise, or by any dishonest concealment of material facts, fraudulently induces or attempts to induce any person to borrow money or to agree to the terms on which money is or is to be borrowed, he shall be guilty of a misdemeanour, and shall be liable on indictment to imprisonment, with or without hard labour, for a term not exceeding two years, or to a fine not exceeding five hundred pounds, or to both.

Definition of money-lender s. 6

The expression "money-lender" in this Act shall include every person whose business is that of money-lending, or who advertises or announces himself or holds himself out in any way as carrying on that business; but shall not include-

(a) any pawnbroker in respect of business carried on by him in accordance with the provisions of the Acts for the time being in force in relation to pawnbrokers; or

(b) any registered society within the meaning of the Friendly Societies Act, 1896, or any society registered or having rules certified under sections two or four of that Act, or under the Benefit Buildings Societies Acts, 1836, or the Loan Societies Act, 1840, or under the Building Societies Acts, 1874 to 1894; or

(c) any body corporate, incorporated or empowered by a special Act of Parliament to lend money in accordance with such special Act; or

(d) the holder of a licence for the time being in force granted under section 9 of the Central Bank Act, 1971, or any person *bona fide* and otherwise carrying on the business of banking, or *bona fide* carrying on the business of insurance or *bona fide* carrying on any business not having for its primary object the lending of money, in the course of which and for the purposes whereof he lends money; or

(dd) a company to which a certificate has been given by the Minister for Finance under section 39B of the Finance Act, 1980 (inserted by the Finance Act, 1987), and which has not been revoked; or

(e) any class or classes of body corporate in respect of which the Minister for Industry and Commerce, by order made from time to time declares that, from such date as he may specify in such order, this Act does not apply; or

(f) any class or classes of industrial and provident society in respect of which the Minister for Industry, and Commerce, by order made from time to time declares that, from such date as he may specify in such order, this Act does not apply.

The 1933 Act provides as follows:

Moneylender's licence s. 5

(1) Every moneylender, whether carrying on business alone or as a partner in a firm, shall take out annually in respect of every address at which he carries on his business as such a licence.

(5) If any person-

(a) takes out a moneylender's licence in any name other than his true name; or

(b) carries on business as a moneylender, without having in force a proper moneylender's licence authorising him so to do, or, being licensed as a moneylender, carries on business as such in any name other than his authorised name, or at any other place than his authorised address or addresses; or

(c) enters into any agreement in the course of his business as a moneylender with respect to the advance or repayment of money, or takes any security for money in the course of his business as a moneylender, otherwise than in his authorised name;

such person shall be guilty of an offence.

Implying a banker s. 8

If any moneylender, for the purposes of his business as such, issues or publishes, or causes to be issued or published, any advertisement, circular or document of any kind whatsoever containing expressions which might reasonably be held to imply that he carried on banking business he shall be guilty of an offence.

Penalties

The penalty for the offences under sections 5 and 8 above on summary conviction shall be:

(i) in the case of a first offence, an excise penalty of one hundred pounds, and (ii) in the case of a second or subsequent offence an excise penalty of one hundred pounds and or three months imprisonment in the case of an individual; or an excise penalty of five hundred pounds in the case of a company.

Bankruptcy Act, 1988

The Act at Part VII provides for offences.

Fraudulent debtors s. 123

(1) Subject to subsection (2), If a bankrupt or arranging debtor-

(a) fails to disclose to the Court, or to the Official Assignee or to such person or persons as the Court from time to time directs, all his property and how and to whom and for what consideration and when he disposes of any part thereof, except such part as has been disposed of in the ordinary way of his trade (if any) or laid out in the ordinary expense of his family, or

(b) fails to deliver up to the Official Assignee, or as he or the Court directs, all such part of his property as is in his possession or under his control, and which he is required by law to deliver up, or

(c) fails to deliver up to the Official Assignee, or as he or the Court directs, all books and papers in his possession or under his control relating to his estate and which he is required by law to deliver up, or

(d) conceals any part of his property to the value of £500 or upwards, or conceals any debt due to or from him, or

(e) fraudulently removes any part of his property to the value of £500 or upwards, or

(f) fails to file or deliver a statement of affairs as required by section 19(c) or makes any material omission in any statement relating to his affairs, or

(g) knowing or believing that a false debt has been proved by any person under the bankruptcy or arrangement, fails for the period of a month to inform the Official Assignee thereof, or

(h) prevents the production of any book or paper affecting or relating to his estate, or

(i) conceals, destroys, mutilates or falsifies or is privy to the concealment, destruction, mutilation or falsification of any book or paper affecting or relating to his estate, or

(j) makes or is privy to the making of any false entry in any book or paper affecting or relating to his estate, or

(k) fraudulently parts with, alters or makes any omission in, or is privy to the fraudulent parting with, altering or making any omission in, any document affecting or relating to his estate, or

(l) attempts to account for any part of his property by fictitious losses or expenses, or

(m) obtains, by any fraud or false representation, any property on credit, or

(n) obtains, under the false pretence of carrying on business and, if a trader, of dealing in the ordinary way of his trade, any property on credit, or

(o) pawns, pledges or disposes of any property which he has obtained on credit, unless, in the case of a trader, such pawning, pledging or disposing is in the ordinary way of his trade, (by subsection (4) every person who takes in pawn or pledged or otherwise receives the property knowing it to be pawned, pledged or disposed of in such circumstances as aforesaid shall be guilty of a like offence.) or

(p) is guilty of any fraud or false representation for the purpose of obtaining the consent of his creditors or any of them to an agreement with reference to his affairs of the bankruptcy or arrangement;

he shall be guilty of an offence.

Defence

(2) It shall be a good defence to a charge under any of paragraph (a), (b), (c), (d), (f), (n) and (o) if the accused proves that he had no intent to defraud and to a charge under any of paragraphs (h), (i) and (j) of that subsection if he proves that he had no intent to conceal the state of his affairs or to defeat the law

Absconding debtors s. 124

If any person with intent to defraud his creditors leaves the State and takes with him, or attempts or makes preparation to leave the State and take with him, any part of his property to the amount of £500 or upwards, he shall be guilty of an offence.

Corrupt agreements with creditors s. 125

If any creditor of a bankrupt or an arranging debtor or any other person as an inducement for forbearing to oppose or for accepting any offer of composition or proposal or any modification thereof made by or on behalf of the bankrupt or arranging debtor, the claim of the creditor shall be void an irrecoverable and the creditor and such other person (if any) shall each be guilty of an offence.

False claim s. 126

If any creditor, or any person claiming to be a creditor, in any bankruptcy or arrangement with intent to defraud makes any false claim or any proof, declaration or statement of account which is untrue in any material particular, he shall be guilty of an offence.

Non-disclosure of after-acquired property s. 127

A bankrupt who fails to disclose to the Official Assignee any after-acquired property shall be guilty of an offence.

Obstructing officers s. 128

Any person who knowingly and wilfully resists, hinders or obstructs the Bankruptcy Inspector or any of his assistants or any other person in the execution of his duties under the Act shall be guilty of an offence.

Obtaining credit or trading under other name s. 129

A bankrupt or an arranging debtor who-

(a) either alone or jointly with any other person obtains credit to the extent of £500 or upwards from any person without informing him that that he is a bankrupt or an arranging debtor, or

(b) engages in any trade or business under a name other than that under which he was adjudicated bankrupt or granted protection without disclosing to all persons with whom he enters into any business transaction the name under which he was so adjudicated or granted protection,

shall be guilty of an offence.

Inserting advertisement without authority s. 130

Any person who wilfully inserts or causes any advertisement under the Act to be inserted in Iris Oifigiuil or in any newspaper without authority under the Act, or knowing the same to be false in any material particular, shall be guilty of an offence.

Criminal liability after annulment s. 131

Where a bankrupt or arranging debtor has been guilty of any offence, he shall not be exempt from being proceeded against for the offence by reason that his bankruptcy has been discharged or annulled or that his proposal has been carried into effect.

Punishment of offences s. 132

(1) Every person guilty of an offence under the Act shall be liable -

(a) on summary conviction, to a fine not exceeding £500 or, at the discretion of the court, to imprisonment for a term not exceeding twelve months or to both the fine and the imprisonment, or

(b) on conviction on indictment, to a fine not exceeding £1,000 or, at the discretion of the Court, to imprisonment for a term not exceeding five years or to both the fine and the imprisonment.

See also section 183 of the Companies Act, 1963 at page 161.

Chapter 20

Offences under the Companies Acts

The law relating to registered companies is contained in:
> Companies Act, 1963;
> Companies (Amendment) Act, 1977;
> Companies (Amendment) Act, 1982;
> Companies (Amendment) Act, 1983;
> Companies (Amendment) Act, 1986;
> Companies (Amendment) Act, 1990;
> Companies Act, 1990.

These statutes are collectively referred to as the "Companies Acts". There are 819 sections in total, together with many schedules. The 1963 Act (the Principal Act) had 399 sections, the 1990 Acts had 37 and 262 sections. A number of sections have been amended or repealed by subsequent acts. A large body of recent legislation has been influenced and necessitated by membership of the European Economic Community.

A great number of offences are created under these statutes, those for which there is a penalty of imprisonment are touched upon in this and the following chapter. There is a general penalty provision in section 240 of the Companies Act, 1990. Within sections of the acts, subsections create offences. It would be prolific to list entire sections where the subsection details the offence, thus the appropriate subsection only is listed.

This chapter deals with the 1963, 1983 and 1986 Acts, the following chapter deals with the Companies Act, 1990. It is beyond the scope of this book to give a detailed consideration of the many offences that are created, such would require an exploration into accountancy and taxation.

Companies Act, 1963

Statement in lieu of prospectus s. 35
(6) If default is made in complying with subsection (2) [re-registration of a private company as a public limited company], (3) [re-registration of a private company as a public unlimited company] or (5) [requirement as to written statement], the company and every officer of the company who is in default shall be guilty of an offence and shall be liable on summary conviction to a £500 fine.

(7) Where a statement in lieu of prospectus, delivered to the registrar under subsection (3) [re-registration of a private company as a public unlimited company] includes any untrue statement, any person who authorised the delivery of the statement in lieu of prospectus for registration shall be guilty of an offence and shall be liable-

159

(a) on indictment a £2,500 fine and or 2 years imprisonment; or

(b) on summary conviction a £500 fine and or 6 months imprisonment;

Defence

unless he proves either that the untrue statement was immaterial or that he had reasonable ground to believe and did, up to the time of delivery for registration of the statement in lieu of prospectus, believe that the untrue statement was true.

Misstatements in the Prospectus s. 50

(1) Where a prospectus ... includes any untrue statement, any person who authorised the issue of the prospectus shall be liable

(a) on conviction on indictment to two years imprisonment and or £2,500 fine fine;

(b) On summary conviction 6 months imprisonment and or £500 fine;

Defence

unless he proves either that the statement was immaterial or that he had reasonable ground to believe and did, up to the time of the issue of the prospectus, believe that the statement was true.

(2) a person shall not be deemed for the propose of this section to have authorised the issue of a prospectus by reason only of his having given the consent required by Section 46 (Expert's consent to issue of prospectus containing statement by him) of this Act to the inclusion therein of a statement purporting to be made by him as an expert.

At section 2 of the Act prospectus is defined as "any prospectus, notice, circular, advertisement or other invitation, offering to the public for subscription or purchase any shares or debentures of a company"

False declaration on assistance for purchase of shares s. 60

(5) Any director of a company making the statutory declaration (re. giving of financial assistance by a company for the purchase of any shares in the company) without having reasonable grounds for the opinion that the company having carried out the transaction whereby such assistance is to be given will be able to pay its debts in full as they become due, shall be liable to 6 months imprisonment and or £500 fine; and

Presumption

if the company is wound up within the period of 12 months after the making of the statutory declaration and its debts are not paid or provided for in full within the period of 12 months after the commencement of the winding up, it shall be presumed until the contrary is shown that the director did not have reasonable grounds for his opinion.

Personation of shareholder s. 90

If any person falsely and deceitfully personates any owner of any share or interest in any company, or of any share warrant or coupon, issued in pursuance of this Act, and thereby obtains or endeavours to obtain any such share or interest or share warrant or coupon, or receives or endeavours to receive any money due to any such owner, or votes at any meeting, as if the offender were the true and lawful owner, he shall be liable, on conviction on indictment to 2 years imprisonment and or a £2,500 fine, or on summary conviction to 6 months imprisonment and or a £500 fine.

Profit and Loss account for Annual General Meeting s. 148

(1) The directors of every company shall at some date not later than 18 months after the incorporation of the company and subsequently once at least in every calendar year lay before the annual general meeting of the company a profit and loss account ...

(3) If any person being a director of a company fails to take all reasonable steps to comply with the provisions of this section, he shall, in respect of each offence, be liable on summary conviction to 6 months imprisonment and or a £500 fine in respect of each offence,

Defence

However that -

(a) in any proceeding against a person in respect of an offence under this section, it shall be a defence to prove that he had reasonable ground to believe and did believe that a competent and reliable person was charged with the duty of seeing that this section was complied with and was in a position to discharge that duty; and

Committed wilfully

(b) a person shall not be sentenced to imprisonment for such an offence unless, in the opinion of the court dealing with the case, the offence was committed wilfully.

Section 149 of the 1963 Act has like provisions and similar penalties in respect of contents and form of accounts; computation and treatment of profits and losses.

Section 150 of the 1963 Act has like provisions and similar penalties in respect of obligation to lay group accounts before holding company.

Section 158 of the 1963 Act has like provisions and similar penalties in respect of directors' report to be attached to balance sheet and contents of such report.

Prohibition of undischarged bankrupts acting as directors or other officers of companies s. 183

(1) ... if any person being an undischarged bankrupt acts as officer, auditor, liquidator or examiner of, or directly or indirectly takes part or is concerned in the promotion, formation or management of, any company except with the leave of the court, he shall be guilty of an offence.

(3) In this section "company" includes a company incorporated outside the State which has an established place of business within the State.

Offences under the Companies Act, 1963

The general penalty applies: on summary conviction a £1,000 fine and or 12 months imprisonment, or on indictment a £10,000 fine and or 3 years imprisonment.

See also Bankruptcy Act, 1988, at page 155.

Offences by officers of companies in liquidation s. 293

(1) ..., if any person, being a past or present officer of a company which at the time of the commission of the alleged offence is being wound up, whether by the court or voluntarily, or is subsequently ordered to be wound up by the court or subsequently passes a resolution for voluntary winding up *(following are abbreviated)*-

(a) does not to the best of his knowledge and belief fully and truly disclose disclose all property to the liquidator; or

(b) does not deliver up property to the liquidator; or

(c) does not deliver up all books and property to the liquidator; or

(d) within 12 months next before the commencement of the winding up or at any time thereafter, conceals any property or debts due to the company; or

(e) within 12 months next before the commencement of the winding up or at any time thereafter, fraudulently removes any part of the property of the company; or

(f) makes any material omission in any statement relating to the affairs of the company; or

(g) fails to inform liquidator of any false debt; or

(h) prevents the production of any book or paper affecting the affairs of the company; or

(i) within 12 months next before the commencement of the winding up or at any time thereafter, conceals, destroys, mutilates or falsifies or is privy to such of any book or paper affecting the affairs of the company; or

(j) within 12 months next before the commencement of the winding up or at any time thereafter, make any false entry in any book or paper affecting the affairs of the company; or

(k) within 12 months next before the commencement of the winding up or at any time thereafter, fraudulently parts with any document affecting the affairs of the company; or

(l) after the commencement of the winding up or at any meeting of the creditors of the company within 12 months attempts to account for any part of the property of the company by fictitious losses or expenses; or

(p) is guilty of any false representation or other fraud for the purpose of obtaining the consent of the creditors of the company or any of them to an agreement with reference to the affairs of the company or to the winding up;

he shall be liable on conviction on indictment to 2 years imprisonment and or a £2,500 fine, or on summary conviction to 6 months imprisonment and or a £500 fine.

In the case of the following:

(m) has within 12 months next before the commencement of the winding up or at any time thereafter, by any false representation or other fraud, obtained any property for on behalf of the company on credit which the company does not subsequently pay for; or

(n) within 12 months next before the commencement of the winding up or at any time thereafter, under the false pretence that the company is carrying on its business, obtains on credit for on behalf of the company, any property which the company does not subsequently pay for; or

(o) within 12 months next before the commencement of the winding up or at any time thereafter pawns, pledges or disposes of any property of the company which has been obtained on credit and has not been paid for, unless such pawning, pledging or disposing is in the ordinary way of business of the company;

he shall be liable on conviction on indictment to 5 years imprisonment and or a £5,000 fine, or on summary conviction to 6 months imprisonment and or a £500 fine.

Defence

(2) It shall be a good defence to a charge under any of paragraphs (a), (b), (c), (d), (f), (n) and (o), if the accused proves that he had no intent to defraud and to a charge under any of paragraphs (h), (i) and (j) if he proves that he had no intent to conceal the state of affairs of the company or to defeat the law.

(4) For the purposes of this section, "officer" shall include any person in accordance with whose directions or instructions the directors of a company have been accustomed to act.

Fraud by officers of companies which have gone into liquidation s. 295

If any person, being at the time of the commission of the alleged offence an officer of a company which is subsequently ordered to be wound up by the court or subsequently passes a resolution for voluntary winding up-

(a) has by false pretences or by means of any other fraud induced any person to give credit to the company;

(b) with intent to defraud creditors of the company, has made or caused to be made any gift or transfer of or charge on, or has caused or connived at the levying of any execution against, the property of the company;

(c) with intent to defraud creditors of the company, has concealed or removed any part of the property of the company since or within 2 months before the date of any unsatisfied judgment or order for payment of money obtained against the company;

he shall be liable, on conviction on indictment to 2 years imprisonment and or a £2,500 fine, or on summary conviction to 6 months imprisonment and or a £500 fine.

Fraudulent trading s. 297

(1) If any person is knowingly a party to the carrying on of the

business of a company with intent to defraud creditors of the company or creditors of any other person or for any fraudulent purpose, that person shall be guilty of an offence.

(2) Any person who is convicted of an offence under this section shall be liable:

(a) on summary conviction, to imprisonment for a term not exceeding 12 months or to a fine not exceeding £1,000 or to both, or

(b) on conviction on indictment, to imprisonment for a term not exceeding 7 years or to a fine not exceeding £50,000 or to both.

Contents of statement to be submitted to receiver s. 320

(5) If any person to whom subsection (2) applies makes default in complying with the requirement of this section, he shall, unless he can prove to the satisfaction of the court that it was not possible for him to comply with the requirements of the section, be liable -

(a) on summary conviction a £1,000 fine and or 6 months imprisonment, or

(b) on indictment a £5,000 fine and or 3 years imprisonment

(2) persons included: the directors and secretary of the company and others-

(a) who are or have been officers of the company;

(b) who have taken part in the formation of the company at any time within one year before the date of the receiver's appointment;

(c) who are in the employment of the company or have been in the employment of the company within the said year, and are in the opinion of the receiver capable of giving the information required;

(d) who are or have been within the said year officers of or in the employment of the company which is, or within the said year was, an officer of the company to which the statement relates.

Sale of shares and offers of shares for sale s. 365

Any person who is knowingly responsible for the issue, circulation or distribution of a prospectus or for the issue of a form of application for shares and debentures, in contravention of any of the provisions of sections 361 to 364 shall be liable on conviction on indictment to 2 years imprisonment and or a £2,500 fine, or on summary conviction to 6 months imprisonment and or a £500 fine.

The relevant sections are:

361. Prospectuses relating to companies incorporated outside the State.
362. Exclusion and relaxation in case of certain prospectuses.
363. Provisions as to expert's consent and allotment.
364. Registration of prospectus.

Companies (Amendment) Act, 1983

Pre-emption rights s. 24

(6) A person who knowingly or recklessly authorises or permits the inclusion in a statement circulated under subsection (5) [such written statement being required to precede special resolution as to the allotting of equity securities] of any matter which is misleading, false or deceptive in a material particular shall be guilty of an offence.

Experts reports s. 31

(3) Any person who knowingly or recklessly makes a false statement which-

(a) is misleading, false or deceptive in a material particular, and

(b) is a statement to which this subsection applies,

shall be guilty of an offence.

(4) Subsection (3) applies to any statement made (whether orally or in writing) to any person carrying out a valuation or making a report under section 30 [Experts' reports on non-cash consideration before allotment of shares], being a statement which conveys or purports to convey any information or explanation which that person requires, or is entitled to require, under subsection (1)

Obligation to convene e. g. m. in event of loss of capital s. 40(1)

(1) ..., where the net assets of a company are half or less of the amount of the company's called-up share capital, the directors of the company shall, not later than 28 days from the earliest day on which that fact is known to a director of the company, duly convene an extraordinary general meeting of the company for a date not later than 56 days from that day for the purpose of considering whether any, and if so what measures should be taken to deal with the situation.

(2) If there is a failure to convene an extraordinary general meeting of a company as required by subsection (1), each of the directors of the company who-

(a) knowingly and wilfully authorises or permits that failure; or

(b) after the expiry of the period during which that meeting should have been convened, knowingly and wilfully authorises or permits that failure to continue,

shall be guilty of an offence.

The penalty for the above offences under the 1983 Act are on summary conviction a £500 fine and or 6 months imprisonment, or on conviction on indictment a £2,500 fine and or 2 years imprisonment.

Companies (Amendment) Act, 1986

The Companies (Amendment) Act, 1986 implements the E.E.C. Fourth Directive on Company Law of 25th July 1978. The 1986 Act has been amended by the 1990 Act. The directive was based upon Article 54(3)(g) of the E. E. C. Treaty.

Accounting principles s. 5

This section sets out the accounting principles on which the accounts of a company should be prepared.

Departure from the accounting principles s. 6

The directors of a company may depart from the accounting principles above if they have special reasons for so doing but they must state the particulars and reasons for such departure in a not for the relevant financial year.

Documents to be annexed to annual return s. 7

Every company is required to attach a copy of the report of the auditors and the report of the directors, which reports must be certified by a director and the secretary of the company to be a true copy as must the balance sheet and profit and loss account as laid before the annual general meeting of the company held during the period to which the annual return relates.

Exemption for small companies from certain provisions s. 10

This section exempts a small company from the necessity of preparing and publishing the full set of accounts.

Exemption for medium-sized companies s. 11

This section exempts a medium-sized company from from certain provisions.

Information regarding subsidiary and associated companies s. 16

This section requires that particulars regarding a company's holding company in subsidiaries and associated companies be disclosed in the notes to the company's accounts.

Documents delivered to registrar of companies s. 18

This section sets out procedures for small and medium sized companies which have claimed the specified exemptions in delivering documents to the Registrar of Companies.

Publication of full or abbreviated accounts s. 19

This section is to ensure that where abbreviated accounts are published they shall be distinguished from full accounts filed with the Registrar of Companies.

Penalties s. 22(1)

(a) If a company fails to comply with a provision of sections 5, 6, 7, 10, 11, 16, 18 or 19 of this Act, the company and every officer of the company who is in default shall be liable on summary conviction to a fine not exceeding £1,000.

(b) Proceedings for an offence under this subsection, in relation to sections 7, 10, 11, 16 or 18 of this Act, may be brought and prosecuted by the registrar of companies.

General provisions in relation to accounts s. 3

These provisions govern the form and contents of the balance sheet, profit and loss account, and additional information to be provided by way of notes to the annual accounts. The accounts must give a true and fair view of the company's affairs.

Format of accounts s. 4

This section requires that every balance sheet and profit and loss account should show the items listed in the various headings set out in the schedule to the Act. By subsection (3) the same formats as set out in the schedule shall be adopted in subsequent years unless, there are special reasons for a change. By subsection (13) arrangement of headings and sub-headings may be assigned Arabic numbers.

Penalties s. 22(2)

If any person, being a director of a company, fails to take all reasonable steps to secure compliance with the requirements of section 3 or section 4 (other than subsections (3) and (13)) of this Act or to comply with the provisions of subsection (3) or (13) of section 4 or section 13 or 14 of this Act, he shall in respect of each offence be liable on summary conviction to imprisonment for a term not exceeding 6 months, or, at the discretion of the court to a fine not exceeding £1,000 or to both so, (however that,) ...

Defence s. 22(2)

(a) in any proceedings against a person in respect of an offence under this subsection, it shall be a defence to prove that he had reasonable grounds to believe and did believe that a competent and reliable person was charged with the duty of ensuring that the provisions of the said section 3 or section 4 (other than subsections (3) and (13)), as may be appropriate, were complied with and that the latter person was in a position to discharge that duty, and

(b) a person shall not be liable to be sentenced to imprisonment for such an offence unless, in the opinion of the court, the offence was committed wilfully.

Wilfully making a false statement s. 22(3)

If any person in any return, report, certificate, balance sheet or other documents required by or for the purposes of any of the provisions of this Act wilfully makes a statement false in any material particular, knowing it to be false, he shall be liable -

(a) on conviction on indictment, to imprisonment for 3 Years and or £2,500 fine

(b) on summary conviction, 6 months imprisonment and or £1,000 fine

"director" and "officer" s. 22(5)

In this section "director" and "officer" includes any person in accordance with whose directions or instructions the directors of the company are accustomed to act.

Chapter 21

Offences under the Companies Act, 1990

Part II Investigations
This part is concerned with company investigation, it contains provisions empowering the Minister to ascertain the true ownership of limited companies, it also enables the Minister to require information directly from companies in certain circumstances without the need to launch a formal investigation of its affairs. Important powers to require the production of a company's books and papers for inspection are created. Section 21 throws a cloak of confidentiality around information obtained under these procedures.

Information as to persons interested in shares and debentures s. 15

(1) Where it appears to the Minister that it is necessary -

(a) for the effective administration of the law relating to companies;

(b) for the effective discharge by the Minister of his functions under any enactments; or

(c) in the public interest;

to investigate the ownership of any shares in or debentures of a company and that it is unnecessary to appoint an inspector for the purpose, he may require any person whom he has reasonable cause to believe to have or to be able to obtain any information as to the present and past interests in those shares or debentures and the names and addresses of the persons interested and of any persons who act or have acted on their behalf in relation to the shares or debentures to give any such information to the Minister.

(3) Any person who fails to give any information required of him under this section or who in giving any such information makes any statement which he knows to be false in a material particular, shall be guilty of an offence.

Restrictions on shares and debentures s. 16

(1) Where in connection with an investigation or enquiry under section 14 (Appointment and powers of inspectors to investigate ownership of company) or 15 it appears to the Minister that there is difficulty in finding out the relevant facts about any shares (whether issued or to be issued), the Minister may by notice in writing direct that the shares shall until further notice be subject to the restrictions imposed by this section.

(14) Any person who-

(a) exercises or purports to exercise any right to dispose of any shares which, to his knowledge, are for the time being subject to the said restrictions or of any right to be issued with any such shares; or

(b) votes in respect of any such shares, whether as holder or proxy, or anoints a proxy to vote in respect thereof; or

(c) being the holder of any such shares, fails to notify of their being subject to the said restrictions any person whom he does not know to be aware of that fact but does know to be entitled, apart from the said restriction, to vote in respect of those shares whether as holder or proxy; or

(d) being the holder of any such shares, or being entitled to any such right as is mentioned in subsection (4) enters into an agreement which is void by virtue of subsection (3) or (4);

shall be guilty of an offence.

Entry and search of premises s. 20

(4) A person who obstructs the exercise of a right of entry or search conferred by virtue of a warrant issued under this section or who obstructs the exercise of a right so conferred to take possession of any books or documents, shall be guilty of an offence.

Provision for security of information s. 21

(1) No information, book or document relating to a body which has been obtained under section 19 or 20 shall, without the previous consent in writing of that body, be published or disclosed, except to a competent authority, unless the publication or disclosure is required-

(2) A person who publishes or discloses any information, book or document in contravention of this section shall be guilty of an offence.

Part III Transactions involving directors

This part is concerned with situations where a director might put his own interests ahead of that of the company. It applies to directors and persons connected with directors as well as "shadow directors". The main focus is on loans to directors and similar transactions such as service contracts and property transactions. Section 52 (not listed below) requires directors to have regard to the interests of employees.

Particular transactions involving conflict of interests

Penalisation of dealing by director s. 30

(1) A director of a company who buys-

(a) a right to call for delivery at a specified price and within a specified time of a specified number of relevant shares or a specified amount of relevant debentures; or

(b) a right to make delivery at a specified price and within a specified time of a specified number of relevant shares or a specified amount of relevant debentures; or

(c) a right (as he may elect) to call for delivery at a specified price and within a specified time or to make delivery at a specified price and within a specified time of a specified number of relevant shares or a specified amount of relevant debentures;

shall be guilty of an offence.

Prohibition of loans, etc. s. 31

(1) Except as provided by sections 32 to 37, a company shall not-

(a) make a loan or a quasi-loan to a director of the company or of its holding company or to a person connected with such a director;

(b) enter into a credit transaction as creditors for such a director or a person so connected;

(c) enter into a guarantee or provide any security in connection with a loan, quasi-loan or credit transaction made by any other person for such a director or a person so connected.

(2) A company shall not arrange for the assignment to it or the assumption by it of any rights, obligations or liabilities under a transaction which, if it had been entered into by the company, would have contravened subsection (1); but for the purposes of this part the transaction shall be treated as having been entered into on the date of the arrangement.

(3) A company shall not take part in any arrangement whereby-

(a) another person enters into a transaction which, if it had been entered into by the company, would have contravened subsection (1) or (2); and

(b) that other person, in pursuance of the arrangement, has obtained or is to obtain any benefit from the company or its holding company or a subsidiary of the company or its holding company.

Criminal penalties s. 40

(1) An officer of a company who authorises or permits the company to enter into a transaction or arrangement knowing or having reasonable cause to believe that the company was thereby contravening section 31 shall be guilty of an offence.

(2) A person who procures a company to enter into a transaction or arrangement knowing or having reasonable cause to believe that the company was thereby contravening section 31 shall be guilty of an offence.

Part IV Disclosure of interests in shares

This part makes provision for the disclosure of interests in shares. The extent of the disclosure will vary according to whether the company is a public limited company or whether it is a private company and also whether the person involved is a director or a secretary or merely an individual shareholder in the company.

It is divided into three chapters. Chapter one deals with share dealing by directors, secretaries and their families and the duty on companies to notify these dealings. Chapter two covers individual and group acquisitions and chapter three covers disclosure orders in relation to companies other than public liability companies.

It was partly designed to give effect to the E. E. C. directive of December 1988, whose purpose was to make adequate information of investors in the field of transferable securities available and thus improve investor protection and to increase investor's confidence in the securities markets.

Obligation to notify interests in shares or debentures s. 53

(1) Subject to the provisions of this section a person who, at the commencement of this section is a director or secretary of a company and is then interested in shares in, or debentures of, the company or any other body corporate, being the company's subsidiary or holding company or a subsidiary of the company's holding company or thereafter becomes a director or secretary of a company and, at the time when he becomes a director or secretary of a company, is so interested, shall notify the company in writing -

(a) of the subsistence of his interests at that time, and

(b) of the number of shares of each class in, and the amount of debentures of each class of, the company or any such other body corporate as aforesaid in which each interest of his subsists at that time.

(2) A director or secretary of a company shall notify the company in writing of the occurrence, while he is a director or secretary, of any of the following events and the date on which it occurred -

(a) Any event in consequence of whose occurrence he becomes, or ceases to be, interested in shares in, or debentures of, the company or any other body corporate, being the company's subsidiary or holding company or a subsidiary of the company's holding company;

(b) the entering into by him of a contract to sell any such shares or debentures;

(c) the assignment by him of a right granted to him by the company to subscribe for shares in, or debentures of, the company; and

(d) the grant to him by another body corporate, being the company's subsidiary or holding company or a subsidiary of the company's holding company, of a right to subscribe for shares in, or debentures of, that other body corporate, the exercise of such a right granted to him and the assignment by him of such a right so granted;

stating the number or amount, and class, of shares or debentures involved.

Other provisions relating to notification s. 58

(1) Where a person authorises any other person ("the agent") to acquire or dispose of, on his behalf, interests in shares in, or debentures of a company, he shall secure that the agents notifies him immediately of acquisitions or disposals of interests in or debentures effected by the agent which will or may give rise to any obligation on his part to make a notification under this Chapter with respect to his interest in those shares or debentures.

(7) A person who fails without reasonable excuse to comply with subsection (1) shall be guilty of an offence.

Extension of section 53 to spouses and children s. 64

(6) A person who fails to fulfil, within the proper period, an obligation to which he is subject under subsection (3) shall be guilty of an offence.

Duty of company to notify the stock exchange s. 65

(1) Whenever a company in the case of whose shares or debentures dealing facilities are provided by a recognised stock exchange is notified of any matter by a director or secretary in consequence of the fulfilment of an obligation imposed on him by section 53 or 64, and that matter relates to shares or debentures for which such dealing facilities are provided, the company shall be under an obligation to notify that stock exchange of that matter; and the stock exchange may publish, in such manner as it may determine, any information received by it under this subsection.

(2) An obligation imposed by subsection (1) must be fulfilled before the end of the day next following that on which it arises.

(3) If default is made in complying with this section, the company and every officer of the company who is in default shall be guilty of an offence.

Obligation of disclosure s. 67

(1) Where a person either-

(a) to his knowledge acquires an interest in shares comprised in a public limited company's relevant share capital, or ceases to be interested in shares so comprised (whether or not retaining an interest in other shares so comprised), or

(b) becomes aware that he has acquired an interest in shares so comprised or that he has ceased to be interested in shares so comprised in which he was previously interested,

then, subject to the provisions of sections 68 to 79, he shall be under an obligation ("the obligation of disclosure") to make notification to the company of the interests which he has, or had, in its shares.

(2) In relation to a public limited company, "relevant share capital" means the company's issued share capital of a class carrying rights to vote in all circumstances at general meetings of the company and it is hereby declared for the avoidance of doubt that

Interest to be disclosed s. 68

(1) For the purposes of the obligation of disclosure, the interests to be taken into account are those in relevant share capital of the company concerned.

(2) A person has a notifiable interest at any time when he is interested in shares comprised in that share capital of an aggregate nominal value equal to or more than the percentage of the nominal value of that share capital which is for the time being the notifiable percentage.

(3) All facts relevant to determining whether a person has a notifiable interest at any time (or the percentage level of his interest) are taken to

be what he knows the facts to be at that time.

Other provisions relating to notification s. 79
(1) Where a person authorises any other person ("the agent") to acquire or dispose of, on his behalf, interests in shares comprised in relevant share capital of a public limited company, he shall secure that the agents notifies him immediately of acquisitions or disposals of interests in shares so comprised effected by the agent which will or may give rise to any obligation on his part to make a notification under this Chapter with respect to his interest in that share capital.

(7) A person who-

(a) fails to fulfil, within the proper period, an obligation of disclosure imposed on him by this Chapter, or

(b) fails to fulfil within the proper period, an obligation to give any other person a notice required by section 75, or

(c) fails without reasonable excuse to comply with subsection (1),
shall be guilty of an offence.

Part V Insider dealing

This Part was designed to give effect to the E. E. C. directive of 13th November 1989 for the purpose of "co-ordinating regulations on insider dealing".

The directive is founded on Article 100a of the E. E. C. Treaty.

Interpretation s. 107
In this Part, except where the context otherwise requires-

Dealing
"dealing" , in relation to securities means (whether as principal or agent) acquiring, disposing of, subscribing for or underwriting the securities, or making or offering to make, or inducing or attempting to induce a person to make or to offer to make, an agreement -

(a) for or relating to acquiring, disposing of, subscribing for or underwriting the securities; or

(b) the purpose or purported purpose of which is to secure a profit or gain to a person who acquires, disposes of, subscribes for or underwrites the securities or to any of the parties to the agreement in relation to the securities;

See also section 113 in respect of agency transactions.

Director
"director" includes a shadow director ...

Officer
"Officer", in relation to a company, includes-

(a) a director, secretary or employee;

(b) a liquidator;

(c) any person administering a compromise or arrangement made between the company and its creditors;

(d) an examiner;

(e) an auditor; and

(f) a receiver;

Public office

"public office" means an office or employment which is remunerated out of the Central Fund or out of moneys provided by the Oireachtas or money raised by local taxation or charges, or an appointment to or employment under any commission, tribunal, board or body established by the Government or any Minister of the Government or by or under any statutory authority;

Recognised stock exchange

"recognised stock exchange" includes, in particular, any exchange prescribed by the Minister which provides facilities for the buying and selling of rights or obligations to acquire stock;

This means the Irish Stock Exchange.

Related company

"related company" in relation to a company, means any body corporate which is the company's subsidiary or holding company, or a subsidiary of the company's holding company;

Relevant authority

"relevant authority", in relation to a recognised stock exchange, means-

(i) its board of directors, committee of management or other management body, or

(ii) its manager, however described;

Securities

"securities" means-

(a) shares, debentures or other debt securities issued or proposed to be issued, whether in the State or otherwise, and for which dealing facilities are, or are to be, provided by a recognised stock exchange;

(b) any right, option or obligation in respect of any such shares, debentures or other debt securities referred to in paragraph (a);

(c) any right, option or obligation in respect of any index relating to any such shares, debentures or other debt securities referred to in paragraph (a); or

(d) such interests as may be prescribed;

Underwrite

"underwrite" includes sub-underwrite.

Unlawful dealings in securities by insiders s. 108

(1) It shall not be lawful for a person who is, or at any time in the preceding 6 months has been, connected with a company to deal in any securities of that company if by reason of his so being, or having been, connected with that company he is in possession of information that is not generally available, but, if it were, would be likely materially to affect the price of those securities

(2) It shall not be lawful for a person who is, or at any time in the preceding 6 months has been, connected with a company to deal in any securities of any other company if by reason of his so being, or having been, connected with the first-mentioned company he is in possession of information that-

(a) is not generally available but, if it were, would be likely materially to affect the price of those securities and

(b) relates to any transaction (actual or contemplated) Involving both those companies or involving one of them and securities of the other, or to the fact that any such transaction is no longer contemplated.

(3) Where a person is in possession of any such information as is mentioned in subsection (1) or (2) that if generally available would be likely materially to affect the price of securities but is not precluded by either of those subsections from dealing in those securities, it shall not be lawful for him to deal in those securities if he has received the information, directly or indirectly, from another person and is aware, or ought reasonably to be aware, of facts or circumstances by virtue of which that other person is then himself precluded by subsection (1) or (2) from dealing in those securities.

(4) It shall not be lawful for a person at any time when he is precluded by subsection (1), (2) or (3) from dealing in any securities, to cause or procure any other person to deal in those securities.

(5) It shall not be lawful for a person, at any time when he is precluded by subsection (1), (2) or (3) from dealing in any securities, by reason of his being in possession of any information, to communicate that information to any other person if he knows, or ought reasonably to know, that the other person will make use of the information for the purpose of dealing, or causing or procuring another person to deal, in those securities.

person
This means a human person and not an artificial person such as a company.

information
The person must have been in possession of information relating to a transaction (actual or contemplated), that is not generally available, but, if it were, would be likely materially to affect the price of securities.

unlawful act
It shall not be lawful for a person to deal in any securities, where he is in possession or receipt of information.

cause or procure

A person is not excused by reason of not having completed the deal himself.

communicate

Communication of information in appropriate circumstance is itself unlawful.

position of companies

(6) Without prejudice to subsection (3), but subject to subsections (7) and (8), it shall not be lawful for a company to deal in any securities at a time when any officer of that company is precluded by subsection (1), (2) or (3) from dealing in those securities.

(7) Subsection (6) does not preclude a company from entering into a transaction at any time by reason only of information in the possession of an officer of that company if -

(a) the decision to enter into the transaction was taken on its behalf by a person other than the officer;

(b) it had in operation at that time written arrangements to ensure that the information was not communicated to that person and that no advice relating to the transaction was given to him by a person in possession of the information; and

(c) the information was not communicated and such advice was not so given.

(8) Subsection (6) does not preclude a company from dealing in securities of another company at any time by reason only of information in the possession of an officer of the first-mentioned company, being information that was received by the officer in the course of the performance of his duties as an officer of the first-mentioned company and that consists only of the fact that the first-mentioned company proposes to deal in securities of that other company.

(9) This section does not preclude a person from dealing in securities, or rights or interests in securities, of a company if-

(a) he enters into the transaction concerned as agent for another person pursuant to a specified instruction of that other person to effect that transaction; and

(b) he has not given any advice to the other person in relation to dealing in securities, or rights or interests in securities, of that company that are included in the same class as the first-mentioned securities.

(10) This section does not preclude a person from dealing in securities, if while not otherwise taking advantage of his possession of information referred to in subsection (1) -

(a) he gives at least 21 days' notice to a relevant authority of the relevant stock exchange of his intention to deal, within the period referred to in paragraph (b), in the securities, of the company concerned, and

(b) the dealing takes place within a period beginning 7 days after the publication of the company's interim or final results, as the case may be and ending 14 days after such publication, and

(c) the notice referred to in paragraph (a) is published by the exchange concerned immediately on its receipt.-

(11) For the purposes of this section, a person is connected with a company if, being a natural person-

(a) he is an officer of that company or a related company;

(b) he is a shareholder in that company or in a related company; or

(c) he occupies a position (including a public office) that may reasonably be expected to give him access to information of a kind to which subsection (1) and (2) apply by virtue of-

(i) any professional, business or other relationship existing between himself (or his employer or a company of which he is an officer) and that company or a related company; or

(ii) his being an officer of a substantial shareholder in that company or in a related company.

Exempt transactions s. 110

(1) Nothing in section 108 shall prevent a person from -

(a) acquiring securities under a will or on the intestacy of another person; or

(b) acquiring securities in a company pursuant to an employee profit sharing scheme -

(i) approved by the Revenue Commissioners for the purposes of the Finance Acts, and

(ii) the terms of which were approved by the company in general meeting, and

(iii) under which all permanent employees of the company are offered the opportunity to participate on equal terms relative to specified objective criteria;

(c) entering in good faith into a transaction to which subsection (2) applies.

(2) This subsection applies to the following kinds of transactions-

(a) the obtaining by a director of a share qualification under section 180 of the Principal Act;

(b) a transaction entered into by a person in accordance with his obligations under an underwriting agreement;

(c) a transaction entered into by a personal representative of a deceased person, a trustee, or liquidator, receiver or examiner in the performance of the functions of his office; or

(d) a transaction by way of, or arising out of, a mortgage of or charge on securities or a mortgage, charge, pledge, or lien on documents of title to securities.

(3) This part shall not apply to transactions entered into in pursuit of monetary, exchange rate, national debt management or foreign exchange reserve policies by any Minister of the Government or the Central Bank, or by any person on their behalf.

Criminal liability s. 111

A person who deals in securities in a manner declared unlawful by section 108 shall be guilty of an offence.

Restriction on dealing s. 112

(1) Subject to subsection (2), a person convicted of an offence under section 111 or this section shall not deal within the period of 12 months from the date of the conviction.

(2) Where a person convicted of an offence under subsection (1) has before the date of his conviction, initiated a transaction under which some element of performance remains to be rendered, subsection (1) shall not prohibit him from completing the transaction where a relevant authority of a recognised stock exchange has indicated in writing, to the parties to the transaction, its satisfaction that-

(a) the transaction was initiated but not completed before the date of the conviction, and

(b) if the transaction were not concluded, the rights of an innocent third party would be prejudiced, and

(c) the transaction would not be unlawful under any other provisions of this part.

(3) A person who contravenes this section shall be guilty of an offence.

Duty of agents in relation to unlawful dealing s. 113

(1) A person shall not deal on behalf of another person if he has reasonable cause to believe or ought to conclude that the deal would be unlawful, within the meaning of section 108.

(2) A person who contravenes this section shall be guilty of an offence.

Penalties s. 114

(2) A person who commits an offence under this Part shall be liable-

(a) on summary conviction, to imprisonment for a term not exceeding 12 months or to a fine not exceeding £1,000 or to both, or

(b) on conviction on indictment, to imprisonment for a term not exceeding 10 years or to a fine not exceeding £200,000 or to both.

Obligation of professional secrecy s. 118

(1) Information obtained by any of the following persons by virtue of the exercise by a recognised stock exchange of its functions under this part shall not be disclosed except in accordance with law, namely-

(a) a relevant authority of the exchange,

(b) an authorised person, or

(c) any person employed or formerly employed by the exchange.

(2) Subsection (1) shall not prevent a relevant authority of a recognised stock exchange from disclosing any information to the Minister, whether pursuant to a request under section 115(5) or

otherwise, or to a similar authority in another Member State of the European Communities.

(3) Any person who contravenes subsection (1) shall be guilty of an offence.

Part VI Winding up and related matters

This Part deals with winding up and related matters, it made a number of changes in the 1963 Act.

Provisions applicable to a Creditors Voluntary Winding Up.

Creditors voluntary winding up s. 131

(7) If a liquidator without reasonable excuse fails to comply with this section, he shall be guilty of an offence.

Part VII Disqualification and Restrictions: Directors and other officers

This part is designed to make it more difficult for persons responsible for the failure of one company with limited liability to immediately recommence trading through the medium of another company.

Chapter 1. Restriction on directors of insolvent companies

Chapter 2. Disqualification generally

Chapter 3. Enforcement

Penalty for acting contrary to provisions of chapter 1 or 2 s. 161

(1) Any person who, in relation to any company, acts in a manner or capacity which, by virtue of being a person to whom section 150 applies or being subject or deemed to be subject to a disqualification order, he is prohibited from doing shall be guilty of an offence.

Penalty for acting under directions of disqualified person s. 164

(1) If any person while a director or other officer or a member of a committee of management or trustee of any company acts in accordance with the directions or instructions of another person knowing that such other person is disqualified or that, in giving the directions or instructions, he is acting in contravention of any provision of this Part he shall be guilty of an offence.

Information to be given by directors to the court s. 166

(1) Where-

(a) a director of a company is charged with an offence or civil proceedings are instituted against such a director, and

(b) the charge or proceedings relate to the company or involve alleged fraud or dishonesty.

the director shall, by notice in writing to the court lodged before the hearing of the case-

(i) give the names of all companies of which he is a director at the date of the notice,

(ii) give the names of all companies of which he was a director within a period commencing not earlier than 12 months prior to the commencement of proceedings and ending at the date of the notice,

(iii) state whether he is at the date of the notice or ever was subject or deemed to be subject to a disqualification order, and

(iv) give the dates and duration of each period in respect of which he is or was disqualified.

(2) This section applies to shadow directors as it applies to directors.

(3) Any person who contravenes subsection (1) shall be guilty of an offence.

Part X Accounts and audit

This part strengthens the law governing company accounts and audit. It implements the Eight E. E. C. Directive concerning company law harmonisation on the qualification of auditors which is based upon Article 54(3)(g) of the E. E. C. Treaty.

Resignation of auditors s. 185

(1) An auditor of a company may, by a notice in writing ... served on the company and stating his intention to do so, resign from the office of auditor to the company; and the resignation shall take effect on the date on which the notice is so served or on such later date as may be specified in the notice.

(7) If default is made in complying with (a statement of circumstances connected with the resignation), the company concerned, and every officer of such company who is in default, shall be guilty of an offence.

By section 186. A notice served by a resigning auditor may requisition a general meeting of the company. if default is made in respect of any further statement it is an additional offence.

Duty of auditors if proper books of account not being kept s. 194

(1) If, at any time, the auditors of a company form the opinion that the company is contravening, or has contravened, section 202 by failing to cause to be kept proper books of account (within the meaning of that section) in relation to the matters specified in subsections (1) and (2) of that section, the auditors shall-

(a) serve a notice on the company as soon as may be stating their opinion, and

(b) not later than 7 days after the service of such notice on the company, notify the registrar of companies in the prescribed form of the notice.

(4) A person who contravenes subsection (1) shall be guilty of an offence.

Prohibition on acting in relation to audit while disqualification order in force s. 195

(1) If a person who is subject or is deemed to be subject to a

disqualification order (as provided for in section 159)-

(a) becomes or remains after 28 days from the date of the making of the order, a partner in a firm of auditors,

(b) gives directions or instructions in relation to the conduct of any part of the audit of the accounts of a company, or

(c) works in any capacity in the conduct of an audit of the accounts of a company,

he shall be guilty of an offence.

Penalty for false statement to auditors s. 197

(1) An officer of a company who knowingly or recklessly makes a statement to which this section applies that is misleading, false or deceptive in a material particular shall be guilty of an offence.

(2) This section applies to any statement made to the auditors of a company (whether orally or in writing) which conveys, or purports to convey, any information or explanation which they require under the Companies Acts, or are entitled so to require, as auditors of the company.

(3) An officer of a company who fails to provide to the auditors of the company or of the holding company of the company, within two days of the making of the relevant requirement, any information or explanations that the auditors require as auditors of the company or of the holding company of the company and that is within the knowledge of or can be procured by the officer shall be guilty of an offence.

(4) In a prosecution for an offence under this section, it shall be a defence for the defendant to show that it was not reasonably possible for him to comply with the requirement under subsection (3) to which the offence relates within the time specified in that subsection but that he complied therewith as soon as was reasonably possible after the expiration of such time.

(5) In this section "officer", in relation to a company, includes any employee of the company.

There are additional offences in relation to auditors in sections:

199. Transitional provisions concerning register.
200. Duty to keep registrar informed.

Keeping of books of account s. 202

(1) Every company shall cause to be kept proper books of account, whether in the form of documents or otherwise, ...

(10) A company that contravenes this section and a person who, being a director of a company, fails to take all reasonable steps to secure compliance by the company with the requirements of this section, or has by his own wilful act been the cause of any default by the company thereunder, shall be guilty of an offence: ...

Liability of officers where proper books of account not kept s. 203
(1) If-
(a) a company that is being wound up and that is unable to pay all of its debts, has contravened section 202, and
(b) the court considers that such contravention has contributed to the company's inability to pay all of its debts or has resulted in substantial uncertainty as to the assets and liabilities of the company or has substantially impeded the orderly winding up thereof,
every officer of the company who is in default shall be guilty of an offence and liable-
(i) on summary conviction to £1,000 fine and or 6 months imprisonment, or
(ii) on conviction on indictment to a £10,000 fine and or 5 years imprisonment.
(2) In a prosecution for an offence under this section it shall be a defence for the person charged with the offence to show that-
(a) he took all reasonable steps to secure compliance by the company with section 202, or
(b) he had reasonable grounds for believing and did believe that a competent and reliable person, acting under the supervision or control of a director of the company who has been formally allocated such responsibility, was charged with the duty of ensuring that that section was complied with and was in a position to discharge that duty.

Part XI Acquisition of own shares and shares in holding company
This part allows a company to purchase its own shares, subject to certain safeguards and conditions.

There are offences specific to companies and their officers.
The relevant sections are:
226. Return to be made to registrar.
228. Regulations as to purchase of shares.
229. Duty of company to notify stock exchange.

Acquisition of own shares and shares in holding company s. 234(1)
A company which contravenes any of the following provisions shall be guilty of an offence, namely sections 207 to 211, 218 and 222 to 224.
The relevant sections are:
207. Power to issue redeemable shares;
208. Cancellation of shares on redemption;
209. Treasury shares;
210. Power to convert shares into redeemable shares
211. Power of company to purchase own shares;
218. Incidental payments with respect to purchase of own shares;
222. Retention and inspection of documents;
223. Dealings by company in its own securities;
224. Holding by subsidiary of shares in holding company.

(2) Section 241 (see below) shall apply to an offence under this Part.

Part XII General

Penalty for offences under the Companies Acts s. 240

(1) A person guilty under any provisions of the Companies Acts of an offence for which no punishment is specifically provided shall be liable-

(a) On summary conviction to a £1,000 fine and or 12 months imprisonment;

(b) On conviction on indictment a £10,000 fine and or 3 years imprisonment

(2) A person guilty under any provisions of the Companies Acts of an offence made punishable by a fine of an unspecified amount shall be liable-

(a) On summary conviction to a £1,000 fine;

(b) On conviction on indictment a £10,000 fine.

(3) Every offence under the Companies Acts made punishable by a fine not exceeding £1,000 or by imprisonment for a term not exceeding 12 months, or by both may be prosecuted summarily.

(4) Summary proceedings in relation to an offence under the Companies Acts may be brought and prosecuted by the Director of Public Prosecutions or the Minister.

Offences by certain bodies s. 241

(1) Where an offence under section 19, 21, 79 or 242 which is committed by a body to which any such section applies is proved to have been committed with the consent or connivance of or to be attributable to any neglect on the part of any person being a director, manager, secretary or other officer of the body, or any person who was purporting to act in any such capacity, that person shall also be guilty of an offence under that section.

(2) Where the affairs of a body are managed by its members, subsection (1) shall apply in relation to the acts and defaults of a member in connection with his functions of management as if he were a director or manager of the body.

Furnishing false information s. 242

(1) A person who, in purported compliance with any provisions of the Companies Acts, answers a question, provides an explanation, makes a statement or produces, lodges or delivers any return, report, certificate, balance sheet or other document false in a material particular, knowing it to be false, or recklessly answers a question, provides an explanation, makes a statement or produces, lodges or delivers any such document false in a material particular shall be guilty of an offence.

(2) Where a person is guilty of an offence under subsection (1) and the court is of opinion that any act, omission or conduct which constitutes that offence has-

(a) substantially contributed to a company being unable to pay its debts;

(b) prevented or seriously impeded the orderly winding-up of the company; or

(c) substantially facilitated the defrauding of the creditors of the company or creditors of any other person,

that person shall be liable on indictment to a £10,000 fine and or 7 years imprisonment.

Penalisation of destruction, mutilation, falsification of documents s. 243

(1) A person being an officer of (a company, a body corporate or an insurance undertaking) who destroys, mutilates or falsifies, or is privy to the destruction, mutilation or falsification of any book or document affecting or relating to the property or affairs of the body, or makes or is privy to the making of a false entry therein, shall unless he proves that he had no intention to defeat the law, be guilty of an offence.

(2) Any such person who fraudulently either parts with, alters or makes an omission in any such book or document, or who is privy to fraudulent parting with, fraudulent altering or fraudulent making of an omission in, any such book or document, shall be guilty of an offence.

Part XIII Investment companies.

This part establishes a new machinery for investment companies with variable capital and facilitates their establishment in the International Finance Services Centre. As such companies are exempt from certain principles of company law; such as capital maintenance they are required to operate under the supervision of the Central Bank.

Offences in relation to investment companies s. 262

Where a company contravenes-

(a) any of the provisions of this Part, or

(b) any regulation made in relation thereto (whether under this Part or under any other enactment), or

(c) any condition in relation to its authorisation or business imposed by the Bank under section 257 (Powers of Central Bank),

the company and every officer thereof who is in default shall be guilty of an offence.

Chapter 22

Criminal Damage

The Criminal Damage Act, 1991 simplified and modernised the law of criminal damage to property by replacing the multiplicity of offences of damage to specific kinds of property contained in the Malicious Damage Act, 1861. The Act is based, in the main, on the recommendations of the Law Reform Commission in Report LRC 26-1988. It created the following offences:

> Damage to another's property
> Damage to any property
> Damage with intent to defraud
> Arson
> Threat to damage property
> Possessing any thing with intent to damage property
> Unauthorised accessing of data

All references below are to the Criminal Damage Act, 1991.

Interpretation s. 1

"to damage" includes -

(a) in relation to property other than data (but including a storage medium in which data are kept), to destroy, deface, dismantle or, whether temporarily or otherwise, render inoperable or unfit for use or prevent or impair the operation of,

(c) to do any act within the State that damages property outside the State,

(d) to do any act outside the State that damages property within the State, and

(e) to make an omission causing damage,

and cognate words shall be construed accordingly;

"property" means -

(a) property of a tangible nature, whether real or personal, including money and animals that are capable of being stolen,

(b) data.

Property shall be treated for the purposes of the Act as belonging to any person-

(a) having lawful custody or control of it,

(b) having in it any proprietary right or interest (not being an equitable interest arising only from an agreement to transfer or grant an interest), or

(c) having a charge over it.

Damage to another's property s. 2(1)

A person who without lawful excuse damages any property belonging to another intending to damage any such property or being reckless as to whether any such property would be damaged shall be guilty of an offence.

Damage to any property s. 2(2)

A person who without lawful excuse damages any property, whether belonging to himself or another -

(a) intending to damage any property or being reckless as to whether any property would be damaged, and

(b) intending by the damage to endanger the life of another or being reckless as to whether the life of another would be thereby endangered,

shall be guilty of an offence.

R V Steer (1987)

The defendant went to the house of a former partner, against whom he had a grudge, and fired several shots at the house with a rifle. There were no injuries caused to the partner or his wife inside the house and there was no suggestion that any shots had been aimed at either of them. The defendant was charged and convicted of an offence similar to section 2(2).

On the appeal to the House of Lords it was held that for a person to be guilty of the offence of damaging any property with intent to endanger the life of another <u>by</u> the damage or being reckless whether the life of another would be thereby endangered the prosecution had to prove that the danger to life resulted from the damage to the property and it was not sufficient for the prosecution to prove that the danger to life resulted from the act which caused the damage. The defendant was not guilty of the offence charged.

Damage with intent to defraud s. 2(3)

A person who damages any property, whether belonging to himself or another, with intent to defraud shall be guilty of an offence.

Arson s. 2(4)

An offence committed under this section by damaging property by fire shall be charged as arson.

By section 14(1): the common law offence of arson is hereby abolished

R V Miller (1983)

A vagrant who was squatting in a house, awoke to find that a cigarette he had been smoking had set fire to the mattress on which he was lying. He did not attempt to extinguish the fire but moved to anther room. The house caught fire. He was convicted of arson.

The House of Lords answered the following question in the affirmative "Whether the *actus reus* of the offence of arson is present when a defendant accidentally starts a fire and thereafter, intending to .. damage property belonging to another or being reckless as to whether any such property would be .. damaged, fails to take any steps to extinguish the fire or prevent damage to such property by that fire."

Penalties s. 2(5)

A person guilty of an offence under the section shall be liable-

(a) on summary conviction, to a fine not exceeding £1,000 or imprisonment for a term not exceeding 12 months or both, and

(b) on conviction on indictment-

(i) in case the person is guilty of arson under subsection (1) or (3) or of an offence under subsection (2) (whether arson or not), to a fine or imprisonment for life or both, and

(ii) in case the person is guilty of any other offence under this section, to a fine not exceeding £10,000 or imprisonment for a term not exceeding 10 years or both.

Reckless s. 2(6)

For the purposes of this section a person is reckless if he has foreseen that the particular kind of damage that in fact was done might be done and yet has gone on to take the risk of it.

R V Caldwell (1982)

The defendant felt a grievance against the proprietor of a hotel. After having got drunk one night, he took his revenge in the early hours of the following morning by setting fire to the hotel, where ten guests were staying. He was charged with arson, similar to section 2(2)(a) and (b) of the Act.

In giving evidence the defendant admitted that he intended to damage the hotel but said that he was so drunk at the time that it never crossed his mind that there might be people in the hotel whose lives might be endangered if it were set on fire.

It was held by the House of Lords that a man was "reckless" as to a possible consequence if two requirements were both satisfied:

(1) he did an act which, in fact, created an obvious risk that that consequence would come about and

(2) when he did that act he either had not given any thought to the possibility of their being any such risk or had recognised that there was some risk involved and had nevertheless gone on to do it.

It was further held, that self-induced intoxication was no defence to a crime (of basic intent) in which recklessness was enough to constitute the necessary *mens rea*.

Threat to damage property s. 3

A person who without lawful excuse makes to another a threat, intending that that other would fear it would be carried out-

(a) to damage any property belonging to that other or a third person, or

(b) to damage his own property in a way which he knows is likely to endanger the life of that other or a third person.

shall be guilty of an offence and shall be liable-

(i) on summary conviction, to a fine not exceeding £1,000 or imprisonment for a term not exceeding 12 months or both, and

(ii) on conviction on indictment, to a fine not exceeding £10,000 or imprisonment for a term not exceeding 10 years or both.

Possessing any thing with intent to damage property s. 4

A person (in the section referred to as the possessor) who has any thing in his custody or under his control intending without lawful excuse to use it or cause or permit another to use it-

(a) to damage any property belonging to some other person, or

(b) to damage his own or the intended user's property-

(i) in a way which he knows is likely to endanger the life of a person other than the possessor, or

(ii) with intent to defraud,

shall be guilty of an offence and shall be liable-

(A) on summary conviction, to a fine not exceeding £1,000 or imprisonment for a term not exceeding 12 months or both, and

(B) on conviction on indictment, to a fine not exceeding £10,000 or imprisonment for a term not exceeding 10 years or both.

Unauthorised accessing of data s. 5

(1) A person who without lawful excuse operates a computer-

(a) within the State with intent to access any data kept either within or outside the State, or

(b) outside the State with intent to access any data kept within the State,

shall, whether or not he accesses any data, be guilty of an offence and shall be liable on summary conviction to a fine not exceeding £500 or imprisonment for a term not exceeding 3 months or both.

(2) Subsection (1) applies whether or not the person intended to access any particular data or any particular category of data or data kept by any particular person.

By section 1(1)(b) *"to damage"* includes in relation to data-

(i) to add to, alter, corrupt, erase or move to another storage medium or to a different location in the storage medium in which they are kept (whether or not property other than data is damaged thereby), or

(ii) to do any act that contributes towards causing such addition, alteration, corruption, erasure or movement,

Note that an attempt is the complete offence.

Without lawful excuse s. 6

(1) This section applies to-

(a) any offence under section 2 (1) or 5,

(b) any offence under section 3 other than one involving a threat by the person charged to damage property in a way which he knows is likely to endanger the life of another, and

(c) any offence under section 4 other than one involving an intent by the person charged to use, or cause or permit the use of, something in his custody or under his control to damage property in such a way as aforesaid.

(2) A person charged with an offence to which this section applies shall, whether or not he would be treated for the purposes of this Act as having a lawful excuse apart from this subsection, be treated for those purposes as having a lawful excuse-

(a) if at the time of the act or acts alleged to constitute the offence he believed that the person or persons whom he believed to be entitled to consent to or authorise the damage to (or, in the case of an offence under section 5, the accessing of) the property in question had consented, or would have consented to or authorised it if he or they had known of the damage or the accessing and its circumstances,

(b) in the case of an offence under section 5, if he is himself the person entitled to consent to or authorise accessing of the data concerned, or

(c) if he damaged or threatened to damage the property in question or, in the case of an offence under section 4, intended to use or cause or permit the use of something to damage it, in order to protect himself or another or property belonging to himself or another or a right or interest in property which was or which he believed to be vested in himself or another and, at the time of the act or acts alleged to constitute the offence, he believed-

(i) that he or that other or the property, right or interest was in immediate need of protection, and

(ii) that the means of protection adopted or proposed to be adopted were or would be reasonable having regard to all the circumstances.

(3) For the purposes of this section it is immaterial whether a belief is justified or not if it is honestly held.

(4) For the purposes of subsection (2) a right or interest in property includes any right or privilege in or over land, whether created by grant, licence or otherwise.

(5) This section shall not be construed as casting doubt on any defence recognised by law as a defence to criminal charges.

The damage to property that results in each of the above offences referred to, is an offence only if done with the appropriate intent, or recklessly, or without lawful excuse. The term "without lawful excuse" replace "unlawfully" which is used in earlier statutes. See "recklessness" (pages 9, 57, 72) and intention (pages 9, 47). These are the states of mind that make up the *mens rea* of the offences.

Jaggard V Dickinson (1981)

The defendant had a relationship with Mr. H. such that she had his permission at any time to treat his property as her own. One evening after being out drinking she took a taxi to his house, no. 67. She was put down outside No. 35, which had an identical appearance to no. 67. Being in a state of self-induced intoxication she thought that no. 35 was no. 67 and when she was unable to get in she broke windows in order to do so.

It was held that the provision similar to section 6(3) required the court to consider the accused's actual belief; the belief could be honestly held even though caused by self-induced intoxication; section 6(2) and (3) therefore provided the defendant with a statutory defence to which the principles established by *D. P. P. V Majewski* (page 32) did not apply.

Proceedings s. 7

(1) Proceedings for an offence under section 2 or 5 alleged to have been committed by a person outside the State in relation to data kept within the State or other property so situate may be taken, and the offence may for all incidental purposes be treated as having been committed, in any place in the State.

(2) (a) Where a person is charged with an offence under section 2, 3 or 4 in relation to property belonging to another-

(i) it shall not be necessary to name the person to whom the property belongs, and

(ii) it shall be presumed, until the contrary is shown, that the property belongs to another.

(b) Where a person is charged with an offence under section 2 in relation to such property as aforesaid, it shall also be presumed, until the contrary is shown, that the person entitled to consent to or authorise the damage concerned had not consented to or authorised it, unless the property concerned is data and the person charged is an employee or agent of the person keeping the data.

(c) Paragraph (b) shall apply in relation to a person charged with an offence under section 5 as if the reference to damage were a reference to access and with any necessary modifications.

(3) A person charged with an offence under section 2 in relation to data or an attempt to commit such an offence may, if the evidence does not warrant a conviction for the offence charged but warrants a conviction for an offence under section 5, be found guilty of that offence.

Jurisdiction of District Court s. 8

No rule of law ousting the jurisdiction of the District Court to try offences where a dispute of title to property is involved shall preclude that court from trying offences under this Act.

Arrest without warrant s. 12

(1) This section applies to an offence under this Act other than section 5 or 13(4).

(2) Any person may arrest without warrant anyone who is or whom he, with reasonable cause, suspects to be in the act of committing an offence to which this section applies.

(3) Where an offence to which this section applies has been committed, any person may arrest without warrant anyone who is or who he, with reasonable cause, suspects to be guilty of the offence.

(4) Where a member of the Garda Síochána, with reasonable cause, suspects that an offence to which this section applies or an offence under

section 13(4) has been committed, he may arrest without warrant anyone whom he, with reasonable cause, suspects to be guilty of the offence.

(5) A member of the Garda Síochána may arrest without warrant anyone who is or who he, with reasonable cause, suspects to be about to commit an offence to which this section applies.

(6) For the purpose of arresting a person under any power conferred by this section a member of the Garda Síochána may enter (if need be, by force) and search any place where that person is or where the member, with reasonable cause, suspects him to be.

(7) This section shall apply to an attempt to commit an offence as it applies to the commission of that offence.

(8) This section shall not prejudice any power of arrest conferred by law apart from this section.

Search warrant s. 13

(1) if a justice of the District Court is satisfied by information on oath of a member of the Garda Síochána that there is reasonable cause to believe that any person has in his custody or under his control or on his premises any thing and that it has been used, or is intended for use, without lawful excuse-

(a) to damage property belonging to another,

(b) to damage any property in a way likely to endanger the life of another or with intent to defraud, or

(c) to access, or with intent to access, data,

the justice may issue a search warrant mentioned in subsection (2).

(2) A search warrant issued under this section shall be expressed and operate to authorise a named member of the Garda Síochána, accompanied by such other members of the Garda Síochána as may be necessary, at any time or times within one month of the date of issue of the warrant, to enter if need be by force the premises named in the warrant, to search the premises and any persons found therein, to seize and detain anything which he believes to have been used or to be intended for use as aforesaid and, if the property concerned is data or the search warrant has been issued on a ground referred to in subsection (1)(c), to operate, or cause to be operated by a person accompanying him for that purpose, any equipment in the premises for processing data, inspect any data found there and extract information therefrom, whether by the operation of such equipment or otherwise.

(3) The Police (Property) Act, 1897, shall apply to property which has come into the possession of the Garda Síochána under this section as it applies to property which has come into the possession of the Garda Síochána in the circumstances mentioned in that Act.

Obstruction s. 13(4)

A person who-

(a) obstructs or impedes a member of the Garda Síochána acting under the authority of a search warrant issued under this section, or

(b) is found on or at the premises specified in the warrant by a member of the Garda Síochána acting as aforesaid and who fails or refuses to give the member his name and address when required by the member to so so or gives him a name or address that is false or misleading,

shall be guilty of an offence and shall be liable on summary conviction-

(i) in the case of an offence under paragraph (a), to a fine not exceeding £1,000 or imprisonment not exceeding 12 months or both, and

(ii) in the case of an offence under paragraph (b), to a fine not exceeding £500.

Chapter 23

Malicious Damage

The law relating to malicious damage is contained in the Malicious Damage Act, 1861 (most of which has been repealed). The Larceny Act, 1861 makes it a felony to destroy or damage; a valuable security (five years imprisonment), documents of title (five years imprisonment), wills (life imprisonment), and records (five years imprisonment).

The Malicious Damage Act, 1861 now makes the following provisions:

Maliciously obstructing railways s. 35

Whosoever shall unlawfully and maliciously put, place, cast, or throw upon or across any railway any wood, stone or other matter or thing, or shall unlawfully and maliciously take up, remove, or displace any rail, sleeper, or other matter or thing, belonging to any railway, or shall unlawfully and maliciously, turn, move or divert any points or other machinery belonging to any railway, or shall unlawfully and maliciously make or show, hide, or remove, any signal or light upon or near to any railway, or shall unlawfully or maliciously do or cause to be done any other matter or thing, with intent, in any of the cases aforesaid, to obstruct, upset, overthrow, injure, or destroy any engine, tender, carriage, or truck using such railway, shall be guilty of felony, and liable to life imprisonment.

Unlawfully obstructing railways s. 36

Whosoever by any unlawful act, or by any wilful omission or neglect, shall obstruct or cause to be obstructed, any engine or carriage using any railway, or shall aid or assist therein, shall be guilty of misdemeanour and liable to two years imprisonment.

Destroying telegraphs s. 37

Whosoever shall unlawfully and maliciously cut, break, throw down, destroy, injure, or remove any battery, machinery, wire, cable, post, or other matter or thing whatsoever being part of or being used or employed in or about any electric or magnetic telegraph, or in the working thereof, or shall unlawfully and maliciously prevent or obstruct in any manner whatsoever the sending, conveyance, or delivery of any communication by any such telegraph, shall be guilty of a misdemeanour and liable to two years imprisonment.

By section 38 the penalty for an attempt is a £10 fine and or three months imprisonment

Killing or maiming cattle s. 40

Whosoever shall unlawfully and maliciously kill, maim, or wound any cattle shall be guilty of felony. The penalty on summary conviction is a £1,000 fine and or 12 months imprisonment, or on conviction on indictment is a £10,000 fine and or 10 years imprisonment.

Killing or maiming animals other than cattle s. 41
Whosoever shall unlawfully and maliciously kill, maim, or wound any dog, bird, beast, or other animal not being cattle, but being either the subject of larceny at common law, or being ordinarily kept in a state of confinement, or for any domestic purpose shall be guilty of an offence.

The penalty on summary conviction is a £1,000 fine and or 12 months imprisonment, or on conviction on indictment is a £10,000 fine and or 10 years imprisonment.

Exhibiting false signals to shipping s. 47
Whosoever shall unlawfully mask, alter, or remove any light or signal, or unlawfully exhibit any false light or signal, with intent to bring any ship, vessel, or boat, into danger, or shall unlawfully and maliciously do anything tending to the immediate loss or destruction of any ship, vessel, or boat, and for which no punishment is hereinbefore provided, shall be guilty of felony and liable to life imprisonment.

Cutting away buoys etc. s. 48
Whosoever shall unlawfully and maliciously cut away, cast adrift, remove, alter, deface, sink, or destroy, or shall unlawfully and maliciously do any act with intent cut away, cast adrift, remove, alter, deface, sink, or destroy, or shall in any other manner unlawfully and maliciously injure or conceal any boat, buoy, buoy-rope, perch, or mark used or intended for the guidance of seamen for the purpose of navigation, shall be guilty of felony and liable to seven years imprisonment

Malice against owner of property unnecessary s. 58
Every punishment and forfeiture by this Act imposed on any person maliciously committing any offence, whether the same be punishable upon indictment or upon summary conviction, shall equally apply and be enforced, whether the offence shall be committed from malice conceived against the owner of the property in respect of which it shall be committed, or otherwise.

The expression "maliciously" imports *mens rea*, i.e. it must be proved that the defendant foresaw that his conduct was likely to result in damage to property.

This offence is the unlawful and malicious damage to property with intent. The mode of causing the damage is not relevant as long as the intention to damage is present.

Fitzgerald V Limerick Corporations (1985)
The applicant's motor car was taken without his permission by a person unknown and was later found, abandoned and crashed. It was held by the Supreme Court that; since the act of taking the car constituted a criminal offence (as in section 112, Road Traffic Act,

1961), and since the driver of the car at the time off the crash was committing the continuing offence of using the car without the owner's permission, the damage caused by the crash was caused in the course of the committing of a crime against the property damaged within the extended meaning of "maliciously" in section 5 of the Malicious Injuries Act, 1981.

Shennick Lodge V Monaghan County Council (1986)

It was held by the Supreme Court that; The test to be applied in deciding whether a crime is a crime against property damaged is firstly to ascertain whether the crime is in general against a person, and secondly, in the light of the particular penal section, what property it is intended to protect, and in applying this test to section 23A of the Larceny Act, 1916, its provisions are intended to protect buildings, persons and goods therein.

Unlawfully

In certain circumstances a person is entitled to damage or destroy property belonging to another, as for example: a person is entitled to kill a dog attacking him or his animals, a person may dismantle and remove a building unlawfully put up on his premises, a person carrying out a lawful arrest or executing a search warrant may break down doors after admittance has been demanded and refused.

Damage

The expression "damage" means perceptible damage. To walk across a lawn will not normally cause any perceptible damage and thus not be an offence, to trample down long grass has, been held to be sufficient.

Claim of right

If a person honestly but erroneously believes that he is damaging his own property, or the property of the person who has instructed him to damage it, he has a good defence. See also page 101.

Where a person is entitled to damage property, or where he thinks that he is entitled to damage property, there is still a limitation on the amount of damage that he may inflict.

R V Clemens (1898)

The defendants honestly but erroneously believed that they were entitled to demolish a hut on land over which they thought they had a right to wander at pleasure. They were not content with demolishing the hut, they threw it over a cliff into the sea. On appeal the Court of Crown Cases Reserved agreed that the jury might properly have found that the defendants did more damage than was reasonably necessary (accepting for this purpose that they had a right to demolish it) and affirmed the conviction.

The Electricity (Supply) Act, 1927, provides:

Malicious Injury s. 111
Any person who unlawfully and maliciously cuts or injures any electric wires or works, damage any electric wires or work with intent to cut off or diminish any supply of electricity shall be guilty of felony, and be liable to five years p/s or two years imprisonment.

Chapter 24

Forcible entry

The Prohibition of Forcible Entry and Occupation Act, 1971, created offences in relation to forcible entry an occupation of property.

Interpretation s. 1

"forcibly" means using or threatening to use force in relation to person or property, and for this purpose participation in action or conduct with others in numbers or circumstances calculated to prevent by intimidation the exercise by any person of his rights in relation to any property shall constitute a threat to use force, and "forcible" shall be construed accordingly.

"land" includes-

(a) messuages and tenements of any tenure,

(b) land covered by water,

(c) houses or other buildings or structures whatsoever,

(d) incorporeal hereditaments of any tenure.

"owner", in relation to land, includes the lawful occupier, every person lawfully entitled to the immediate use and enjoyment of unoccupied land, any person having an estate or interest in land (including a person who remains in occupation of land after the determination of his tenancy therein), the owner of the servient tenement (in relation to an easement or *profit a prendre*), the owner of an easement or *profit a pendre* (in relation to the servient tenement) and, in relation to land or a vehicle, any person acting on behalf of the owner, and "ownership" shall be construed accordingly;

"vehicle" means an aircraft not in flight, a train, an omnibus or a boat, ship or other vessel in any port or harbour, or any river or lake, in the State or anywhere in territorial waters.

Forcible entry s. 2

A person who forcibly enters land or a vehicle shall be guilty of an offence unless:-

(a) he is the owner of the land or vehicle, or

(b) if he is not the owner, he does nor interfere with the use and enjoyment of the land or vehicle by the owner and, if requested to leave, by the owner or by a member of the Garda Siochana in uniform, he does so with all reasonable speed and in a peaceable manner, or

(c) he enters in pursuance of a *bona fide* claim of right.

Remaining in forcible occupation s. 3

(1) A person who remains in forcible occupation of land or a vehicle shall be guilty of an offence unless he is the owner or so remains thereon in pursuance of a *bona fide* claim of right.

Forcible entry

(2) In this section "forcible occupation of land or a vehicle" includes-

(a) the act of locking, obstructing or barring any window, door or other entry to or means of exit from land or a vehicle with a view to preventing or resisting a lawful attempt to enter the land or vehicle,

(b) the act of erecting a physical obstacle to an entry to or means of exit from land or a vehicle with a view to preventing or resisting a lawful attempt to enter the land or vehicle,

(c) the act of physically resisting a lawful attempt at ejection from land or a vehicle.

Encouragement and advocacy s. 4

(1) A person who encourages or advocates the commission of an offence under section 2 or 3 of the Act shall be guilty of an offence.

(2) Where a statement in contravention of subsection (1) of this section is made by or on behalf of a group of persons, every person who is a member of the group and who consented to the making of the statement shall be guilty of an offence under that subsection.

(3) In a prosecution of a person (in this subsection referred to as the defendant) as a member of a group for an offence under subsection(1) in relation to a statement made by or on behalf of the group, if, having regard to all the circumstance (including the constitution and rules, if any, of the group, and the extent to which the defendant had participated in the activities of the group), the court thinks it reasonable to do so, it may regard proof of the defendant's membership of the group and of the making of the statement by or on behalf of the group as proof of consent on the part of the defendant in the absence of any adequate explanation by him.

Penalties s. 7

Every person who commits an offence under the Act shall be liable-

On summary conviction in this case of a first offence £50 and or six months imprisonment,

On summary conviction in the case of a second or subsequent offence £100 fine and or twelve months imprisonment.

On conviction on indictment £500 fine and or three years imprisonment.

By section 6 the court, in coming to a decision as to the penalty, may take the damage (caused by the owner or gardai entering) to property into account as if that damage had been caused by the defendant and may have regard to whether or not the defendant has compensated the owner in respect of that damage.

Power of arrest s. 9

A member of the Garda Siochana may arrest a person without warrant where-

(a) the member knows or has reasonable cause for suspecting that the person is committing and offence under section 3, and

(b) the owner of the land or vehicle to which the offence relates represents to any member of the Garda Siochana, and the member proposing to make the arrest reasonably believes, that, as a result of the continuance of the offence, serious damage to the land or vehicle or serious interference with the lawful rights of the owner in relation thereto, or serious inconvenience to the public or a section thereof, is being or will be caused, and

(c) the member proposing to make the arrest reasonably believes that the arrest is necessary to prevent the damage, interference or inconvenience, and

(d) it is not reasonably practicable to apply for a warrant.

Common law

At common law: a forcible entry is when a person enters into lands or tenements and a forcible detainer is when a person who has entered peaceably maintains his possession by force.

Forcible Entry Act, 1786

Section 64 provides in respect of agrarian disturbances.

That if any person or persons shall, forcibly and without due process of law take the possession of any house, land, or tenement, and forcibly and without due authority by law, hold such possession so taken by force, or shall forcibly oppose or resist the execution of any process of law for giving or quitting the possession ... shall be guilty of felony and liable to seven years penal servitude.

Chapter 25

Forgery

The law as to forgery and related matters is contained in many statutes, this chapter considers the following:

Forgery Act, 1861; Forgery Act, 1913; Merchandise Marks Act, 1887; Central Bank Act, 1942; Decimal Currency Act, 1969 and Hallmarking Act, 1981.

In addition there is a Coinage Offences Act, 1861 and a Coinage Act, 1870, which deal with false or counterfeit coins.

The Forgery Act, 1861, provides:

Making false entries of stock etc. s. 5

Whosoever shall wilfully make any false entry in, or wilfully alter any word or figure in any of the books of account kept by ... the Bank of Ireland .. in which books the accounts of the owners of any stock, annuities, or other public funds, which now are or hereafter may be transferable at the Bank of Ireland ... shall be entered and kept, or shall in any manner wilfully falsify any of the accounts of any of such owners in any of the said books, with intent in any of the cases aforesaid to defraud, or shall wilfully make any transfer of any share or interest of or in any stock, annuity, or other public fund which now is or hereafter may be transferable at the Bank of Ireland ... in the name of any person not being the true and lawful owner of such share or interest, with intent to defraud, shall be guilty of felony, and being convicted thereof shall be liable to imprisonment for life.

Making false dividend warrants s. 6

Whosoever, being a clerk, officer, or servant of or other person employed or intrusted by ... the Bank of Ireland ... shall knowingly make out or deliver any dividend warrant, or warrant for payment of any annuity, interest, or money payable at the Bank of Ireland for a greater or less amount than the person on whose behalf such warrant shall be made out is entitled to, with intent to defraud, shall be guilty of felony, and being convicted thereof shall be liable to imprisonment for seven years.

Destruction of registers of birth, etc. s. 36

Whosoever shall unlawfully destroy, deface or injure, or cause or permit to be destroyed, defaced, or injured, any register of births, baptisms, marriage, deaths, or burials, ..., or shall knowingly and unlawfully insert or permit to be inserted in any such register, or in any certified copy thereof, any false entry of any matter relating to any birth, baptism, marriage, death, or burial, or shall knowingly and unlawfully give any false certificate relating to any birth, baptism, marriage, death,

201

or burial, ... shall be guilty of felony and liable to imprisonment for life.

Making false entries in copies of registers sent to registrar s. 37

Whosoever shall knowingly and wilfully insert, or cause or permit to be inserted, in any copy of any register directed or required by law to be transmitted to any registrar or other officer, any false entry of any matter relating to any baptism, marriage or burial, or shall knowingly and wilfully sign or verify any copy of any register so directed or required to be transmitted as aforesaid, which copy shall be false in any part thereof, knowing the same to be false, or shall unlawfully destroy, deface, or injure, or shall for any fraudulent purpose take from its place of deposit or conceal any such copy of any register, shall be guilty of felony and liable to imprisonment for life.

Intent to defraud s. 44

It shall be sufficient in any indictment for (forging, altering, uttering, offering, disposing of, or putting off any instrument whatsoever) where it shall be necessary to allege an intent to defraud, to allege that the party accused did the act with intent to defraud, without alleging an intent to defraud any particular person; and on the trial of any such offence it shall not be necessary to to prove that the party accused did the act charged with an intent to defraud.

The Forgery Act, 1913

The forging or uttering of forged documents is governed by the 1913 Act, which was passed to consolidate, simplify and amend the law relating to forgery and kindred offences. In brief forgery is the making of a false document in order that it may be used as genuine, with intent to defraud or deceive.

Documents

There is no definition of document in the Act. Certain things are clearly documents, such as wills or deeds, and some things are clearly not documents such as statues and paintings. The Act lists a large number of documents in sections 2 and 3. Section 4 operates as a "catch-all" provision in that it make it an offence to forge any document. In addition to documents seals and dies can be forged

Decisions of the courts as to what was a document at common law may also be referred to.
R V Closs (1858)

The accused a picture-dealer was indicted for selling a copy of one of the pictures of the artist John Linnell, on which copy "was unlawfully painted and forged the name of John Linnell".

Cockburn C.J. said: "A forgery must be some document or writing, and this was merely in the nature of a mark put upon the painting with a view of identifying it, and was no more than if the painter put any other arbitrary mark as a recognition of the picture being his."

R V Pryse-Hughes (1958)

The accused tried to sell a painting as a Constable and gave a forged authentication certificate purporting to come from an authority on Constable.

He was convicted of forgery.

R V Smith (1858)

The accused sold his baking powder and egg powder in printed wrappers resembling the wrappers used by Borwick.

Pollock C.B. said: "In the printing of these wrappers there is no forgery; nor could the man who printed them be indicted. ... They are merely wrappers, and in their present shape I doubt whether they are anything like a document or instrument which is the subject of forgery at common law".

Documents have been classified as being either of a private or public nature. Documents of a private character where the intent must be to defraud, such documents include wills, codicils and other testamentary documents, deeds, bonds, bank notes, valuable securities, documents of title to land or goods, powers of attorney, policies of insurance, endorsements and assignments (all felonies) and forgeries of any other document of a like character. Documents of a public official character where the intent must be to defraud or deceive, this would include forgeries of all public and judicial documents, records, registers, and licences.

Mens rea

The *mens rea* of forgery is the "intent to defraud or deceive". The accused must have committed the forgery with intent to defraud or, in the case of public documents, with intent to defraud or deceive. This distinction has been considered in the courts;

Re London, etc. Finance Corporation Ltd. (1903)

Buckley J. said: "To deceive is, I apprehend, to induce a man to believe that a thing is true which is false, and which the person practising the deceit knows or believes to be false. To defraud is to deprive by deceit: it is by deceit to induce a man to act to his injury. More tersely it may be put, that to deceive is by falsehood to induce a state of mind; to defraud is by deceit to induce a course of action."

This was discussed further in:

Welham V D. P. P. (1960)

The accused was charged with uttering certain hire-purchase documents, knowing them to be forged, with intent to defraud, contrary to section 6. He was a sales manager with a firm of motor dealers who had obtained loans from the Consortium finance Company on the basis of documents which purported to be signed by one J. Murray. It was proved that the signatures were, to Welham's knowledge forged. His defence was that he had no intent to defraud the finance company but merely to circumvent restrictions on borrowing.

In the House of Lords, Lord Denning referred to the definition given by East in his *Pleas of the Crown* vol. 2, p. 852 "To forge, (a metaphorical expression borrowed from the occupation of the smith), means, properly speaking, no more than to make or form: but in our law it is always taken in the evil sense; and therefore Forgery at common law denotes a false making (which includes every alteration of our addition to a true statement), a making *malo animo*, of any written instrument for the purpose of fraud and deceit." and then went on to say: "The important thing about this definition is that it is not limited to the idea of economic loss, nor to the idea of depriving someone of something of value. It extends generally to *the purpose of fraud and deceit*. Put shortly, 'with intent to defraud' means 'with intent to practise a fraud' on someone or other. It need not be anyone in particular. Someone in general will suffice. If anyone may be prejudiced in any way by the fraud, that is enough. At this point it becomes possible to point the contrast in the statute between an 'intent to deceive' and an 'intent to defraud'. 'To deceive' here conveys the element of deceit, which induces a state of mind, without the element of fraud, which induces a course of action or inaction." The conviction of the accused was upheld.

Thus knowledge of the forgery is essential.

People (D. P. P.) V Harrington (1990)

The applicant was charged with two others of possession of forged banknotes contrary to section 13, his defence was that he had been asked whether he would like to make a few pounds for moving a few bags. It was accepted that he played a minor part and knew that was involved was not straight but that he did not know that it would involve thousands of forged banknotes. It was also accepted that it was necessary under section 11 to establish knowledge on his part that notes were forged. The trial judge convicted on basis that he had been involved in a common design and that he had been aware in broad terms of what he was doing.

It was held by the Court of Criminal Appeal that while the applicant may have been aware that the transaction involved illegality, the prosecution had failed to establish beyond reasonable doubt that he had been aware that the bank notes were forgeries and so the conviction could not stand.

Definition of forgery s. 1

(1) For the purposes of this Act, forgery is the making of a false document in order that it may be used as genuine, and in the case of the seals and dies mentioned in this Act the counterfeiting of a seal or die, and forgery with intent to defraud or deceive, as the case may be, is punishable as in this Act provided.

(2) A document is false within the meaning of this Act if the whole or any material part thereof purports to be made by or on behalf or on account of a person who did not make it nor authorise its making; or if,

though made by or on behalf or on account of the person by whom or by whose authority it purports to have been made, the time or place of making, where either is material, or, in the case of a document identified by number or mark, the number or any distinguishing mark identifying the document, is falsely stated therein; and in particular a document is false:-

(a) if any material alteration, whether by addition, insertion, obliteration, erasure, removal, or otherwise, has been made therein;

(b) if the whole or some material part of it purports to be made by or on behalf of a fictitious or deceased person;

(c) if, though made in the name of an existing person, it is made by him or by his authority with the intention that it should pass as having been made by some person, real or fictitious, other than the person who made or authorised it,

(3) For the purposes of this Act-

(a) it is immaterial in what language a document is expressed or in what place within or without the State it is expressed to take effect;

(b) Forgery of a document may be complete even if the document when forged is incomplete, or is not or does not purport to be such a document as would be binding or sufficient in law;

(c) The crossing on any cheque, draft on a banker, post office money order, postal order, coupon, or other document the crossing of which is authorised or recognised by law, shall be a material part of such cheque, draft, order, coupon, or document.

Forgery is the making of a false document, using such a document is the separate offence of uttering (See section 6).

Forgery of certain documents with intent to defraud s. 2

(1) Forgery of the following documents, if committed with intent to defraud, shall be felony and punishable with penal servitude for life:-

(a) Any will, codicil, or other testamentary document, either of a dead or of a living person, or any probate or letters of administration, whether with or without the will annexed;

(b) Any deed or bond, or any assignment at law or in equity of any deed or bond, or any attestation of the execution of any deed or bond;

(c) Any bank note, or any indorsement on or assignment of any bank note.

(2) Forgery of the following documents, if committed with intent to defraud, shall be felony and punishable with penal servitude for any term not exceeding fourteen years:-

(a) Any valuable security or assignment thereof or endorsement thereon, or where the valuable security is a bill of exchange, any acceptance thereof;

(b) Any document of title to lands or any assignment thereof or endorsement thereon;

(c) Any document of title to goods or any assignment thereof or endorsement thereon;

(d) Any powers of attorney or other authority to transfer any shares or interest in any stock, annuity, or public fund of the State or of any foreign state or country or to transfer any share or interest in the debt of any public body, company, or society, Irish or foreign, or in the capital stock of any such company or society, or to receive any dividend or money payable in respect of such share or interest or any attestion of any such power of attorney or other authority;

(e) Any entry in any book or register which is evidence of the title of any person to any share or interest hereinbefore mentioned or to any dividend or interest payable in respect thereof;

(f) Any policy of insurance or any assignment thereof or endorsement thereon;

(g) Any charter-party or any assignment thereof;

(h) Any declaration, warrant, order, affidavit, affirmation, certificate, or other document required or authorised to be made by or for the purposes of the Government Annuities Act, 1829, or the Government Annuities Act, 1832 or by the National Debt Commissioners acting under the authority of the said Acts;

(i) Any certificate of the Revenue Commissioners ..

Forgery of certain documents with intent to defraud or deceive s. 3

(2) Forgery of the following documents, if committed with intent to defraud or deceive, shall be felony and punishable with penal servitude for any term not exceeding fourteen years:-

(a) Any register or record of births, baptisms, namings, dedications, marriages, deaths, burials, or cremations, which now is, or hereafter may be, by law authorised or required to be kept in the State, relating to any birth, baptism, naming, dedication, marriage, death, burial, or cremation, or any part of any such register, or any certified copy of any such register or of any part thereof;

(b) Any copy of any register of baptisms, marriages, burials, or cremations, directed or required by law to be transmitted to any registrar or other officer;

(c) Any register of the birth, baptism, death, burial or cremation of any person to be appointed a nominee under the provisions of the Government Annuities Act, 1829, or any copy or certificate of any such register, or the name of any witness to any such certificate;

(e) Any wrapper or label provided by or under the authority of the Revenue Commissioners.

(3) Forgery of the following documents, if committed with intent to defraud or deceive, shall be felony and punishable with penal servitude for any term not exceeding seven years:-

(a) Any official document whatsoever of or belonging to any court of justice, or made or issued by any judge, magistrate, officer, or clerk of any such court;

(b) Any register or book kept under the provisions of any law in or under the authority of any court of justice;

(c) Any certificate, office copy, or certified copy of any such document, register, or book or of any part thereof;

(d) Any document which any magistrate or any master or registrar in lunacy is authorised or required by law to make or issue;

(e) Any document which any person authorised to administer an oath under the Commissioners for Oaths Act, 1889, is authorised or required by law to make or issue;

(f) Any document made or issue by an officer of state or law officer of the State, or any document upon which, by the law or usage at the time in force, any court of justice or any officer might act;

(g) Any document or copy of a document used or intended to be used in evidence in any Court of Record, or any document which is made evidence by law;

(h) Any certificate required by an Act for the celebration of marriage;

(i) Any licence for the celebration of marriage which may be given by law;

(j) Any certificate, declaration, or order under any enactment relating to the registration of births or deaths;

(k) Any register book, builder's certificate, surveyor's certificate, certificate of registry, declaration, bill of sale, instrument of mortgage, or certificate of mortgage or sale under Part I of the Merchant Shipping Act, 1894, or any entry or endorsement required by the said Part of the said Act to be made in or on any of those documents;

(l) Any permit, certificate, or similar document made or granted by or under the authority of the Revenue Commissioners.

Forgery of other documents with intent to defraud or deceive s. 4

(1) Forgery of any document, which is not made felony under this or any other statute for the time being in force, if committed with intent to defraud, shall be a misdemeanour punishable with two years imprisonment

(2) Forgery of any public document, which is not made felony under this or any other statute for the time being in force, if committed with intent to defraud, shall be a misdemeanour punishable with two years imprisonment

Forgery of seals and dies s. 5

1) Forgery of the following seals, if committed with intent to defraud or deceive, shall be felony and punishable with penal servitude for life:-

(c) The seal of any court of record;

(d) The seal of the office of the Registrar-General of Births, Deaths, and Marriages.

(2) Forgery of the following seals, if committed with intent to defraud or deceive, shall be felony and punishable with penal servitude for any term not exceeding fourteen years:-

(a) The seal of any register office relating to births, baptisms, marriages, or deaths;

(b) The seal of any burial board or of any local authority performing the duties of a burial board;

(c) The seal of or belonging to any office for the registry of deeds or titles to lands.

(3) Forgery of the following seals, if committed with intent to defraud or deceive, shall be felony and punishable with penal servitude for any term not exceeding seven years:-

(a) The seal of any court of justice other than a court of record;

(b) The seal of the office of any master or registrar in lunacy.

(4) Forgery of the following dies, if committed with intent to defraud or deceive, shall be felony and punishable with penal servitude for any term not exceeding fourteen years:-

(a) Any die provided, made, or used by the Revenue Commissioners

(b) Any die which is or has been required or authorised by law to be used for the marketing or stamping of gold or silver plate, or gold or silver wares. (Note 1981 Act below)

(5) Forgery of the following die, if committed with intent to defraud or deceive, shall be felony and punishable with penal servitude for any term not exceeding seven years:-

Any stamp or die provided, made, or used in pursuance of the Local Stamp Act, 1869.

Uttering s. 6

(1) Every person who utters any forged document, seal, or die shall be guilty of an offence of the like degree (whether felony or misdemeanour) and on conviction thereof shall be liable to the same punishment as if he himself had forged the document, seal, or die.

(2) A person utters a forged document, seal or die, who knowing the same to be forged, and with either of the intents necessary to constitute the offence of forging the said document, seal, or die, uses, offers, publishes, delivers, disposes of, tenders in payment or exchange, exposes for sale or exchange, exchanges, tenders in evidence, or puts off the said forged document, seal or die.

(3) It is immaterial where the document, seal, or die was forged.

Demanding property on forged document, &c. s. 7

Every person shall be guilty of felony and on conviction thereof shall be liable to fourteen years imprisonment, who, with intent to defraud, demands, receives, or obtains, or causes or procures to be delivered, paid or transferred to any person, or endeavours to receive or obtain or to cause or procure to be delivered, paid or transferred to any person any money, security for money or other property, real or personal:-

(a) under, upon, or by virtue of any forged instrument whatsoever, knowing the same to be forged; or

(b) under, upon, or by virtue of any probate or letters of administration, knowing the will, testament, codicil, or testamentary writing on which such probate or letters of administration shall have been obtained to have been forged, or knowing such probate or letters of administration to have been obtained by any false oath, affirmation, or affidavit.

Possession of forged documents, seals and dies s. 8

(1) Every person shall be guilty of felony and on conviction thereof shall be liable to fourteen years imprisonment, who, without lawful authority or excuse, the proof whereof shall lie on the accused purchases or receives from any person, who has in his custody or possession, a forged bank note, knowing the same to be forged.

(2) Every person shall be guilty of felony and on conviction thereof shall be liable to fourteen years imprisonment, who, without lawful authority or excuse, the proof whereof shall lie on the accused, and knowing the same to be forged and has in his possession-

(a) any forged die required or authorised by law to be used for the marking of gold or silver plate, or of gold or silver wares, or any ware of gold silver or base metal bearing the impression of any such forged die; (Note Hallmarking Act, 1981, section 13 below.)

(b) any forged stamp or die, as defined by the Stamp Duties Management Act, 1891;

(c) any forged wrapper or label provided by or under the authority of the Revenue Commissioners.

(3) Every person shall be guilty of felony and on conviction thereof shall be liable to seven years imprisonment, who, without lawful authority or excuse, the proof whereof shall lie on the accused, and knowing the same to be forged, has in his custody or possession:-

Any forged stamp or die, resembling or intended to resemble either wholly or in part any stamp or die which at any time whatever has been or may be provided, made, or used by or under the direction of the local authority for the purposes of the Local Stamp Act, 1869.

Making or having in possession paper or implements s. 9

Every person shall be guilty of felony and on conviction thereof shall be liable to seven years imprisonment, who, without lawful authority or excuse, the proof whereof shall lie on the accused:-

(a) Makes, uses, or knowingly has in his custody or possession, any paper intended to resemble and pass as-

(i) Special paper such as is provided and used for making any bank note, Treasury bill,

(ii) Revenue paper;

(b) Makes, uses, or knowingly has in his custody or possession, any frame, mould, or instrument for making such paper, or for producing in or on such paper any words, figures, letters, marks, lines, or devices peculiar to and used in or on any such paper;

(c) Engraves or in anywise makes upon any plate, wood, stone, or other material, any words, figures, letters, marks, lines, or devices, the print whereof resembles in whole or in part any words, figures, letters, marks, lines or devices peculiar to and used in or on any bank note, or in or on any document entitling or evidencing the title of any person to any share or interest in any public stock, annuity, fund, or debt of the State or any foreign state, or in any stock, annuity, fund, or debt of any body corporate, company, or society, whether within or without the State;

(d) Uses or knowingly has in his custody or possession any plate, wood, stone, or other material, upon which any such words, figures, letters, marks, lines, or devices have been engraved or in anywise made as aforesaid;

(e) Uses or knowingly has in his custody or possession any paper upon which any such words, figures, letters, marks, lines, or devices have been printed or in anywise made as aforesaid.

Purchasing or having in possession certain paper s. 10

Every person shall be guilty of a misdemeanour and on conviction thereof shall be liable to two years imprisonment, who, without lawful authority or excuse, the proof whereof shall lie on the accused, purchase, receives, or knowingly has in his custody or possession-

(a) Any special paper provided and used for making Treasury bills .. or any Revenue paper before such paper has been duly stamped, signed, and issued for public use;

(b) Any die peculiarly used in the manufacture of any such paper.

Accessories and abettors s. 11

Any person who knowingly and wilfully aids, abets, counsels, causes, procures or commands the commission of an offence punishable under this Act shall be liable to be dealt with, indicted, tried and punished as a principal offender.

Criminal possession s. 15

Where the having of any document, seal, or die in the custody or possession of any person is in this Act expresses to be an offence, a person shall be deemed to have a document, seal or die in his custody or possession if he-

(a) has it in his personal custody or possession; or

(b) knowingly and wilfully has it in the actual custody or possession of any other person, or in any building, lodging, apartment, field, or other place, whether open or enclosed, and whether occupied by himself or not.

It is immaterial whether the document, matter, or thing is had in such custody, possession, or place for the use of such person or for the use or benefit of another person.

Forgery

The Merchandise Marks Act, 1887, provides:

Offences as to trade marks and trade descriptions s. 2

(1) Every person who-

(a) forges any trade mark; or

(b) falsely applies to goods any trade mark or any mark so nearly resembling a trade mark as to be calculated to deceive; or

(c) makes any die, block, machine, or other instrument for the purpose of forging or of being used for forging a trade mark; or

(d) in the course of any trade, business or profession, applies any false trade description to goods, or

(e) disposes of or has in his possession any die, block, machine, or other instrument for the purpose of forging a trade mark; or

(f) causes any of the things above in this section mentioned to be done, shall, subject to the provisions of this Act, and unless he proves that he acted without intent to defraud, be guilty of an offence against this Act.

(2) Every person who sells, or exposes for, or has in his possession for, sale, or any purpose of trade or manufacture, any goods or things to which any forged trade mark or false trade description is applied, or to which any trade mark or mark so nearly resembling a trade mark as to be calculated to deceive is falsely applied, as the case may be, shall, unless he proves-

(a) That having taken all reasonable precautions against committing an offence against this Act, he had at the time of the commission of the alleged offence no reason to suspect the genuineness of the trade mark, mark, or trade description; and

(b) That on demand made by or on behalf of the prosecutor, he gave all the information in his power with respect to the persons from whom he obtained such goods or things; or

(c) That otherwise he had acted innocently;

be guilty of an offence against this Act.

(3) Every person guilty of an offence against this Act shall be liable-

(i) on conviction on indictment, to imprisonment, with or without hard labour, for a term not exceeded two years, or to fine, or to both imprisonment and fine; and

(ii) on summary conviction to imprisonment, with or without hard labour, for a term not exceeding four months, or to a fine not exceeding twenty pounds, and in the case of a second or subsequent conviction to imprisonment, with or without hard labour, for a term not exceeding six months, or to a fine not exceeding fifty pounds; and

(iii) in any case, to forfeit to *the State* every chattel, article, instrument, or thing by means of or in relation to which the offence has been committed.

(4) The court before whom any person is convicted under this section may order any forfeited articles to be destroyed or otherwise disposed of as the court thinks fit.

(5) If any person feels aggrieved by any conviction made by a court

of summary jurisdiction, he may appeal therefrom to a court of quarter sessions.

(6) Any offence for which a person is under this Act liable to punishment on summary conviction may be prosecuted, and any articles liable to be forfeited under this Act by a court of summary jurisdiction may be forfeited, in manner provided by the Summary Jurisdiction Acts: Provided that a person charged with an offence under this section before a court of summary jurisdiction shall, on appearing before the court, and before the charge is gone into, be informed of his right to be tried on indictment, and if he requires be so tried accordingly.

Note Hallmarking Act, 1981, section 5 below.

Forging trade marks s. 4

A person shall be deemed to forge a trade mark who either -

(a) without the assent of the proprietor of the trade mark makes that trade mark or a mark so nearly resembling that trade mark as to be calculated to deceive; or

(b) falsifies any genuine trade mark, whether by alteration, addition, effacement, or otherwise;

and any trademark or mark so made or falsified is in this Act referred to as a forged trade mark.

Provided that in any prosecution for forging a trade mark the burden of proving the assent of the proprietor shall lie on the defendant.

The Central Bank Act, 1942, provides:

Definition of "bank note" s. 52

In this part of this Act the expression "bank note" has the same meaning as it has in the Forgery Act, 1913, as amended or expanded by the Currency Act and by this part of this Act.

Extension of the Forgery Act, 1913 s. 53(1)

(1) Currency notes issued by or on behalf of the government of any country outside the State shall be deemed to be bank notes within the meaning of the Forgery Act, 1913.

(2) In the foregoing subsection of this section the expression "currency note" includes any notes (by whatever name they are called) which are legal tender in the country in which they are issued.

Making, etc. a document purporting to be ... a banknotes s. 55(1)

If any person makes, or causes to be made, or uses for any purpose whatsoever, or utters any document purporting to be, or in any way resembling, or so nearly resembling as to be calculated to deceive, a bank note, he shall be guilty of an offence for which the penalty on summary conviction is a £1,000 fine and or 12 months imprisonment or on indictment is a £10,000 fine and or five years imprisonment.

The Decimal Currency Act, 1969, provides:

Counterfeiting copper coins s. 14(1)

Except coins issued under this Act, no piece of metal or mixed metal of any value whatsoever shall be made or issued in the State as a coin or token for money or as purporting that the holder thereof is entitled to demand any value denoted thereon.

Every person who does so shall be guilty of an offence for which the penalty on summary conviction is a £1,000 fine and or 12 months imprisonment or on indictment is a £5,000 fine and or two years imprisonment.

See also the Coinage Offences Act, 1861, as amended by the Coinage Act, 1870, and secion 8 of the Currency Act, 1927. The relevant provisons of these Acts have been adapted and applied by the 1969 Act.

The Hallmarking Act, 1981 provides:

False descriptions of certain articles s. 5

... a person who in the course of trade or business applies to any article which is not of precious metal a description indicating or specifying that the article is made wholly or partly of gold, silver or platinum, or who supplies or offers to supply or has in his possession for sale such an article to which such a description is applied is guilty of an offence under section 2 of the Merchandise Marks Act, 1887 of applying a false trade description.

Penalty for forgery, etc. of certain dies and stamps s. 13

(1) Notwithstanding anything in the Act of 1913, the penalty for forgery under section 5(4) of the Act of 1913 shall be in the case of summary conviction a £500 fine and or twelve months imprisonment and on conviction on indictment is a £5,000 fine and or five years imprisonment.

(2) Notwithstanding anything in the Act of 1913, the penalty for forgery under section 8(2)(a)) of the Act of 1913 shall be in the case of summary conviction a £500 fine and or twelve months imprisonment and on conviction on indictment is a £5,000 fine and or five years imprisonment.

(3) Notwithstanding anything in the Plate Assay (Ireland) Act 1807 or in any other enactment, the penalty for felony under section 16 of that Act or for any other offence under that section shall be,, in the case of summary conviction a £500 fine and or twelve months imprisonment and on conviction on indictment is a £5,000 fine and or five years imprisonment.

The Plate Assay (Ireland) Act, 1807, provides:

Persons forging, casting, or counterfeiting any mark or stamp s. 16
Person forging, casting, or counterfeiting any mark or stamp used by the Assay Master under this Act for the marking. etc., of gold or silver plate or causing such to be done, or marking or causing to be marked gold or silver plate, etc., with any such forged mark or stamp, or removing or causing to be removed from one such article to another any such mark or stamp, or who shall knowingly sell, expose for sale or export any such article with such forged or counterfeited or removed stamp, or shall wilfully or knowingly have in possession any such forged or counterfeited stamp shall be guilty of felony.

Chapter 26

Road traffic offences

The law as to road traffic is contained in the Road Traffic Act, 1961 (the principal Act); which has been amended by:

Road Traffic Act, 1968;
Road Traffic (Amendment) Act, 1978;
Road Traffic (Amendment) Act 1984;
Dublin Transport Authority (Dissolution) Act, 1987.

There are other statutes relating to specific areas (such as "road tax"), there are regulations made by the Minister under the principal Act, such as the Road Traffic General Bye Laws 1964 and the Road Traffic (Insurance Disc) Regulations 1984 and there are in addition E. E. C. Regulation in the area of insurance.

All of the offences under the Road Traffic Acts are not dealt with in this chapter. There are in excess of one hundred and twenty-seven sections in the principal Act and a detailed consideration would be beyond the scope of this book.

All references below are to the 1961 Act unless otherwise stated.

Interpretation s. 3

This section interprets a number of words and phrases used throughout the Acts; they include:

"driving" includes managing and controlling;

"footway" means that portion of any road which is provided primarily for the use of pedestrians;

"mechanically propelled vehicle" means a vehicle intended or adapted for propulsion by mechanical means, including -

(a) a bicycle or tricycle with an attachment for propelling it by mechanical power, whether or not the attachment is being used,

(b) a vehicle the means of propulsion of which is electrical or partly electrical and partly mechanical;

"owner" when used in relation to a mechanically propelled vehicle which is subject of a hire-purchase agreement, means the person in possession of the vehicle under the agreement;

"park" in relation to a vehicle, means keep or leave stationary, and cognate words shall be construed accordingly;

"public place" means any street, road or other place to which the public have access with vehicles whether as of right or by permission and whether subject to or free of charge;

"public road" means a road the responsibility for the maintenance of which lies on a road authority;

"road" includes any bridge, pipe, arch, gully, footway, pavement, fence, railing or wall forming part thereof;

"use" in relation to a vehicle, includes park and cognate words shall be construed accordingly.

Part V of the 1961 Act contains the principal driving offences. Section 51A was inserted by the 1968 Act, sections 52, 53 (part of) and 55 (part of) were substituted by the 1968 Act. All penalties have been increased by the 1984 Act.

Driving when unfit s. 48

(1) A person shall not drive or attempt to drive a mechanically propelled vehicle in a public place when he is, to his knowledge, suffering from any disease or physical or mental disability which would be likely to cause the driving of the vehicle by him in a public place to be a source of danger to the public.

(2) A person who contravenes (1) shall be guilty of an offence and shall be liable on summary conviction for a first offence to a £150 fine and or one months imprisonment; in the case of a second or subsequent offence, a £350 fine and or three months imprisonment. An ancillary disqualification order (see below), may be made, however there is a mandatory disqualification in the case of a second or subsequent offence within three years. Otherwise the court may endorse a person's licence, however there is a mandatory endorsement of a person's license for a second offence within three years.

"drive or attempt to drive" an attempt at driving as well as driving itself is covered by this offence.

"public place" is not defined in the Act. It must be read as meaning a place to which the public have access. The parking of cars in a private place by some members of the public will not make a place public, however a private place may become public on a temporary basis.

A. G. (McLaughlin) V Rhatigan (1966)

R. was charged under Section 49 and 52 of 1961 Act. The only evidence adduced by the State as to the place where the offences were said to have happened was that it was described as a private car park near a licensed premises.

It was held in the High Court by Davitt P. that the onus is on the prosecution to establish by proper evidence that the offences were committed in a public place and that the prosecution had not proved that the place in question was one to which the public had access and thus failed to prove an essential element of each offence.

Stanbridge V Healy (1985)

It was held by the High Court that; "public" means the public generally and not any particular class of the public. In this civil case on the evidence, the public at large did not have access to the place where the accident happened, and therefore it was not a "public place".

Sandy V Martin (1974)

The accused parked his van at a car park of a public house. An hour after closing time he was found near the van in a drunken condition and was charged with being in charge while above the prescribed limits.

It was held on appeal that the car park was a public place during the time it was open to the public and used by customers, but that there was no evidence that the licensee's invitation or permission continued one hour after closing time and the charge was dismissed.

"to his knowledge" This requirement of knowledge on the part of an accused shows the need for a *mens rea* in this offence.

"any disease or .." The type of diseases or disability may be mental or physical. The degree of incapacity is judged by an objective standard, i.e. danger to the public, expert medical evidence would probably be required.

Attorney General V Kenny (1960)

Lavery J. stated in the Supreme Court "where the physical or mental condition is the very fact in issue, to admit an expression of opinion involves the danger that the judgment of the Court may be seriously affected by the judgment of the witness".

"a source of danger to the public" see dangerous driving below.

Driving without reasonable consideration s. 51A

(1) A person shall not drive a mechanically propelled vehicle in a public place without reasonable consideration for, other person's using that place.

(2) A person who contravenes (1) shall be guilty of an offence and shall be liable to the general penalties set out in section 102.

"without reasonable consideration" this would be of an objective standard and would involve *mens rea*. See *McCrone V Riding* below.

"other persons using the place" Other persons must be affected by the actions of the accused.

Pawley V Wharldall (1966)

This phrase includes a passenger in the vehicle driven by the accused person.

The penalties involved show that this is a lesser offence than careless driving, see below.

Careless driving s. 52

(1) A person shall not drive vehicle in a public place without due care and attention.

(2) A person who contravenes (1) shall be guilty of an offence and shall be liable on summary conviction to a £350 fine and or three months imprisonment. An ancillary disqualification order may be made, however there is a mandatory disqualification in the case of a third or subsequent offence within three years. Otherwise the court may endorse a person's licence, however there is a mandatory endorsement of a person's license for a second offence within three years.

"without due care and attention" The standard of driving would be objective and has been considered in:

McCrone V Riding (1938)

"That standard is an objective standard, impersonal and universal, fixed in relation to the safety of other users of the highway. It is in no way related to the degree of proficiency or degree of experience attained by the individual driver.

Where a person is charged of the offence of dangerous driving below, it may be reduced to a charge of careless driving.

Dangerous driving s. 53

(1) A person shall not drive a vehicle in a public place in a manner (including speed) which having regard to all the circumstances of the case (including the condition of the vehicle, the nature, condition and use of the place and the amount of traffic, which then actually is, or might reasonably be expected then to be therein) is dangerous to the public.

(2) A person who contravenes (1) shall be guilty of an offence and-

(a) in case the contravention causes death or serious bodily harm, he shall be liable on conviction on indictment to five years penal servitude and or £3,000 fine;

(b) in any other case, he shall be liable, on summary conviction to a £1,000 fine and or six months imprisonment.

(3) In a prosecution for an offence under this section, it shall not be a defence to prove that the speed at which the accused person was driving was not in excess of an ordinary, general, built up area or special speed limit applying in relation to the vehicle.

(4) Where, when a person is tried on indictment or summarily for an offence under this section, the jury, or, in the case of a summary trial, the District Court, is of opinion that he was not guilty of an offence under section 52, the jury or court may find him guilty of an offence under section 52 and he may be sentenced accordingly.

(5) A person liable to be charged with an offence under this section shall not, by reference to the same occurrence, be liable to be charged with an offence under section 35 of the Offences against the Person Act, 1861.

(6) Where a member of the Garda Siochana is of the opinion that a person has committed an offence under this section, he may arrest the person without a warrant.

"vehicle" this offence is not confined to a mechanically propelled vehicle.

An ancillary disqualification order may be made, however there is a mandatory disqualification in the case of a second offence within three years, where a mechanically propelled vehicle was involved and such disqualification must be for not less than six months. Otherwise the court may endorse a person's licence, however there is a mandatory endorsement of a person's license for a second offence within three years.

Dangerous driving causing death or serious bodily harm s. 53

This is the same offence as Dangerous Driving above, with the proviso

that either death or serious bodily harm has been caused to another person. It creates a specific offence, of what would otherwise be manslaughter.

The penalty for conviction on indictment is a £3,500 fine and or five years imprisonment. There is a mandatory disqualification where and such disqualification must be for not less than six months?.

People (A. G.) V Gallagher (1972)

It was held by the Court of Criminal Appeal that proof that the dangerous driving of a motor vehicle by an accused is one of the causes of the death of another person is sufficient to support the conviction of an accused.

Driving of dangerously defective vehicle s. 54

(2) Where a mechanically propelled vehicle is driven in a public place while there is a defect affecting the vehicle which the owner thereof knows of or could have discovered by the exercise of ordinary care and which is such that the vehicle is, when in motion a danger to the public, such owner shall be guilty of an offence.

(3) Where a person is charged with an offence under (2). it shall be a good defence to the charge for him to show that the vehicle was driven on the occasion in question by another person and that such driving was unauthorised.

"defect" The defect must be one which affects the vehicle when driven and in motion.

"owner thereof knows" The owner, who need not be the registered owner (see also interpretation above) must have had knowledge of the defect, this is the *mens rea* required.

The penalty is a £350 fine and or three months imprisonment. An ancillary disqualification order may be made, however there is a mandatory disqualification in the case of a third or subsequent offence within three years. Otherwise the court may endorse a person's licence, however there is a mandatory endorsement of a person's license for a second offence within three years.

Dangerous parking s. 55(1)

(1) A person shall not park a vehicle in a public place if, when so parked, the vehicle would be likely to cause danger to other persons using that place.

(2) A person who contravenes subsection(1) shall be guilty of an offence and shall be liable on summary conviction-

(a) in the case of-

(i) a first offence during lighting-up hours, or

(ii) a second or subsequent offence is

a £350 fine and or three months imprisonment, and

(b) in any other case a £150 fine and or one months imprisonment.

(3) Where a member of the Garda Siochana is of opinion that a person is committing or has committed an offence under this section, he may

arrest the person without warrant.

"Lighting-up time" is defined in the Road Traffic (Lighting of Vehicles) Regulations 1963, Art 3 as the period commencing one-half hour after the sunset and lasting to one-half hour before sunrise on the following day.

The Road Traffic General Bye-laws 1964, contains "Rules for parking" at bye-law 26 which include:

When parking a driver shall ensure that the vehicle-

(a) is not likely to cause inconvenience, to obstruct or endanger other traffic, or to obstruct the view of another driver at or near a road junction, corner or bend or at or near a brow of a hill, or to prevent another driver from seeing a traffic sign;

(b) will not obstruct or interfere with an entrance to, or an exit from, a fire brigade station or ambulance station;

(c) will not interfere with the normal flow of traffic;

(d) will not wholly or partly on a zebra crossing or within thirty feet of a zebra crossing or pedestrian lights;

(f) will not obstruct an entrance for vehicles to premises, save when the occupier of the premises consents;

(h) will not, in such a way as to interfere with the free movement of pedestrians along a footway, be wholly or partly on the footway or projecting over the footway, or be wholly or partly on a cycle track;

These rules would give an indication of the type of parking that would not come within the section.

Driving offences while under the influence of alcohol or drugs

The law governing the driving or being in charge of a vehicle while under the influence of an intoxicant, is to be found in sections 49, 50 and 51 of Part V of the 1961 Act as amended by the 1978 Act; and the breath / blood / urine tests and procedure relating to same are to be found in the 1978 Act.

Driving while under the influence s. 49

1(a) A person shall not drive or attempt to drive a mechanically propelled vehicle in a public place while he is <u>under the influence</u> of an intoxicant to such an extent as to be incapable of having proper control of the vehicle.

(b) In this subsection "intoxicant" includes alcohol and drugs and any combination of drugs or of drugs and alcohol.

2. A person shall not drive or attempt to drive a mechanically propelled vehicle in a public place while there is present in his body a quantity of alcohol such that, within three hours of so driving or attempting to drive the concentration of alcohol in his <u>blood</u> will exceed a concentration of 100 milligrammes of alcohol per 100 millilitres of blood.

3. A person shall not drive or attempt to drive a mechanically

propelled vehicle in a public place while there is present in his body a quantity of alcohol such that, within three hours of so driving or attempting to drive the concentration of alcohol in his <u>urine</u> will exceed a concentration of 135 milligrammes of alcohol per 100 millilitres of urine.

(6) a member of the Garda Siochana may arrest without warrant a person who in the member's opinion is committing or has committed an offence under this section.

The contravention of subsection (1), (2) or (3) is an offence, for which the penalty on summary conviction is £1,000 fine and or six months imprisonment. There is a mandatory disqualification and such disqualification must be for not less than one year in the case of a first offence and not less than three years in the case of a second or any subsequent offence.

Where a person is charged with an offence under section 49, he may be found guilty of an offence under section 50 below.

Distinct offences

Section 49 creates six of distinct offences:

To drive, or to attempt to drive

(1) under the influence of an intoxicant.

(2) with a certain concentration of alcohol in the blood.

(3) with a certain concentration of alcohol in the urine.

Attempt

State (Prendergast) V Porter (1961)

The accused was charged with attempting to drive while drunk. He had attempted to turn the starting handle of the vehicle, then seemed to touch the dashboard. Having again turned the starting handle, he sat on the driving seat and the engine turned over but did not start. On a case stated it was held that these actions amounted to an attempt to drive.

Section 49(1)

Attorney General (Ruddy) V Kenny (1960)

The Supreme Court held that a Garda may give evidence of his opinion that the driver of a vehicle was drunk.

State (McGroddy) V Carr (1975)

It was held by the Supreme Court that in section 49, the reference to intoxicating liquor or a drug creates a single offence.

State (Collins) V Kelleher (1983)

It was held by the Supreme Court that, a charge brought under 1(a) of section 49 and one brought under 3. of that section are alternative charges.

Section 49 (2) & (3)

Director of Public Prosecutions V O'Connor (1985)

These offences require proof based entirely on chemical analysis

221

showing a concentration, beyond a permitted level, of alcohol in the blood or urine (as the case may be).

Garda power of arrest

There is much case law in this area:

Hobbs V Hurley (1980)

It was held by the High Court that a Garda making an arrest is not required to have in mind any of the specific offences created by the section. The opinion upon which an arrest is based must be a reasonable one and must result from an honest belief arrived at after facts have been ascertained and considered. In forming this opinion a Garda is entitled to rely on his own observations alone or on those observations together with the positive finding on the alcolyser test. However a breath test is not necessary to justify an arrest.

Director of Public Prosecutions V Gilmore (1981)

The Supreme Court held that a positive result on the breath testing apparatus referred to in section 12 of the 1978 Act is sufficient to justify the forming of an opinion of the Garda that a person is in breach of Section 49 (2) or (3)..

Director of Public Prosecutions V O'Connor (1985)

The Supreme Court held that when a Garda stated that he was arresting a defendant, this should be taken to mean that he had formed the required opinion.

Director of Public Prosecutions V Corrigan (1986)

The High Court stated that an arrest is not unlawful merely because it did not occur in a public place or because Gardai were in law trespassers.

Director of Public Prosecutions V Gaffney (1987)

The defendant was charged with a number of offences under the 1961 Act. He had driven through a Garda checkpoint was followed and stopped in the driveway of a dwelling house. He was requested to stop, refused to do so and continues into the house. The Gardai made two requests to enter the house, but were refused by the defendant's brother (whom they subsequently arrested for assault). On a third occasion the Gardai entered the dwelling and arrested the defendant.

It was held by the Supreme Court:

1. The arrest of the defendant was in violation of Article 40.5 of the Constitution, in view of the fact that they had twice been refused entry there could be no presumption that there was an invitation to enter, either as a matter of fact or law merely because there was no express refusal.

2. Section 107 did not authorise the Gardai to enter a dwelling without the owner's consent, since its terms only authorised arrest without warrant where there was a refusal to give specified information.

Director of Public Prosecutions V Donoghue (1987)

Where an opinion has been reasonably arrived at and honestly held, it must be accepted.

Forgery

Director of Public Prosecutions V Lynch (1990)

In the District Court it was accepted that there had been no evidence to validate an arrest under section 49 since the Garda had not informed the respondent that he (the Garda) had formed the relevant opinion.

It was held by O'Hanlon J. in the High Court that the District Justice was correct in dismissing the charge. It was not sufficient for a Garda to state to the person under arrest merely that he was being arrested under section 49, and that the Court should not always infer that the Garda had concurrently formed the opinion that the person placed under arrest is committing or has committed an offence under section 49; and it was only where the surrounding circumstances clearly indicated that such opinion must have been formed that the court could draw such an inference in the absence of positive evidence to that effect.

Director of Public Prosecutions V McCreesh (1991)

The defendant failed to stop for a Garda patrol car, he was followed to the driveway of his house.

A Garda from the patrol car approached the door of the Defendant's house, the defendant told the Garda he was a trespasser and that he should leave. An arrest was made under section 49 and there was a subsequent charge under section 13 of the 1978 Act. It was argued on behalf of the defendant that the arrest was invalid, it being a breach of Article 40.5 of the Constitution which provides: The dwelling of every citizen is inviolable and shall not be forcibly entered save in accordance with law.

It was held by the Supreme Court that since section 49 did not confer a power of arrest on the Gardai where they were trespassing the charge must be dismissed.

Director of Public Prosecutions V Brady (1991)

It was held by O'Hanlon J. in the High Court that if the Defendant had been charged with the offence of failure to provide a breath test under section 12 of the 1978 Act, it would be a good defence if no evidence had been adduced to show that the Garda had formed the necessary opinion that the defendant had consumed intoxicating liquor before requiring the defendant to undergo the breath test.

Director of Public Prosecutions V Mooney (1992)

It was held by Blancy J. in the High Court that the arrest by a Garda under section 49(6), on his suspicion of the suspect committing or having committed and offence under subsections (2) or (3) is not invalidated where the reason given was that he was being arrested "for drunken driving"; technical or precise language is not required

Per Curiam Since the person arrested does not need to be informed of the reason for his arrest if the circumstances as such that he must know the general nature of the alleged offence for which he is detained, it is doubtful if an arrest is invalid where no reason is given but where the suspect had blown into a breathalyser and the reading had been positive: he must therefore have been aware of the reason for his arrest.

Garda need not give evidence that he had formed opinion.

Director of Public Prosecutions V O'Suilleabhain (1993)

The defendant was involved in a road traffic accident. A Garda arrived on the scene, he gave evidence that he got a smell of intoxicating liquor from the defendant's breath and formed the opinion that he had consumed intoxicating liquor. The Garda informed the defendant that he was arresting him under section 49(6) for offences under section 49 (2) and (3).

It was held by Carroll J. in the High Court that all the circumstances known to the Garda at the time of the arrest amounted to sufficient evidence to form the opinion that an offence under section 49 (2) or (3) had been committed and the Garda showed that he had formed this opinion by arresting him.

Being in charge while drunk s. 50

(1) (a) a person shall be guilty of an offence who, when in charge of a mechanically propelled vehicle in a public place with intent to drive or attempt to drive the vehicle (but not driving or attempting to drive it), is under the influence of an intoxicant to such an extent as to be incapable of having proper control of the vehicle.

(b) In this subsection "intoxicant" includes alcohol and drugs and any combination of drugs or of drugs and alcohol.

(2) A person shall be guilty of an offence who is in charge of a mechanically propelled vehicle in a public place with intent to drive or attempt to drive the vehicle (but not driving or attempting to drive it) and in whose body there is present a quantity of alcohol such that, within three hours after having been so in charge of the vehicle, the concentration of alcohol in his blood will exceed a concentration of 100 milligrammes of alcohol per 100 millilitres of blood.

(3) A person shall be guilty of an offence who is in charge of a mechanically propelled vehicle in a public place with intent to drive or attempt to drive the vehicle (but not driving or attempting to drive it) and in whose body there is present a quantity of alcohol such that, within three hours after having been so in charge of the vehicle, the concentration of alcohol in his urine will exceed a concentration of 135 milligrammes of alcohol per 100 millilitres of urine.

Whether a person is or is not "in charge" is a question of fact to be decided in each case:

Crichton V Burrell (1951)

It was held that the reference must be to a person in *de facto* control, even though he may not be at the time actually driving or attempting to drive.

Leach V Evans (1952)

It was held that an intending driver may be in charge of his vehicle before he enters it to drive it.2

Haines V Roberts (1953)

It was held that a person who takes a vehicle out on to the road remains in charge of it until he puts someone else in charge of it.

(5) In a prosecution for an offence under this section it shall be presumed that the defendant intended to drive or attempt to drive the vehicle until he show the contrary.

(8) A member of the Garda Siochana may arrest without warrant a person who in the member's opinion is committing or has committed an offence under this section.

The penalty on summary conviction, in the case of a first offence is a £350 fine and or three months imprisonment or in the case of a second or subsequent offence is £1,000 fine and or six months imprisonment.

Where a person is charged with an offence under section 50, he may be found guilty of an offence under section 49 above.

Reduction in concentrations

A Road Traffic Bill may be introduced by the Government it is to propose the reduction in the proportion of alcohol in respect of the above offences. The reduction in respect of blood is expected to be from 100 milligrammes to 80 milligrammes and in respect of urine is expected to be from 135 milligrammes to 107 milligrammes.

Driving of animal drawn vehicle or pedal cycle s. 51

1 A person shall not, in a public place;

(a) drive or attempt to drive, or be in charge of an animal drawn vehicle, or

(b) drive or attempt to drive a pedal cycle.

While he is under the influence of intoxicating liquor or a drug to such an extent as to be incapable of having proper control of the vehicle or cycle.

(4) Where a member of the Garda Siochana is of opinion that a person is committing or has committed an offence under this section, he may arrest the person without warrant.

The penalty on summary conviction in the case of a first offence which relates to an animal drawn vehicle is a £150 fine and or one months imprisonment, in the case of any other offence under this section the penalty is £350 fine and or three months imprisonment.

Obligation to provide preliminary breath specimen s. 12 (1978 Act)

(1) Whenever a member of the Garda Siochana is of the opinion that a person in charge of a mechanically propelled vehicle in a public place has consumed intoxicating liquor, he may require the person to provide, by exhaling into an apparatus for indicating the presence of alcohol in the breath a specimen of his breath and may indicate the manner in which he is to comply with the requirement.

(2) A person who refuses or fails to comply forthwith with a requirement under this section, or to comply forthwith with such a requirement in a manner indicated by a member of the Garda Siochana, shall be guilty of an offence and liable on summary conviction to a £1,000 fine and or six months imprisonment.

(3) A member of the Garda Siochana may arrest without warrant a person who in the member's opinion is committing or has committed an offence under this section.

(4) In a prosecution for an offence under this section it shall be presumed until the contrary is shown that an apparatus provided by a member of the Garda Siochana for the purpose of enabling a person to provide a specimen of breath is an apparatus for indicating the presence of alcohol in the breath.

It is not an offence to have a positive breath test.

Director of Public Prosecutions V Joyce (1985)

It was held by the Supreme Court that a request by a Garda to require any person to provide a specimen of his breath must be in a public place and that person must then be in charge of a mechanically propelled vehicle in such public place. Section 12 is limited to these powers.

See D. P. P. V Gilmore (1981) above.

Obligation to provide specimen at Garda Station s. 13 (1978 Act)

(1) Where a person arrested under section 49(6) for driving while drunk or under Section 12(3) above has been brought to a Garda Station, a member of the Garda Siochana may at his discretion do either or both of the following:

(a) require the person to provide, by exhaling into an apparatus for indicating the concentration of alcohol in breath or blood, a specimen of his breath,

(b) require the person either to permit a designated registered medical practitioner to take from the person a specimen of his blood or, at the option of the person, to provide for the designated registered medical practitioner a specimen of the persons urine.

(2) A person who, refuses or fails to comply forthwith with a requirement, under subsection (1)(a) shall be guilty of an offence and liable on summary conviction to a £1,000 fine and or six months imprisonment.

(3) A person who, following a requirement under subsection 1(b)-

(a) refuses or fails to comply with such a requirement, or

(b) refuses or fails to comply with a requirement, of a designated registered medical practitioner in relation to the taking under this section of a specimen of blood or the provision under this section of a specimen of urine,

shall be guilty of an offence and liable on summary conviction to a £1,000 fine and or six months imprisonment.

(4) In a prosecution for an offence under this section it shall be presumed until the contrary is shown that an apparatus provided by a member of the Garda Siochana for the purpose of enabling a person to provide a specimen of breath is an apparatus for indicating the presence of alcohol in the breath or blood.

Section 14 of the 1978 Act makes similar provisions in respect of a person arrested under section 50(8) of the 1961 Act (see above).

Prohibition of driving without a driving licence s. 38

(1) A person shall not drive a mechanically propelled vehicle in a public place unless he holds a driving licence for the time being having effect and licensing him to drive the vehicle.

(2) (a) A person who contravenes subsection (1) of this section shall be guilty of an offence.

(b) In a prosecution for an offence under this subsection, it shall be presumed, until the contrary is shown by the defendant, that he did not, at the time he drove the vehicle, hold a driving licence then having effect and licensing him to drive the vehicle.

(3) The owner of a mechanically propelled vehicle shall not employ a person to drive the vehicle in a public place unless the person holds a driving licence for the time being having effect and licensing him to drive the vehicle.

(4) (a) A person who contravenes subsection (3) of this section shall be guilty of an offence.

(b) In a prosecution for an offence under this subsection, it shall be presumed, until the contrary is shown by the defendant, that the person employed to drive the vehicle did not, at the time he drove the vehicle, hold a driving licence then having effect and licensing him to drive the vehicle.

(5) A person-

(a) who is summarily convicted of the offence of contravening subsection (1) and was at the time he committed the offence-

(i) disqualified for holding a driving licence, or

(ii) a person required to produce a certificate of competency or a certificate of fitness before obtaining a driving licence,

shall be liable in lieu of the punishment mentioned in section 102 (the general penalty) to a £1,000 fine and or six months imprisonment.

A contravention of this section, otherwise than is mentioned in subsection (5) is subject to the general penalty outlined in section 102.

Prohibition on applying for a licence when disqualified s. 39

(1) A person shall not apply for a driving licence if he is disqualified for applying therefor.

(2) A person who contravenes subsection (1) shall be guilty of an offence and shall be liable on summary conviction to a £1,000 fine and or six months imprisonment.

Compulsory insurance s. 56

(1) A person shall not use in a public place a mechanically propelled vehicle unless either a vehicle insurer or an exempted person would be liable for injury caused by the negligent use of the vehicle by him at that time or there is in force at that time, an approved policy of insurance covering (exclusive of excepted persons) the negligent use of the vehicle

at that time by the user, in accordance with this Act.

(3) Where a person contravenes subsection (1) he, and if he is not the owner of the vehicle, such owner shall each be guilty of an offence and liable on summary conviction is a £1,000 fine and or six months imprisonment.

(4) Where, in a prosecution under this section, it is shown that, a demand having been made under section 69 (Production of certificate on demand) of the Act-

(a) the person on whom the demand was made refused or failed to produce a certificate of insurance or certificate of exemption then and there, or

(b) such person, having duly produced such certificate consequent upon the demand, refused or failed to permit the member of the Garda Siochana to whom such certificate was produced to read and examine it.

it shall be presumed until the contrary is shown by the defendant, that the vehicle was used in contravention of this section.

(5) Where a person charged under this section is the owner of the vehicle, it shall be a good defence for such person to show that the vehicle was used without his consent and either that he had taken all reasonable precautions to prevent its being used or that it was used by his servant contrary to his orders.

(6) Where a person charged under this section was the servant of the owner of the vehicle, it shall be a good defence for such person to show that he was using the vehicle in obedience to the express orders of the owner.

Insurance Disc

The Road Traffic (Insurance Disc) Regulations 1984, which are made under the provisions of sections 5 and 11 of the 1961 Act, provide at 3(1) Where a certificate of insurance is issued to a person the vehicle insurer shall issue to such person one insurance disc for each vehicle to which the certificate relates. Which disc must be displayed on the vehicle.

By section 11 of the 1961 Act, the non-compliance by a person using a vehicle in a public place of regulations made by the Minister is an offence and is liable to the general penalty provided for in the Act.

Motor tax

The Finance (Excise Duties)(Vehicles) Act, 1952 at section 1 requires that vehicle excise duty be paid on motor vehicles, "vehicle excise duty" means the duty of excise charged and levied under that Act. Where vehicle excise duty is chargeable and is unpaid, then any person, who at any time while the duty remains unpaid, uses parks or otherwise keeps the vehicle in a public place or causes another person to do such, shall be guilty of an offence. The word "use" includes keeping or leaving a vehicle stationary.

The Roads Act, 1920, section 13(1) provides that if a person uses a vehicle for which a license is not in force, he shall be liable to an excise penalty of £20 or an excise penalty equal to three times the amount of duty payable in respect of the vehicle, whichever is the greater. This excise penalty may be recovered and enforced upon an information by any member of the Garda Siochana before a court of summary jurisdiction.

Other motor vehicle offences

Speed s. 47

A person shall not drive a mechanically propelled vehicle at a speed exceeding a speed limit applying in relation to the vehicle and to do so shall be an offence.

In this section "speed limit" means a limit which is:

(a) an ordinary speed limit,

(b) a general speed limit,

(c) the built-up area speed limit, or

(d) a special speed limit.

Obstruction of traffic s. 98

(1) A person shall not do any act (whether of commission or omission) which causes or is likely to cause traffic any public place to be obstructed.

(2) A person who contravenes subsection (1) of this section shall be guilty of an offence.

(3) Where a person is charged with an offence under this section, it shall be a good defence to show that there was lawful authority for the act complained of or that it was due to unavoidable accident.

The general penalty applies in the case of this offence.

O'Connor V Leonard

It was held that the section was not an absolute and unqualified prohibition, and the test of reasonableness had to be applied.

Taking vehicle without authority s. 112

(1) (a) A person shall not use or take possession of a mechanically propelled vehicle without the consent of the owner thereof or other lawful authority.

(b) Where possession of a vehicle has been taken in contravention of this subsection, a person who knows of the taking shall not allow himself to be carried in or on it without the consent of the owner thereof or other lawful authority.

(2) A person who contravenes subsection (1) shall be guilty of an offence for which the penalty (a) on summary conviction is a £1,000 fine and or twelve months imprisonment, and (b) on conviction on indictment a £2,000 fine and or five years imprisonment.

(3) A person shall not use or take possession of a pedal cycle without the consent of the owner thereof or other lawful authority.

(4) A person who contravenes subsection (3) shall be guilty of an offence.

(5) Where a person is charged with an offence under this section, it shall be a good defence to the charge for him to show that, when he did the act alleged to constitute the offence, he believed, and had reasonable grounds for believing, that he had lawful authority for doing that act.

(6) Where a member of the Garda Siochana has reasonable grounds for believing that a person is committing or has committed an offence under this section, he may arrest the person without warrant,

(7) Where, when a person is tried on indictment or summarily for the larceny of a vehicle, the jury, or, in the case of a summary trial, the District Court, is of opinion that he was not guilty of the larceny of the vehicle but was guilty of an offence under this section in relation to the vehicle, the jury or court may find him guilty of that offence and he may be sentenced accordingly.

Unauthorised interference with vehicle s. 113

(1) A person shall not, without lawful authority or reasonable cause, interfere or attempt to interfere with the mechanism of a mechanically propelled vehicle while it is stationary in a public place, or get on or into or attempt to get on or into the vehicle while it is so stationary.

(2) A person who contravenes subsection (1) shall be guilty of an offence for which the penalty on summary conviction is a £350 fine and or three months imprisonment,

(3) Where a member of the Garda Siochana has reasonable grounds for believing that a person is committing or has committed an offence under this section, he may arrest the person without warrant,

(4) This section shall not apply to a person taking, in relation to a mechanically propelled vehicle which is obstructing his lawful entry or exit to or from any place, such steps as are reasonably necessary to move the vehicle by human propulsion sufficient to end the obstruction.

(5) Where a person is charged with an offence under this section, it shall be a good defence to the charge for him to show that, when he did the act alleged to constitute the offence, he believed, and had reasonable grounds for believing, that he had lawful authority for doing that act.

Unlawful seizure of vehicles

By the Criminal Law (Jurisdiction) Act, 1976 section 10, a person who unlawfully by force, or by any other form of intimidation, seizes or exercises control of any vehicle shall be guilty of an offence, for which the penalty is fifteen years imprisonment.

Giving false particulars s. 115

(1) Where a person is required by this Act or regulations made thereunder to furnish particulars in connection with an application for the grant or issue of a licence plate or certificate or otherwise in connection with a licence plate, certificate or vehicle, he shall not furnish

pursuant to the requirement any particulars which to his knowledge are false or in any material respect misleading.

(2) A person who contravenes subsection (1) shall be guilty of an offence.

(3) Where, in a prosecution under subsection (2) with respect to particulars in connection with an application for the grant or issue of a licence plate or certificate, such grant or issue and an application therefor are proved, it shall be presumed, until the contrary is shown by the defendant, that the person to whom the licence plate or certificate was granted or issued made the application.

(4) A person shall not forge or fraudulently alter or use, or fraudulently lend to, or allow to be used by, any other person, any licence, plate, badge or certificate issued under this Act or under Regulations thereunder or a special permit under regulations under section 13 of this Act.

(5) Where a person contravenes subsection (4) shall be guilty of an offence.

(6) A person who is guilty of an offence under this section shall be liable on summary conviction to a £350 fine and or six months imprisonment.

The Road Traffic (Construction, Equipment and Use of Vehicles) (Amendment) (No. 2) Regulations, 1978, made under the provisions of sections 5 and 11 of the Act; make it obligatory for the driver and front seat passengers in cars, station wagons and light goods vehicles first registered on or after the 1st June 1971, to wear safety belts of prescribed standards. Provision is also made for the obligatory wearing of crash helmets of prescribed standards by the drivers of motor cycles and their passengers. In both cases the general penalty applies where there is a breach of the regulations.

Safety belts

5.(1) A person driving a vehicle to which this part of these Regulations applies and a person occupying a front seat of such a vehicle as a passenger shall, ... wear a safety belt.

6. The driver of a vehicle ... shall not permit a person to occupy a front seat-

(a) where the person is under 17 years of age and is over 150 centimetres in height unless the person is wearing a safety belt;

(b) where the person is under 12 years of age and is under 150 centimetres in height unless a means of restraint for the safety of the person is used,

unless in each case, no reasonable alternative seating accommodation is available for the person.

7. Where a person has been found not to have complied with article 5(1) of these Regulation and the person so found produces to a member of the Garda Siochana, a certificate of a registered medical practitioner

that, because of physical or mental disability or for medical or psychological reasons, it was undesirable or inadvisable for the person to wear a safety belt on the occasion in question, the person shall not be regarded as being in breach of the requirements.

8.(1) In a prosecution of a person for an offence under article 5(1) or (6), it shall be a good defence for the defendant to satisfy the court that he had a special and substantial reason for not wearing a safety belt or that it was undesirable or inadvisable for him to wear a safety belt because of physical or mental disability or because of medical or psychological considerations, or that it would because of inconvenience or risk to person or property, have been unreasonable for him to wear a safety belt having regard to nature of the use of the vehicle at the time of the alleged offence.

(2) In a prosecution of a person for an offence under article 5(1) or (6), it shall be a good defence for the defendant to satisfy the court that the safety belt being used at the time of the alleged offence afforded a level of protection not less than that afforded by a safety belt as defined in article 4.

Crash helmets

10. The driver of a motor cycle and a passenger carried on the motor cycle shall each wear a crash helmet while the motor cycle is used in a public place.

11. The driver of a motor cycle shall not, while using it in a public place, permit a passenger to be carried on the motor cycle unless the passenger is wearing a crash helmet.

12. In a prosecution for an offence under article 10 or 11 it shall be a good defence to satisfy the court that the driver, or, in the case of an offence under article 11, the passenger was wearing a helmet at the time of the alleged offence which afforded a level of protection not less than that afforded by a crash helmet as defined in article 9.

Additional provisions

Consequential disqualification order s. 26

(1) Where a person is convicted of an offence specified in the Second Schedule to this Act, the court shall make an order (in this act referred to as a consequential disqualification order) declaring him to be disqualified from holding a driving licence.

(2) A disqualification under this section shall disqualify the convicted person for holding any driving licence whatsoever during a specified period or during a specified period and thereafter until he has produced to the appropriate licensing authority a certificate of competency or a certificate of fitness or both.

(3)(a) The period of a disqualification specified in a consequential disqualification order shall, where the person to whom the order relates is convicted of-

(i) an offence under section 49 of this Act,

(ii) an offence under section 53 of this Act where the contravention caused death or serious bodily harm to another person,

(iii) an offence under section 13 (2) or (3) (of the 1978 Act)

be not less than one year in the case of a first offence and not less than three years in the case of a second or any subsequent offence.

(4) The period of disqualification specified in a consequential disqualification order shall, in a case not coming within subsection(3) of this section, be not less than six months on a conviction of an offence.

Ancillary disqualification order s. 27

(1) (a) Where a person is convicted of an offence under this Act or otherwise in relation to a mechanically propelled vehicle or the driving of any such vehicle (other than an offence in relation to which section 26 applies) or a crime or offence in the commission of which a mechanically propelled vehicle was used, the court may, without prejudice to the infliction of any other punishment authorised by law, make an order declaring the person convicted to be disqualified for holding a driving licence.

(b) A disqualification under this subsection-

(i) shall disqualify the convicted person either for holding any driving licence whatsoever or for holding a driving licence in respect of a class or classes of mechanically propelled vehicles, and

(ii) shall so disqualify him during a specified period or during a specified period and thereafter until he has produced to the appropriate licensing authority a certificate of competency or a certificate of fitness or both.

Special disqualification orders s. 28

(1) Where an officer of the Garda Siochana has reasonable grounds for believing that a person who is the holder of a driving licence is by reason of disease or physical or mental disability unfit to drive any mechanically propelled vehicle whatsoever or any class or classes of mechanically propelled vehicles covered by such licence, such officer may apply to the District Court having jurisdiction in the place in which such person ordinarily resides for an order under this subsection, and if the Judge is satisfied that such person is by reason of disease or physical or mental disability unfit to drive any mechanically propelled vehicle whatsoever or any class or classes of mechanically propelled vehicles as are within the terms of the application, he may make the appropriate order declaring such person to be disqualified for holding a driving licence until he produces to the appropriate licensing authority a certificate of fitness.

(2) Where an officer of the Garda Siochana has reasonable grounds for believing that a person who is the holder of a driving licence is incompetent to drive any mechanically propelled vehicle whatsoever or any class or classes of mechanically propelled vehicles covered by such

licence, such officer may apply to the District Court having jurisdiction in the place in which such person ordinarily resides for an order under this subsection, and if the Judge is satisfied that such person is incompetent to drive any mechanically propelled vehicle whatsoever or any class or classes of mechanically propelled vehicles as are within the terms of the application, he may make the appropriate order declaring such person to be disqualified for holding a driving licence until he produces to the appropriate licensing authority a certificate of fitness.

Removal of orders s. 29

(1) A person in respect of whom a consequential or ancillary disqualification order specifying a period of disqualification exceeding six months has been made may, at any time and from time to time after the expiration of three months from the beginning of the period of disqualification and before the expiration of that period, apply to the court which made the order, for the removal of the disqualification, and that court, if it considers that circumstances exist which justify such a course, may by order remove the disqualification as from a specified date not earlier than six months after the beginning of the period of disqualification.

People (D. P. P.) V O'Byrne (1989)

It was held by the Court of Criminal Appeal (on an application under section 29) in allowing the application and restoring the driving licence, that disqualification from driving was not a primary punishment but an adjudication on an accused's fitness to drive. In this case the wrong principles were applied by the trial judge to the disqualification and its removal. Matters which the court must consider in deciding whether or not to restore a driving licence include the applicant's fitness to drive, the nature of the offence, and his conduct sine the original conviction.

Order for endorsement s. 36

(1) Where a person is convicted of an offence under the Act or otherwise in relation to a mechanically propelled vehicle or the driving of any such vehicle or of a crime or offence in the commission of which a mechanically propelled vehicle was used, the court, if it does not make a consequential or ancillary disqualification order, may (and in the case of an offence which would be an offence which such as is specified in paragraph 1, 2, 3, 5, 5A, 5B, 7, 8, 9, 10 or 11 or subparagraph (b) of paragraph 6 of the second schedule to this Act if it were a second or any subsequent offence within any period of three years, shall) by order direct particulars of the conviction to be endorsed on the driving licence held by such a person or, if he is not the holder of a driving licence but subsequently a driving licence is granted to him, on that driving licence.

Offences under the Act involving consequential disqualification orders as contained in second schedule:

1. Using mechanically propelled vehicle without test certificate (section 18(2));

2. Driving mechanically propelled vehicle before remedying dangerous defect (section 20(10));
3. Driving mechanically propelled vehicle when unfit (section 48);
5. Being in charge while under influence of intoxicating liquor or drugs (section 50);
5A. Blood and urine tests (section 13 & 14 1978);
5B. Careless driving (section 52);
6(b). Dangerous driving of mechanically propelled vehicle;
7. Driving of dangerously defective vehicle (section 54);
8. Parking mechanically propelled vehicle in dangerous position (section 55);
9. Use of mechanically propelled vehicle not insured or guaranteed (section 56);
10. Failure to fulfil duties on occurrence of accident (section 106);
11. Taking mechanically propelled vehicle without authority (section 112(2)).

Director of Public Prosecutions V O'Brien (1989)

It was held by the Supreme Court, that on a construction of section 52 of the Act, a conviction of an offence under that section led to a mandatory endorsement pursuant to the provisions of section 36, of the particulars of the offence on the defendant's driving licence.

General penalty s. 102

(1) Where a person is guilty of an offence under any section or subsection of a section of this Act and, apart from this section and disregarding any disqualifications that may be capable of being imposed, no penalty is provided for the offence, such person shall be liable on summary conviction-

(a) In the case of a first offence a £150 fine,

(b) In the case of a second offence under that section or subsection, or a third, or subsequent offence other than an offence referred to in the next paragraph, a £350 fine,

(c) In the case of a third or subsequent offence (being so in any period of twelve consecutive months) to a £350 fine and or three month imprisonment

Also note the provisions of section 2 of the Courts (No. 2) Act, 1986 at section 2 regarding imprisonment in default of due payment of fine at page 3.

Notice of offence s. 104

Where a person is charged with an offence under section's 47, 51A, 52, or 53, he shall not be convicted unless either-

(a) He was warned at the time at which the offence is alleged to have been committed, or within twenty four hours thereafter, that the question of prosecuting him would be considered, or

(b) Within fourteen days after the commission of the offence, a summons for the offence was served on him, or

(c) Within fourteen days a notice in writing stating the time and place at which the offence is alleged to have been committed and stating briefly the act or acts alleged to constitute the offence and stating the intention to prosecute him therefor was served personally or by registered post on him or (in the case of a mechanically propelled vehicle) on the registered owner of the vehicle in relation to which the offence is alleged to have been committed:

Provided that-

(i) failure to comply with this requirement shall not be a bar to conviction in a case in which the court is satisfied that-

(I) the accused by his own conduct contributed to the failure, or

(IA) notwithstanding the failure, the accused was at all material times aware of the occurrence in respect of which the prosecution for such an offence is brought,

(II) in case the offence alleged to have been committed is in relation to a mechanically propelled vehicle, neither the name and address of the registered owner of the vehicle could with reasonable diligence have been ascertained in time for a summons to be served or for a notice to be served as aforesaid, or

(III) in case the offence alleged to have been committed is not in relation to a mechanically propelled vehicle, the name and address of the accused could with reasonable diligence have been ascertained in time for a summons to be served or for a notice to be served as aforesaid, and

(ii) it shall be presumed, until the contrary is shown by the defendant, that the requirement of this section has been complied with.

Duties on occurrence of an accident s. 106

(1) Where injury is caused to person or property in a public place and a vehicle is involved in the occurrence of the injury (whether the use of the vehicle was or was not the cause of the injury), the following provisions shall have effect:

(a) If the vehicle is not stationary after the occurrence, the driver of the vehicle shall stop the vehicle;

(b) the driver or other person in charge of the vehicle shall keep the vehicle at or near the place of the occurrence for a period which is reasonable in all the circumstances of the case and having regard to the provisions of this section;

(c) the driver of the vehicle or, if he is killed or incapacitated, the person then in charge of the vehicle shall give on demand the appropriate information to a member of the Garda Siochana or, if no such member is present, to one person entitled under this section to demand same:

(d) if-

(i) injury is caused to property other than that of the driver of the vehicle and for any reason he or, if he is killed or incapacitated, the person then in charge of the vehicle does not at the place of the occurrence give the appropriate information to a person entitled under this section to demand it, or

(ii) injury is caused to a person other than the driver of the vehicle, the driver of the vehicle or, if he is killed or incapacitated, the person then in charge of the vehicle shall, unless he has already given the appropriate information to a member of the Garda Siochana, report the occurrence as soon as possible to such a member and, if necessary, shall go for that purpose to the nearest convenient Garda station and also give on demand the appropriate information to the member.

(2) Where-

(a) a member of the Garda Siochana has reasonable grounds for believing that an injury has been caused to person or property in a public place and that a vehicle was involved in the occurrence of the injury (whether the use of the vehicle was or was not the cause of the injury), and

(b) the member is not aware of the place where the vehicle is being kept, the member may require the owner of the vehicle to state to the member where the vehicle is being kept and the owner shall comply with that requirement.

(3) A person who contravenes subsection (1) or subsection (2) of this section shall be guilty of an offence and shall be liable on summary conviction-

(a) in a case in which injury is caused to person a £1,000 fine and or six months imprisonment, and

(b) in any other case a £350 fine and or three months imprisonment.

(4) In this section "appropriate information" means the name and address of the person required by this section to give such information, the name and address of the owner of the vehicle of which such person is the driver or is in charge, the identification mark of such vehicle under the Roads Act, 1920, or any other enactment and particulars of the insurance of the vehicle pursuant to this Act.

(5) The persons entitled under this section to demand the appropriate information are-

(a) in the case of injury to a person, that person or, where that person is killed or incapacitated, any one other person for the time being having charge of the person so injured by reason of family relationship, the relationship of master and servant or otherwise,

(b) in the case of injury to property, the owner of the property or, where the owner of the property is killed or injured or is not present, any one person having charge of the property,

(c) where there is no person entitled under whichever of the foregoing paragraphs is applicable, any one person who was present when the injury was inflicted and who is not the employer of or in the employment or company of the person required to give the information.

Duty to give information s. 107

(1) Where a member of the Garda Siochana alleges to a person using a mechanically propelled vehicle, that the member suspects that such

person has committed a specified offence under this Act, the member may demand of such person his name and address and may, if such person refuses or fails to give his name and address or gives a name and address which the member has reasonable grounds for believing to be false or misleading, arrest such person without warrant.

(2) Where a member of the Garda Siochana has reasonable grounds for believing that an offence under this Act has been committed and that the vehicle in relation to which the offence was committed does not carry its identification mark under the Roads Act, 1920, or any other enactment, the member may arrest without warrant the person whom he has reasonable grounds for believing was using the vehicle when the offence was so believed to have been committed.

(3) Where a person, when his name and address is demanded of him under this section, refuses or fails to give his name and address or gives a name and address which is false or misleading, such person shall be guilty of an offence.

(4) Where a member of the Garda Siochana has reasonable grounds for believing that there has been an offence under this Act involving the use of a mechanically propelled vehicle-

(a) the owner of the vehicle shall, if required by the member state whether he was or was not actually using the vehicle at the material time and, if he fails to do so shall be guilty of an offence,

(b) if the owner of the vehicle states that he was not actually using it at the material time, he shall give such information as he may be required by the member to give as to the identity of the person who was actually using it at the time and, if he fails to do so, shall be guilty of an offence unless he shows to the satisfaction of the court that he did not know and could not with reasonable diligence have ascertained who that person was,

(c) any person other than the owner of the vehicle shall, if required by the member, give any information which it is in his power to give and which may lead to the identification of the person who was actually using the vehicle at the material time and, if he fails to do so, shall be guilty of an offence.

(5) A person who is guilty of an offence under this section shall be liable on summary conviction to a £350 fine and or three months imprisonment.

See *D. P. P. V Gaffney* above.

Obligation to stop s. 109

(1) A person driving a vehicle in a public place shall stop the vehicle on being so required by a member of the Garda Siochana.

(2) A person who contravenes subsection (1) shall be guilty of an offence.

A Garda has a common law power to sop a vehicle:

Road traffic offences
Director of Public Prosecutions V Fagan (1993)
It was held by Carney J. that it is a necessary implication from section 109 that a member of the Garda Siochana is authorised to stop a motor vehicle without having a particular reason to do so in order to ascertain if the vehicle is being driven in contravention of section 49.

In addition a Garda has a common law power to operate random road checks involving the stopping of traffic even though there is no immediate suspicion that an offence has been committed.

Identification of member of the Garda Siochana s. 111
Where, in exercise of any power or the performance of any duty conferred or imposed by or under this Act, any member of the Garda Siochana makes in a public place a request, requirement or demand of, or gives an instruction to, any person, such person shall not be bound to comply with the request, requirement, demand or instruction unless the member either-

(a) is in uniform, or

(b) produces, if requested by such person, an official identification card or such other evidence of his identity as may be prescribed.

The Offences against the Person Act, 1861, provides:

Injuring persons by furious driving s. 35
Whosoever, having the charge of any carriage or vehicle shall, by wanton or furious driving or racing, or other wilful misconduct, or by wilful neglect, do or cause to be done any bodily harm to any person whatsoever, shall be guilty of a misdemeanour and being convicted thereof shall be liable to imprisonment for two years.

This is an alternative to section 53 of the 1961 Act.

Attorney General V Joyce (1955)
The accused while driving a horse-drawn vehicle came into collision with a motor cycle. The driver and pillion passenger of the motor cycle were killed. The vehicle of the accused was unlighted and he was charged under section 35 of the 1861 Act.

It was held by the Circuit Court, that the failure to have a light was sufficient evidence, for a jury to find "wilful neglect".

Chapter 27

Misuse of drugs

The law relating to the misuse of dangerous or harmful drugs and the regulation of such drugs is contained in the Misuse of Drugs Act, 1977 (the Principal Act) as amended and in the Misuse of Drugs Act, 1984.

All references are to the 1977 Act unless otherwise indicated.

Interpretation s. 1

"cannabis" (except in "cannabis resin") means any plant of the genus Cannabis or any part of any such plant (by whatever name designated) but includes neither cannabis resin nor any of the following products after separation from the rest of any such plant, namely-

(a) mature stalk of any such plant,

(b) fibre produced from such mature stalk, or

(c) seed of any such plant;

"cannabis resin" means the separated resin, whether crude or purified, obtained from any plant of the genus Cannabis;

"supply" includes giving without payment

Controlled Drugs s. 2

A controlled drug means any substance, product or preparation which is either specified in the Schedule to the Act or has been declared by the Government to be such. The Government may by order remove or vary substances, product or preparation within the classification of controlled drugs. The substances set out in the schedule to the 1977 Act include: amphetamine, cannabis and cannabis resin, cocaine, diamorphine (heroin), lysergide (L.S.D.) and opium, whether raw, prepared or medicinal.

Regulations permitting possession of controlled drugs

By section 4 the Minister for Health may make regulations enabling any person or persons, to possess a controlled drug subject to conditions.

Regulations to prevent misuse of controlled drugs

By sections 5 the Minister for Health may make regulations enabling any person or persons, to possess a controlled drug, subject to such conditions as may be prescribed and may for the purpose of preventing the misuse of controlled drugs make regulations prohibiting absolutely, or otherwise:

(i) the manufacture, production or preparation of controlled drugs,

(ii) the importation or exportation of controlled drugs,

(iii) the supply, the offering to supply or the distribution of controlled drugs,

(iv) the transportation of controlled drugs,

The Minister in exercise of the powers conferred on him has issued Regulations which include the following:

Misuse of Drugs Act, 1977 (Controlled Drugs)(Declaration) Order, 1987 (S.I. 251) which declares certain substances to be controlled drugs;

Misuse of Drugs (Safe Custody) Regulations, 1982 (S.I. 321) which prescribe minimum standards for the safes and cabinets to be used in pharmacies for the safe custody of drugs;

Misuse of Drugs Regulations 1988 (S.I. 328), which regulate the production, supply, importation, exportation, possession of, and documentation and record keeping of controlled drugs.

Possession

The possession of controlled drugs is the fundamental offence under the Acts. It is not possible for a person or persons, who are not in possession to manufacture, produce, prepare, import, export, supply, distribute or transport controlled drugs.

Restriction of possession s. 3

(1) Subject to subsection (3) and section 4(3), a person shall not have a controlled drug in his possession.

(2) A person who has a controlled drug in his possession in contravention of subsection (1) shall be guilty of an offence.

(3) The Minister may by order declare that subsection (1) shall not apply to a controlled drug specified in the order, and for so long as an order under this subsection is in force the prohibition contained in the said subsection (1) shall not apply to a drug which is a controlled drug specified in the order.

(4) The Minister may by order amend or revoke an order under this section (including an order made under this subsection).

State (Gleeson) V District Justice Connellan (1988)

It was held by the Supreme Court that section 3 created only one offence of possession *simpliciter*; the question of the use of the drug was not an ingredient of the offence and arose only in relation to the penalty to be imposed under section 27.

This is an offence of strict liability, however note the defence available under section 29(2) below.

What is "possession" has been considered in:

Warner V Metropolitan Police Commissioner (1968)

The defendant was charged with being in possession. He had been given two boxes, one containing perfume and the other a controlled drug. He said that he thought they both contained perfume. The House of Lords held that *mens rea* was necessary regarding the possession, but not regarding the knowledge that what he possessed was a dangerous drug; as long as the defendant knew he possessed the container with something in it, it did not matter that he did not know, and could not reasonably have known, that the contents was a prohibited drug. Lord

Pearce stated: "One may, therefore, exclude from the 'possession' intended by the Act....... the physical control of articles which have been 'planted' on him without his knowledge; but how much further is one to go? If one goes to the extreme length of requiring the prosecution to prove that 'possession' implies a full knowledge of the name and nature of the drug concerned, the efficacy of the Act is seriously impaired, since many drug pedlars may in truth be unaware of this. I think the term 'possession' is satisfied by a knowledge only of the existence of the thing itself and not its qualities, and that ignorance or mistake as to its qualities is not an excuse."

An accused person is not "in possession" of a controlled drug, if he has consumed it, even though traces are discovered in his urine after arrest. This arose in:

Hambleton V Callinan (1968)

Parker C.J. stated: "..... once one had consumed something and its whole character had alerted and no further use could be made of it, as in this case, a man could not be said to be in possession of a prohibited substance..."

R V Peaston (1979)

It was held that where a controlled drug was delivered to an accused by post at his request, he became the possessor as soon as it was put through the letter box, even though he was not aware of its arrival. The possession of a small quantity of a controlled drug, though it may be too small for use, does not rule out the possibility of a conviction.

R. V Boyesen (1982)

Lord Scarman stated: "It is a perfectly sensible view that the possession of any quantity, which is visible, tangible, measurable and 'capable of manipulation'...... is a serious matter to be prohibited...."

R V Lewis (1988)

The defendant was convicted of possessing controlled drugs. He was the sole tenant of a house where the police had discovered the drugs. He claimed that the tenancy was a device to obtain social security and he had never spent any time in the house. The Court of Appeal held that the jury should decide whether the defendant had possession rather than mere control by considering all the circumstances in which the custody commenced and what knowledge as to the presence of the substance the defendant had up to the time he was found with it. The question to be determined was whether the defendant had been proved to have, or ought to have imputed to him, the intention to possess, or the knowledge that he did possess, what was in fact a prohibited substance. It is not necessary that he should also know the nature of the substance.

Possession for unlawful sale or supply s. 15

(1) Any person who has in his possession, whether lawfully or not, a controlled drug for the purpose of selling or otherwise supplying it to another in contravention of regulations under section 5 made by the Minister, shall be guilty of an offence.

(2) Subject to section 29(3), in any proceedings for an offence under subsection (1), where it is proved that a person was in possession of a controlled drug and the court, having regard to the quantity of the controlled drug which the person possessed or to such other matter as the court considers relevant, is satisfied that it is reasonable to assume that the controlled drug was not intended for the immediate personal use of the person, he shall be presumed until the court is satisfied to the contrary, to have been in possession of the controlled drug for the purpose of selling or otherwise supplying it to another in contravention of regulations under section 5.

This offence is distinguished from the offence of possession under section 3, in that it is not relevant whether the possession is lawful or not, and possession must be for the purpose of selling or otherwise supplying to another, hence self-administration of a controlled drug is not within the section.

A court until it is satisfied to the contrary, will assume having regard to the quantity of a controlled drug in the possession of an accused, that it was not intended for the immediate personal use of the accused, but that it was for the purpose of selling or otherwise supplying to another. This was considered in :

People (D. P. P.) V Lawless (1985)

The applicant was convicted of possession, contrary to section 15. A premises was forcibly entered by the Gardai. At the time of the entry the applicant was in the toilet, the sound of flushing was heard. A detective found seventeen packets of heroin at the manhole.

It was held by the Court of Criminal Appeal having regard to the presumption in section 15(2), there was no evidence that the applicant was a drug addict, or a person who required it "for immediate personal use" and further with the incriminating circumstances of the attempted destruction. There was clearly evidence of guilt.

R V Adepoju and R V Lubren (1988)

The question of what was meant by "another" was considered. Two defendants were charged with supplying to another. They appealed on the basis that the third defendant could not be charged with supplying drugs to herself.

The Court of Appeal held that "another" could not be a person included in the indictment.

Penalties s. 27

The penalties for offences are contained in section 27 of the Act as amended. Every person guilty of an offence under section 3 shall be liable -

(a) where the controlled drug is cannabis or cannabis resin and the court is satisfied that the person was in possession of such drug for his personal use.

(I) first offence: on summary conviction, a £300 fine, on conviction on indictment, a £500 fine

(II) second offence: on summary conviction, a £400 fine, on conviction on indictment, a £1000 fine

(b) in any other case -

on summary conviction, a £1000 fine and or twelve months imprisonment, on conviction on indictment, an unlimited fine and or seven years imprisonment.

Every person guilty of an offence under section 15 shall be liable; on summary conviction, £1000 fine and or twelve months imprisonment, on conviction on indictment, unlimited fine and or life imprisonment.

Other offences

Opium s. 16

(1) A person shall not-

(a) smoke or otherwise use prepared opium,

(b) frequent a place used for the purpose of smoking or otherwise using prepared opium, or

(c) have in his possession-

(i) any pipes or other utensils made or adopted for use in connection with the smoking of opium, being pipes or utensils which have been used by him or with his knowledge or permission in that connection or which he intends to use or permit others to use in that connection, or

(ii) any utensils which have been used by him or with his knowledge and permission in connection with the preparation of opium for smoking.

(2) A person who contravenes a provision of subsection (1) shall be guilty of an offence:

It will be noted that the "use" of opium, unlike the use of most controlled drugs, is a criminal offence. Section 29(5) makes provision for a possible defence (see below).

Cultivation of opium poppy or cannabis plant s. 17

(1) A person shall not cultivate opium poppy, any plant of the genus Cannabis, or any plant of the genus Erythroxylon, except under and accordance with a licence issued by the Minister.

(2) Every person who cultivates opium poppy, a plant of the genus Cannabis, or any plant of the genus Erythroxylon in contravention of subsection (1) shall be guilty of an offence.

R V Champ (1981)

The accused had pleaded that she taught that the plant been cultivated was hemp. It was held that the burden of proof was on the accused to prove that she did not know that the plant she was cultivating was cannabis.

Forged or fraudulently altered prescriptions s. 18

(1) A person shall not forge a document purporting to be a prescription issued by a practitioner (which document is in this Act

referred to as a forged prescription),

(2) A person shall not with intent to deceive either alter or use a prescription which has been duly issued by a practitioner (which document is in this Act referred to as a duly issued prescription),

(3) A person shall not have in his possession either a forged prescription or a duly issued prescription which has been altered with intent to deceive.

(4) The Minister may by regulation declare that in circumstances specified in regulations subsection (3) shall not apply in relation to persons who are of a prescribed class or description, and for so long as regulations under this subsection are in force the said subsection (3) shall be construed in accordance with and have effect subject to the regulations.

(5) A person who contravenes a provision of this section) shall be guilty of an offence.

Occupiers permitting certain activities s. 19

(1) A person who is the occupier or is in control or is concerned in the management of any land, vehicle or vessel and who knowingly permits any of the following to take place, on the land, vehicle or vessel namely-

(a) the cultivation contrary to section 17 of opium poppy or any plant of the genus Cannabis,

(b) the preparation of opium for smoking,

(c) the preparation of cannabis for smoking,

(d) the smoking of cannabis, cannabis resin or prepared opium,

(e) the manufacture, production or preparation of a controlled drug in contravention of regulations made under section 5,

(f) the importation or exportation of a controlled drug in contravention of such regulations,

(g) the sale, supply or distribution of a controlled drug in contravention of such regulations,

(h) any attempt so to contravene such regulations,

(i) the possession of a controlled drug in contravention of section 3,

shall be guilty of an offence.

Sweet V Parsley (1969)

The defendant was a landlady who did not live on the premises, but only visited occasionally. Her lodgers smoked cannabis and she was charged with being concerned in the management of premises which were used for the purpose of smoking cannabis. It was not proved that she knew of the smoking, she was nevertheless found guilty, it being held that no *mens rea* was necessary.

The House of Lords quashed the conviction and said that this was not an offence of strict liability. In relation to "knowingly permits" Lord Diplock stated : "The word 'permit' used to define the prohibited act, in itself connotes as a mental element of the prohibited conduct knowledge or grounds for reasonable suspicion on the part of the occupier that the premises will be used by someone for that purpose and an unwillingness on his part to take means available to him to prevent it"

R V Mogford (1970)

Two sister aged twenty and fifteen, were charged as the occupiers of premises, with permitting the premises to be used for the purpose of smoking cannabis. Their parents were on holidays at the relevant time. It was held that the parents did not have sufficient control to be occupiers.

R V Tao (1976)

The accused was an undergraduate living in a college hostel. It was held that a person was an occupier of a room if he is entitled to its exclusive possession, and his degree of control over the room is such that he is capable of excluding any person likely to commit an offence.

Offences relating to acts outside the State s. 20

(1) Any person who aids, abets, counsels or induces the commission in a place outside the State of an offence punishable under a corresponding law in force in that place shall be guilty of an offence

(2) In this section "a corresponding law" means a law stated in a certificate purporting to be issued by or on behalf of the government of a country outside the State to be a law providing for the control or regulation in that country of the manufacture, production, supply, use, exportation or importation of dangerous or otherwise harmful drugs in pursuance of any treaty, convention, protocol or other agreement between states and prepared or implemented by, or under the auspices of, the League of Nations or the United Nations Organisation and which for the time being in force.

(3) Any statement in a certificate mentioned in subsection (2), of this section as to the effect of the law mentioned in the certificate of in any such statement that any facts constitute an offence against the law so mentioned shall, for the purposes of any proceedings under this Act, be evidenced of the matters stated.

Every person guilty of any of the above offences shall be liable, on summary conviction, £1,000 fine and or twelve months imprisonment, and on conviction on indictment an unlimited fine and or fourteen years imprisonment

Printing s. 5 (1984 Act)

(1) (a) A person shall not print, publish, cause or procure to be printed or published, sell or expose or offer or keep for sale, distribute or offer or keep for distribution, any book, periodical or other publication which either -

(i) advocates or encourages, or might reasonably be supposed to advocate or encourage, whether expressly or by implication, the use of any controlled drug prescribed for the purposes of this section, or any product or preparation containing any such controlled drug, otherwise than in the course of professional treatment by a practitioner, or

(ii) contains any advertisement advertising any use of a pipe, utensil or other thing for use by persons, for or in in connection with the use of a controlled drug so prescribed or such a product or preparation, which is a use other than a use described in paragraph (b) of this subsection.

(b) The use lastly referred to in paragraph (a) of this subsection is a use (being the use of a pipe, utensil or other thing)-

(i) which is described in the relevant advertisement, and

(ii) which any person reading the relevant advertisement would-

(I) take to be a use relating to a controlled drug prescribed for the purposes of this section or a product or preparation containing such a controlled drug, and

(II) take to be, and only to be, a use to be availed of in the course of professional treatment by a practitioner.

(2) A person who contravenes subsection (1) shall be guilty of an offence.

(3) If any person, for the purpose of enabling or assisting another person to obtain, otherwise than on foot of a prescription issued by a practitioner, a controlled drug prescribed for the purposes of this section or a product or preparation containing such a drug communicates to that person any information, he shall be guilty of an offence.

(4) If any person, with intent to commit or to aid, abet, cause or procure the commission of an offence under subsection (3), has in his possession or under his control any document of such a nature that the dissemination of copies thereof would constitute such an offence, he shall be guilty of an offence.

(5) In any proceedings for an offence under subsection (2) it shall be a defence for the defendant to prove that-

(a) at the time of the alleged offence he carried on the business of selling or distributing books, periodicals or other publications, and

(b) the act alleged to constitute such offence was committed by him in the ordinary course of his said business, and

(c) he could not by the exercise of reasonable care have known or ascertained the contents of the book, periodical or other publication in respect of which the act was committed.

(6) Where in proceedings for an offence under subsection (4) it is proved that the defendant had at the time of the alleged offence in his possession or under his control a document described in the said subsection (4), then, unless there is sufficient other evidence to raise an issue as to whether the defendant so had the document with the intent referred to in the said subsection (4), he shall be treated as having had such time the document in his possession or under his control with such intent.

Every person guilty of this offence is liable on summary conviction to a £1,000 fine.

Attempts s. 21(1)

(I) A person who attempts to commit an offence under the Act, or who aids, abets, counsels or procures the commission of an offence under the

Act, or who solicits or incites any other person to commit an offence under the Act, shall be guilty of an offence.

Every person guilty of this offence shall be liable to be punished, on summary conviction, and on conviction on indictment, as if he were guilty of the substantive offence.

Contravening regulations and other offences s. 21

(2) Any person who, whether by act or omission, contravenes or fails to comply with regulations under the Act shall be guilty of an offence.

(3) A person who, in purported compliance with any obligation to give information to which he is subject by virtue of regulations made under this Act, gives any information which he knows to be false in a material particular or recklessly gives information which is so false shall be guilty of an offence.

(4) Any person who by act or omission impedes or obstructs a member of the Garda Siochana or a person duly authorised under this Act in the lawful exercise of a power conferred by this Act shall be guilty of an offence and if, in the case of a continuing offence, the impediment or obstruction is continued after conviction, he shall be guilty of a further offence.

(5) Any person who conceals from a person lawfully exercising a power under section 24 any controlled drug, or who without reasonable excuse fails to produce any book, record or other document which he has been duly required to produce under that section, shall be guilty of an offence.

(6) Any person who contravenes a condition attached to a licence, permit or authorisation granted or issued by the Minister under this Act (other than section 24) or under regulations made under this Act shall be guilty of an offence.

(7) Any person who, for the purpose of obtaining, whether for himself or another, the grant, issue or renewal of a licence, permit or authorisation, under this Act or under regulations made under this Act-

(a) makes any statement or gives information which he knows to be false in a material particular or recklessly gives information which is so false, or

(b) produces or otherwise makes use of any any book, record or other document which to his knowledge contains any statement or information which he knows to be false in a material particular,

shall be guilty of an offence.

Powers of Garda Siochana

Power to search persons, vehicles, vessels or aircraft s. 23A

(1) A member of the Garda Siochana who with reasonable cause suspects that a person is in possession in contravention of this Act of a controlled drug, may without warrant-

(a) search the person and, if he considers it necessary for that purpose, detain the person for such time as is reasonably necessary for making the search.

(b) search any vehicle, vessel or aircraft in which he suspects that a controlled drug may be found (and any substance, article or other thing on or in the vehicle, vessel or aircraft) and for the purpose of carrying out the search may, if he thinks fit, require the person who for the time being is in control of such vehicle, vessel or aircraft to bring it to a stop and when stopped to refrain from moving it, or in case such vehicle, vessel or aircraft is already stationary, to refrain from moving it, or

(c) examine (by opening or otherwise) and seize and detain anything found in the course of a search under this section which with such cause appears to him to be something which might be required as evidence in proceedings for an offence under this Act.

(1A) Where a member of the Garda Siochana decides to search a person under this section, he may require the person to accompany him to a Garda station for the purpose of being so searched at the station.

(1B) Where a member of the Garda Siochana decides to search a vehicle, vessel or aircraft under this section he may as regards the person who appears to him to be the owner or in control or charge for the time being of the vehicle, vessel or aircraft make any one or more or all of the following requirements:

(a) require such person, pending the commencement of the search, not to remove from the vehicle, vessel or aircraft as may be appropriate, any substance, article or other thing,

(b) in case the decision relates to a vehicle and the place at which he finds the vehicle is in his reasonable opinion unsuitable for such search, require such person forthwith to take the vehicle or cause it to be taken to a place which he considers suitable for such search and which is specified by him,

(c) require the person to be in or on or to accompany the vehicle, vessel or aircraft, as may be appropriate, for so long as the requirement under the paragraph remains in force.

(1C) Where there is a failure to comply with a requirement made under this section the following provisions shall apply-

(a) in case the requirement was made under subsection (1A) of this section, the member of the Garda Siochana concerned may arrest without warrant the person of whom the requirement was made, and

(b) in case the requirement is a requirement mentioned in paragraph (b) of subsection (1B) of this section, such member may take the vehicle concerned, or cause it to be taken, to a place which he considers suitable for a search under this section.

(1D) Where a requirement is made of a person under this section-

(a) in case the requirement is a requirement mentioned in paragraph (c) of subsection (1B) of this section, if at any time while the requirement is in force the person of whom it was made is neither in nor on nor accompanying the vehicle, vessel or aircraft, as may be appropriate, in relation to which the requirement was made, he shall be guilty of an offence,

(a) in case the requirement is a requirement mentioned in paragraph (c) of subsection (1B) of this section, if at any time while the requirement is in force the person of whom it was made is neither in nor on nor accompanying the vehicle, vessel or aircraft, as may be appropriate, in relation to which the requirement was made, he shall be guilty of an offence,

(b) in case any other requirement mentioned under this section, the person who fails to comply with the requirement shall be guilty of an offence,

(1E) A requirement mentioned in paragraph (c) of subsection (1B) of this section shall remain in force until the search in relation to which it is made is completed.

(1F) Where a requirement described in paragraph (a) of subsection (1B) of this section is made of a person, the search in relation to which the requirement is made shall be carried out as soon as is practicable.

(2) Nothing in this section shall operate to prejudice any power to search, or to seize or detain property which may be exercised by a member of the Garda Siochana apart from this section.

At common law there is no power to search someone to see whether or not they have committed a crime, hence any search carried out must be in strict conformity with the section.

"reasonable cause" This is a question of law not of fact.

Powers to Inspect

By section 24 for the purpose of enforcing the Act and regulations made thereunder, a member of the Garda Siochana or a person authorised by the Minister may at all reasonable times enter any building, require any person to produce any controlled drugs or, books records or other documents and inspect the same.

Power of Arrest   s. 25

(1) Where with reasonable cause a member of the Garda Siochana suspects that an offence under section 15 (Possession of controlled drugs for unlawful sales or supply) has been committed and so suspected a person having committed the offence, he may arrest the person without a warrant.

(2) Where with reasonable cause a member of the Garda Siochana. (a) suspects that an offence under this Act, other than an offence under section 15, has been committed or attempted, and

(b) suspects a person of having committed the offence or having made the attempt,

then if the member,

(c) with reasonable cause suspects that the person unless he is arrested either will abscond for the purposes of evading justice or will obstruct the course of justice, or

(d) having enquired of the person, has reasonable doubts as to the persons identity or place of abode or

(e) having enquired of the person, knows that the person does not ordinarily reside in the State, or has reasonable doubts as to whether the person so resides

he may arrest the person without warrant.

Search warrant s. 26

(1) If a Judge of the District Court or a Peace Commissioner is satisfied by information on oath of a member of the Garda Siochana that there is reasonable grounds for suspecting that -

(a) a person is in possession in contravention of this Act on any premises of a controlled drug, a forged prescription or a duly issued prescription which has been wrongfully altered and that such drug or prescription is on a particular premises or other land, or

(aa) opium poppy, a plant of the genus Cannabis or a plant of the genus Erythroxylon is being cultivated contrary to section 17 of the Act or in any premises or other land, or

(b) documents directly or indirectly relating to, or connected with, a transaction or dealing which was, or was an intended transaction or dealing which would if carried out be, an offence under this Act, or in the case of a transaction or dealing carried out or intended to be carried out in a place outside the State, an offence against a provision of a corresponding law within the meaning of section 20 of this Act and in force in that place, is in the possession of a person on any premises,

he may issue a search warrant.

Byrne V Grey (1988)

Hamilton P. in the High Court held that a District Justice or a peace commissioner issuing a warrant under section 26 must himself be satisfied that there is reasonable ground for suspicion and is not entitled to rely on a mere averment by a member of the Garda Siochana that he has such ground for suspicion.

People (D. P. P.) V Kenny (1990)

It was held by the Supreme Court that an information required to obtain a search warrant under section 26(1) must state facts from which a district justice or peace commissioner could be satisfied there were reasonable grounds for the issue thereof. In the absence of an independent decision by a Judge of the District Court or a peace commissioner that a search warrant is justified beyond a suspicion by members of the Garda Síochána that controlled drugs are on the premises, there may be a failure to adequately protect the inviolability of the dwelling under Article 40.5 of the Constitution of Ireland.

Officers of Customs and Excise

The Customs and Excise (Miscellaneous Provisions) Act, 1988 at section 2 provides that Officers of Customs and Excise have similar power of search in the vicinity of any port or airport or the land frontier in relation to controlled drugs suspected of being illegally imported or exported. Section 3 of that Act makes provision for the obtaining of search warrants. See later.

General

Onus of proof s. 22

(1) In any proceeding for an offence under this Act, it shall not be necessary to negative by evidence the existence of any-

(a) order made under section 2 or 3 of this Act,

(b) licence, permit or authorisation under this Act,

and accordingly the onus of proving the existence of any such licence, permit or authorisation shall be on the person seeking to avail himself thereof.

(2) In any proceedings for an offence under this Act it shall not be necessary for the prosecutor to prove that at the time of the offence-

(a) a defendant was not a person to whom regulations made under section 4 of this Act applied,

(b) a defendant was a person to whom an exception under regulations made under section 5 of this Act applied and

in case a defendant claims that-

(i) by virtue of the said section 4 he had lawfully in his possession a controlled drug,

(ii) he is a person to whom such an exception applied,

the onus of proving such lawful possession, or that he is such a person, as may be appropriate, shall be on the defendant.

However note defences generally in section 29 below.

Evidence s. 10 (1984 Act)

In any proceeding for an offence under the Principal Act or section 5 of this Act, the production of a certificate purporting to be signed by an officer of the Forensic Science Laboratory of the Department of Justice and relating to an examination, inspection, test or analysis, as the case may be, specified in the certificate of a controlled drug or other substance, product or preparation so specified shall, until the contrary is proved be evidence of any fact thereby certified without proof of any signature thereon or that such signature is that of such an officer.

The burden of proving that a substance is a controlled drug rests on the prosecution; which may be proved by the expert opinion of an analyst. Where an accused pleads guilty an unsupported admission would be sufficient evidence:

Bird V Adams (1972)

It was held that in the absence of expert evidence, an admission by an accused (who also admitted being a drug pedlar) that a substance was a controlled drug was *prima facie* evidence that such substance was a controlled drug.

R V Chatwood (1980)

An experienced drug user admitted possession of a substance which he identified as a controlled drug. It was held that his statements, whether made orally to the police or reduced into writing, having regard to the circumstances of the case, provided *prima facie* evidence of the identity of the substance in question.

Remand s. 28

By section 28, a court has power to remand persons convicted under section 3, 15, 16, 17, or 18 of the Act and to obtain a report and in certain cases to arrange for the medical treatment or for the care of such persons.

Defences generally s. 29

(1) In any proceeding for an offence in which it is proved that the defendant had in his possession or supplied a controlled drug, the defendant shall not be acquitted of the offence charged by reason only of proving that he neither knew nor suspected nor had reason to suspect that the substance, product, or preparation in question was the particular controlled drug alleged.

(2) In any such proceeding in which it is proved that the defendant had in his possession a controlled drug, or a forged prescription, or duly issued prescription altered with intent to deceive,, it shall be a defence to prove that -

(a) he did not know and had no reasonable grounds for suspecting -

(i) that what he had in his possession was a controlled drug or such a prescription, as may be appropriate, or

(ii) that he was in possession of a controlled drug or such a prescription, or

(b) he believed the substance, product or preparation to be a controlled drug, or a controlled drug of a particular class or description, and that, if the substance, product or preparation had in fact been that controlled drug or a controlled drug of that class or description, he would not at the material time have been committing an offence, or

(c) knowing or suspecting it to be such a drug or prescription, he took or retained possession of it for the purpose of -

(i) preventing another from committing or continuing to commit an offence in relation to the drug or document, as may be appropriate, or

(ii) delivering it into custody of a person lawfully entitled to take custody of it,

and that as soon as practicable he took steps to destroy the drug or document or to deliver it into the custody of such a person.

(3) In any proceeding for an offence under under section 15 a defendant may rebut the presumption raised by subsection (2) of that section by showing that at the time of the alleged offence he was by virtue of regulations made under section 4 lawfully in possession of the controlled drug to which the proceedings relate.

(4) In any proceeding for an offence under section 19 it shall be a defence to show that the defendant took steps to prevent the occurrence

or continuance of the activity or contravention to which the alleged offence relates and that, in the particular circumstances, the steps were taken as soon as practicable and were reasonable.

(5) In any proceedings for an offence under section 16, 17, or 21(2), it shall be a defence for the defendant to prove that he neither knew of nor suspected nor had reason to suspect the existence of some fact alleged by the prosecutor which it is necessary for the prosecutor to prove if he is to be convicted of the offence charged.

(6) In any proceedings for an attempt to commit an offence under this Act, the defences mentioned in subsection (2) or (5) shall, with the necessary modifications, be open to the defendant.

(7) Subject to subsection (1) nothing shall prevent a person raising a defence which, apart from this section, would be open to him to raise in proceedings for an offence under this Act.

Forfeiture s. 30

(1) Subject to subsection (2), a court by which a person is convicted of an offence under this Act may order anything shown to the satisfaction of the court to relate to the offence to be forfeited and either destroyed or dealt with in such manner as the court thinks fit.

(2) A court shall not order anything to be forfeited under this section if a person claiming to be the owner of or otherwise interested in it applies to be heard by the court, unless an opportunity has been given to him to show cause why the order should not be made.

Offences in relation to bodies corporate s. 31

Where an offence under this Act is committed by a body corporate or by a person purporting to act on behalf of a body corporate and is proved to have been so committed with the consent, connivance or approval of, or to have been facilitated by any neglect on the part of, any director, manager, secretary or other official of such body, such person shall also be guilty of an offence.

Chapter 28

Offences against the public peace and order

The offences considered in this chapter are:
>Unlawful assembly;
>Rout;
>Riot;
>Riotous assembly;
>Affray;
>Challenges;
>Public nuisance;
>Indecent exposure;
>Public indecency

References is also made to offences created by the following statutes:
>Vagrancy Act, 1824;
>Dublin Police Act, 1842
>Town Improvement (Ireland) Act, 1854;
>Refreshment Houses (Ireland) Act, 1854;
>Pedlars Act, 1871;
>Licensing Act, 1872;
>Habitual Drunkards Act, 1879.

Unlawful Assembly

Unlawful Assembly is committed where three or more persons gather together for the purpose of committing or preparing to commit a crime involving the use of violence, or in order to carry out a lawful or unlawful purpose in such a way as to lead to alarm being caused to bystanders of ordinary courage, that there will be a breach of the peace as a direct result of their conduct.

An assembly which was originally lawful may become unlawful, if a proposal is made at the meeting to do an act of violence to the disturbance of the public and the proposal is acted upon. The offence will have been committed even though the parties involved have departed without having done anything to carry out their purpose.

The moment when persons in a crowd begin to act for some shared common purpose and thus causing alarm the assembly becomes unlawful, alarm is likely to be caused by, the tone of any speeches, or the carrying of any offensive weapons, or the late hour of the meeting.

An unlawful assembly need not take place in public. Private citizens may on their own initiative disperse an unlawful assembly forcibly. Unlawful assembly is an indictable misdemeanour at common law punishable by imprisonment.

Rout

Rout is a misdemeanour at common law it stands midway between unlawful assembly and a riot, it is committed when an unlawful assembly makes some move towards the execution of its common purpose.

Riot

A rout becomes a riot when an unlawful assembly executes its common purpose. It does not matter whether the purpose is lawful or not or whether the Riot Act, (see below) has been read or not. It is a misdemeanour at common law, the elements of which are:

(1) three or more persons,

(2) such persons must have a common purpose,

(3) they must have begun to execute such purpose,

(4) they must have an intent to help one another by force if necessary against any person who may oppose them,

(5) force or violence must be displayed in such a manner as to alarm at least one person of reasonable firmness and courage.

The degree of force used to suppress a riot must be reasonable and proportionate to the circumstances of the case, as the rioters are guilty only of a misdemeanour.

Riotous assembly

Riotous Assembly is a statutory offence created by the Riot Act, 1787, By this Act if an unlawful assembly of twelve or more persons do not disperse within an hour after a Justice of the Peace has read or has attempted to read, a proclamation calling on them to disperse, they become felons.

In such circumstances the rioters become liable to any amount of force, including military or armed police. However such force that is to be used must be proportionate to that of the rioters, a riotous assembly may be fired upon but only where this is necessary as a last resort to preserve life. Any persons hindering the making of such proclamation are deemed felons.

Lynch V Fitzgerald & Others (1938)

The Plaintiff claimed damages for the death of his son who was killed at Marsh's Yard, Copley Street, Cork by a bullet fired by one of a group of detectives of the Special Branch. The defendants were detailed for the protection of prospective buyers whose lives had been threatened. A lorry filled with men carrying stick came through the crowd and crashed into the gate of the yard. When the lorry came through the gate the defendants opened fire and killed a fifteen year old onlooker behind the lorry.

Hanna J. found that: The onslaught made by the lorry and the men in it upon the gate turned what was a lawful assembly into an unlawful assembly which could of course be repelled and subdued by force. He held that armed force however whether police or military, can fire upon an unlawful or riotous assembly only where such a course is necessary as a last resort to preserve life.

Offences against the public peace and order

Breach of the peace

Breach of the peace is not a separate offence, but it is a constituent part of a number of offences discussed below. As a general rule a breach of the peace is an offence against public order such as riot, affray, challenging, being armed in public without lawful authority in such a manner as to alarm the public, threatening another with bodily injury etc.

Attorney General V Cunningham (1932)

It was held by the Court of Criminal Appeal that in order to constitute a breach of the peace, an act must be such as to cause reasonable alarm and apprehension to members of the public.

Affray

Affray is a misdemeanour at common law it consists of fighting in some public place, by one or more persons, or a display of force by one or more persons, in such a manner as to frighten reasonable people.

Fighting in a private place, or at some distance from the public road where no one else is present other than those who are aiding and abetting, does not amount to an affray, but an assembly for such a purpose is unlawful, and the parties concerned may be convicted of an assault, or of taking part in an unlawful assembly.

Before a person can be convicted of an affray, even as an aider and abettor, it must be proved that he was at least encouraging the participants in a fight, his mere presence even if he intended to participate is not enough.

A person acting in self-defence cannot be guilty of an affray by fighting.

Any person may arrest others guilty of an affray if it is actually continuing in his presence or he has a reasonable ground to believe that it will be renewed, or the arrest is upon fresh pursuit immediately after the affray.

Challenges

It is a misdemeanour at common law punishable by fine and imprisonment to either verbally or in writing to challenge a person to fight or to attempt to provoke a person to give such a challenge.

Public nuisance

Public nuisance is a misdemeanour at common law, It consists of an unlawful act or omission which obstructs or causes inconvenience or damage to the public. An example would be the emission of noise or smells from a factory in such a way as to cause serious inconvenience. Where special damage is caused as the result of a public nuisance, a civil action for damages can be brought. Public nuisance is an exception to the general rule that a master is not vicariously liable for crimes committed by his servants.

257

Indecent exposure

At common law it is a misdemeanour to commit an act outraging public decency in public and in such a way that more than one person sees, or is at least able to see, the act. The more usual way of committing this offence is by indecently exposing the body. It is not necessary to prove any sexual motive or any intention to insult or annoy. It may be committed by a female and the exposure need not necessarily be to a person of the opposite sex.

Public indecency

The Criminal Law Amendment Act, 1935, section 18 provides that: Every person shall commit, at or near or in sight of any place along which the public habitually pass as of right or by permission, any act in such a way as to offend modesty or cause scandal or injure the morals of the community shall be guilty of an offence and shall on summary conviction be liable to a £2 fine and or one months imprisonment.

Pedlars

The Pedlars Act, 1871 as amended by the Pedlars Act, 1881 provides:

By section 3 of the Act; the term "pedlar" means any hawker, pedlar, petty chapman, tinker, caster of metals, mender of chairs, or other person who, without any horse or other beast bearing or drawing burden, travels and trades on foot and goes from town to town or to other men's houses, carrying to sell or exposing for sale any goods, wares, or merchandise, or procuring orders for goods, wares, or merchandise immediately to be delivered or selling or offering for sale his skills in handicraft.

By section 4 of the Act an offence is committed where a person acts as a pedlar without a proper certificate. the penalty is a 50p fine or a £1 fine in the case of a second or subsequent offence.

Dublin Police Act, 1842

The Dublin Police Act, 1842, (which applies in the Dublin Metropolitan District of the Garda Siochana) makes the following provisions in respect of nuisances in public thoroughfares at section 14.

And be it enacted, that every person shall be liable to a penalty not exceeding Forty Shillings (£2) within the Limits of the Police District, shall in any Thoroughfare of Public Place commit any of the following Offences; (that is to say,)

Animals
2. Every person who shall turn loose any horses or cattle.
3. Every person who by negligence or ill-usage in driving cattle shall cause any mischief to be done by such cattle or who shall in anyway

misbehave himself in the driving, care or management of such cattle; and also every person, not being hired or employed to drive such cattle who shall wantonly and unlawfully drive or hunt any such cattle.

Posting bills

10. Every Person who, without the Consent of the Owner or Occupier, shall affix any Posting Bill or other Paper against or upon any Building, Wall, Fence, or Pale, or write upon, soil, deface, or mark any such Building, Wall, Fence, or Pale with Chalk or Paint or in any other way whatsoever, or wilfully break, destroy or damage any Part of any such Building, Wall, Fence, or Pale or any Fixture of Appendage there unto, or any Tree, Shrub, or Seat, in any public Walk, Park or Garden.

Loitering in a public place

11. Every common prostitute or night-walker loitering or being in any thoroughfare or public place for the purpose of prostitution or solicitation, to the annoyance of the inhabitants or passengers.

Mooney V Corporation of Dublin (1939)

A Garda arrested a woman on a charge of soliciting for the purposes of prostitution in a public thoroughfare contrary to section 14(11). It was held by the High Court, that the soliciting in question was neither a breach of the public peace nor likely to lead to a breach of the public peace, and therefore the woman in question was not a disturber of the public peace.

Profane, indecent, or obscene book, etc.

12. Every person who shall sell, or distribute, or offer for sale or Distribution, of exhibit to public view, any profane, indecent, or obscene book, paper, print, drawing, painting, or representation, or sing any profane, indecent, or obscene song or ballad,or write or draw any indecent or obscene word, figure or representation, or use any profane, indecent or obscene language, to the annoyance of the inhabitants or passengers.

The Post Office Act, 1908 prohibits the sending of indecent prints through the post see section 63 of that Act at page 266.

Words

13. Every person who shall use any threatening, abusive, or insulting words or behaviour, with intent to provoke a breach of the peace, or whereby a breach of the peace may be occasioned.

Stone, missiles etc.

15. Every person who shall wantonly discharge any firearm or throw or discharge any stone or other missile, to the damage or danger of any person, or make any bonfire or throw or set fire to any fireworks.

Offences against the public peace and order

Ringing of doorbells

16. Every person who shall wilfully and wantonly disturb any inhabitant by ringing any doorbell or knocking at any door without lawful excuse, or unlawfully extinguish any public light.

Playing games

17. Every person who shall play at any game to the annoyance of the inhabitants or passengers, or who shall make or use any slide on ice or snow in any street or other thoroughfare to the common danger of passengers.

Any Garda may arrest without warrant any person who shall commit any such offence within his view.

Director of Public Prosecutions V Rooney (1992)

The defendant was stopped and searched and found to be in possession of forged £20 notes contrary to section 8 of the Forgery Act, 1913.

The district judge submitted a consultative case seeking the opinion of the High Court whether a member of the Garda Siochana proposing to exercise the power of search under section 29 of the Dublin Police Act, 1842 must:

(a) inform the suspect of his suspicion that he has or conveyed in any manner "any thing stolen or unlawfully obtained";

(b) first arrest the suspect prior to exercising the said power of search;

(c) inform the suspect of his suspicion that he has or conveyed in any manner "any thing stolen or unlawfully obtained" and tell the suspect of the said power under section 29 of the Dublin Police Act, 1842 " .. and every such constable may also stop, search and detain ... any person who may be reasonably suspected of having or conveying in any manner anything stolen or unlawfully obtained"

It was held by O'Hanlon J. in the High Court in answering (a) and (c) in the affirmative and (b) in the negative that a suspect is entitled to be informed of the nature and description of the statutory power which is being invoked.

Towns Improvement Act (Ireland) 1854

The Towns Improvement Act (Ireland) 1854, which applies in a large number of urban areas (those with a population of 1,500 or more in the 1851 census) outside of Dublin, makes provisions similar to those contained in the Dublin Police Act for those towns.

Offences against the public peace and order
Vagrancy

The Vagrancy Act, 1824 was extended to Ireland by section 15 of the Prevention of Crimes Act, 1871.

The Act creates three classes of vagrants.

Idle and disorderly person s. 3

A person shall be deemed to be an idle and disorderly person where such person :

(1) causes his family to become a charge on the parish,
(2) hawks goods without a pedlars licence,
(3) is a common prostitute,
(4) begs in a public place.

An idle and disorderly person is liable to a £5 fine and or one months imprisonment.

A rogue and a vagabond s. 4

A person shall be deemed to be a rogue and a vagabond where such person :

(1) tells fortunes,
(2) exposes to public view any obscene print or picture,
(3) exposes his person with intent to insult any female,
(It has been held that "person" means penis).
(4) exposes wounds to gather alms,
(5) procures charitable contributions under fraudulent pretence,
(6) runs away and leaves his family as a charge on the parish,
(7) is found in a building for an unlawful purpose,
(8) is twice convicted as an idle and disorderly person.

A rogue and a vagabond is liable to a £25 and or three months imprisonment.

Incorrigible rogue s. 5

A person shall be deemed to be an incorrigible rogue where such person :

(1) escapes from legal confinement,
(2) commits an offence under section 4 above, having been previously convicted as a rogue and a vagabond,
(3) when apprehended as a rogue and a vagabond, he violently resists any constable.

An incorrigible rogue shall be imprisoned until the next court session.

Wandering abroad and begging

The Vagrancy (Ireland) Act, 1847 at section 3 provides as follows: That every person wandering abroad and begging, or placing himself in any public place, street, highway, court, or passage to beg, or gather alms, or causing or procuring, or encouraging any child or children to do so, shall be guilty of an offence and liable to one months imprisonment.

Offences against the public peace and order

Smith V McCabe (1912)
In this case it was held that the begging need not be in a public place. See also Obstruction at General Post Office at section 68 of the Post Office Act, 1908 at page 267.

Drunkenness

Drunkenness is not of itself a criminal offence, but being drunk in certain circumstances can constitute an offence, as where it violates public peace and order.

Habitual drunkards
There are, certain provisions which enable a criminal habitual drunkard to be dealt with on indictment.

The Habitual Drunkards Act, 1879, at section 3 declares that a "Habitual Drunkard" means a person who, not being amenable to any jurisdiction in lunacy, is notwithstanding, by reason of habitual intemperate drinking of intoxicating liquor, at times dangerous to himself or herself or to others, or incapable of managing himself or herself, and his or her affairs.

A person who commits any of certain offences, as is mentioned in the first schedule to the Inebriates Act, 1898, and who within the previous twelve months has been convicted summarily at least three times, and who is a habitual drunkard, is liable on conviction on indictment to be detained for three years.

Amongst the offence contained in the schedule to the 1898 Act are:
Being found drunk in a highway or other public place, whether a building or not, or on a licensed premises.

Being guilty while drunk of riotous or disorderly behaviour in a highway or other public place, whether a building or not.

Being drunk while in charge, on any highway or other public place, of any carriage, horse, cattle, or steam-engine.

The Dublin Police Act, 1842 provides as follows :

Disorderly conduct in houses of public resort s. 7
Every person who shall have or keep any house, shop, room or place of public resort (within the Dublin Police District) wherein provisions, liquors, or refreshments of any kind shall be sold or consumed (whether the same shall be kept or retailed therein or procured elsewhere) and who shall wilfully or knowingly permit drunken or other disorderly conduct therein, or knowingly suffer any unlawful games or any gaming whatsoever therein, or knowingly permit or suffer persons of notoriously bad character to meet and remain therein is guilty of an offence for which the penalty is a £5 fine.

Offences against the public peace and order

Drunkards guilty of riotous or Indecent behaviour s. 15
And be it enacted that every person who shall be found drunk in any street or public Thoroughfare within the Police District, and who while drunk shall be guilty of any riotous or indecent behaviour, and also any person who shall be guilty of any violent or indecent behaviour in any Police station house, shall be liable to a penalty of 40/- for every such offence, or may be committed for 7 days.

The Towns Improvement (Ireland) Act, 1854, makes similar provision.

The Refreshment Houses (Ireland) Act, 1860, provides:

Permitting drunkenness s. 31
Every person licensed to sell wine by retail who shall permit any person to be guilty of drunkenness or other disorderly conduct in the premises mentioned in such licence, or who shall himself be guilty of any disorderly conduct shall be guilty of an offence for which the penalty is a £5 fine.

The Licensing Act, 1872 provides as follows:

Persons found drunk s. 12
Every person found drunk on any highway or other public place whether a building or not, or on any licensed premises shall be guilty of an offence for which the penalty on a first offence is £1; on a second offence within 12 months £2 and on a third offence within 12 months £4.
Every person who in any highway or other public place, whether a building or not, is guilty while drunk of riotous or disorderly behaviour, or who is drunk while in charge on any highway or other public place of any carriage, horse, cattle or steam engine, or who is drunk while in possession of any loaded firearm, may be apprehended, and is guilty of an offence for which the penalty is a £50 fine and or one months imprisonment.

Permitting drunkenness s. 13
If any licensed person permits drunkenness or any violent, quarrelsome, or riotous conduct to take place on his premises, or sells any intoxicating liquor to any drunken person, he shall be guilty of an offence for which the penalty is a £200 fine.
It is not necessary to show that drink has been supplied in order to constitute this offence. A person may be convicted upon evidence that someone who had been drinking on such premises was found drunk at a distance away. Knowledge or belief of the condition of the person alleged to be drunk is not necessary to constitute the offence of selling drink to a drunken person, although it is necessary in the case of a complaint for permitting drunkenness.

Chapter 29

Postal, telecommunication and broadcasting offences

The Post Office Act, 1908 makes provision for offences in relation to the postal service. The penalties in respect of section's 51 and 53 and section 55 of the Act have been amended by the Larceny Act, 1990.

Postal and Telecommunications Service Act, 1983

The Postal and Telecommunications Service Act, 1983, divided the former Department of Posts and Telegraphs into two, setting up a postal company and a telecommunications company, An Post and Bord Telecom Eireann. This Act also amended the 1908 Act.

Penalties

The Act at section 4 makes provision for a general penalty in respect of various offences which include-

Sections 53A and 62 of the 1908 Act;

Sections 37, 63, 84, 87, 98 and 99 of the 1983 Act; and

Section 13 of the Post Office (Amendment) Act, 1951.

The penalties in respect of the above offences are; on summary conviction a £800 fine and or twelve months imprisonment; and on conviction on indictment a £50,000 fine and or five years imprisonment.

Prohibition on unauthorised disclosure of information s. 37

(1) A person shall not disclose confidential information obtained by him while performing duties as a director or member of staff of, or an advisor or consultant to, the postal company or the telecommunications company or as a postmaster unless he is duly authorised to do so.

(2) A person who contravenes (1) shall be guilty of an offence.

(3) In this section-

"confidential" means that which is expressed to be confidential either as regards particular information or as regards information of a particular class or description;

"duly authorised" means authorised by the company or by some person authorised in that behalf by the company.

Postal offences

All reference below are to the Post Office Act, 1908 as amended unless otherwise stated.

Exclusive privilege of the postal company s. 63 (1983 Act)

(5) A postal packet originating within the State shall not be taken or sent outside the State with a view to having the packet posted from outside the State to an address within the State for the purpose of evading the exclusive privilege of the company.

(6) A person who breaches the exclusive privilege granted by this section, or who attempts to breach that privilege or who aids, abets, counsels or procures such a breach, or who conspires with, solicits or incites any other person to breach that privilege, shall be guilty of an offence.

In any proceeding in relation to that offence it shall lie upon the person proceeded against to prove that the act or omission in respect of which the offence is alleged to have been committed was done in conformity with this section

Unlawfully taking away or opening the mail s. 51

If any person unlawfully takes away or opens a mail bag sent by any vessel employed by or under An Post for the transmission of postal packets under contract, or unlawfully takes a postal packet in course of transmission by post out of a mail bag so sent, he shall be guilty of felony and be liable on conviction on indictment to imprisonment of a term not exceeding 10 years or to a fine or to both.

Fraudulent retention of mail bag or postal packet s. 53

If any person fraudulently retains, or wilfully secretes or keeps, or detains or, when required by an officer of An Post, neglects or refuses to deliver up-

(a) any postal packet which is in course of transmission by post and which ought to have been delivered to any other person, or

(b) any postal packet in course of transmission by post or any mail bag, which shall have been found by him or by any other person,

he shall be guilty of an offence and be liable on conviction on indictment to imprisonment of a term not exceeding 2 years or to fine or to both.

Inviolability of mail s. 53A

Any person who unlawfully and maliciously damages or interferes with a mail box shall be guilty of an offence. See general penalty above.

Secreting or destroying by officer of An Post of postal packet s. 55

If any officer of An Post for any purpose whatsoever secrets or destroys a postal packet in course of transmission by post, he shall be guilty of felony, and shall be liable on conviction on indictment to imprisonment for a term not exceeding 10 years or to a fine or to both.

Opening or delaying postal packets s. 56(1)

If any officer of An Post, contrary to his duty, opens or procures or suffers to be opened any postal packet in course of transmission by post, or wilfully detains or delays, or procures or suffers to be detained or delayed, any such postal packet, he shall be guilty of a misdemeanour, and being convicted thereof shall be liable, at the discretion of the court, to imprisonment with or without hard labour, or to a fine, or to both such imprisonment and fine.

Carelessness, negligence, or misconduct etc.
By section 57 of the Act a variety of acts including any carelessness, negligence, or misconduct of persons while employed to convey or deliver postal packets, shall be an offence for which the penalty on summary conviction is a £20 fine.

Issuing money orders with fraudulent intent s. 58
(1) If any officer of An Post grants or issues any money order with a fraudulent intent, he shall be guilty of felony, and be liable to seven years p.s. or two years imprisonment.

(2) If any officer of An Post re-issues a money order previously paid, he shall be deemed to have issued the order with a fraudulent intent under this section.

Forgery and stealing of money orders s. 59(2)
If any person, with intent to defraud, obliterates, adds to, or alters any such lines or words on a money order as would, in the case of a cheque, be a crossing of that cheque, or knowingly offers, utters, or disposes of any money order with such fraudulent obliteration, addition, or alteration, he shall be guilty of a felony and be liable to the like punishment as if the order were a cheque.

Placing injurious substances in or against post office letter boxes s. 61
(1) A person shall not place or attempt to place in or against any post office letter box any fire, match, any light, any explosive substance, any dangerous substance, any filth, any noxious or deleterious substance, or any fluid, and shall not commit a nuisance in or against any post office letter box, and shall not do or attempt to do anything likely to injure the box, appurtenances or contents.

(2) A contravention is a misdemeanour, for which the penalty on summary conviction is a £10 fine and indictment is twelve months imprisonment.

Affixing placards, notices, &c., on post office letter box, &c. s. 62
(1) A person shall not, without due authority, affix or attempt to affix any placard, advertisement, notice, list, document, board, or thing, in or on, or in association or conjunction with or paint or tar, any post office, post office letter box, telegraph post, or other property belonging to or used by or on behalf of An Post, and shall not in any way disfigure any such office, box, post, or property.

(2) If any person acts in contravention of this section, he shall be guilty of an offence.

Additional offences under the 1908 Act
Section 63 provides that; Sending by post explosive, inflammable, or

deleterious substances, or indecent prints, words, etc. is a misdemeanour for which the penalty on summary conviction is a £10 fine or on conviction on indictment is twelve months imprisonment.

Section 64 provides that; Imitation of post office stamps, forms and marks, is an offence for which the penalty on summary conviction is a £2 fine.

Section 65 prohibits fictitious stamps for which the penalty on summary conviction is a £20 fine.

Section 66 provides that; The displaying without lawful authority the words "Post Office" or "Telegraph Office", or "Letter Box", etc., is an offence for which the penalty on summary conviction is a £2 fine plus 25p each day that the offence continues.

Section 67 provides that; Obstructing an officer of An Post, or of an Bord Telecom Eireann in the execution of his duty, or obstructing the course of business of An Post is an offence for which the penalty is a £2 fine. Any officer of An Post may require person offending under this section to leave a Post Office, and if he refuses he is liable to a further fine (£5) and may be removed by any officer of An Post, and all members of the Garda Siochana are required on demand to remove or assist in removing such person.

Section 68 provides:

(1) A hackney carriage shall not stand or ply for hire opposite the G.P.O. in Dublin and if any driver or person having the management of any hackney carriage, permits that same to stand or ply for hire opposite the G.P.O. he shall be guilty of an offence,

(3) In any hawker, newsvendor, or idle or disorderly person stops or loiters on the flagway or pavement opposite the G.P.O., he shall be guilty of an offence.

The penalty on summary conviction is a £5 fine.

Endeavouring to procure the commission of any offence s. 69

If any person solicits or endeavours to procure any other person to commit an offence punishable on indictment under this Act, he shall be guilty of a misdemeanour, and be liable to two years imprisonment.

Definitions s. 89

"mail" includes every conveyance by which postal packets are carried, whether it be a carriage, coach, cart, horse, or any other conveyance, and also a person employed in conveying or delivering postal packets, and also any vessel:

"mail bag" includes a bag, box, parcel, or any other envelope or covering in which postal packets in course of transmissions by post are conveyed, whether it does or does not contain any such packets:

"postal packet" means a letter, post card, reply post card, newspaper, book packet, pattern or sample packet, or parcel, and every packet or article transmissible by post, and includes a telegram.

Postal, telecommunication and broadcasting offences

Opening or delaying postal packets s. 84 (1983 Act)

A person who-

(a) opens or attempts to open a postal packet addressed to another person or delays or detains any such postal packet or does anything to prevent its due delivery or authorises, suffers or permits another person (who is not the person to whom the postal packet is addressed) to do so, or

(b) discloses the existence or contents of any such postal packet, or

(c) uses for any purpose any information obtained from any such postal packet, or

(d) tampers with any such postal packet,

without the agreement of the person to whom the postal packet is addressed shall be guilty of an offence.

This section does not apply to a person who is acting under lawful authority.

Telecommunications offences

Offensive telecommunication messages

The Post Office (Amendment) Act, 1951 at section 13(1) as amended provides that if any person:

(a) sends by means of the telecommunications system operated by Bord Telecom Eireann, any message or other matter which is grossly offensive or of an indecent, obscene or menacing character, whether addressed to an operator or any other person, or

(b) sends by those means, for the purpose of causing annoyance, inconvenience, or needless anxiety to another, a message which he knows to be false, or persistently makes use of those means for that purpose,

shall be guilty of an offence.

This has been amended by the 1983 Act, as it stood originally it was confined to telephone messages, but now it is much broader in scope and would cover fax and modems.

Interception of telecommunications messages s. 98(1)

A person who-

(a) intercepts or attempts to intercept, or

(b) authorises, suffers or permits another person to intercept, or

(c) does anything that will enable him or another person to intercept, telecommunications messages being transmitted by the company or who discloses the existence, substance or purport of any such message which has been intercepted or uses for any purpose any information obtained from any such message shall be guilty of an offence.

Subsection (1) does not apply to persons acting under lawful authority.

Postal, telecommunication and broadcasting offences

The Interception of Postal Packets and Telecommunications Messages (Regulation) Bill, 1992 (No. 6) proposes at section 13(2):

The following subsection in section 98:

(2A) A person employed by the company who discloses to any person any information concerning the use made of telecommunications services provided for any other person by the company shall be guilty of an offence unless the disclosure is made -

(a) at the request or with the consent of that other person,

(b) for the prevention or detection of crime or for the purpose of any criminal proceedings,

(c) in the interests of the security of the State,

(d) in pursuance of an order of a court,

(e) for the purpose of civil proceedings in any court, or

(f) to another person to whom he is required, in the course of his duty as such employee, to make such disclosure.

Fraudulent use of telecommunications system s. 99

(1) A person who wilfully causes the company to suffer loss in respect of any rental, fee or charge properly payable for the use of the telecommunications system or any part of the system or who by any false statement or misrepresentation or otherwise with intent to defraud avoids or attempts to avoid payment of any such rental, fee or charge shall be guilty of an offence.

(2) A person who connects or causes to be connected any apparatus or device to, or places or causes to be placed any apparatus or device in association with or conjunction with, the telecommunications system operated by Bord Telecom Eireann or any part of the system the effect of which might result in the provision by Bord Telecom Eireann of a service to any person without payment of the appropriate rental, fee or charge shall be guilty of an offence.

Broadcasting Act, 1990

Interception of communications s. 9

(1) No person, other than a duly authorised officer of the Minister shall, in relation to a service provided by a licensee or a service provider-

(a) intercept the service,

(b) suffer or permit or do any thing that enables such interception by any person,

(c) possess, manufacture, assemble, import, supply, or offer to supply, any equipment which is designed or adapted to be used for the purpose of enabling such interception by any person, or

(d) publish information with the intention of assisting or enabling any person to intercept such a service.

(2) No person shall-

(a) knowingly install or attempt to install or maintain any equipment which is capable of being used or designed or adapted to be used for the purpose of enabling such interception by any person, or

(b) wilfully damage or attempt to damage a system or part of a system operated by a licensee or service provider.

(3) A person who contravenes any provision of subsection (1) or (2) shall be guilty of an offence.

(4) In this section "intercept" in relation to a service means receive, view, listen to, record by any means or acquire the substance or purport of the service or part thereof supplied by a licensee or service provider without the agreement of the licensee or service provider.

By section 11 a person guilty of an offence under section 9 shall be liable;

(a) on summary conviction to a £1,000 fine and or three months imprisonment;

(b) on conviction on indictment to a £20,000 fine and or two years imprisonment.

Chapter 30

Miscellaneous statutory offences of a public nature

This chapter deals with offences under the following Acts:
> Gaming and Lotteries Act, 1956
> Defamation Act, 1961
> Litter Act, 1982
> Control of Dogs Act, 1986
> Incitement to Hatred Act, 1989
> Video Recording Act, 1989
> Electoral Act, 1992

Gaming and Lotteries Act, 1956

Unlawful gaming s. 4

(1) No person shall promote or assist in promoting or provide facilities for any kind of gaming-

(a) in which by reason of the nature of the game, the chances of all the players, including the banker, are not equal, or

(b) in which any portion of the stakes is retained by the promoter or is retained by the banker otherwise than as winnings on the result of the play, or

(c) by means of any slot-machine.

(2) Such gaming is in this Act referred to as unlawful gaming.

(3) Gaming shall not be unlawful if no stake is hazarded by the players with the promoter or banker other than a charge for the right to take part in the game, provided that -

(a) only one such charge is made in respect of the day on which the game is played, and

(b) the charge is of the same amount for all the players, and

(c) the promoter derives no personal profit from the promotion of the game.

See *D. P. P. V Flanagan (1979)* in respect of (c).

Use of buildings for unlawful gaming s. 5

No person shall open, keep or use any buildings, room or place, enclosed or unenclosed, or permit it to be opened, kept or used for unlawful gaming or take part in the care and management of or in any way assist in conducting the business of any building, room or place so opened, kept or used.

Gaming on licensed premises s. 9

The licensee of premises licensed for the sale of intoxicating liquor shall not permit gaming on the premises.

271

Cheating s. 11

Every person who by any fraud or cheat in promoting or operating or assisting in promoting or operating or in providing facilities for any game or in acting as banker for those who play or in playing at, or in wagering on the event of, any game, sport pastime or exercise wins from any other person or causes or procures any person to win from another anything capable of being stolen shall be deemed guilty of obtaining such thing from such other person by a false pretence, with intent to defraud, within the meaning of section 10 of the Criminal Justice Act, 1951, and on conviction shall be punished accordingly. See also page 143.

Proof s. 43

It shall not be necessary in support of a prosecution in relation to unlawful gaming to prove that any person found playing at any game was playing for any money, wager or stake.

Offences s. 44

A person who contravenes any provision of this Act for which a penalty is not specifically provided shall be guilty of an offence and shall on summary conviction thereof be liable to a £100 fine and or three months imprisonment.

Defamation Act, 1961

The Defamation Act, 1961 at Part II makes provision for criminal proceedings for libel.

Competence of jury to give general verdict s. 5

(1) On every trial of an indictment for making or publishing any libel to which a plea of not guilty is entered, the jury may give a general verdict of guilty or not guilty upon the whole matter put in issue on the indictment, and the jury shall not be required or directed by the court to find the person charged guilty merely on proof of the publication by him of the paper charged to be a libel and of the sense ascribed to such paper in the indictment.

(2) On every such trial the court shall, according to its discretion, give its opinion and directions to the jury on the matter in issue in like manner as in other criminal cases.

(3) Subsections (1) and (2) of this section shall not operate to prevent the jury from finding a special verdict, in their discretion as in other criminal cases.

Plea of truth of matters charged publication for public benefit s. 6

On the trial of any indictment for a defamatory libel, the person charged having pleaded such plea as hereinafter mentioned the truth of the matters charged may be inquired into but shall not amount to a defence, unless it was for the public benefit that the said matters charged should be published; and, to entitle the defendant to give evidence of the truth of such matters charged as a defence to such indictment, it shall be necessary for the person charged, in pleading to the said indictment, to allege the truth of the said matters charged, in the manner required in pleading a justification to an action for defamation, and further to allege that it was for the public benefit that the said matters charged should be published, and the particular fact or facts by reason of which it was for the public benefit that the said matters charged should be published, to which plea the prosecutor shall be at liberty to reply generally, denying the whole thereof; and if, after such plea, the person charged is convicted on such indictment, the court may, in pronouncing sentence, consider whether his guilt is aggravated or mitigated by the said plea and by the evidence given to prove or to disprove the same: provided that-

(a) the truth of the matters charged in the alleged libel complained of by such indictment shall in no case be inquired into without such plea of justification;

(b) in addition to such plea of justification, the person charged may enter a plea of not guilty;

(c) nothing in this section shall take away or prejudice any defence under the plea of not guilty which it is competent to the person charged to make under such plea to any indictment for defamatory libel.

Evidence to rebut *prima facie* case of publication by agent s. 7

Whenever, upon the trial of an indictment for the publication of a libel, a plea of not guilty having been entered, evidence is given establishing a presumption of publication against the person charged by the act of any other person by his authority, it shall be competent for the person charged to prove that the publication was made without his authority, consent or knowledge and that the publication did not arise from want of due care or caution on his part.

Order of Judge required for prosecution of newspaper s. 8

No criminal prosecution shall be commenced against any proprietor, publisher, editor or any person responsible for the publication of a newspaper for any libel published therein without the order of a Judge of the High Court sitting *in camera* being first had and obtained, and every application for such order shall be made on notice to the person accused, who shall have an opportunity of being heard against the application.

Inquiry as to libel being for public benefit or being true s. 9

A Judge of the District Court, upon the hearing of a charge against a proprietor, publisher or editor or any person responsible for the publication of a newspaper for a libel published therein, may receive evidence as to the publication being for the public benefit, as to the matters charged in the libel being true, as to the report being fair and accurate and published without malice and as to any matter which, under this or any other Act or otherwise, might be given in evidence by way of defence by the person charged on his trial on indictment, and the Judge, if of the opinion after hearing such evidence that there is a strong or probable presumption that the jury on the trial would acquit the person charged, may dismiss the case.

Summary conviction for libel s. 10

If a Justice of the District Court is of the opinion that, the libel was of a trivial character may with the consent of the accused deal with the case summarily and impose a fine not exceeding £50.

Penalty for maliciously publishing defamatory libel s. 11

Every person who maliciously publishes any defamatory libel, shall on conviction on indictment be liable to a £200 fine and or one year imprisonment.

Penalty for maliciously publishing libel known to be false s. 12

Every person who maliciously publishes any defamatory libel, knowing the same to be false, shall on conviction on indictment be liable to a £500 fine and or two years imprisonment.

Also see chapter 33 for reference to section 13 (blasphemous or obscene libel).

Must be published

To make a writing a libel it must be published, i.e. communicated to some person. In a criminal prosecution communication to a single person, even the person libelled is a sufficient publication even if it be contained in a private letter. Any person who is concerned in the writing or publishing of a libel is liable to conviction, unless his part in the transaction is innocent or is a lawful act.

Criminal libel at common law

A criminal libel is a malicious defamation expressed either in printing or writing or by signs or pictures, tending either to blacken the memory of one who is dead or the reputation of one who is alive and thereby exposing him to public hatred, contempt, ridicule. Because of its tendency to provoke a breach of the peace such a libel is criminal. A criminal libel is a misdemeanour at common law.

Litter Act, 1982

Prohibition of creation of litter s. 3

(1) A person shall not-

(a) deposit anywhere, whether in a receptacle or not, any substance, material or thing for collection by or on behalf of a local authority, or

(b)(i) otherwise place or leave, anywhere, or

(ii) throw down, anywhere, any substance, material or thing,

so as to create or tend to create litter in a public place or litter that is visible from a public place.

(2) A person shall not load, transport, unload or otherwise handle or process any substance, material or thing, or carry on a trade, in a manner that creates or tends to create litter in a public place or litter that is visible from a public place.

(3) A person who contravenes subsections (1) or (2) shall be guilty of an offence.

Duty of occupiers of land in relation to litter s. 4

(1) The occupier of any land (not being a public road or a building or other structure) that is a public place shall keep the land free of litter.

(2) The occupier of any land (other than a building or other structure) that is not a public place shall keep the land free of litter that is visible from a public place.

(5) A person who contravenes subsections (1) or (2) ... shall be guilty of an offence.

(6) In a prosecution for an offence under this section, it shall be a good defence to show that reasonable steps were taken to keep free of litter the land to which the prosecution relates.

Provisions regarding certain offences s. 5

(1) Where a litter warden has reasonable grounds for believing that a person is committing or has committed an offence under section 3, a notice requiring a payment of £25 may be given to such person.

Penalty s. 15

A person guilty of an offence under this Act shall be liable on summary conviction to a £800 fine.

Control of Dogs Act, 1986

The Control of Dogs (Amendment) Act, 1992 amended the 1986 Act to provide additional powers to deal with the problem of dangerous dogs, the provisions of the 1986 Act below are as amended.

"general dog licence" s. 1
"general dog licence" means a licence means a licence entitling a person to keep an unspecified number of dogs at a premises specified in the premises only being so specified

Prohibition on keeping a dog without a licence s. 2
It shall be unlawful for any person to-
(a) keep a dog unless he holds either-
(i) a dog licence for that dog, or
(ii) a general dog licence.
Failure to comply is an offence for which the penalty is £100 fine for each dog.

Effectual control of dogs s. 9(1)
The owner or any other person in charge of a dog shall not permit the dog to be in any place other than
(a) the premises of the owner, or
(b) the premises of such other person in charge of the dog, or
(c) the premises of any other person, with the consent of that person,
unless such owner or such other person in charge of the dog accompanies it and keeps it under effectual control. A failure to comply is an offence for which the penalty is a £500 fine and/or one months imprisonment.

Worrying livestock s. 9(2)
If a dog worries livestock, the owner or any other person in charge of the dog shall be guilty of an offence unless it is established that at the material time the dog worried the livestock for the purpose of removing trespassing livestock and that having regard to all the circumstances the action was reasonable and necessary. A person guilty of an offence shall be liable to a £500 fine and/or one months imprisonment.

Prohibition of Incitement to Hatred Act, 1989

The Prohibition of Incitement to Hatred Act, 1989 was passed to prohibit incitement to hatred on account of race, religion, nationality or sexual orientation. It enables Ireland to ratify the United Nations Covenant on Civil and Political Rights, which was adopted on 16th December 1966. The Bill as initiated was amended to include hatred against a group of persons on account of their membership of the travelling community or sexual orientation.

At common law incitement to hatred could constitute a criminal libel, now new offences have been created by statute.

Actions likely to stir up hatred s. 2

It shall be an offence for a person -

(a) to publish or distribute written material,

(b) to use words, behave or display written material -

(i) in any place other than inside a private residence, or

(ii) inside a private residence so that the words, behaviour or material are heard or seen by persons outside the residence, or

(c) to distribute, show or play a recording of visual images or sounds,

if the written material, words, behaviour, visual images or sounds, as the case may be, are threatening, abusive or insulting and are intended or, having regard to all the circumstances, are likely to stir up hatred.

Hatred

Hatred means hatred against a group of persons in the State or elsewhere on account of their race, colour, nationality, religion, ethnic or national origins, membership of the travelling community or sexual orientation.

Group of persons

It should be noted that hatred must be directed against a "group" of persons, rather than individual persons.

Private residence

By section 2(3), private residence does not include any part not used as a dwelling, or any part in which a public meeting is being held; "public meeting" means a meeting at which the public are entitled to be present, on payment or otherwise and as a right or by virtue of an express or implied permission.

State or elsewhere

In relation to this offence and an offence under section 4 below and given the definition of hatred, all offence created by the Act are of an extra jurisdictional effect.

Defence

By sub-section 2, if the accused person is not shown to have intended to stir up hatred, it shall be a defence for him to prove that he was not aware of the content of the material or recording concerned and did not suspect, and had no reason to suspect, that the material or recording was threatening, abusive or insulting.

Prohibition of Incitement to Hatred Act, 1989

In relation to b(i), it shall be a defence for the accused person -

(i) to prove that he was inside a private residence at the relevant time and had no reason to believe that the words, behaviour or material concerned would be heard or seen by a person outside the residence, or

(ii) if he is not shown to have intended to stir up hatred, to prove that he did not intend the words, behaviour or material concerned to be, and was not aware that they might be, threatening, abusive or insulting.

Broadcasts likely to stir up hatred s. 3

If an item involving threatening, abusive or insulting visual images or sounds is broadcast, each of the persons mentioned below is guilty of an offence if he intends thereby to stir up hatred or, having regard to all the circumstances, hatred is likely to be stirred up thereby.

The persons referred to are:

(a) the person providing the broadcasting service concerned,

(b) any person by whom the item concerned is produced or directed,

(c) any person whose words or behaviour in the item concerned are threatening, abusive or insulting.

Defence

In proceedings against a person referred to in paragraph (a) or (b) for an offence, if the person is not shown to have intended to stir up hatred, it is a defence for him to prove-

(a) that he did not know and had no reason to suspect that the item concerned would involve the material to which the offence relates, or

(b) in a case other than (a) relates, that, having regard to the circumstances in which the item was broadcast, it was not reasonably practicable for him to secure the removal of the material aforesaid.

In proceedings against a person referred to in (b), it is a defence for the person to prove that he did not know and had no reason to suspect -

(a) that the item would be broadcast, or

(b) that the circumstances in which the item would be broadcast would be such that hatred would be likely to stirred up.

In proceedings against a person referred to in (c), it is a defence for the person to prove that he did not know and had no reason to suspect -

(a) that an item involving the use of the material to which the offence relates would be broadcast, or

(b) that the circumstances in which such an item would be broadcast would be such that hatred would be likely to be stirred up.

It shall be a defence for him to prove that he did not know, and had no reason to suspect, that the material to which the offence relates was threatening, abusive or insulting.

Powers of Garda Síochána

If a member of the Garda Síochána not below the rank of superintendent has reasonable grounds for suspecting -

(i) that an offence under section 3 has been committed by a person in respect of an item included in a broadcast, or

278

(ii) that an item is to be so included and that an offence under the section is likely to be committed by a person in respect of the item,

he may make an order in writing authorising any member of the Garda Síochána, to require any person named in the order to produce, if such thing exists-

(A) a script, or (B) a recording, and if produced, to require the person to afford him an opportunity of causing a copy thereof to be made.

Any person who without reasonable excuse fails or refuses to comply with a requirement made shall be guilty of an offence.

Preparation and possession of material s. 4

It shall be an offence for a person-

(a) to prepare or be in possession of any written material with a view to it being distributed, displayed, broadcast or otherwise published, in the State or elsewhere, whether by himself or another, or

(b) to make or be in possession of a recording of sounds or visual images with a view to its being distributed, shown, played, broadcast or otherwise published, in the State or elsewhere, whether by himself or another,

if the material or recording is threatening, abusive or insulting and is intended or, having regard to all the circumstances, including such distribution, display, broadcasting, showing, playing or other publication thereof as the person has, or it may reasonably be inferred that he has, in view, is likely to stir up hatred.

This section of the Act was included to deal with the situation where racist material was being prepared in the State for distribution outside the State.

Defence

If the accused is not shown to have intended to stir up hatred, it shall be a defence for him to prove that he was not aware of the content of the material or recording concerned and did not suspect, and had no reason to suspect, that the material or recording was threatening, abusive or insulting. Where it is proved that the accused person was in possession of material or a recording such as is referred to above and it is reasonable to assume that the material or recording was not intended for the personal use of the person, he shall be presumed, until the contrary is proved, to have been in possession of the material or recording in contravention of the above offence.

Penalties s. 6

A person guilty of an offence under section 2, 3 or 4 shall be liable

(a) on summary conviction, to a fine not exceeding £1,000 or to imprisonment for a term not exceeding 6 months or to both, or

(b) on conviction on indictment, to a fine not exceeding £10,000 or to imprisonment for a term not exceeding two years or to both.

Consent of Director of Public Prosecutions s. 8

Where a person is charged with an offence under section 2, 3, or 4 no further proceedings in the matter (other than any remand in custody or on bail) shall be taken except by or with the consent of the Director of Public Prosecutions.

Search and seizure s. 9

If a justice of the District Court or a Peace Commissioner is satisfied on the sworn information of a member of the Garda Síochána not below the rank of sergeant that there are reasonable grounds for suspecting that an offence under sections 3 or 4 has been or is being committed on any premises, he may issue a warrant.

Powers of arrest s. 10

If a member of the Garda Síochána reasonably suspects that a person has committed an offence :

(i) under section 2(1)(b), he may arrest him without warrant.

(ii) referred to above, he may require him to give him his name and address and, if the person fails or refuses to do so or gives a name or address that the member reasonably suspects to be false or misleading, the member may arrest him without warrant.

Forfeiture

By section 11 of the Act, the court by or before which a person is convicted of an offence under section 2, 3 or 4 may order any written material or recording shown to the satisfaction of the court to relate to the offence to be forfeited and either destroyed or otherwise disposed of in such manner as the court may determine.

Video Recordings Act, 1989

The Video Recordings Act, 1989 makes provision for the control and regulation of the supply and importation of video recordings.

Exempted supply s. 2
"exempted supply" includes a supply of a video recording-
(a) that is neither a supply for reward nor a supply in the course or furtherance of a business, or...

Supply certificate s. 3
The Official Censor shall, on application to him in relation to a video work, grant a supply certificate declaring the work to be fit for viewing.

Prohibition of supply of uncertificated video works s. 5
(1) A person who supplies or offers to supply a video recording containing a video work in respect of which a supply certificate is not in force for the time being shall be guilty of an offence unless-
(a) the supply is, or would if it took place be, an exempted supply, or
(b) the work is an exempted work.
(2) It shall be a defence to a charge of committing an offence under this section to prove that the accused believed on reasonable grounds-
(a) that the video work concerned ... was either an exempted work or a work in respect of which a supply certificate was in force at the time of the commission of the offence alleged, or
(b) that the supply concerned was, or would if it took place be, an exempted supply.
(3) A person guilty of an offence under this section shall be liable-
(a) on summary conviction to a £1,000 fine and/or 12 months imprisonment, or
(b) on conviction on indictment to a fine and/or 3 years imprisonment.

Prohibition orders s. 7
If the Official Censor, having examined a video recording containing a video work, is of opinion that the work is unfit for viewing, he may make a prohibition order.

Prohibition of supply of video recordings of prohibited works s. 8
(1) A person who supplies or offers to supply a video recording containing a video work in respect of which a prohibition order is in force for the time being shall be guilty of an offence unless the supply is, or would if it took place be, an exempted supply.
(2) It shall be a defence to a charge of committing an offence under this section to prove that the accused believed on reasonable grounds-
(a) that the video work/recording concerned ... was not a work in respect of which a prohibition order was in force at the time of the commission of the offence alleged, or

(b) that the supply concerned was, or would if it took place be, an exempted supply.

(3) A person guilty of an offence under this section shall be liable-

(a) on summary conviction to a £1,000 fine and/or 12 months imprisonment, or

(b) on conviction on indictment to a fine and/or 3 years imprisonment.

Prohibition of possession for supply contrary to section 8 s. 9

(1) A person who has in his possession for the purpose of supplying it a video recording containing a video work in respect of which a prohibition order is in force for the time being shall be guilty of an offence unless he has it in his possession for the purposes only of a supply that, if it took place would be, an exempted supply.

(2) It shall be a defence to a charge of committing an offence under this section to prove that the accused believed on reasonable grounds-

(a) that the video work/recording concerned ... was not a work in respect of which a prohibition order was in force at the time of the commission of the offence alleged, or

(b) had the video recording concerned in his possession for the purposes only of a supply that he believed on reasonable grounds would, if it took place be, an exempted supply.

(3) A person guilty of an offence under this section shall be liable-

(a) on summary conviction to a £1,000 fine and/or 12 months imprisonment, or

(b) on conviction on indictment to a fine and/or 3 years imprisonment.

Prohibition of exhibition of certain video works s. 11

... a person who causes or permits, or is concerned in causing or permitting, a video work in respect of which-

(a) a supply certificate is not in force for the time being, or

(b) a prohibition order is in force for the time being,

to be viewed-

(i) elsewhere than in a private dwelling,

(ii) in a private dwelling for reward, or

(iii) in a private dwelling by persons other than himself, the occupier of the private dwelling where it is viewed, members of the family or the household of himself or of such occupier or *bona fide* guests of himself or such occupier,

shall be guilty of an offence, and liable on summary conviction to a £1,000 fine.

Prohibition of false indication as to supply certificate s. 13

(1) A person who supplies, offers to supply or has in his possession for the purpose of supplying it a video recording containing a video work in respect of which a supply certificate is not in force for the time being shall be guilty of an offence if the recording, or any spool, case or other thing on or in which it is kept, contains an indication that such a

certificate is in force for the time being.

(2) A person who supplies, offers to supply or has in his possession for the purpose of supplying it a video recording containing a video work in respect of which a supply certificate is not in force for the time being shall be guilty of an offence if the recording, or any spool, case or other thing on or in which it is kept, contains an indication that the classification of the work is a higher classification than that in force for the time being.

A person guilty of an offence under this section shall be liable on summary conviction to a fine not exceeding £1,000.

Restriction of importation of certain video recordings s. 16

A person shall not, except under and in accordance with a permit, import into the State a video recording containing a video work in respect of which a prohibition order is in force for the time being. To do so is an offence. A person guilty of an offence under this section shall be liable on summary conviction to a fine not exceeding £1,000.

Prohibition of sale or letting on hire by unlicensed persons s. 19

(1) Subject to the provisions of this section, a person shall not sell, or let on hire, a video recording except in accordance with a licence for the time being in force. To do so is an offence. A person guilty of an offence under this section shall be liable on summary conviction to a fine not exceeding £1,000.

Prohibition of possession for sale or hire contrary to section 19 s. 20

(1) A person who has in his possession a video recording for the purpose of selling it or letting it on hire contrary to section 19 shall be guilty of an offence.

A person guilty of an offence under this section shall be liable on summary conviction to a £1,000 fine and/or 12 months imprisonment.

Prohibition of false information and alteration of licences s. 21

(1) A person shall not knowingly give false information to the Official Censor in relation to an application for a licence.

(2) A person shall not forge a document purporting to be a licence, or use any such document, with intent to deceive.

(3) A person shall not alter or use a licence, or use an altered licence, with intent to deceive.

A person who contravenes this section shall be guilty of an offence under this section shall be liable on summary conviction to a £1,000 fine and/or 12 months imprisonment.

Powers of arrest s. 26

(1) If a member of the Garda Síochána reasonably suspects that a person has committed an offence under this Act, he may require him to give him his name and address and, if the person fails or refuses o do so

or gives a name and address that the member reasonably suspects to be false or misleading, the member may arrest him without warrant.

Offences by bodies corporate s. 27

(1) Where an offence under this Act has been committed by a body corporate and is proved to have been committed with the consent or connivance of or to be attributable to any neglect on the part of a person being a director, manager, secretary or other officer of the body corporate, or a person who was purporting to act in any such capacity, that person as well as the body corporate shall be guilty of the offence and be liable to be proceeded against and be punished accordingly.

Forfeiture of video recordings s. 28(1)

If a person is convicted of an offence under the Act (other than an offence under section 21 or 22) or an offence referred to in section 16(2), the court may order a video recording that is shown to the satisfaction of the court to relate to the offence to be forfeited and either destroyed or otherwise disposed of in such manner as the court may determine.

Electoral Act, 1992

Part XXII of the Electoral Act, 1992 deals with electoral offences, all references below are to that Act.

Personation s. 134

(1) A person who-

(a) at a Dail election applies for a ballot paper in the name of some other person, whether that name be the name of a living person or of a dead person or of a fictitious person, or

(b) having obtained a ballot paper once at a Dail election applies at the same election for a ballot paper in his own name otherwise than under section 102,

shall be guilty of the offence of personation.

(2) For the purposes of this section a person to whom a ballot paper has been issued pursuant to section 68 shall be deemed to have obtained a ballot paper.

(3) A person who aids, abets, counsels or procures the commission of the offence of personation shall be guilty of an offence.

Bribery s. 135

(1) A person shall not, in relation to a Dail election-

(a) give valuable consideration to induce a voter to vote, or to procure the election of any person or the vote of any voter, or on account of a voter having voted; or

(b) procure by means of, or in consequences of, valuable consideration, the election of any person or the vote of any voter, or

(c) withdraw or refrain from withdrawing, in consequences of any valuable consideration, from being a candidate; or

(d) induce, by means of, or in consequence of, valuable consideration, any person to withdraw or to refrain from withdrawing from being a candidate; or

(e) receive, agree or contract to receive, valuable consideration for voting or agreeing to vote.

(2) A person who contravenes subsection (1) shall be guilty of an offence.

(3) A person who aids, abets, counsels or procures the commission of an offence under this section shall be guilty of an offence.

(4) In this section-

"give", "induce" and "procure" include agreeing or promising or attempting to give, induce or procure, as the case may be, and whether directly or indirectly;

"valuable consideration" includes the giving, lending or agreeing to give or lend, or the offer or promise to procure or to attempt to procure, any money, money's worth or valuable security or any valuable consideration or any office, place or employment to or for any person;

"vote" includes voting in a particular way or refraining from voting.

Undue influence s. 136

A person who, in relation to a Dail election, directly or indirectly makes use of or threatens to make use of any force, violence or restraint against or inflicts or causes or threatens to inflict or cause any temporal or spiritual injury or loss on or to any person, or attempts by abduction, duress, or fraud-

(a) to induce or compel any person to vote or refrain from voting, or to vote or refrain from voting for a particular person or in a particular way, or

(b) to induce or compel any person to withdraw, or to refrain from withdrawing, from being a candidate, or

(c) to induce or compel any person to be a candidate or to impede or prevent any person from being a candidate, or

(d) to impede or prevent the free exercise of the franchise by any Dail elector,

shall be guilty of an offence.

Disorderly conduct at election meeting s. 139

(1) A person shall be guilty of an offence if, between the date of the issue of a writ for the election of a member or members of the Dail for a constituency and the date on which the return is made to the Clerk of the Dail under section 39, he acts in a disorderly manner at a lawful public meeting held in connection with the election.

(2) A person who aids, abets, counsels or procures the commission of an offence under this subsection (1) shall be guilty of an offence.

Nominating or withdrawing a candidate without consent s. 141

(1) A person shall not-

(a) nominate another person for election under this Act to the Dail, or

(b) withdraw the candidature of another person for such election to the Dail,

save with the consent of that person.

(2) A person who contravenes subsection (1) shall be guilty of an offence.

Forged certification of political affiliation s. 142

A person who produces to a returning officer a certificate such as is referred to in section 46 which that person knows to be false, shall be guilty of an offence.

False declaration on nomination paper s. 143

(1) In case a person who, being a candidate or the proposer of a candidate at a Dail election, makes a declaration on a nomination paper that he has read the notes on the nomination paper and believes the candidate to be eligible for election under this Act then if the candidate is not eligible for election under this Act the person shall be guilty of an offence.

(2) In a prosecution for an offence under subsection (1), it shall be a good defence for the defendant to show that he had reasonable grounds for believing that the candidate was eligible for election.

Obstruction of nomination or poll s. 145

A person who at a Dail election obstructs by violence the nomination of candidates or the poll shall be guilty of an offence.

Obstruction of or interference with electors s. 147

(1) A person shall not interfere with or obstruct or impede an elector going or coming from or in the vicinity of or in a polling station.

(2) During the period commencing 30 minutes before the time appointed for the taking of a poll at an election, including a poll which has been adjourned under section 107, and ending 30 minutes after the close of the said poll, a person shall not, in or in the curtilage of a polling station or in any place within 100 metres of such station, for the purpose of promoting the interest of a political party or furthering the candidature of a candidate or candidates or soliciting votes for a candidate or candidates or for any contrary purpose, do any or all of the following things:

(a) loiter or congregate with other persons;

(b) attempt to induce, by any means whatsoever, an elector to vote for a candidate or candidates or vote in a particular way or refrain from voting;

(c) display or distribute any notice, sign or poster (other than a notice, sign or poster displayed by the returning officer) or card, circular or other document relating to the election; or

(d) use or cause to be used any loud-speaker or other public address mechanism to broadcast matter relating to the election.

(3) For the purpose of this section, a polling station shall be deemed to include all parts of the building and any land within the curtilage of the building in which the polling station is situate and the distance referred to in subsection (2) shall be measured from any entrance to the polling station or to the curtilage thereof.

(4) A person who contravenes subsections (1) or (2) shall be guilty of an offence.

Prohibition on voting by person registered when not entitled s. 149

(1) A person-

(a) who is registered in the register of Dail electors for the time being in force for a constituency but is not entitled to be so registered, or

(b) who is not registered in that register,

shall not vote in that constituency.

(2) A person who contravenes subsection (1) shall be guilty of an offence.

False statement of withdrawal or death of a candidate s. 151

A person who, between the date of the issue of a writ for the election of a member or members of the Dail for a constituency and the date on which the return is made to the Clerk of the Dail under section 39, knowingly publishes a false statement of the withdrawal or death of a candidate at the Dail election shall be guilty of an offence.

Corrupt withdrawal of petition s. 155

A person who makes any agreement or enters into any undertaking in relation to the withdrawal of a petition in consideration of any payment or the cesser of membership of the Dail or for any substantial reason not stated in the affidavit referred to in Rule 8 of the Third Schedule shall be guilty of an offence.

Penalties s. 157

(1) Where a person is guilty of an offence under this Act, other than an offence mentioned in subsection (2), such person shall be liable

(a) on summary conviction to a £1,000 fine and or six months imprisonment, or

(b) on conviction on indictment to a £2,500 fine and or two years imprisonment

(2) Where a person is guilty of an offence under sections 133, 140, 148 or 153 such person shall be liable on summary conviction to a £500 fine and or three months imprisonment.

Chapter 31

Corruption

The statute law is contained in the following:
>Public Bodies Corrupt Practices Act 1889,
>Prevention of Corruption Act 1906,
>Prevention of Corruption Act 1916

The three Acts should be read as one and have been supplemented by the Central Bank Act, 1989.

Corruption in public bodies s. 1 (1889 Act)

(1) Every person who shall by himself or by or in conjunction with any other person corruptly solicit, or receive or agree to receive, for himself or any other person, any gift, loan, fee, reward, or advantage whatsoever as an inducement to, or reward for, or otherwise on account of any member, officer, or servant of a public body doing or forbearing to do anything in respect of any matter or transaction whether actual or proposed in which the said public body is concerned, shall be guilty of a misdemeanour.

(2) Every person who shall by himself or by or in conjunction with any other person corruptly give, promise or offer any gift, loan, fee, reward, or advantage whatsoever to any person, whether for the benefit of that person or of another person, as an inducement to, or reward for, or otherwise on account of any member, officer, or servant of a public body doing or forbearing to do anything in respect of any matter or transaction whether actual or proposed in which the said public body is concerned, shall be guilty of a misdemeanour. The penalty on conviction is £500 fine and or two years imprisonment, together with the return of any gift etc.

corruptly
means a deliberate offering of cash or something similar with the intention that it should operate on the mind of the person to whom it is offered to persuade him to enter into the contract.

public body
means any council of a county, or council of a city or town, also any board of Commissioners which has power to act under any Act relating to Local Government or the public health, or otherwise to administer money raised by rates in pursuance of any public general Act.

advantage
includes any office or dignity and any forbearance to demand any money or money's worth or valuable thing, and includes any aid, consent, vote or influence or pretended aid, vote consent or influence and also includes any promise or procurement of or agreement or endeavour to procure, or the holding out of any expectation of any gift, loan fee, reward or advantage as defined.

289

Corruption of and by agents s. 1 (1906 Act)

(1) If any agent corruptly accepts or obtains, or agrees to accept or attempts to obtain, from any person, for himself or for any other person, any gift or consideration as an inducement or reward for doing or forbearing to do, .. or forborne to do, any act in relation to his principal's affairs or business, or for showing or forbearing to show favour or disfavour to any person in relation to his principal's affairs or business;, or if any person corruptly gives or agrees to give or offers any gift or consideration to any agent as an inducement or reward for doing or forbearing to do,,, done or forborne to do, any act in connection with his principal's business he shall be guilty of a misdemeanour. The penalty on indictment is £500 fine and or two years imprisonment and on summary conviction is £50 and or four months imprisonment.

"agent" in this Act and in the Act of 1916 includes any person employed by or acting for another.

State contracts s. 1 (1916 Act)

A person convicted on indictment of a misdemeanour under the Act of 1889 or the Act of 1906 may be liable to a greater penalty of seven years imprisonment in certain cases where State contracts are involved.

A prosecution shall not be instituted under either of the above Acts without the consent of the Director of Public Prosecutions. In addition if it is proved that any money gift or other consideration has been paid or given to or received by any person in the employment of any Government department or public body, by or from a person, or his agent holding or seeking to obtain a contract from any Government department or public body, the money gift or other consideration shall be deemed to have been paid or given and received corruptly as such inducement or reward as is mentioned in the Acts, unless the contrary is proved.

Prevention of corruption s. 17 (1989 Act)

... the provisions of the above Acts shall apply to every person to whom section 16 of the 1989 Act relates and accordingly section 1(3) of the 1906 Act and section 2 of the 1916 Act shall be construed as if there were included, after the reference to a person holding an office remunerated out of the Central Fund or moneys provided by the Oireachtas, a reference to a person to whom section 16 of the Central Bank Act, 1989 relates

Disclosure of information s. 16 (1989 Act)

(1) A person, who is, Governor or a Director, officer or servant of the Central Bank of Ireland or who is employed by the such bank in any other capacity, shall not disclose, during his term of office or employment or at any time thereafter, any information concerning-

(a) the business of any person or body (whether corporate or unincorporate) which came to his knowledge by virtue of his office o⁻

employment, or

(b) the Central Bank's activities in respect of the protection of the integrity of the currency or the control of credit,

unless such disclosure is to enable the Central Bank to carry out its functions under the Central Bank Acts, 1942 to 1989, or under any enactment amending those Acts.

A contravention is an offence for which the penalty on summary conviction is a £1,000 fine and or 12 months imprisonment, or on conviction on indictment £25,000 fine and or five years imprisonment.

Sub-section (2) provides that the provisions as to non-disclosure shall not apply in particular cases.

Chapter 32

Bigamy

Nature of the offence

Bigamy means being married twice; but in law is used as synonymous with polygamy (i.e. being married to several persons at the same time). It was originally an ecclesiastical offence. In an English Act of 1603 it was made a felony due to it being "to the great dishonour of God,".
R V Allen (1872)

Cockburn J. stated "It involves an outrage on public decency and morals, and creates a public scandal by the prosecution of a solemn ceremony, which the law allows to be applied only to a legitimate union, to a marriage at best but colourable and fictitious, and which may be made and too often is made, the means of the most cruel and wicked deception."

The Offences against the Person Act, 1861, provides:

Bigamy s. 57

Whosoever, being married, shall marry any other person during the life of the former husband or wife, whether the second marriage shall have taken place in Ireland or elsewhere, shall be guilty of felony, and shall be liable on conviction to seven years penal servitude.

Provided that nothing in this section contained shall extend to any second marriage contracted elsewhere than in Ireland by any other than a citizen of Ireland or to any person marrying a second time, whose husband or wife shall have been continually absent from such person for the space of seven years then last past, and shall not have been known by such person to be living within that time, or shall extend to any person who, at the time of such second marriage, shall have been divorced from the bond of the first marriage, or to any person whose former marriage shall have been declared void by the sentence of any court of competent jurisdiction,

"elsewhere" means any other part of the world. Thus a citizen of Ireland who goes through a second marriage anywhere in the world commits an offence.

If the other party is aware of the bigamous nature of the marriage he or she is a principal in the second degree. A clergyman who knowingly assists in a bigamous marriage is liable as an aider and abettor. It would not be a defence for a clergyman to claim that the first marriage was invalid having regard to a decree of nullity being granted by the church to which he belongs.

Statutory exceptions

The proviso to section 57 gives statutory exceptions as follows:
1. Where the second marriage has been contracted outside of Ireland

by someone who is not a citizen of Ireland, thus an American, who is already married in Ireland can marry again abroad with impunity despite the still existing prior marriage.

2. Where in the case of a person marrying a second time their husband or wife shall have been continually absent for seven years, and shall not have been known by such person to be living within that time.

R V Taylor (1950)

This defence is always available even though several bigamous ceremonies have been gone through, the phrase "a second time" is not limited to a second ceremony; it may refer to a third ceremony which forms the basis of the indictment.

3. Where a person has been divorced. Because of the provisions of Article 41.3.3, it is not possible for a marriage to be dissolved by the courts in the State, however there are circumstances where a divorce obtained abroad may be recognised. See Domicile and Recognition of Foreign Divorces Act, 1986, section 5.

4. Where the former marriage of a person has been declared void by any court of competent jurisdiction and a decree of nullity granted. The decree may be granted in any country; whether Ireland or elsewhere. There are a number of grounds upon which a marriage may be declared to be void as distinct from voidable, however their consideration is beyond the scope of this work.

Proof required

In order to prove the offence of bigamy the prosecution must show:

(a) Celebration of the first marriage of the accused. There must be evidence of the ceremony itself, i.e. by production of a certified copy of the marriage register, also evidence of the identity of the parties must be given. It is necessary to prove that the first marriage was validly celebrated.

(b) Proof of the validity of the first marriage. The second marriage is not bigamous unless the first marriage was valid; and the validity of the first marriage must be proved by the prosecution. The law will not presume such in the case of bigamy, as in civil cases.

(c) The subsistence of the first marriage. The prosecution must prove that the spouse of the accused was alive at the date of the second ceremony of marriage. Where the evidence shows only that the first spouse was alive at some time before the second ceremony, the jury must decide whether or not the spouse was alive at the date of that ceremony.

(d) Proof of the second ceremony of marriage. The second ceremony must be proved as was the first. It is no defence that the second marriage was itself void independently of its bigamous character.

R V Brawn (1843)

Lord Denman stated: "It is the appearing to contract a second marriage and the going through the ceremony which constituted the crime of bigamy, otherwise it would never exist in the ordinary cases"

Mens rea

An intention on the part of an accused to go through a second ceremony of marriage would be sufficient to constitute the *mens rea* of the offence. It follows from the doctrine of *mens rea*, that the defendant would not be guilty of bigamy where, he mistakenly thought that:

(a) his spouse had died. Where a person believed that his spouse was dead, however such belief must be reasonable.

R V Tolson (1889)

T. heard that her husband, who had deserted her, had been lost at sea. Five years after she had last saw him, and reasonably believing him to be dead, she remarried. On appeal her conviction for Bigamy was quashed, it was held that, despite the absence from the section of any word such as "knowingly" or "intentionally", a common law rule applied, The rule was that an honest and reasonable belief in the existence of circumstances which, if true, would make the accused's an innocent act, was a good defence.

(b) his first marriage had been dissolved or annulled. It was formerly believed that a mistaken belief that a first marriage was dissolved was not a good defence.

R V Gould (1968)

The Court of Appeal held that the statute should not be construed literally but as subject to the presumption that a crime is not committed if the mind of the person was innocent.

(c) his first marriage was void.

R V King (1964)

An honest and reasonable belief by the defendant, that his first marriage was invalid is a good defence. The mistake must be one of fact and not of law.

There is no modern Irish case law on this offence, an offence which is often committed (due to the absence of divorce legislation); though less often prosecuted.

Chapter 33

Offences concerning religion

Blasphemy

At common law Blasphemy is the denial God and religion. As defined a mere denial constitutes blasphemy, however the courts have not been as strict to convict on such evidence as that alone.

Ramsay and Foote (1883)

"If the decencies of controversy are observed, even the fundamentals of religion may be attached without the writer being guilty of blasphemy. "

Thus the denial of God or religion will not be held criminal if it is expressed in decent and temperate language and not in terms as are likely to lead to a breach of the peace.

The Constitution at Article 40.6.1.i. provides: The State guarantees liberty for the exercise, subject to public order and morality, the right of the citizens to express freely their convictions and opinions. The publication or utterance of blasphemous, seditious, or indecent matter is an offence which shall be punishable in accordance with law.

The offence is not confined to the Christian religions.

Quinn's Supermarket V A. G. (1972)

It was stated in the Supreme Court by Walsh J. that the Constitution reflects a firm conviction that we are (a) religious people .... (Article 44.1) acknowledges that the homage of public worship is due to Almighty God but it does so in terms which do not confine the benefits of that acknowledgement to members of the Christian faith.

The Defamation Act, 1961, provides:

Publishing blasphemous or obscene libel s. 13

(1) Every person who composes, prints or publishes any blasphemous or obscene libel shall, on conviction thereof on indictment, be liable to a £500 fine and or two years imprisonment / seven years penal servitude.

2(a) In every case in which a person is convicted of composing, printing or publishing a blasphemous libel, the court may make an order for the seizure and carrying away and detaining in safe custody, in such manner as shall be directed in the order, of all copies of the libel in the possession of such person or of any other person named in the order for his use, evidence upon oath having previously been given to the satisfaction of the court that copies of the said libel are in the possession of such other person for the use of the person convicted.

Utterance of a blasphemy

There is no statutory provision for the offence of uttering a blasphemy, however in the light of the constitutional provision it would be open to the courts to recognise the utterance of a blasphemy as an offence. It is likely that such an utterance would have to be contemptuous in order to secure a conviction.

The Ecclesiastical Courts Jurisdiction Act, 1860, provides:

Disturbing religious worship s. 2
Any person who shall be guilty of riotous, violent or indecent behaviour in any place of religious worship, whether during the celebration of divine service or at any other time, or in any churchyard or burial ground, or who shall molest, disturb, vex or trouble, or, by any other unlawful means, disquiet or misuse any preacher duly authorised to preach therein, or any clergyman in holy orders ministering or celebrating any sacrament or any divine service, rite or office, in any cathedral, church or chapel, or in any churchyard or burial ground, shall be guilty of of an offence for which the penalty is a £5 fine and or 2 months imprisonment.

This offence can be committed by a clergyman who acts in a violent or indecent way in his own church. An offender may be apprehended immediately after commission of the offence. This offence is known as "brawling".

The Offences against the Person Act, 1861, provides:

Obstructing a clergyman s. 36
Whosoever shall, by threats or force, obstruct or prevent, or endeavour to obstruct or prevent any clergyman, or other minister in or from celebrating divine service, or otherwise officiating in any church, chapel, meeting-house, or other place of divine worship, or in or from the performance of his duty in the lawful burial of the dead in any churchyard or other burial place, or shall strike or offer any violence to, or shall, upon any civil process, or under the pretence of executing any civil process, arrest any clergyman or other minister who is engaged in, or, to the knowledge of the offender, is about to engage in, any of the rites or duties in this section aforesaid, or who to the knowledge of the offender shall be going to perform the same, or returning from the performance thereof, shall be guilty of a misdemeanour. The penalty is two years imprisonment.

Amongst the offences created here are:
Obstructing any clergyman
     (a) officiating in a church, or
     (b) in the performance of his duty at a burial,
or to the knowledge of the offender
     (e) in the above duties of a clergyman, or
     (d) with a clergyman going to or coming from the above.

It must be proved that the person obstructed was a clergyman and that the accused obstructed or prevented him from preforming duties as outlined.

The Burial Laws Amendment Act, 1880, provides:

Violent behaviour at a burial s. 7

All burials under this Act, whether with or without a religious service, shall be conducted in a decent and orderly manner; and ever person ... who shall .. deliver any address, not being part of or incidental to a religious service permitted by this Act, and not otherwise permitted by any lawful authority, or who shall, under colour of any religious service or otherwise, in any such churchyard or graveyard, wilfully endeavour to bring into contempt or obloquy the Christian religion, or the belief or worship of any church or denomination of Christians, or the members or any minister of any such church or denomination, or any other person, shall be guilty of a misdemeanour.

any ever person guilty of any riotous, violent, or indecent behaviour at any burial under this Act, or wilfully obstructing such burial, or any service as aforesaid, ... shall be guilty of misdemeanour.

Assault in a church or environs

It is an indictable misdemeanour at common law to strike any person in a church or churchyard.

Obscenity

Obscenity means something that is filthy, lewd, or disgusting. It has been held to apply to matters of a sexual nature.

Obscene or indecent performance

It is an offence at common law to show an obscene or indecent performance. In general all open lewdness, grossly scandalous, and whatever openly outrages decency or is offensive and disgusting, or is injurious to public morals by tending to corrupt the mind and destroy the love of decency, morality and good order, is a misdemeanour indictable at common law.

See also the the Dublin Police Act, 1842, section 14(12) regarding the sale, distibution, or exhibition of any profane, indecent, or obscene book, etc., at page 259 and the Post Office Act, 1908, section 63 which prohibits the sending of indecent prints through the post at page 266.

The Censorship of Publications Act, 1929, provides:

Indecent publications s. 14(1)

It shall not be lawful to print or publish or cause to procure to be printed or published in relation to any judicial proceedings -

(a) any indecent matter the publication of which would be calculated to injure public morals, or

(b) any indecent medical, surgical or physiological details the publication of which be calculated to injure public morals.

Chapter 34

Offences against Government

The present Irish State deals severely with any threat to it's authority. The Crown was sacrosanct at common law, however the current provisions are statutory. The law in this area is codified and contained in the following:

> Treason Act, 1939;
> Official Secrets Act, 1963;
> Emergency Powers Act, 1976.

The legislation that is used most frequently in this area is the Offences against the State Acts, which are dealt with in the following chapter.

Treason

The Constitution at Article 39 defines treason and provides:

Treason shall consist only in levying war against the State, or assisting any State or persons or inciting or conspiring with any person to levy war against the State, or attempting by force of arms or other violent means to overthrow the organs of Government established by this Constitution, or taking part in or being concerned in or inciting or conspiring with any person to make or take part or be concerned in any such attempt.

It can be seen that an attempt at treason is itself treason.

The Treason Act, 1939 was passed to give effect to this provision of the Constitution. The 1939 Act has been amended by the Criminal Justice Act, 1990 in respect of punishment. All references below are to the 1939 Act, unless otherwise stated.

Penalty for treason s. 1

(1) Every person who commits treason within the State shall be sentenced on conviction thereof to imprisonment for life.

(2) Every person who, being an Irish citizen or ordinarily resident within the State, commits treason outside the State shall be sentenced on conviction thereof to imprisonment for life.

The use of "shall" denotes that no lesser penalty may be passed.

Court of trial s. 1(3)

Treason is to be tried by the Central Criminal Court.

Uncorroborated evidence s. 1(4)

No person shall be convicted of treason on the uncorroborated evidence of one witness.

Treason felony s. 2

(1) Every person who encourages, harbours, or comforts any person whom he knows or has reasonable grounds for believing to be engaged

in committing treason shall be guilty of a felony.

(2) No person shall be convicted of treason felony on the uncorroborated evidence of one witness.

The penalty for treason felony is a £500 fine and or twenty years imprisonment.

Misprision of treason s. 3

Every person who, knowing that any act the commission of which would be treason is intended or proposed to be, or is being, or has been committed, does not forthwith disclose the same, together with all particulars thereof known to him, to a Judge of the District Court, or officer of the Garda Siochana or some other person lawfully engaged on duties relating to the preservation of peace and order shall be guilty of the felony of misprision of treason. The penalty for misprision of treason is five years penal servitude or two years imprisonment.

The Official Secrets Act, 1963

The law relating to official secrets is contained in the Official Secrets Act, 1963, which by section 3 repealed the earlier Acts of 1911 and 1920. All references below are to the 1963 Act unless otherwise stated.

Expressions s. 2

"official document" includes a passport, official pass, permit, document of identity, certificate, licence or other similar document, whether or not completed or issued for use, and also includes an endorsement thereon or addition thereto;

"official information" means any secret official code word or password, and any sketch, plan, model, article, note, document or information which is secret or confidential or is expressed to be either and which is or has been in the possession, custody or control of a holder of a public office, or to which he has or had access, by virtue of his office, and includes information recorded by film or magnetic tape or by any other recording medium;

"public office" means an office or employment which is wholly remunerated out of the Central Fund or out of moneys provided by the Oireachtas, or an appointment to, or employment under, any commission, committee or tribunal set up by the Government or a Minister for the purposes of any inquiry but does not include membership of either House of the Oireachtas;

"State authority" means the Attorney General, the Comptroller and Auditor General, the Revenue Commissioners, the Commissioners of Public Works in Ireland.

Part II of the Act deals with official information

Unlawful Communication of Official Information s. 4

(1) A person shall not communicate any official information to any other person unless he is duly authorised to do so or does in the course of and in accordance with his duties as the holder of a public office or when it is his duty in the interest of the State to communicate it.

(2) A person to whom subsection (1) applies shall take reasonable care to avoid any unlawful communication of such information.

(3) A person shall not obtain official information where he is aware or has reasonable grounds for believing that the communication of such information to him would be a contravention of subsection (1).

(4) In this section "duly authorised" means authorised by a Minister or State authority or by some person authorised in that behalf by a Minister or State authority.

Confidential information s. 5

(1) A person who is or has been

(a) a party to a contract with a Minister or State authority or with any person on behalf of a Minister or State authority, or

(b) employed by such party,

shall not communicate to any third party any information relating to the contract and expressed therein to be confidential.

(2) A person to whom subsection (1) applies shall take reasonable care to avoid any unlawful communication of such information.

(3) It shall be a good defence to a prosecution for a contravention of this section to prove that the communication was authorised in writing by the Minister or State authority or by the party contracting on behalf of the Minister or State authority.

Retention of information s. 6

(1) A person shall not retain any official document or anything which constitutes or contains official information when he has no right to retain it or when not required by his duty as the holder of a public office to retain it.

(2) A person shall comply with all directions issued by a Minister or the Secretary of a Department or any person authorised by a Minister under seal as to the return or disposal of any official document or anything which constitutes or contains official information and which is in his possession or under his control.

(3) The Taoiseach may give directions as to the return or disposal of any original document specified which contain official information and which are in the possession or under the control of any person who formerly held office as a Minister or Parliamentary Secretary/Minister of State.

(4) Subsections (1) and (2) shall not apply to a person who formerly held an office to which subsection (3) applies.

Possession of official dies s. 7

(1) A person shall not-

(a) use or have in possession, or under his control, without lawful authority or excuse, any official die, seal or stamp, or any die seal or stamp so nearly resembling it as to be calculated to deceive, or

(b) counterfeit any official die, seal or stamp, or

(c) use or have in his possession or under his control, without lawful authority or excuse, any such counterfeit die, seal or stamp, or

(d) manufacture or sell or have in his possession for sale, without lawful authority or excuse, any official die, seal or stamp.

(2) In this section "official die, seal or stamp" means a die, seal or stamp of or belonging to, or used, made or provided by a Minister or State authority or any diplomatic or consular agent or other authority appointed by or acting under authority of the Government.

Forging official documents s. 8

A person shall not-,

(a) forge or, without lawful authority or excuse, alter or tamper with any official document, or

(b) use or have in his possession or under his control, without lawful authority or excuse any forged, altered or irregular official document.

Part III of the Act deals with communication of information to the prejudice of the safety or preservation of the State

Acts contrary to the Safety or Preservation of the State s. 9

(1) A person shall not, in any manner prejudicial to the safety or preservation of the State-

(a) obtain, record, communicate to any other person or publish, or

(b) have in his possession or under his control any document containing, or other record whatsoever of,

information relating to-

(i) the number, description, armament, equipment, disposition, movement or condition of any of the Defence Forces or of any vessels or aircraft belonging to the State,

(ii) any operations or projected operations of any of the Defence Forces or of the Garda Siochana or any of the vessels or aircraft belonging to the State,,

(iii) any measures for the defences or fortification of any place on behalf of the State,

(iv) munitions of war, or

(v) any other matter whatsoever information as to which would or might be prejudicial to the safety or preservation of the State.

(2) When a person is charged with a contravention of this section it shall be a good defence to prove that the act in respect of which he is charged was authorised by a Minister or by some person authorised in that behalf by a Minister or was done in the course of and in accordance

with his duties as the holder of a public office.

Communication with foreign agents ... s. 10

(1) Where a person is charged with contravening section 9, the fact that he has (whether within or outside the State) been in communication with or attempted to communicate with a foreign agent or with a member of an unlawful organisation shall be evidence that the act with which he is charged has been done in a manner prejudicial to the safety or preservation of the State.

(2) A person shall, unless he proves the contrary, be deemed to have been in communication with a foreign agent or a member of an unlawful organisation if he has (whether within or outside the State) visited the address of a foreign agent or a member of an unlawful organisation or consorted or associated with such agent or member, or if (whether within or outside the State) the name or address or any other information regarding a foreign agent or a member of an unlawful organisation has been found in his possession or has been supplied by him to any other person or has been obtained by him from any other person.

(3) Any address (whether within or outside the State) reasonably suspected of being an address used for the receipt of communications intended for a foreign agent or a member of an unlawful organisation, or any address at which such a person resides, or to which he resorts for the purpose of giving or receiving communications, or at which he carries on any business, shall be deemed to be the address of a foreign agent or a member of an unlawful organisation and communications addressed to that address to be communications with a foreign agent or a member of an unlawful organisation.

(4) In this section-
"foreign agent" includes any person who is or has been or is reasonably suspected of being or having been employed by a foreign power either directly or indirectly for the purpose of committing an act (whether within or outside the State) prejudicial to the safety or preservation of the State, or who has or is reasonably suspected of having (whether within or outside the State) committed or attempted to commit any such act;
"member of an unlawful organisation" means any person who is or has been or is reasonably suspected of being or having been a member of an unlawful organisation within the meaning and for the purpose of the Offences against the State Act, 1939.

Harbouring offenders and failure to report offences s. 11

(1) A person shall not knowingly harbour any person whom he knows or has reasonable grounds for supposing to have contravened or to be about to contravene section 9.

(2) A person who becomes aware that there has been or is about to be a contravention of section 9 shall forthwith disclose to a member of the

Garda Siochana or the Defence Forces any information in relation thereto which it is in his power to give.

Proceedings in camera s. 12

If in the course of proceedings, including proceedings on appeal, for an offence under section 9 or for an offence under Part II (in relation to the unlawful communication of official information) committed in a manner prejudicial to the safety or preservation of the State, application is made by the prosecution on the ground that the publication of any evidence or statement to be given or made during any part of the hearing would be prejudicial to the safety or preservation of the State, that that part of the hearing shall be in camera, the court shall make an order to that effect,, but the verdict and sentence (if any) shall be announced in public.

Part IV of the Act deals with legal proceedings and supplementary matters.

Penalties s. 13

(1) A person who contravenes or attempts to contravene any provision of this Act shall, without prejudice to any other enactment, be guilty of an offence, penalty a £100 fine and or six months imprisonment.

(3) A person <u>shall</u> be triable on indictment for any offence under Section 9 or under Part II committed in a manner prejudicial to the safety or preservation of the State, and on conviction shall be liable to two years imprisonment or seven years penal servitude

Consent of Attorney General s. 14

(1) Proceedings for any offence under this Act shall not be instituted except by or with the consent of the Attorney General.

(2) Before such consent is obtained a person charged with an offence under section 9 may be arrested, or a warrant for his arrest may be issued and executed, and he may be remanded in custody or on bail, but not in any case later than eight days after he has been first remanded, and no further proceedings shall be taken until such consent is obtained.

The Prosecution of Offences Act, 1974, at section 3(5) provides that where a person is charged with an offence under section 3 of the Geneva Convention Act, 1962 the Official Secrets Act, 1963 or the Genocide Act, 1973, no further proceedings in the matter except remands in custody or on bail as the court may think necessary shall be taken without the consent of the Attorney General.

The remainder of the Act deals with apprehension and detention (section 15); search warrants (section 16) and failure to give information (section 17).

Emergency Powers Act, 1976

The Constitution at Article 28.3.3 provides:

Nothing in this Constitution shall be invoked to invalidate any law enacted by the Oireachtas which is expressed to be for the purpose of securing the public safety and the preservation of the State in time of war or armed rebellion, or to nullify any act done or purporting to be done in time of war or armed rebellion in pursuance of any such law.

Each of the House of the Oireachtas resolved that a national emergency existed on the first day of September 1976 in relation to the Emergency Powers Act, 1976.

When in force s. 1(1)

Section 2 of this Act shall remain in force only until the expiry of the period of twelve months beginning with the passing of this Act, unless it is continued in force or is again brought into force by an order under this section. At the time of writing section 2 is not in force.

Detention s. 2

(1) A member of the Garda Siochana (on production of his identification card, if demanded where he is not in uniform) may without warrant stop, search, question and arrest any person, if he suspects with reasonable cause that that person has committed an offence under the Offences against the State Act, 1939, or an offence which is a scheduled offence under Part V of the Act, or if he suspects with reasonable cause that the person is carrying anything, or is in possession of information relating to such an offence.

(2) Any vehicle or vessel which he suspects may also be stopped.

(3) Whenever a person is arrested, he may be kept in custody for 48 hours and may, if a member of the Garda Siochana not below the rank of chief superintendent so directs, be kept in custody for another five days.

(4) A detained person may be charged before the District Court, the Special Criminal Court or be released at the end of the detention period.

(5) The powers conferred by section 30 of Offences against the State Act, 1939, shall not be exercisable during a period when this section is in force.

Also see the Criminal Law Act, 1976, section 7 at page 316.

Comparison with Section 30 of Offences against the State Act

The major difference between Section 2 of this Act and Section 30 of the Offences against the State Act, 1939 are the detention period a maximum of seven days rather than two days (section 30) and the use of the words "suspects with reasonable cause" rather than "suspects" (section 30).

State (Hoey) V Garvey (1978)

It was held by the High Court that section 2 did not authorise the arrest and detention of a person on a second occasion, if the second arrest was grounded on the same suspicion as had justified the first arrest, even though the police had acquired further information between the dates of the two arrests.

Customs Consolidation Act, 1876

The Customs Consolidation Act, 1876, is particularly concerned with smuggling; references below are to that Act unless otherwise stated.

Smuggling

Smuggling consists in bringing on shore, or in carrying from the shore, dutiable goods, wares, or merchandise for which duty has not been paid, or goods the importation of which is prohibited. Smuggling across the land frontier of the State is an offence.

Melling V O'Mathghamhna (1962)

It was held by the Supreme Court that smuggling offences are criminal offences and are minor which may be tried summarily.

Land frontier

The Adaptation of Enactments Act, 1922, section 13 provides that the Minister of Finance may make regulations to apply to the importation and exportation of any goods into and from the State by land, any of the provisions of the Customs Act. He may prohibit the importation and exportation of all goods or of any classes of goods except by such routes within the State and during such hours as may be prescribed. Such regulations are contained in the Customs (Land Frontier) Regulations 1968.

Prohibited goods

The Customs (Amendment) Act, 1942 at section 2(a) provides:

The expression "prohibited goods" includes and always included goods the export of which is prohibited as well as goods the import of which is prohibited.

Forfeiture s. 177

Any goods brought into the State without clearance, shall be forfeited together with any goods which shall be found packed with or used in concealing them.

Ships may be searched within the limits of the ports s. 182

Any officer of customs or other person duly employed for the prevention of smuggling may go on board any ship or boat which shall be within the limits of any port, and rummage and search the cabin and all other parts of such ship or boat for prohibited or uncustomed goods, and remain on board such ship or boat so long as she shall continue within the limits of such port.

Powers of search s. 184

Section 184 as amended by the Customs and Inland Revenue Act 1881, section 12 provides;

Any officer of customs or other person duly employed for the prevention of smuggling may search any person on board any ship or boat within the limits of any port, or any person who shall have landed from any ship or boat, provided such officer or other person has good reason to suppose that such person is carrying or has in his possession uncustomed or prohibited goods about his person.

Any person who

(1) staves, breaks or destroys any goods to prevent the seizure thereof by any officer of customs;

(2) rescues, staves, breaks or destroys any goods seized by a customs officer; or

(3) rescues any person arrested for any customs offence; or

(4) prevents the arrest of any such person; or

(5) assaults or obstructs any customs officer or other person duly employed in the prevention of smuggling, acting in the execution of his duty; or

(6) attempts or endeavours to commit or aids, abets or assists in committing any of the above offences.

commits an offence, for which the penalty is a £100 fine.

Penalty s. 186

Every person who shall illegally import, remove or shall knowingly harbour, keep or conceal upon his premises or person any dutiable or prohibited goods which shall have been illegally unshipped or removed without payment of duty; or shall be in any way knowingly concerned in carrying, removing, depositing, concealing, or in any manner dealing with any such goods with intent to, or shall evade the duties of customs, is liable to the penalty of treble the value or the goods, or £100, and may be detained or proceeded against by summons.

The Finance Act, 1963 section 34(4)(c)(i) provides that in case treble the estimated value of goods exceeds £100, the offence shall be triable on indictment.

Assembling to run goods s. 188

All persons to the number of three or more who shall assemble for or having so assembled shall unship, run, carry, convey, or conceal any spirits, tobacco, or prohibited, restricted, or uncustomed goods shall each forfeit a penalty not exceeding £500 nor less than £100.

Procuring or hiring persons to assemble to run goods s. 189

Every person who shall by any means procure or hire, or shall depute or authorise any other person to procure or hire, any person or persons to assemble for the purpose of being concerned in the landing or unshipping, or carrying, conveying, or concealing any goods which are prohibited to be imported, or the duties for which have not been paid or secured shall be guilty of a misdemeanour for which the penalty is twelve months imprisonment, however if offensive weapons are involved the penalty is three years imprisonment.

Persons shooting at boats belonging to the navy s. 193

Any person maliciously shooting at boats belonging to navy or revenue service, or maliciously shoots at anyone employed in the prevention of smuggling shall be guilty of a felony for which the penalty is five years penal servitude or two years imprisonment.

The Censorship of Publications Act, 1946 provides:

Prohibited book or periodical publication s. 18

(1) No person shall, except under and in accordance with a permit, import any prohibited book or any prohibited periodical publication

(2) Where a person is charged, under section 186 with the importation of a prohibited book or a prohibited periodical publication it shall be a good defence for him to prove that the book or prohibited periodical publication was imported otherwise than for sale or distribution or that it was not a prohibited book or prohibited periodical publication at the time he ordered it.

Chapter 35

Offences against the State Acts

The Offences Against the State Acts make provisions in relation to actions and conduct calculated to undermine public order and the authority of the State, they are as follows:
> Offences Against the State Act, 1939 (the principal Act);
> Offences Against the State (Amendment) Act, 1940;
> Offences Against the State (Amendment) Act, 1972;
> Offences Against the State (Amendment) Act, 1985;

and are supplemented by the following:
> Criminal Law Act, 1976;
> Criminal Law (Jurisdiction) Act, 1976;
> Criminal Justice Act, 1984;
> Criminal Justice (Forensic Evidence) Act, 1990.

The offences against the State created by the Acts are contained in Part II of the principal Act and are as follows;

Usurpation of functions of government s. 6

(1) Every person who usurps or unlawfully exercises any function of government, executive, legislative or judicial, or by forming, maintaining, or being a member of an armed force or a purported police force not legally authorised, or by any other action or conduct whatsoever, shall be guilty of a felony and liable to 20 years imprisonment.

(2) To attempt or aid or abet or conspire to do or attempt to do any such thing or to advocate or encourage the doing of any such thing shall be guilty of a misdemeanour for which the penalty is 20 years imprisonment.

Obstruction of government s. 7

(1) Every person who prevents or obstructs, or attempts or is concerned in an attempt to prevent or obstruct, by force of arms or other violent means or by any form of intimidation the carrying on of the government of the State or any branch (whether legislative, judicial, or executive) of the government of the State or the exercise or performance by any member of the legislature, the judiciary, or the executive or by any officer or employee (whether civil (including police) or military) of the State of any of his functions, powers, or duties shall be shall be guilty of a felony for which the penalty is 20 years imprisonment.

(2) To aid or abet or conspire to do any such thing or advocate or encourage same shall be guilty of a misdemeanour for which the penalty is 20 years imprisonment.

People (D. P. P.) V Kehoe (1983)

The accused was convicted in the Special Criminal Court of this offence. There was evidence that he had used a pole, to aim blows at a Garda, who was guarding the British embassy. It was held by the Court of Criminal Appeal, that the conduct of the accused, as established by the evidence, constituted the commission of the offence.

Obstruction of the President s. 8

(1) Every person who prevents or obstructs, or attempts or is concerned in an attempt to prevent or obstruct, by force of arms or other violent means, or by any form of intimidation the exercise or performance by the President of any of her functions, powers, or duties shall be guilty of a felony and liable 7 years p.s. / 2 years imprisonment.

(2) Every person who aids or abets or conspire with another person to do thing the doing of which is a felony under the foregoing subsection or advocates or encourages the doing of any such thing shall be guilty of a misdemeanour for which the penalty is 2 years imprisonment.

Interferences with military or other employees s. 9

(1) Every person who shall with intent to undermine public order or the authority of the State commit any act of violence against or of interference with a member of a lawfully established military or police force (whether such member is or is not on duty) or shall take away, injure, or otherwise interfere with the arms or equipment, or any part of the arms or equipment, of any such member shall be guilty of a misdemeanour for which the penalty is 2 years.

(2) Every person who shall incite or encourage any person employed in any capacity by the State to refuse, neglect, or omit (in a manner or to an extent calculated to dislocate the public service or a branch thereof) to perform his duty or shall incite or encourage any person so employed to be negligent or insubordinate (in such manner or to such extent as aforesaid) in the performance of his duty shall be guilty of a misdemeanour and shall be liable to 2 years imprisonment.

(3) Every person who attempts to do any thing the doing of which is a misdemeanour under either of the foregoing sub-sections of this section or who aids or abets or conspires with another person to do or attempt to do any such thing or advocates or encourages the doing of any such thing shall be guilty of a misdemeanour for which the penalty is 12 months imprisonment.

Prohibition of printing of certain documents s. 10

(1) It shall not be lawful to set up in type, print, publish, send through the post, distribute, sell, or offer for sale any document-
(a) which is or contains or includes an incriminating document, or
(b) which is or contains or includes a treasonable document, or
(c) which is or contains or includes a seditious document.
Section 2 of the Act, defines such documents as follows:

"incriminating document" means a document, issued by or emanating from an unlawful organisation or appearing to be so issued or so to emanate or purporting or appearing to aid or abet any such organisation or calculated to promote the formation of an unlawful organisation.

"treasonable document" includes a document which relates directly or indirectly to the commission of treason.

"seditious document" includes-

(a) a document consisting of or containing matter calculated or tending to undermine the public order or the authority of the State, and

(b) a document which alleges, implies, or suggests or is calculated to suggest that the government functioning under the Constitution is not the lawful government of the State or that there is in existence in the State any body or organisation not functioning under the Constitution which is entitled to be recognised as being the government of the country, and

(c) a document which alleges, implies, or suggests or is calculated to suggest that the military forces maintained under the Constitution are not the lawful military forces of the State, or that there is in existence in the State a body or organisation not established and maintained by virtue of the Constitution which is entitled to be recognised as a military force, and

(d) a document in which words, abbreviations, or symbols referable to a military body are used in referring to an unlawful organisation.

(2) Any letter etc. in any newspaper etc. on behalf of an unlawful organisation is prohibited

(3) Every person who shall contravene either of the foregoing sub-sections of this section shall be guilty of an offence for which the penalty is £100 fine and or 6 months imprisonment.

Foreign newspapers, etc. s. 11

The Minister for Justice may prohibit the importation of any foreign periodicals which he considers seditious or contains any matter the publication of which is a contravention of the Act.

Possession of documents s. 12

(1) It shall not be lawful for any person to have any, treasonable document, seditious documents, or incriminating document in his possession or on any lands or premises owned or occupied by him or under his control.

(2) Every person who has a treasonable document, seditious documents, or incriminating document in his possession or on any lands or premises owned or occupied by him or under his control shall be guilty of an offence and liable on summary conviction to a £50 fine and or 3 months imprisonment.

(3) Where a person is charged with an offence under this section it shall be a good defence to such charge for such person to prove:

(a) that he is an officer of the State and had possession or custody of the document in respect of which the offence is alleged to have been committed in the course of his duties as such officer, or,

(b) that he did not know that the said document was in his possession or on any lands or premises owned or occupied by him or under his control, or,

(c) that he did not know the nature or contents of the said document.

(4) Every person who has in his possession a treasonable document, seditious document, or incriminating document shall, when so requested by a member of the Garda Siochana, deliver up to such member the said document and every copy thereof in his possession, and if he fails or refuses so to do he shall be guilty of an offence and liable on summary conviction to three months imprisonment.

Documents printed for reward s. 13

It shall be a summary offence, for a person who prints documents for reward not to retain for six months the name and address of his client in order that it may be available to the Garda Siochana. The penalty is £25 fine in the case of a first offence and £50 fine in case of a second or subsequent offence.

Obligation to print printer's name and address s. 14

A person who prints documents for reward, if such document consists only of one page or sheet printed on one side only, is required to print his own name and address on such documents. An omission to do so is a summary offence, for which the penalty is £25 fine in the case of a first offence and £50 fine in case of a second or subsequent offence.

Unauthorised military exercises prohibited s. 15

(1) Save as authorised by a Minister of State under this section, and subject to the exceptions hereinafter mentioned, it shall not be lawful for any assembly of persons to practise or to train or drill themselves in or to be trained or drilled in the use of arms or the performance of military exercises, evolutions, or manoeuvrers nor for any persons to meet together or assemble for the purpose of so practising or training or drilling or being trained or drilled.

(2) A Minister of State may at his discretion by order, subject to such limitations, qualifications and conditions as he shall think fit to impose and shall express in the order, authorise the members of any organisation to meet together and do such one or more of the following things as shall be specified in such order, that is to say, to practise or train or drill themselves in or be trained or drilled in the use of arms or the performance of military exercises, evolutions, or manoeuvres.

(3) If any person is present at or takes part in or gives instruction to or trains or drills an assembly of persons who without or otherwise than in accordance with an authorisation granted by a Minister of State under this section practise, or train or drill themselves in, or are trained or

drilled in the use of arms or the performance of any military exercise, evolution or manoeuvre or who without or otherwise than in accordance with such authorisation have assembled or met together for the purpose of so practising, or training or drilling or being trained or drilled, such person shall be guilty of a misdemeanour, for which the penalty is two years imprisonment.

(4) This section shall not apply to any assembly of members of any military or police force lawfully maintained by the Government.

(5) In any prosecution under this section the burden of proof that any act was authorised under this section shall lie on the person prosecuted.

Secret societies in army or police s. 16

(1) Every person who shall-

(a) form, organise, promote, or maintain any secret society amongst or consisting of or including members of any military or police force lawfully maintained by the Government, or

(b) attempt to form, organise, promote, or maintain any such secret society, or

(c) take part, assist, or be concerned in any way in the formation, organisation, promotion, management, or maintenance of any such society, or

(d) induce, solicit, or assist any member of a military or police force lawfully maintained by the Government to join any secret society whatsoever,

shall be guilty of a misdemeanour and liable to five years penal servitude or two years imprisonment.

Administering unlawful oaths s. 17

(1) Every person who shall administer, or cause to be administered or take part in, be present at, or consent to the administering or taking in any form or manner of any oath, declaration, or engagement purporting or intended to bind the person taking the same to do all or any one of the following things that is to say:-

(a) to commit or to plan, contrive, promote, assist, or conceal the commission of any crime or any breach of the peace, or

(b) to join or become a member of or associated with any organisation having for its object or one of its objects the commission of any crime, or breach of the peace, or

(c) to abstain from disclosing or giving information of the existence or formation or proposed or intended formation of any such organisation, association, or other body as aforesaid or from informing or giving evidence against any member of or person concerned in the formation of any such organisation, association, or other body, or

(d) to abstain from disclosing or giving information of the commission or intended or proposed commission of any crime, breach of the peace, or from informing or giving evidence against the person who committed such an act,

312

shall be guilty of a misdemeanour for which the penalty is two years imprisonment.

(2) Every person who shall take any such oath, declaration, or engagement as is mentioned above shall be guilty of a misdemeanour for which the penalty is two years imprisonment unless he can show-

(a) that he was compelled by force or duress to take such oath, declaration, or engagement (as the case may be), and

(b) that within four days after the taking of such oath, declaration, or engagement, if not prevented by actual force or incapacitated by illness or other sufficient cause, or where so prevented or incapacitated then within four days after the cessor of the hindrance caused by such force, illness or other cause, he declared to an officer of the Garda Siochana the fact of his having taken such oath, declaration, or engagement, and all the circumstances connected therewith and the names and descriptions of all persons concerned in the administrating thereof so far as such circumstances, names, and descriptions were known to him.

Unlawful organisations
Part III of the Act deals with unlawful organisations

Unlawful organisations s. 18
In order to regulate and control in the public interest the exercise of the constitutional right of citizens to form associations, it is hereby declared that any organisation which-

(a) engages in, promotes, encourages, or advocates the commission of treason or any activity of a treasonable nature, or

(b) advocates, encourages, or attempts the procuring by force, violence, or other unconstitutional means of an alteration of the Constitution, or

(c) raises or maintains or attempts to raise or maintain a military or armed force in contravention of the Constitution or without constitutional authority, or

(d) engages in, promotes, encourages, or advocates the commission of any criminal offence or the obstruction of or interference with the administration of justice or the enforcement of the law, or

(e) engages in, promotes, encourages, or advocates the attainment of any particular object, lawful or unlawful, by violent, criminal, or other unlawful means, or

(f) promotes, encourages, or advocates the non-payment of moneys payable to the Central Fund or any other public fund or the non-payment of local taxation,

shall be an unlawful organisation within the meaning and for the purposes of this Act, and this Act shall apply and have effect in relation to such organisation accordingly.

Suppression order s. 19
(1) If and whenever the Government are of opinion that any particular organisation is an unlawful organisation, it shall be lawful for the

Government by order (a suppression order) to declare that such organisation is an unlawful organisation and ought in the public interest, to be suppressed.

Prohibition of membership of an unlawful organisation s. 21

(1) It shall not be lawful for any person to be a member of an unlawful organisation.

(2) Every person who is a member of an unlawful organisation shall be guilty of an offence and be liable:

(a) on summary conviction to a £50 fine and or three months imprisonment, or

(b) on conviction on indictment. up to seven years imprisonment.

(3) It shall be a good defence for a person charged with such membership to show-

(a) that he did not know that such organisations was an unlawful organisation, or,

(b) he had ceased to be a member thereof and dissociated himself therefrom.

Proof of membership of unlawful organisation s. 24

On the trial of a person charged with the offence of being a member of an unlawful organisation, proof to the satisfaction of the court that an incriminating document relating to the said organisation was found on such person or in his possession or on lands or in premises owned or occupied by him or under his control shall, without more, be evidence until the contrary is proved that such person was a member of the said organisation at the time alleged in the said charge.

People V O'Leary (1988)

The appellant was convicted in the Special Criminal Court on a count which charged him with being a member of an unlawful organisation contrary to section 21 and on a count which charged him with possessing incriminating documents contrary to section 12.

The Gardai found on the appellant's premises, thirty-seven copes of a poster which was held to be incriminating, and this was taken to be evidence of membership of an unlawful organisation.

It was held on appeal that the appellant had failed to displace the *prima facie* evidence furnished by his possession of such documents. The conviction was upheld.

Evidence of membership s. 3 (1972 Act)

1(a) Any statement made orally in writing or otherwise, or any conduct, by an accused person implying or leading to a reasonable inference that he was at a material time a member of an unlawful organisation shall, in proceedings under section 21 of the Act of 1939, be evidence that he was then such a member.

(b) In paragraph (a) of this subsection "conduct" includes omission by the accused person to deny published reports that he was a member of an unlawful organisation, but the fact of such denial shall not by itself be conclusive.

(2) Where an officer of the Garda Siochana, not below the rank of Chief Superintendent, in giving evidence in proceedings relating to an offence under the said section 21, states that he believes that the accused was at a material time a member of an unlawful organisation, the statement shall be evidence that he was then such a member.

(3) Subsection (2) shall only be in force as long as Part V of the 1939 Act is in force.

Unlawful public meetings s. 27

It shall not be lawful to hold a public meeting on behalf of an unlawful organisation. In addition any meeting may be rendered unlawful by a member of the Garda Siochana not below the rank of Chief Superintendent by giving notice of such.

See also the Offences against the State (Amendment) Act, 1972, section 4 at page 339.

Prohibition of meetings near Oireachtas s. 28

It shall not be lawful for any public meeting to be held or any procession to pass within one half of a mile of a sitting of either house of the Oireachtas.

Where:

(a) An officer of the Garda Siochana not below the rank of Chief Superintendent has by notice prohibited such, or

(b) A member of the Garda Siochana

has called on persons taking part to disperse.

Section 30-arrest and detention of suspected persons

(1) A member of the Garda Siochana (if he is not in uniform on production of his identification card if demanded) may without warrant stop, search, interrogate and arrest any person, or do any one or more of those things in respect of any person, whom he suspects of having committed or being about to commit or being or having been concerned in the commission of an offence under this Act or an offence which is a scheduled offence for the purposes of Part V of this Act or whom he suspects of carrying a document relating to the commission or the intended commission of any such offence as aforesaid or whom he suspects of being in possession of information relating to the commission or the intended commission of any such offence as aforesaid.

(2) Any member of the Garda Siochana (if he is not in uniform on production of his identification card if demanded) may for the purpose of the exercise of any of the powers in sub-section 1, stop and search (if necessary by force) any vehicle or any ship, boat, or other vessel which he suspects to contain a person whom he is empowered to arrest without warrant.

Offences Against the State Act, 1939

(3) Whenever a person is arrested under this section, he may be removed to and detained in custody in a Garda Siochana station, a prison, or some other convenient place for a period of twenty-four hours from the time of his arrest and may if an officer of the Garda Siochana not below the rank of Chief Superintendent so directs, be so detained for a further period of twenty-four hours.

(4) A person detained may, at any time during such detention, be charged before the District Court, or a Special Criminal Court with an offence or be released by direction of an officer of the Garda Siochana, and shall, if not so charged or released, be released at the expiration of the detention period.

Power to question person ... s. 2 (1972 Act)

Where a member of the Garda Siochana -

(a) has reasonable grounds for believing that an offence which is for the time being a scheduled offence for the purposes of Part V of the Act of 1939 is being or was committed in any place,

(b) has reasonable grounds for believing that any person whom he finds at or near the place at the time of the commission of the offence or soon afterwards knows, or knew at that time, of its commission, and

(c) informs the person of his belief as aforesaid.

the member may demand of the person his name and address and an account of his recent movements and, if the person fails or refuses to give the information or gives information that is false or misleading, he shall be guilty of an offence and shall be liable on summary conviction to a £200 fine and or twelve months imprisonment.

The Criminal Law Act, 1976, provides:

Power of Garda Siochana in relation to certain arrested persons s. 7

(1) Where a person is in custody under the provisions of under section 30 or section 2 of the Emergency Powers Act, 1976, a member of the Garda Siochana may do all or any of the following in respect of him:

(a) demand of him his name and address;

(b) search him or cause him to be searched;

(c) photograph him or cause him to be photographed;

(d) take, or cause to be taken, his fingerprints and palm prints;

(f) seize and retain for testing anything that he has in his possession

(2) Any person who obstructs or attempts to obstruct any member of the Garda Siochana or any other person acting under the powers conferred by subsection (1), or who fails or refuses to give his name and address when demanded, or gives a name or address which is false or misleading, shall be guilty of an offence and be liable-

(a) on summary conviction to a £1,000 fine and or twelve months imprisonment.

Application of Criminal Justice Act, 1984

Section 9 of the Criminal Justice Act, 1984 makes application to persons in custody under section 30. The effect of which is as follows:

(a) any time for medical attention whether after arrest or during detention will be discounted in reckoning the lawful maximum period of detention.

(b) access to a solicitor and notification of detention provisions apply.

(c) powers to photograph a person arrested, or to take fingerprints or palmprints may be taken only with the authority of a Garda not below the rank of superintendent.

(d) the power to search does not empower a Garda to require a person to remove underclothing unless there is a reasonable suspicion that an explosive substance is concealed on his person and such a search has been authorised by a member of the Garda Siochana not below the rank of superintendent.

Case law on section 30

People (D. P. P.) V McCaffrey (1986)

A Garda gave evidence that he had arrested the accused on suspicion of having committed a scheduled offence, namely, having possession of a firearm and ammunition with intent to endanger life. The Garda witness agreed under cross-examination that he had no suspicion of his own with regard to the accused but that the source of his suspicion was a direction by the officer in charge of the investigation to arrest the accused on suspicion of having committed a crime which had involved firearms and ammunition. The Court of Criminal Appeal held that the arresting officer, in stating in evidence that the arrest under section 30 was on suspicion that a scheduled offence had been committed, had sufficiently complied with the requirements of the section; all that was necessary for the arresting officer to show was that at the time of the arrest, he had the required suspicion, however arrived at.

Trimbole V Governor of Mountjoy (1985)

Trimbole an Australian citizen, was arrested under section 30. On the same day the Government applied the Extradition Act 1965, part II to Australia and on his release by the High Court, he was arrested under that Act. It was held by Egan J. in the High Court that since no genuine suspicion grounding the arrest under section 30 existed, the arrest was a misuse of that section amounting to a conscious and deliberate violation of right guaranteed by the Constitution. It was subsequently held by the Supreme Court, that the Courts have a positive duty, to protect persons against invasion of their constitutional rights and to ensure as far as possible that persons acting on behalf of the executive who consciously and deliberately violate the constitutional rights of citizens do not for themselves or their superiors obtain the planned results of that invasion.

People (D. P. P.) V Byrne (1987)

The respondent was arrested under section 30. He was detained in Garda custody for a period of 24 hours, during which time a Chief

Superintendent authorised his detention for a further period of 24 hours. Counsel for the accused objected to the manner in which the validity of the extension order was proved by the prosecution. The Chief Superintendent who had signed the extension order had died prior to the trial.

It was held by the Supreme Court, that the trial judge had been correct in ruling that, in the absence of direct evidence from the Chief Superintendent as to his state of mind when making the extension order, the prosecution had failed to establish that the continued detention of the respondent after the expiration of the initial 24 hour period was lawful; and the evidence of the Garda officer who was present when the Chief Superintendent issued the authorisation was irrelevant to the validity of the respondent's further period of detention.

People (D. P. P.) V Quilligan (1986)

Walsh L. stated that the object of the powers given by section 30 is not to permit the arrest of persons simply for the purpose of questioning but rather for the purpose of investigating the commission or suspected commission of a crime by the person already arrested.

People (D. P. P.) V Howley (1989)

The applicant was arrested under section 30, on suspicion of having committed the scheduled offence of cattle maiming. During a further period of detention the appellant made a statement confessing to a murder, which was subsequently admitted as evidence at his trial.

It was held by the Supreme Court that:

(1) The trial judge was correct in concluding that the arrest in respect of the scheduled offence of cattle maiming was not in any sense a "colourable device" to allow the Gardai an opportunity to question the accused in relation to the alleged murder. There is no requirement that an arrest under section 30 must be predominantly motivated by a desire to investigate a scheduled offence.

(2) There are no grounds for holding that the extension of the period of detention was unlawful. Where the Garda officer empowered to make the extension order *bona fide* suspects the accused person of being involved in the offence for which he was originally arrested, the extended period of detention is lawful.

People (D. P. P.) V Walsh (1988)

It was held by the Court of Criminal Appeal that the provisions of section 30 were clear and unambiguous in their terms and the Government, in making an order providing that offences under the Malicious Damage Act, 1861, be scheduled offences for the purposes of section 30 provided that all offences under the 1861 Act come within the power of arrest under section 30, whether the malicious damage in question was or was not caused for subversive reasons, and the power in section 45 of the 1939 Act vested in the Director of Public Prosecutions to direct a trial in the ordinary courts in respect of a scheduled offence was presumably granted for the purpose of taking account of the distinction between subversive and non-subversive malicious damage.

People (D. P. P.) V Walsh (1989)

The applicant applied for leave to appeal conviction and sentence on charges arising out of the stabbing of two ladies. The principal ground relied on was that the arrest under section 30, on suspicion of having committed a scheduled offence, namely malicious damage, was unlawful and the statements obtained during the ensuing detention was inadmissible. The malicious damage concerned damage to clothing worn by the victims which was pierced in the course of the stabbing.

It was held by the Court of Criminal Appeal:

(1) Section 30 cannot be used as either a pretext or a colourable devise for arrest.

(2) That in this case the Gardai were not justified in availing of the powers of section 30 because the arrest and subsequent interrogation was not directed towards the investigation of an offence of malicious damage to clothing. There must be genuine investigation of a genuine offence of malicious damage which was worthy of investigation in itself.

People (D. P. P.) V McGing (1989)

It was held by the Court of Criminal Appeal: That it is undesirable for persons detained under section 30 to be interviewed for lengthy periods by a single member of the Gardai, and where practicable it was desirable that a Ban Garda should be physically present in the interview room while a female was being interrogated.

People (D. P. P.) V O'Shea (1989)

At the trial of the applicant the Chief Superintendent who made the extension order gave evidence of the making of the said order. Under cross-examination he stated that after some discussions with the officers involved in the investigation it was his opinion that a further period of detention was necessary in the interests of the progress of the investigation and that was guided by the opinions of the investigating officers.

It was held by the Court of Criminal Appeal:

(1) That the Chief Superintendent in deciding whether to make an extension order pursuant to section 30(3) was entitled to rely upon the information and opinions of his subordinate officers with regard to the suspicions they held of the commission of a scheduled offence by the person detained and with regard to the continuance of that same suspicion.

People (D. P. P.) V Quilligan & O'Reilly (1992)

It was held by the Supreme Court: The constitutional guarantee (at Article 40) that all citizens are to be held equal before the law is not breached merely because section 30 permits the detention for up to 48 hours of a person. Although persons suspected of different offences are treated differently the invidious discrimination necessary for such to amount to a breach of the constitutional guarantee has not been established

The Offences Against the State (Amendment) Act, 1940

The Act provides for powers of internment, whenever the Government proclaims that Part II of the Act is to be in force.

Arrest and detention s. 4
(1) Whenever a Minister of State is of opinion that any particular person is engaged in activities which in his opinion are prejudicial to the preservation of public peace and order, or security of the State, such Minister may by warrant under his hand and seal, order the arrest and detention of such person.

(2) Any member of the Garda Siochana may arrest without other warrant such person.

Detained persons s. 5
(1) It shall be lawful for any member of the Garda Siochana to do all or any of the following things in respect of any person who is arrested and detained;

(a) to demand of such person his name and address;
(b) to search such person or cause him to be searched;
(c) to photograph such person or cause him to photographed;
(d) to take or cause to be taken his finger-prints.

Release s. 6
A Minister of State may by writing, order the release of any particular person who is detained under the Act.

Immune from challenge
The Constitution at Article 34.3.3 provides: No court whatever shall have jurisdiction to question the validity of a law, or any provision of a law, the Bill for which shall have been reffered to the Supreme Court by the President under Article 26 of the Constitution, or to question the validity of a provision of a law where the corresponding provision in the Bill for such law shall have been freffered to the Supreme Court by the President under the said Article 26

The Act together with the Criminal Law (Jurisdiction) Act, 1976 and the Emergency Powers Act, 1976 are thus immune from challenge.

re O'Laighleis (1960)
The applicant was detained by warrant of the Minister of Justice under the Act. He obtained in the High Court a conditional order of *habeas corpus* contending that his detention was was unlawful as it contravened the European Convention of Human Rights, to which the State was a party.

It was held by the Supreme Court that the Convention was not part of the domestic law of the State, and that the applicant was detained in accordance with law.

Chapter 36

Firearm, explosive and offensive weapons offences

Firearm offences

Given the use of firearms in the commission of offence, one way of discouraging serious offences against the person is by regulating the use of firearms, and the law on this subject is contained in the following:

Firearms Act, 1925
Firearms Act, 1964
Firearms (Proofing) Act, 1968
Firearms Act, 1971
Firearms (Dangerous Weapons) Order 1972
Firearms Regulations 1976
Firearms and Offensive Weapons Act, 1990

A number of amendments and insertions to the Firearms Acts have been made by the Criminal Law (Jurisdiction) Act, 1976. These statutes have been further added to by the Criminal Justice Act, 1984 which also increased the penalties for offences under the earlier Acts.

Part II of the Firearms and Offensive Weapons Act, 1990 amends and extends the Firearms Acts. The Firearms Acts, 1925 to 1971, and Part II of the 1990 Act may be cited together as the Firearms Acts, 1925 to 1990.

Firearm

By section 4 of the 1990 Act: In the Firearms Acts, 1925 to 1990 "firearm" means -

(a) a lethal firearm or other lethal weapon of any description from which any shot, bullet or other missile can be discharged;

(b) an air gun (which expression includes an air rifle and an air pistol) or any other weapon incorporating a barrel from which metal or other slugs can be discharged;

(c) a crossbow;

(d) any type of stun gun or other weapon for causing any shock or other disablement to a person by means of electricity or any other kind of energy emission;

(e) a prohibited weapon as defined in section 1(1) of the Firearms Act, 1925;

(f) any article which would be a firearm under any of the foregoing paragraphs but for the fact that, owing to the lack of a necessary component part or parts, or to any other defect or condition, it is incapable of discharging a shot, bullet or other missile or of causing a shock or other disablement (as they case may be);

(g) save where the context otherwise requires, any component part of any article referred to in any of the foregoing paragraphs and, for the purposes of this definition, the following articles shall be deemed to be such component parts as aforesaid :

(i) telescope sights with a light beam, or telescope sights with an electronic light amplification device or an infra-red device, designed to be fitted to a firearm specified in paragraph (a), (b), (c), (d), or (e), and

(ii) a silencer designed to be fitted to a firearm specified in paragraph (a), (b) or (e).

This new definition of "firearm" includes crossbows and stun guns.

By the 1925 Act Section 1 (as amended):

ammunition means ammunition for a firearm but also includes grenades, bombs and other similar missiles whether the same are or are not capable of being used with a firearm and also includes any ingredient or component part of any such ammunition or missile.

By the 1964 Act section 25 (as amended): In section 28 of the Larceny Act 1916, offensive weapon shall include a firearm that is not loaded and an imitation firearm.

imitation firearm means anything which is not a firearm but has the appearance of being a firearm.

By section 6 of the 1990 Act: A superintendent of the Garda Síochána may grant an authorisation to hold a defective firearm without a firearm certificate.

Unlawful possession of firearms s. 2 (1925 Act)

It shall not be lawful for any person to have in his possession, use or carry any firearm or ammunition unless authorised by a firearm certificate.

Where a person is guilty of this offence, he shall be liable :

(a) in a case where an offence relates to a sporting firearm or to any firearm in respect of which a firearm certificate was held on summary conviction, in the case of a first offence, to a £50 fine and, in the case of any subsequent offence to a £50 fine and or three months imprisonment.

(b) in any other case, on summary conviction to a £200 fine and or one years imprisonment, or, on conviction on indictment to a £50 fine and or five years imprisonment.

A number of persons may lawfully be in possession of firearms, otherwise a firearm certificate granted by the Garda Superintendent of the district shall be required.

Manufacture, sell or repair s. 10(2) (1925 Act)

It shall not be lawful for any person to manufacture, sell, repair, test, or prove, or expose for sale, or have in his possession for sale.... any firearm or ammunition unless such person is registered in the register of firearm dealers.

Sell, etc. to a prescribed country s. 10(3A) (1925 Act)

A person shall not sell, transfer or otherwise dispose of a firearm or ammunition for a firearm to a person, or to a body, in a country that stands prescribed for the time being for the purposes of this section unless the superintendent of the Garda Síochána of the district in which the firearm or ammunition is kept, being satisfied that the transaction is authorised by the competent authorities of that country, also authorises it.

General penalty s. 25 (1925 Act)
Any person shall be liable-
(a) on summary conviction, to a £50 fine and or 6 months imprisonment;
(b) on conviction on indictment, to a £100 fine and or 2 years imprisonment.
in respect of the two preceding offences.

Possession of firearms in suspicious circumstances s. 27A (1964 Act)
A person who has a firearm or ammunition in his possession or under his control in such circumstances as to give rise to a reasonable inference that such possession or control is not for a lawful purpose, shall be guilty of an offence and be liable to ten years imprisonment.
R V Whelan (1972)
It was held that the finding of a revolver and ammunition in a room in which three brothers were sleeping is not sufficient to found an inference that all three were in possession, nor was there anything to indicate which, if any had possession.
D. P. P. V Kelso and Others (1984)
Three armed R.U.C. men were charged with an offence under the section 27(a). The question was whether the possession of a firearm in all the circumstances obtaining, was for a lawful purpose. The defendants stated that they carried firearms to protect their lives should the necessity arise. The court held that it had been established as a probability that each of the accused reasonably and honestly believed that his life might be in danger and that it's protection required him to carry his gun.

Possession of firearms while taking a vehicle s. 26 (1964 Act)
A person who contravenes section 112 of the Road Traffic Act, 1961 (see page 229) and who at the time has with him a firearm or an imitation firearm shall be guilty of an offence and be liable to fourteen years imprisonment.

Carrying firearms with criminal intent s. 27B (1964 Act)
A person who has with him a firearm or an imitation firearm with intent to commit an indictable offence, or to resist or prevent the arrest of himself or another, shall be guilty of an offence and be liable to fourteen years imprisonment. In a proceeding for an offence under this section proof that the accused had a firearm or imitation firearm with

him and intended to commit an indictable offence or to resist or prevent arrest is evidence that he intended to have it with him while doing so.

See also aggravated burglary at page 128.

Possession of firearms with intent s. 15 (1925 Act)

Any person who has in his possession or under his control any firearms:

(a) with intent to endanger life or cause serious injury to property, or

(b) with intent to enable any other person by means of such firearm to endanger life or cause serious injury to property,

shall, whether any injury to person or property has, or has not been caused thereby, be guilty of felony and liable to life imprisonment.

By the 1971 Act section 4 references to life and property includes references to life and property outside the area of application of the laws enacted by the Oireachtas.

Use of firearms to resist arrest or aid escape s. 27 (1964 Act)

A person shall not use or produce a firearm or an imitation firearm

(a) for the purpose of or while resisting the arrest of such person or of another person by a member of the Garda Siochana, or

(b) for the purpose of aiding of in the course of the escape or rescue of such person or another person from custody.

A person who contravenes this shall be guilty of an offence and be liable to life imprisonment.

Possession, sale, etc., of silencers s. 7 (1990 Act)

A person shall be guilty of an offence if he has in his possession or sells or transfers to another person a silencer unless the possession, sale, or transfer is authorised in writing by the superintendent of the district in which the first-mentioned person resides.

The penalty on summary conviction is a £1,000 fine and or one years imprisonment, or on conviction on indictment is a fine and or five years imprisonment.

Reckless discharge of firearm s. 8 (1990 Act)

A person who discharges a firearm being reckless as to whether any person will be injured or not, shall be guilty of an offence, whether any such injury is caused or not.

The penalty on summary conviction is a £1,000 fine and or twelve months imprisonment, or on conviction on indictment is a fine and or five years imprisonment.

Court of trial

The offences under the Firearms Acts 1925 to 1990 are scheduled offences for the purposes of Part V of the Offences against the State Act, 1939, and as such where a person is charged with such an offence, he is brought before the Special Criminal Court.

Explosive offences

The Criminal Justice Act, 1984, provides:

Withholding information regarding firearms s. 15

(1) Where a member of the Garda Siochana -

(a) finds a person in possession of any firearm or ammunition,

(b) has reasonable grounds for believing that the person is in possession of the firearms or ammunition in contravention of the criminal law, and

(c) informs that person of his belief, he may require that person to give him any information which is in his possession, or which he can obtain by taking reasonable steps, as to how he came by the firearm or ammunition and as to any previous dealings with it, whether by himself or by any other person.

(2) If that person fails or refuses, without reasonable excuse, to give the information or gives information that he knows to be false or misleading,

he shall be guilty of an offence and shall be liable summarily £800 and or twelve months and on indictment £10,000 and or five years imprisonment.

Any information given by a person shall not be admissible in evidence against that person, other than for an offence under sub-section 2

Explosive offences

The law is contained in the Explosive Substances Act, 1875 (and regulations thereunder), the Explosive Substances Act, 1883, as amended by the Criminal Law (Jurisdiction) Act, 1976 and additional offences are contained in the Offences against the Person Act, 1861.

Substances to which this Act applies s. 3 (1875 Act)

This Act shall apply to gunpowder and other explosives as defined by this section. The term "explosive" in this Act -

(1) Means gunpowder, nitro glycerine, dynamite, guncotton, blasting powders, fulminates of mercury or other metals, coloured fires, and every other substance, whether similar to those above mentioned or not used or manufactured with a view to produce a practical effect by explosion or a pyrotechnic effect; and

(2) Includes fog signals, fireworks, fuzes, rockets, percussion caps, detonators, cartridges, ammunition of all descriptions and every adaption or preparation of an explosive as above defined

Section 43 gives powers whereby the Government may by order, prohibit the manufacture, importation, storage and carriage of specially dangerous explosives. ...

Section 104 gives power to the Government for the extension of the definition of explosive to other explosive substances by reason either of its explosive properties, or any process in the manufacture thereof being liable to explosion.

Hardy V Special Criminal Court (1992)

The applicant was convicted of possession of an explosive namely sodium chlorate and sentenced to five years imprisonment. He had been found to be in contravention of the Explosives (Ammonium Nitrate and Sodium Chlorate) Order, 1972 (S.I. 191/72), an order which had been made under the 1875 Act.

The applicant sought an order that sodium chlorate was not an explosive.

It was held by Carroll J. in the High Court in refusing

1. That the word "properties" in the Act of 1875 was not to be given an obsolete meaning; the word referred to attributes, inherent qualities, characteristics or abilities.

2. That in determining whether or not a substance is an explosive within the meaning of the Act of 1875 the test to be applied is whether the substances possesses explosive properties and if it does whether it is especially dangerous to life and property by reason of those explosive properties.

3. That by reason of of sodium chlorate acting as an oxidising agent when mixed with fuels, including innocuous substances, so as to transfer these substances into explosive substances, it had explosive properties which were especially dangerous to life and property ..

Causing explosion to endanger life or property s. 2 (1883 Act)

A person who in the State or (being an Irish citizen) outside the State unlawfully and maliciously causes by any explosive substance an explosion of a nature likely to endanger life, or cause serious injury to property, shall, whether any injury to person or property is actually caused or not, be guilty of an offence and, on conviction on indictment, shall be liable to imprisonment for life.

Intent to cause explosions s. 3 (1883 Act)

A person who in the State or (being an Irish citizen) outside the State unlawfully and maliciously-

(a) does any act with intent to cause, or conspire to cause, by an explosive substance an explosion of a nature likely to endanger life, or cause serious injury to property, whether in the State or elsewhere, or

(b) makes or has in his possession or under his control an explosive substance with intent by means thereof to endanger life, or cause serious injury to property, whether in the State or elsewhere, or to enable any other person so to do, shall whether any explosion does or does not take place, and whether any injury to person or property is actually caused or not, be guilty of an offence and, on conviction on indictment liable to twenty years imprisonment.

Possession under suspicious circumstances s. 4(1) (1883 Act)

Any person who makes or knowingly has in his possession or under his control any explosive substance, under such circumstances as to give rise to a reasonable suspicion that he is not making it or does not have it in his possession or under his control for a lawful object shall, unless he can show that he made it or had it in his possession or control for a lawful object, shall be guilty of felony and on conviction liable to fourteen years imprisonment.

Explosive substance s. 9 (1883 Act)

This expression shall be deemed to include any materials for making any explosive substance; also any apparatus, machine, implement, or materials used, or intended to be used, or adapted for causing, or aiding in causing, any explosion in or with any explosive substance; also any part of any such apparatus, machine, or implement.

Causing bodily injury by gunpowder s. 28 (1861 Act)

Whosoever shall unlawfully and maliciously, by explosion of gunpowder or other explosive substance, burn, maim, disfigure, or do grievous bodily harm to any person, shall be guilty of felony and on conviction liable to life imprisonment.

Causing gunpowder to explode s. 29 (1861 Act)

Whosoever shall unlawfully and maliciously, cause any gunpowder or other explosive substance to explode, or send or deliver to or cause to be taken or received by any person any explosive substance or any other dangerous or noxious thing, or put or lay at any place, or cast or throw at or upon or otherwise apply to any person, any corrosive fluid or any destructive or explosive substance, with intent in any of the cases aforesaid to burn, maim, disfigure, or do grievous bodily harm to any person, shall, whether any bodily injury is effected or not, be guilty of felony and on conviction liable to life imprisonment.

Placing gunpowder near a building with intent s. 30 (1861 Act)

Whosoever shall unlawfully and maliciously place or throw in, into, upon, against, or near any building, ship, or vessel any gunpowder or other explosive substance, with intent to do any bodily injury to any person, shall, whether or not any explosion take place, and whether or not any bodily injury be effected be guilty of felony and on conviction liable to fourteen years imprisonment.

Offensive weapons

Part III of the Firearms and Offensive Weapons Act, 1990 introduced controls on the availability and possession of Offensive weapons and other articles.

By section 9 of the Act, there are a number of offences of possession of knives and other articles.

Offensive weapons

Possession of knives etc.
(1) Where a person has with him in any public place any knife or other article which has a blade or which is sharply pointed, he shall be guilty of an offence.

The penalty on summary conviction is a £1,000 fine and or twelve months imprisonment.

It shall be a defence for a person charged with an offence to prove that he had good reason or lawful authority for having the article with him in a public place. It shall be a defence to prove that he had the article with him for use at work or for a recreational purpose.

"public place" includes any highway and any other premises or place to which at the material time the public have or are permitted to have access, whether on payment or otherwise, and includes any club premises and any train, vessel or vehicle used for the carriage of persons for reward.

Possession of flick-knifes etc.
(4) Where a person, without lawful authority or reasonable excuse (the onus of proving shall lie on him), has with him in any public place -

(a) any flick-knife, he shall be guilty of an offence.

The penalty on summary conviction is a £1,000 fine and or twelve months imprisonment, or on conviction on indictment is a fine and or five years imprisonment.

"flick-knife" means a knife -

(a) which has a blade which opens when hand pressure is applied to a button, spring, lever or other device in or attached to the handle, or

(b) which has a blade which is released from the handle or sheath by the force of gravity or the application of centrifugal force and when released is locked in an open position by means of a button, spring, lever or other device.

Possession of any other article made or adopted
(4) Where a person, without lawful authority or reasonable excuse (the onus of proving shall lie on him), has with him in any public place -

(b) any other article whatsoever made or adapted for use for causing injury to or incapacitating a person,

he shall be guilty of an offence.

The penalty on summary conviction is a £1,000 fine and or twelve months imprisonment, or on conviction on indictment is a fine and or five years imprisonment.

Any article with intent
(5) Where a person has with him in any public place any article intended by him unlawfully to cause injury to, incapacitate or intimidate any person either in a particular eventuality or otherwise, he shall be guilty of an offence. The penalty is the same as in the case of flick-knives above.

evidence of intent

In a prosecution for this offence, it shall not be necessary for the prosecution to allege or prove that the intent to cause injury, incapacitate or intimidate was intent to cause injury to, incapacitate or intimidate a particular person; and if, having regard to all the circumstances (including the type of the articie alleged to have been intended to cause injury, incapacitate or intimidate, the time of the day or night, and the place), the court (or the jury as the case may be) thinks it reasonable to do so, it may regard possession of the article as sufficient evidence of intent in the absence of any adequate explanation by the accused.

Trespassing with a knife, weapon of offence etc. s. 10

Where a person is on any premises, he shall be guilty of an offence if he has with him _

(a) any knife or other article which has a blade or which is sharply pointed, or

(b) any weapon of offence

The penalty on summary conviction is a £1,000 fine and or twelve months imprisonment, or on conviction on indictment is a fine and or five years imprisonment.

"premises" means any building, any part of a building and any land ancillary to a building.

"weapon of offence" means any article -

made or adapted for use for causing injury to or incapacitating a person, or intended by the person having it with him for such use.

A court is entitled to take judicial notice of a made article, see *R V Simpson (1983)* at page 132.

An article may be adapted that is altered in some way, e.g. a broken bottle.

Where an article is neither made or adapted, an intention on the part of a person having the article with him to cause injury to another or to incapacitate another will be sufficient.

See also burglary and aggravated burglary in chapter 15 (page 126).

Production of article capable of inflicting serious injury s. 11

Where a person, while committing or appearing to be about to commit an offence, or in the course of a dispute or fight, produces in a manner likely unlawfully to intimidate another person any article capable of inflicting serious injury, he shall be guilty of an offence.

The penalty on summary conviction is a £1,000 fine and or twelve months imprisonment, or on conviction on indictment is a fine and or five years imprisonment.

Power to prohibit manufacture, etc. s. 12

Any person who -

(a) manufactures, sells or hires, or offers or exposes for sale or hire, or by way of business repairs or modifies, or

(b) has in his possession for the purpose of sale or hire or for the purpose of repair or modification by way of business, or

(c) puts on display, or lends or gives to any other person,

a weapon to which this section applies shall be guilty of an offence.

The Minister for Justice may by order direct that this section shall apply to any description of weapon specified in the order except any firearm subject to the Firearms Acts, 1925 to 1990.

The penalty on summary conviction is a £1,000 fine and or twelve months imprisonment, or on conviction on indictment is a fine and or five years imprisonment.

Forfeiture s. 13

Where a person is convicted of an offence under Part III of the Act, the court may order any article in respect of which the offence was committed to be forfeited and either destroyed or otherwise disposed of.

Power of arrest without warrant s. 14

A member of the Garda Síochána may arrest without warrant any person who is, or whom the member, with reasonable cause suspects to be, in the act of committing an offence under section 9, 10 or 11.

Search warrants s. 15

If a judge of the District Court or a Peace Commissioner is satisfied on the sworn information of a member of the Garda Síochána that there are reasonable grounds for suspecting that an offence under section 12 has been or is being committed on any premises, he may issue a warrant.

Power of search s. 16

Where a number of people are congregated in any public place and a breach of the peace is occurring, or a member of the Garda Síochána has reasonable grounds for believing that a breach of the peace has occurred, or may occur, in that place when the people were or are congregated there.

If a member of the Garda Síochána suspect with reasonable cause that a person has with him any article in contravention of section 9, he may search him in order to ascertain whether this is the case.

If a member of the Garda Síochána suspect with reasonable cause that some one or more of the people present has or have with him or them an article or articles in contravention of section 9, then, even if the member has no reason to suspect that any particular one of the people present has with him any such article, the member may search any of those people if he considers that a search is necessary in order to ascertain whether any of them has with him any such article or articles.

Chapter 37

Offences of an international nature

Piracy

Piracy *jure gentium* (piracy at common law) involves an act of armed violence committed upon the high seas within the jurisdiction of the Admiralty, and not being an act of war. The common law offence was supplemented by the Piracy Act, 1837.

Piracy Act, 1837 s. 2

Whosoever, with intent to commit or at the time of or immediately before or immediately after committing the crime of piracy in respect of any ship or vessel, shall assault, with intent to murder, any person being on board of or belonging to such ship or vessel, or shall stab, cut, or wound any such person, or unlawfully do any act by which the life of such person may be endangered, shall be guilty of a felony, the penalty for which is life imprisonment.

Piracy is an offence under international law and can be tried by the courts of any country even though it was not committed within its territorial waters. In Ireland it must be tried by the Central Criminal Court.

War crimes

Geneva Convention Act, 1962

This gives effect to the Geneva Convention of the 12th August 1949.

Whom protected

Those protected by the convention, include the sick, wounded and shipwrecked members of armed forces, prisoners of war and civilians. Prisoners of war may not be compelled to serve in the forces of a hostile power, nor may they be deprived of the right of a fair and regular trial.

War crimes

The wilful killing, torture or inhuman treatment, including biological experimentation, wilfully causing great suffering or serious injury to body or health of persons is prohibited.

The extensive destruction of and appropriation of property, not justified by military necessity and carried out unlawfully and wantonly is prohibited.

Grave breaches s. 3(1)

Any person, whatever his nationality, who, whether in or outside the State, commits, or aids, abets or procures the commission by any other person of any grave breach of the convention shall be guilty of an offence.

Penalties
The penalty where the offence involved a wilful killing is life imprisonment, in any other case the penalty is fourteen years. Proceedings for an offence under this section can only be instituted, with the consent of the Attorney General (see page 303).

Minor breaches s. 4(1)
Any persons, whether in the State or outside the State if a citizen of Ireland, who commits, or aids, or abets or procures the commission by any other person of, any minor breach of the Convention shall be guilty of an offence. The penalty on summary conviction is £60 and or six months imprisonment and on indictment is £300 and or two years imprisonment.

Aircraft crimes

The Tokyo and the Hague Conventions
The Air Navigation and Transport Act, 1973, writes into Irish law, the provisions of the Tokyo Convention on offences and certain other acts committed on board aircraft, of the 14th September 1963 and the Hague Convention for the suppression of unlawful seizure of aircraft, of the 16th. December 1970. The 1973 Act in respect of contraventions by a commander of an aircraft has been amended by the Air Navigation and Transport Act, 1988.

Application of criminal law to aircraft s. 2
(1) Any act or omission which, if taking place in the State, would constitute an offence under the law of the State, shall, if it takes place on board an Irish controlled aircraft while in flight elsewhere than in or over the State, constitute that offence.

(2) Proceedings for an offence under this Act or an offence referred to in subsection (1) of this section may be taken, and the offence may for all incidental purposes be treated as having been committed, in any place in the State. So if, for example a person steals a wallet on board an Irish aircraft while it is in flight over Germany, he may be arrested in Dublin and tried under the Larceny Act, 1916.

Article I(4.) of the Convention on offences and certain other acts committed on board aircraft provides: This Convention shall not apply to aircraft used in military, customs or police services.

Unlawful seizure of aircraft s. 11
A person who on board an aircraft in flight anywhere -
(a) unlawfully, by force or threat thereof, or by any other form of intimidation, seizes or exercises control of or otherwise interference with

the control of that aircraft, or

(b) attempt to perform any such act or aides or abets a person who performs or attempts to perform any such act of counsels or procures the performance of any such act.

shall be guilty of an offence.

By section 16 the penalty is imprisonment for life or such other term as the court considers proper, however such a sentence may not be suspended.

Genocide

The General Assembly of the United Nations on 11th December 1946 declared genocide to be a crime under international law, contrary to the spirit and aims of the United Nations and condemned by the civilised world. A Genocide Convention was drawn up and adopted by the General Assembly on 9th December 1949 which Ireland later adhered to. The Genocide Act, 1973 gives effect in Irish criminal law to the Genocide Convention.

Definition

Genocide is defined in Article II of the Convention and means any of the following acts committed with intent to destroy, in whole or in part, a national, ethnical, racial or religious group, as such:

(a) Killing members of the group;

(b) Causing serious bodily or mental harm to members of the group;

(c) Deliberately inflicting on the group conditions of life calculated to bring about its physical destruction in whole or in part;

(d) Imposing measures intended to prevent births within the group;

(e) Forcibly transferring children of the group to another group.

Acts punishable

By Article III of the Convention the following acts shall be punishable:

(a) Genocide;

(b) Conspiracy to commit genocide;

(c) Direct and public incitement to commit genocide;

(d) Attempt to commit genocide;

(e) Complicity in genocide.

Persons punishable

Article IV of the Convention provides that: Persons committing genocide or any of the acts enumerated in article III shall be punished, whether they are constitutionally responsible rulers, public officials or private individuals.

Penalties s. 2

A person guilty of an offence of genocide shall on conviction on indictment-

Offences of an international nature

(a) in case the offence consists of the killing of any person, be sentenced to imprisonment for life, and

(b) in any other case, be liable to imprisonment for a term not exceeding fourteen years.

Proceedings for an offence of genocide shall not be instituted except by or with the consent of the Attorney General. See the Prosecution of Offences Act, 1974 at page 307.

A person charged with an offence of genocide or any attempt, conspiracy or incitement to commit genocide shall be tried by the Central Criminal Court.

Extradition

Article VII of the Convention and section 3 of the Act provides that genocide is an extraditable offence in any form and it shall not be regarded as a political offence or an offence connected with a political offence for the purposes of the Extradition Act, 1965.

Diplomats

The Diplomatic Relations and Immunities Act, 1967, gives force of law to the Vienna Conventions on diplomatic relations signed on 18th April 1961 and on the 24th April 1963.

Hindering diplomats s. 46

(1) A person who wilfully hinders, restricts or prevents the enjoyment or exercise of inviolability or an exemption, facility, immunity, privilege or right conferred by the Act shall be guilty of an offence, for which the penalty on summary conviction is a £100 fine and or six months imprisonment.

(2) A prosecution for this offence may not be instituted without a certificate from the Minister for Foreign Affairs.

Chapter 38

Offences against the administration of justice

Perjury

Perjury is a misdemeanour at common law, it consists in knowingly giving false evidence on oath in a material matter in a judicial proceeding.

The essential ingredients for the commission of the offence are:

(a) it must have been committed in a judicial proceeding;
(b) the making of an oath:
(c) the evidence given must be something material;
(d) the evidence must be given falsely.

Corroboration is also necessary for a conviction for perjury.

Judicial proceeding

The evidence must be given in a judicial proceeding. This includes the various courts (see chapter 40), any commission established by such courts to hear evidence and all statutory tribunals at which evidence must be given on oath, and proceedings before those who are authorised by law to take evidence.

A statement made for the purpose of a judicial proceeding is treated as a statement made in a judicial proceeding, thus affidavits depositions, answers to interrogatories, and examinations on oath are included.

Oath

The making of the oath must be proved, together with the lawful authority of such oath. An affirmation is of the same force and effect as if an oath had been taken, see below.

Material to the issue

The evidence given must be to something material to the issue. If the statement is not material, then even though it is false, it is not perjury. A statement is material if it is likely to influence a court in making its decision. A statement may be oral or written and must be given by a competent witness.

False evidence

False evidence given by a person who is not competent is not perjury. False evidence need not necessarily be untrue, as a person is only bound to give evidence as to what he knows and believes. Thus a truthful statement which is believed to be false could be perjury. The false statement must be deliberate, negligence will not suffice to constitute the *mens rea* of perjury. The fact that one witnesses contradicts another is not proof that either one of them is guilty of perjury.

The Oaths Act, 1888 provides:

When affirmation may be made instead of oaths s. 1

... and if any person making such affirmation shall wilfully, falsely, and corruptly affirm any matter or thing which, if deposed on oath, would have amounted to wilful and corrupt perjury, he shall be liable to prosecution, indictment, sentence, and punishment in all respects as if he had committed wilful and corrupt perjury.

Subornation of perjury

The counselling, procuring, or inciting of another to commit perjury, where it is actually committed is also a misdemeanour at common law.

An attempt to suborn perjury is also a misdemeanour at common law.
People (D. P. P.) V Murtagh (1990)
In a prosecution for the offence of subornation of perjury, the perjurer is an accomplice of the suborner, and the trial judge must warn the jury that, although they may convict on the evidence of an accomplice, it is dangerous to do so unless it is corroborated. Likewise in a prosecution for an attempt to pervert the course of justice by insisting another person to make a false statement to the Gardai, that other person by allowing himself to be incited, is an accomplice to the accused's crime and the same warning must be give.

In addition to the above provisions at common law, there are many statutes which require the taking of oaths and which provide for the falsity of such oaths.

Statutory Declarations Act, 1835

By section 21 of the Act: Any person wilfully and corruptly making or subscribing to any statutory declaration under this Act knowing same to be untrue in any material particular shall be guilty of a misdemeanour.

Commissioners for Oaths (Ireland) Act, 1872

By section 5 of the Act: Any person swearing falsely in any affidavit taken before a commissioner for oaths is guilty of perjury.

Tribunals of Enquiry (Evidence) Acts, 1921 to 1979

It is an offence for wilfully giving false evidence to a tribunal which is material to the inquiry to which the tribunal relates.

Statutory Declarations Act, 1938

By section 6 of the Act: Every person who makes a statutory declaration which to his knowledge is false or misleading in any material respect is guilty of an offence for which the penalty is a £50 fine and or 3 months imprisonment.

Court of Justice of the European Communities (Perjury) Act, 1975

By section 1 of the Act, A person who before the Court of Justice of the European Communities swears anything which he knows to be false or does not believe to be true shall, whatever his nationality, be guilty of perjury.

Also note the provisions of sections 26(2) and 28(3) of the Criminal Evidence Act, 1992.

Contempt of Court

Contempt of court is an offence against the due administration of justice and may take the following forms:

(a) an act of disobedience to the orders of the court; that is a refusal to obey an order of the court.

(b) disrespect *ex facie* the court, which would include the actual commission of violence or the use of scandalous or threatening words.

(c) the publication of scandalous material of the court.

(d) any act or writing prejudicial to a fair trial or calculated to obstruct the course of justice or process of the courts.

Contempt of court may also be categorised as civil or criminal. Criminal contempt is a misdemeanour at common law punishable by fine and or imprisonment.

At common law

The courts have given consideration as to what is meant by contempt, or more importantly what amounts to contempt.

Keegan V DeBurca (1973)

The defendant refused to answer a relevant question asked by a judge. The Judge thereupon sentenced her to be imprisoned "until she purge her said contempt". The Supreme Court gave consideration to what is meant by contempt of court O'Dalaigh C.J. stated: "The distinction between civil and criminal contempt is not new in law. Criminal contempt consists in behaviour calculated to prejudice the due course of justice, such as contempt in *facie curiae*, words written or spoken or acts calculated to prejudice the due course of justice or disobedience to a writ of *habeas corpus* by the person to whom it is directed to give but some examples of this class of contempt. Civil contempt usually arises where there is a disobedience to an order of the Court by a party to the proceedings and in which the court has generally no interest to interfere unless moved by the party for whose benefit the order was made. Criminal contempt is a common law misdemeanour and, as such, is punishable by both imprisonment and fine at discretion, that is to say without statutory limit, its object is punitive . . ." Accordingly punishment by imprisonment should be imposed by sentencing the defendant to imprisonment for a period of definite duration.

Types of contempt ?

There is no one type of contempt of court and it is established that there is no limitation as to the contempts, that the courts may hold there to be.

M.M. and H.M. (1933)

This case related to criminal contempt by obstruction.

Attorney General V O'Ryan and Boyd (1946)

The High Court has full jurisdiction under Article 34.3(1) of the Constitution to deal with contempt of court where the Circuit Court is scandalised and will, in its discretion, exercise that jurisdiction in a proper case. Such jurisdiction will be exercised in the case of an editor of a newspaper who is liable to be punished for contempt of court in respect of matter published in his newspaper.

State (Quinn) V Ryan (1965)

The carrying away of an arrested person across the border while his legal advisers backs were turned thus denying access to the courts was a contempt of court by the police.

Re: O'Kelly (1974)

The refusal of a journalist to give evidence of an interview he had had with an accused person, on the grounds of journalistic ethics was held to be a contempt.

The criticism of the judgment of a court is permissible, but if it is intemperate and calculated to undermine confidence in the operation and fairness of the courts, it is a criminal contempt.

State (D. P. P.) V Walsh and Conneely (1981)

A newspaper report of the Special Criminal Court "that they had so abused the rules of evidence as to make the court akin to a sentencing tribunal" was held a contempt.

In the matter of Kelly and Deighan (1984)

A witness stated that he had been approached by K. and D., they had attempted to suborn him and also suggested that he not attend to give evidence. It was held by the High Court that; the evidence established that a contempt in the face of the Court had been committed which, in the interests of the proper administration of justice required to be tried summarily and immediately at the instance of the trial judge without reference to the Director of Public Prosecutions. It was held by the Supreme Court that having regard to the sequence of evidence in this case, the necessity for the judge to hear and determine the contempt issue did not exist.

Desmond V Glackin (1992)

It was held by O'Hanlon J. in High Court. While the European Convention on human Rights is not a code of legal principles which is enforceable in the domestic courts, this does not prevent a judgment of in relation to the interpretation of the convention from having persuasive effect before the courts in this jurisdiction when they are called on to consider the common law principles relating to contempt of court in the light of the constitutional guarantee of freedom of expression contained in the Constitution.

"I also consider that in the present state of considerable confusion and uncertainty which exists in relation to the law of contempt of court, and which is being addressed by the Law Reform Commission, the applicants had some justification in seeking to have the matter tested before the court"

The common law on contempt has been supplemented by statute:

Enforcement of Court Orders Act, 1926 s. 24

(1) Every person who resists, obstructs, or impedes an under-sheriff, court messenger, or other person in the lawful execution of an execution order or resists, obstructs, or impedes any member of the Garda Siochana in the lawful execution of an execution order shall be guilty of a misdemeanour.

The penalty on conviction on indictment is a £100 fine and or twelve months imprisonment; on summary conviction is a £50 fine and or six months imprisonment.

Criminal Procedure Act, 1967 s. 17

(1) No person shall publish or cause to be published any information as to any particular preliminary examination other than a statement of fact that such examination in relation to a named person on a specified charge has been held and of the decision thereon.

(2) If it appears to a Judge of the District Court, on the application of the Director of Public Prosecutions, that any person has contravened subsection (1), he may certify to that effect under his hand to the High Court and the Court may thereupon inquire into the alleged offence and after hearing any witnesses who may be produced against or on behalf of that person, and after hearing any statement that may be offered in defence, punish or take steps for the punishment of that person in the like manner as if he had been guilty of contempt of court.

(3) Subsection (1) shall not apply to the publication of such information as the judge by whom the preliminary examination was conducted permits to be published at the request of the accused.

Offences Against the State (Amendment) Act, 1972 s. 4

(1)(a) Any public statement made orally, in writing or otherwise, or any meeting, procession or demonstration in public, that constitute an interference with the course of justice shall be unlawful.

(b) A statement, meeting, procession or demonstration shall be deemed to constitute an interference with the course of justice if it is intended, or is of such a character as to be likely, directly or indirectly to influence any court, person or authority concerned with the institution, conduct or defence of any civil or criminal proceedings (including a party or witness) as to whether or how the proceedings should be instituted, conducted, continued or defended, or as to what should be their outcome.

(2) A person who makes a statement, or who organises, holds or takes part in any meeting, procession or demonstration, that is unlawful under this section shall be guilty of an offence and shall be liable -

(a) on summary conviction is a £200 fine and or twelve months imprisonment:

(b) on conviction on indictment is a £1,000 fine and or five years imprisonment.

(3) Nothing in this section shall affect the law as to contempt of court.

Escape from lawful custody

It is a misdemeanour at common law for a person who is lawfully confined in connection with a criminal offence, whether before or after trial, to escape from confinement. This offence is committed where no force or violence is used to effect an escape.

The prisoner escaping is deemed to have regained his liberty as soon as he gets out of sight of the person from whom he escapes, and not before.

Permitting an escape

It is an offence for an officer of the law or a private person to either voluntarily or negligently permit the escape of a prisoner in his custody, to do so is a misdemeanour. A negligent escape has been defined to be when the party arrested or imprisoned escapes against the will of him in whose custody he is, and is not immediately pursued and taken again before he had been lost sight of.

The offence, is punishable in the same degree as that of which the prisoner is guilty, and for which he is in custody, whether treason, felony, or misdemeanour.

In the case of a prisoner in custody for a felony whose escape is voluntarily permitted by the person who has him in custody such person cannot be punished for the escape until the prisoner has been convicted of the felony that he was in custody for. He would of course be guilty of misdemeanour.

Prison breaking

It is also a misdemeanour at common law for a person who is lawfully confined in connection with a criminal offence, to break out of prison or other building in which he is confined. It is not material whether the accused was innocent or guilty of the offence for which he was imprisonment.

Rescue from lawful custody

Rescue at common law is forcibly liberating a prisoner from lawful custody. The rescuer is liable to the same penalty as the escaped prisoner. The rescue must be effected forcibly and knowingly. If the escaped prisoner is not convicted, the offence is a misdemeanour.

The Criminal Law Act, 1976, provides:

Escape from custody s. 6(1)
(1) Any person who-

(a) aids any person in escaping or attempting to escape from lawful custody or, with intent to facilitate the escape of any person from lawful custody or enable a person after escape to remain unlawfully at large, or with intent to cause injury to persons or property in a place where a person is in lawful custody, conveys any article or thing into or out of such place or to a person in such a place or places any article or thing inside or outside such a place, or

(b) makes, or takes part in, any arrangement for the purpose of enabling a person to escape from lawful custody, facilitating such an escape, enabling a person after escape to remain unlawfully at large, or causing injury to persons or property in a place where a person is in lawful custody,

shall be guilty of an offence, for which the penalty on indictment is ten years imprisonment.

(2) Any person who, contrary to any rules or regulations in force in relation to a prison, conveys or attempt to convey any article or thing into or out of the prison or to a person in the prison, or places any article or thing in any place inside or outside the prison with intent that it shall come into the possession of a person in the prison,

shall be guilty of an offence, for which the penalty on summary conviction shall be a £500 fine and or twelve months imprisonment, and on indictment to five years imprisonment.

Statutory offences

The Forgery Act, 1861, provides:

Uttering false records s. 28
The clerk of any court or other officer having the custody of the records of any court, or being the deputy of any such clerk or officer, uttering any false copy or certificate of any record, knowing the same to be false; or delivering to any person any paper falsely purporting to be any such process or a copy thereof, or to be any judgment, decree or order of any court of law or equity of a copy thereof, knowing the same to be false; or acting or professing to act under any such false process, knowing the same to be false shall be guilty of felony and liable to seven years imprisonment.

Personating bail etc. s. 34
Whosoever, without lawful authority or excuse (the proof whereof shall lie on the party accused), shall, in the name of any other person,

341

acknowledge any recognisance or bail, or any *cognovit actionem* or judgment, or any deed or other instrument, before any court, judge or other person lawfully authorised in that behalf, shall be guilty of felony and liable to seven years imprisonment.

The Garda Siochana Act, 1924 provides:

Personating a Garda s. 15(1)

If any person, not being a member of the Garda Siochana, shall have in his possession any article of clothing or equipment supplied to a member of the Garda Siochana and shall not be able satisfactorily to account for his possession thereof, or shall, without the permission of the Commissioner, put on or wear the uniform of any rank or member of the Garda Siochana or any colourable imitation of such uniform, or shall, for the purpose of doing or procuring to be done any act which such person would not by law be entitled to do or procure to be done of his own authority assume the name, designation or description of any rank or of any member of the Garda Siochana, such person shall on summary conviction be liable in addition to any other punishment to a £50 fine and or six months imprisonment.

The Criminal Law Act, 1976 provides:

Giving false information s. 12

Any person who-

(a) knowingly makes a false report or statement tending to show that an offence has been committed, whether by himself or another person, or tending to give rise to apprehension for the safety of persons or property, or

(b) knowingly makes a false report or statement tending to show that he has information material to any inquiries by the Garda Siochana and thereby cause the time of the Garda Siochana to be wastefully employed,

shall be guilty of an offence for which the penalty on summary conviction is a £500 fine and or 12 months imprisonment and on conviction on indictment is 5 years imprisonment.

Offences at common law

Embracery

Embracery consists in attempting by bribes or any corrupt means whatsoever, other than evidence and argument in open court, to influence or instruct jurors, or to incline them to favour one party to a judicial proceeding. It is a misdemeanour at common law which is punishable by fine and or imprisonment. It may be committed by a party to the cause, his agent or by one of the jurors. A juror who allows himself to be so corrupted or influenced is guilty of the same offence.

Interference with witnesses

At common law interference with witnesses by threats or persuasion to induce them not to give evidence, is a misdemeanour, punishable on indictment or on an information.

The offence seems to be committed whether the prisoner dissuades him from giving evidence at all or dissuades him from giving certain evidence. There is no distinction between the offence of endeavouring to persuade a witness to alter evidence already given, and the offence of attempting to dissuade a witness from giving evidence of a certain character.

The offence is also summarily punishable as a contempt of court, see above. To prevent a witness duly summoned from attending court is punishable as a contempt or, in the event of combination, is indictable as a conspiracy to pervert the course of justice, see conspiracy at page 41.

Personating a member of a jury

To personate a member of a jury, even though there is no intention to pervert the course of justice is a misdemeanour at common law. See also consideration of juries.

Barratry

Barratry arises when a false or groundless action is incited, promoted, or maintained. It is an indictable misdemeanour at common law to be a common barrator, i.e., habitually to move, excite or maintain suits and quarrels either at law or otherwise: The offence is rarely heard of at the present time.

Maintenance

Maintenance is said to consist in the unlawful taking in hand or upholding of or assisting in civil suits or quarrels of others, to the disturbance of common right, and from other than charitable motives. It would seem to be immaterial whether the maintenance is of the plaintiff or of the defendant. A man may lawfully maintain a suit respecting any property in which he has an equitable interest. It is not maintenance to assist another in a criminal prosecution. Maintenance is an indictable misdemeanour at common law, and is punishable by fine and or imprisonment

Champerty

Champerty is a species of maintenance. In champerty the person who assists makes a bargain with a plaintiff or defendant to divide the land or other matter sued for between them, if they prevail at law. The champerter undertakes to carry on the party's suit at his own expense. Champerty is an indictable misdemeanour at common law.

Bribery of public officials

The receiving or offering of any undue reward by or to any person whatsoever, whose ordinary profession or business relates to the administration of public justice in order that his behaviour in office would incline him to act contrary to the known rules of honesty and integrity is a common law misdemeanour An attempt at bribery is also a misdemeanour. See also consideration of corruption at page 289.

Public mischief

The wasteful employment of the police has been held to be a public mischief.

Director of Public Prosecutions (Vizzard) V Carew (1981)

The accused was charged as follows: " For that you ...did by means of certain false statements, to wit, report the larceny of £2,000 in cash, cause officers of an Garda Siochana, maintained at public expense for the public benefit, to devote their time and services to the investigation of false allegations, thereby temporarily depriving the public of the services of these police officers and rendering certain persons liable to suspicion, accusation and arrest, and in doing so did unlawfully effect a public mischief contrary to common law." The District Justice stated a case for the opinion of the High Court as to whether this offence is known to the common law of Ireland. It was held by the court that the offence of effecting a public mischief is known to the common law of Ireland and that the facts set out in the charge prepared against the accused, if established, would constitute the offence.

Chapter 39

The criminal courts

The Constitution at Article 34.1 provides that:

Justice shall be administered in Courts established by law by judges appointed in the manner provided, and save in such special and limited cases as may be prescribed by law, shall be administered in public.

It took the legislature twenty-four years to establish the courts as envisaged by the Constitution, in the meanwhile Article 58 permitted the pre-existing courts to continue. The Courts (Establishment and Constitution) Act, 1961 (the Principal Act) and the Courts (Supplemental Provisions) Act, 1961 gave legislative effect to the provisions of the Constitution. References to the "Act" below are to the Courts (Establishment and Constitution) Act, 1961 unless otherwise stated.

Proceedings otherwise than in public

The "special and limited cases" where justice is administered otherwise than in public are few.

The Criminal Justice Act, 1951 provides in section 20(3):

In any criminal proceedings for an offence which is, in the opinion of the court of an indecent or obscene nature, the court may, subject to a parent or other relative or friend of a young person involved in the case being present, exclude from the court during the hearing all persons except officers of the court, persons directly concerned in the proceedings, *bona fide* representatives of the press and such other persons as the court may, in its discretion, permit to remain.

The Courts (S. P.) Act, 1961 provides in section 45(1):

Justice may be administered otherwise than in public in any of the following cases:

(a) applications of an urgent nature for relief by way of *habeas corpus,* bail, prohibition or injunction;

(b) matrimonial causes and matters;

(c) lunacy and minor matters;

(d) proceedings involving the disclosure of a secret manufacturing process.

The Criminal Procedure Act, 1967 provides in section 16(2):

Where the court is satisfied, because of the nature or circumstances of the case or otherwise in the interests of justice, that it is desirable, the court may exclude the public or any particular person or persons except *bona fide* representatives of the press from the Court during the hearing. The reference here is to the District Court, any members of the press who may be present are not free to report the proceedings.

The presence of *bona fide* representatives of the press does not mean that they are free to report such proceedings.

The Criminal Law (Rape) Act, 1981 at section 6 provides for exclusion

345

of the public, see page 75.

The Courts that now stand established by law are as follows:

District Court
Established by section 5 of the Act, the District Court is a Court of first instance, it is presided over by a Judge who sits without a jury. The Courts Act, 1991 at section 2 amended the Act with regard to the description of District Justices's, "Justice" been replaced by "Judge". The District Court by its nature is restricted by the Constitution which provides in Article 38.2 that minor offences (see Chapter 3) may be tried by courts of summary jurisdiction, and by article 38.5 which provides that save in the case of the trial of certain offences no person shall be tried on any criminal charge without a jury.

Summary trial of indictable offences
The Criminal Justice Act, 1951 at section 2(2)(b) provides:
The District Court may try summarily a person charged with a scheduled offence if -
(i) the Court is of opinion that the facts proved or alleged constitute a minor offence fit to be so tried, and
(ii) the accused, on being informed by the Court of his right to be tried with a jury, does not object to being tried summarily.
The indictable offences which may be dealt with summarily by the District Court and contained in the first schedule includes both felonies and misdemeanours.
The offences triable summarily in this way are public mischief, obstruction of the administration of justice or the enforcement of the law, or perjury, which may not be tried in this way without the consent of the Director of Public Prosecutions.
The other offences which may be tried summarily in this way include; riot or unlawful assembly, assault occasioning actual bodily harm, indecent assault, offences under the Larceny Acts 1861 and 1916 involving property worth not more than £50, assault resisting arrest, concealing the birth of a child, gross indecency where the accused is over sixteen years of age and the other person involved is under sixteen years or is an idiot, an imbecile or a feeble-minded person, and attempted carnal knowledge under sections; 1(2), 2(2), or 4 of the Criminal Law Amendment Act, 1935.

State (Nevin) V Tormey (1976)
It was held by the High Court that
(i) the District Court has no jurisdiction to try a person charged with a scheduled offence unless the Judge has formed the opinion that the facts proved or alleged constitute a minor offence fit to be so tried;
(ii) if he wishes to form such opinion without hearing evidence, the Judge should consider the fact alleged by the prosecution.

State (McDonagh) V O'hUadhaigh (1979)
It was held by the High Court that an inadequate statement of the facts

alleged does not deprive the Judge of the District Court of jurisdiction to embark on the trial of a person for a scheduled offence; however, it would be the duty of the Court to discontinue such trial if the facts proved indicated that the offence is a minor one

State (O'Hagan) V Delap (1982)

The High Court held that an initial acceptance by the District Court to try an offence summarily, being the result of an opinion formed upon alleged facts disclosed to the Judge at the time of such acceptance, did not debar the Court from refusing jurisdiction when it was informed of additional relevant facts.

The Offences against the Person Act, 1861 at section 42 provides in respect of common assault and battery that the District Court may hear and determine such offences. This jurisdiction may be exercised without the consent of the accused person.

The Criminal Procedure Act, 1967 at section 13 provides that: Where an accused pleads guilty in the District Court to an indictable offence, other than an offence under the Treason Act, 1939, murder, attempt to murder, conspiracy to murder, piracy or a grave breach of the Geneva Conventions Act, 1962, or an offence by an accessory before or after the fact. The District Court, if it is satisfied that the accused understands the nature of the offence and if the Director of Public Prosecutions consents may deal with the offence summarily. In this case where a District Court deals with an offence summarily, the accused is liable to a fine and or twelve months imprisonment.

Childrens court

Where an offence has been committed by a child under the age of sixteen years, A Judge of the District Court sits as a Childrens Court and deals in such manner as shall seem just with all offences except those of a very grave nature.

The District Court in addition to its own jurisdiction as outlined above, is responsible for the conducting of the preliminary examination of indictable offences (see later).

Circuit (Criminal) Court

Established by section 4 of the Act, the Circuit Criminal Court (i.e. the Circuit Court exercising its criminal jurisdiction) is a court of first instance. It is presided over by a Judge who may sit with or without a jury.

The Courts (S. P.) Act, 1961 at section 25 outlines the jurisdiction of the Circuit Court in relation to indictable offence. It has subject to a number of exceptions the same jurisdictions as the Central Criminal Court (see below). This jurisdiction is exercisable by the Judge of the circuit in which the offence charged has been committed or in which the accused person has been arrested or resides.

A Judge of the Circuit Court may, on the application of the Director of Public Prosecutions or of an accused, transfer a criminal trial from one part of his circuit to another part of his circuit. A Judge of the Circuit Court is obliged on the application of the Director of Public Prosecutions or of an accused, to transfer a criminal trial to the Central Criminal Court.

An appeal lies from the Circuit Court from a decision of the District Court. A criminal appeal consists of a rehearing of the case and fresh evidence may be introduced. In the case of an appeal, the Circuit Court sits without a jury, it may confirm, vary or reverse the order of the District Court. On appeal the decision of the Circuit Court is final, conclusive and may not itself be appealed.

Central Criminal Court

The Constitution at Article 34.3.1 provides that: The courts of first instance shall include a High Court invested with full original jurisdiction in and power to determine all matters and questions whether of law or fact, civil or criminal.

The Courts (S. P.) Act, 1961 at section 11(1) provides that: the High Court when exercising its criminal jurisdiction shall be known as the Central Criminal Court. (It is questionable whether the legislature can change the name of a court, which is entitled in the Constitution). The jurisdiction of the Central Criminal Court is exercisable by a Judge or Judges of the High Court nominated by the President of the High Court, the High Court may sit with or without a jury. The Central Criminal Court has exclusive jurisdiction in relation to offences under the Treason Act, 1939, major offences under the Offences against the State Act, 1939, murder, attempt to murder, piracy and offences under the Genocide Act, 1973.

The Courts (S. P.) Act, 1961 provides:

Section 51(1) Section 2 of the Summary Jurisdiction Act,, 1857 is extended to enable any party in proceedings in the District Court if dissatisfied with its determination as been erroneous on a point of law to appeal to the High Court.

Section 52(1) A Judge of the District Court shall, if requested by any person before him, unless he considers the request frivolous, refer any question of law to the High Court for determination.

If a case is stated under section 51, appeal lies from the High Court to the Supreme Court. However if a case is stated under section 52, appeal only lies to the Supreme Court with the permission of the High Court.

In respect of inferior tribunals such as the District Court, the Circuit Court, and the Special Criminal Court, the High Court may grant a judicial review of the exercise of their functions.

Court of Criminal Appeal

The Act at section 3, established the Court of Criminal Appeal. It consists of not less than three Judges, one of whom shall be the Chief Justice or an ordinary Judge of the Supreme Court nominated by him, and the other two, Judges of the High Court nominated by the Chief

Justice. The Court of Criminal Appeal has jurisdiction to hear appeals from the Central Criminal Court, the Special Criminal Court and the Circuit Criminal Court. A person convicted on indictment may appeal to the Court of Criminal Appeal, but only where the trial judge gives a certificate for leave to appeal, or where the Court of Criminal Appeal itself grants leave to appeal. The Court of Criminal Appeal may affirm a conviction, reverse it in whole or in part, and reduce or increase the sentence. In exceptional circumstances fresh evidence may be introduced. The Court of Criminal Appeal may also order a new trial.
People (D. P. P.) V Egan (1990)

It was held by the Supreme Court that the Court of Criminal Appeal has no jurisdiction to substitute its own subjective view of evidence for the verdict of a jury. If there is credible evidence to support the verdict of the jury the Court of Criminal Appeal has no power to interfere with it save only where a verdict may be identified as perverse.

Supreme Court

The Constitution at Article 34.4 makes provision for the Supreme Court (established by section 1 of the Act):

1. The Court of final appeal shall be called the Supreme Court.
2. The president of the Supreme Court shall be called the Chief Justice.
3. The Supreme Court shall, with such exceptions and subject to such regulations as may be prescribed by law, have appellate jurisdiction from all decisions of the High Court, and shall also have appellate jurisdiction from such decisions of other courts as may be prescribed by law.
4. No law shall be enacted excepting from the appellate jurisdiction of the Supreme Court cases which involve questions as to the validity of any law having regard to the provisions of this Constitution.

Where an application is made for a judicial review in respect of the District Court, an appeal lies to the Supreme Court in respect of a decision of the High Court.

The Court of Justice Act, 1947 at section 16 provides that: A Judge of the Circuit Court may, on the application of any party to any matter before him, refer any question of law arising in such matter to the Supreme Court by way of case stated.

An appeal lies from the grant or refusal of the High Court for an order of *habeas corpus* to the Supreme Court.

An appeal lies from the Central Criminal Court to the Supreme Court in respect of interlocutory orders.

The Criminal Procedure Act, 1967 at section 34 (1) provides that: Where on a question of law, a verdict in favour of an accused person is found by direction of the trial judge, the Director of Public Prosecutions may without prejudice to the verdict in favour of the accused, refer the question of law to the Supreme Court for determination.

The Court of Justice Act, 1924 at section 29 makes provision that; an accused may appeal from a decision of the Court of Criminal Appeal to the Supreme Court, if the Director of Public Prosecutions or the Court of Criminal Appeal itself certifies that the decision involves a point of law of exceptional public importance and that it is desirable in the public interest that the opinion of the Supreme Court be taken thereon.

In addition to the ordinary courts there are other courts.

Special Criminal Court

The Constitution at Article 38.3 makes provision for Special Courts:

1 Special Courts may be established by law for the trial of offences in cases where it may be determined in accordance with such law that the ordinary courts are inadequate to secure the effective administration of justice, and the preservation of public peace and order.

2 The constitution, powers, jurisdiction and procedure of such special courts shall be prescribed by law.

Part V of the Offences against the State Act, 1939 gives statutory effect to these provisions.

Section 35 of that Act provides that whenever the Government is satisfied that the ordinary courts are inadequate to secure the effective administration of justice and the preservation of public peace and order and that it is necessary that Part V of the Act should come into force, the Government may make a proclamation to that effect. Such a proclamation was made on the 26th day of May 1972.

Section 38 of the Act establishes Special Criminal Courts, at the present time there is only one such court, which sits in Dublin.

Section 39 of the Act outlines the constitution of such courts. The court consists of an uneven number of persons not being less than three; it sits without a jury and delivers only one decision. At present the court is composed of a judge of the High Court, of the Circuit Court and a Judge of the District Court.

Section 43 of the Act gives the Special Criminal Court jurisdiction to try convict, or acquit any person lawfully brought before it.

The offences declared to be scheduled offences for the purposes of Part V of the Act are offences under the following Acts:

> Malicious Damage Act, 1861
> Explosive Substances Act, 1883
> Firearms Acts, 1925 to 1971
> Offences against the State Act, 1939
> Conspiracy and Protection of Property Act, 1875 (s.7)

Section 45 of the Act provides that; Whenever it is intended to charge a person with a scheduled offence, the Director of Public Prosecution may direct that the person be brought before the Special Criminal Court instead of the District Court and such person shall be charged and eventually tried there.

Section 46 of the act provides that; Whenever it is intended to charge a person with an offence which is not a scheduled offence, if the Director of Public Prosecutions certifies that in his opinion that the ordinary courts are not adequate to secure the effective administration of justice and the preservation of public peace and order. The District Court shall transfer the person charged to the Special Criminal Court to be charged and tried.

Cox V Ireland (1991)

Barr J. in the High Court held that for legislation to provide that whenever a person, convicted in the Special Criminal Court of a scheduled offence, is employed in the public service, he shall forfeit his employment and that any such convicted person shall be disqualified from any such employment for a further seven years, is to interfere to an unreasonable and unjustified extent with the personal rights, particularly the right to practise a particular profession or vocation, of those within its wombat. Further, any such legislation also amounts to unfair discrimination contrary to Article 40.1 of the Constitution of Ireland, in that it would be so patently capricious as to be a denial of equality before the law. Accordingly section 34 (1) to (IV) of the Offences against the State Act, 1939 are contrary to the Constitution and are void.

Military tribunals

The Constitution at Article 38.4.1 makes provision for Military Tribunals; Military tribunals may be established for the trial of offences against military law alleged to have been committed by persons while subject to military law, and also to deal with a state of war or armed rebellion.

By virtue of section 39(3) above, a Special Criminal Court may be composed entirely of officers of the Defence Forces not below the rank of commandant.

Court-martials

The Defence Act, 1954, Part V provides for the convening of military courts called courts-martials. This part of the Act also deals with the categories of persons subject to military law and the application of military law. The membership of courts-martial is confined to officers of the Defence Forces.

Section 192(3) of the Act provides that a court-martial may not try a person for treason, murder, manslaughter, or rape unless such person is on active service.

Courts-martial appeal court

The Courts-Martial Appeals Act, 1983 at section 9 established this court, to which a person convicted by a court martial may appeal. The Court shall consist of not less than three judges, i.e. the Chief Justice and two ordinary judges of the Supreme Court nominated by him. An appeal shall not lie to the Supreme Court unless the court itself or the Attorney General certify that the decision involves a point of law of exceptional public importance and that such appeal is desirable in the public interest.

Chapter 40

Jurisdiction of courts

Territorial

The Constitution provides:

Article 2 The national territory consists of the whole island of Ireland, its islands and the territorial seas.

Article 3 Pending the re-integration of the national territory, and without prejudice to the right of the Parliament and Government established by this Constitution to exercise jurisdiction over the whole of that territory, the laws enacted by that Parliament shall have the like area and extent of application as the laws of Saorstat Eireann and the like extra-territorial effect.

Accordingly the criminal jurisdiction of the courts in Ireland, extends to all offences committed within the State and within the territorial seas. The jurisdiction extends within the territorial waters of other states.

The Merchant Shipping Act, 1894, at section 687 provides

All offences against property or persons committed in or at any place either ashore or afloat by any master, seaman or apprentice, who at the time when the offence is committed is, or within three months previously has been employed in any Irish ship shall be deemed to be an offence of the same nature respectively, and be liable to the same punishments respectively and be inquired of, heard, tried, determined, and adjudicated in the same manner and by the same courts and in the same place as if those offences had been committed within the jurisdiction.

People (A. G.) V Thomas (1954)

The accused was convicted of the manslaughter of his friend. The accused and his friend were on board an Irish ship on its way from Liverpool to Dublin. They came into hand grips, as a result of which his friend was thrown into the sea. The body was never recovered. It was held by the Supreme Court, that there was ample evidence before the jury on which they might conclude that the death had been proved, so as to leave no grounds for reasonable doubt. Also, the evidence pointed only to a death by drowning on the high sea and that the act that caused the death occurred on board an Irish ship. The two elements necessary to give jurisdiction were both present and the accused was properly triable in the Central Criminal Court.

The Maritime Jurisdiction Act, 1959 provides:

Section 2 For the purposes of this Act, the territorial seas of the State shall be that portion of the sea which lies between the baseline and the outer limit of the territorial seas.

Section 3 For the purposes of this Act, the outer limit of the territorial seas is the line every point of which is at a distance of twelve nautical miles from the nearest point of the baseline.

Section 10(1) Every offence committed within the territorial seas or internal waters is an offence within the jurisdiction of the State and may be dealt with by a Court of competent jurisdiction although committed on board or by means of a foreign ship and a person who commits such offence may be arrested, tried and punished accordingly.

The Broadcasting (Offences) Act, 1968 at section 2 provides: it is an offence for any person to broadcast from any ship or aircraft registered in the State which is in or over waters adjacent to the State within the territorial waters of the State, or from any ship or aircraft registered in the State which is outside such waters.

The Criminal Law (Jurisdiction) Act, 1976, section 2 extends the jurisdiction of the courts to the whole island of Ireland in respect of certain specified offences, the offences specified in the schedule to the Act include all the major criminal offences.

A person outside the territorial limits of the State may commit a crime within such limits, and for the purpose of criminal jurisdiction a crime may be regarded as having been committed within the territory of the State if completed there, though commenced or in part committed in another State. See *Attorney General V Finegan (1933)* at page 121.

Extra-territorial

In general offences committed by Irish citizens, or by persons who are ordinarily resident within the State outside the State are not triable within the State. There are a number of exceptions to this rule, those which have been referred to elsewhere are:

Conspiracy to murder, section 4 of the Offences against the Person Act, 1861;

Murder or Manslaughter, the Offences against the Person Act, 1861, Section 9;

Misuse of Drugs Act, 1977, section 20;

Prohibition of Incitement to Hatred Act, 1989, section 4;

Treason Act, 1939 section 1(2);

Bigamy: Offences against the Person Act, 1861, section 56;

Explosive Substances Act, 1883, section's 2 and 3;

Piracy;

Geneva Convention Act, 1962, section 3(1);

Air Navigation and Transport Act, 1973, section 2(1);

Criminal Evidence Act, 1992, section 29(4).

Time

At common law there is no time limit for the commencement of proceedings for indictable offences; *nullum tempus occurrit regi*, (time does not run against the Crown). So in the case of all felonies and misdemeanours where no time limit is fixed by statute, a prosecution may be commenced at any length of time after the commission of the offence.

N. O. C. V D. P. P. and Another (1992)

It was held in the High Court; Barr J. A delay of upwards of nine years in the making of a complaint about the applicant was unreasonably long in all the circumstances of the case. This delay had prejudiced the applicant in the preparation of his defence and had deprived him of his constitutional right to fair procedure and a fair trial. (a sexual offences case).

There are a number of statutory exceptions to the common law rule, where prosecution must be commenced within a fixed time period:

Offences under the Riot Act, 1789, by section 12 within twelve months;

Offences under the Merchandise Marks Act, 1887, by section 15 within one or three years;

Offences under the Criminal Law Amendment Act, 1935, by sections 2 and 4 within twelve months;

Offences under the Social Welfare (Consolidation) Act, 1981, by sections 188 and 231 within two years or three months;

Offences under the Electoral Act, 1992, by section 156 within twelve months or two years.

State (O'Connell) V Fawsitt (1986)

Finlay C.J. stated: "A person charged with an indictable offence and whose chances of a fair trial have been prejudiced by excessive delay should not be put to the risk of being arraigned and pleading before the jury".

Hannigan V Clifford & Others & O'Flynn V Clifford & Others (1989)

It was held by the Supreme Court that once a charge has been brought against a person the matter must be prosecuted without undue delay; any other course of action might prejudice the right of such a person to a fair trial.

In relation to summary offences, the Petty Sessions (Ireland) Act, 1851 at section 10(4), provides that: In cases of summary jurisdiction, the complaint shall be made within a six months from the time when the cause of the complaint shall have arisen.

By section 7 of the Criminal Justice Act, 1951, this does not apply to an indictable offence which may be dealt with summarily by a Judge of the District Court as a minor offence.

Some statutes contain specific provisions in relation to particular offences:

Night Poaching Act, 1828, section 4, within six months;

Customs Consolidation Act, 1876, section 257, within three years;

Prevention of Cruelty to Children Act, 1904, section 18, within six months.

Nationality

The Aliens Act, 1935, at section 4 provides:

An alien shall be amenable to and triable under the law of Ireland in the like manner and to the like extent in all respects as a citizen of Ireland.

See also the Court of Justice of the European Communities (Perjury) Act, 1975, section 1, at page 337.

Chapter 41

Law officers

Attorney General

The Constitution at Article 30.1 provides:

There shall be an Attorney General who shall be the advisor of the Government in matters of law and legal opinion, and shall exercise and perform all such powers, functions and duties as are conferred or imposed on him, by this Constitution or by law.

The Criminal Justice (Administration) Act, 1924 at section 9(1) provides: All criminal charges prosecuted upon indictment in any court shall be prosecuted at the suit of the Attorney General ... This must now be seen in the light of the 1974 Act below.

Director of Public Prosecutions

The Prosecution of Offences Act, 1974 at section 2 established this office. By section 3 of the Act the functions of the director are:

(1)   , the Director shall perform all the functions capable of being performed in relation to criminal matters ... by the Attorney General ... and references to the Attorney General in any statute or statutory instrument in force immediately before such commencement shall be construed accordingly.

(3) Nothing in this section shall affect the functions of the Attorney General in relation to any question as to the validity of any law having regard to the provisions of the Constitution.

(4) Notwithstanding anything in this section, the Attorney General may, in addition to the Director exercise the functions conferred on the Attorney General by section 29 of the Courts of Justice Act, 1924, and section 34 of the Criminal Procedure Act, 1967.

State solicitor

The Chief State Solicitor is a civil servant who represents the State in litigation and who instructs barristers on behalf of the State. At county level solicitors in private practise are appointed to act on behalf of the State. These State Solicitors represent the State in both civil and criminal matters.

Garda Siochana

The Garda Siochana are the police force of the State. The Police Forces Amalgamation Act, 1925 brought together the Dublin Metropolitan Police and the former Civic Guard who had replaced the Royal Irish Constabulary outside of Dublin. The Garda Siochana Act, 1924, section 20 gave the force its current name. The prosecution of many less serious offences is a matter for the Garda Siochana

Chapter 42

Legal aid in criminal cases

The Criminal Justice (Legal Aid) Act, 1962 (as amended by the Criminal Evidence Act, 1992) makes provision for the grant by the State of free legal aid to poor persons in certain criminal cases. The Act has been supplemented by the Criminal Procedure (Amendment) Act, 1973 and the Criminal Justice (Legal Aid) Regulations 1965.

Legal aid certificate

If it appears to the Court, that the means of a person charged before it with an offence are insufficient to enable him to obtain legal aid, and by reason of the gravity of the change or of exceptional circumstances it is essential in the interests of justice that he should have legal aid in the preparation and conduct of his defence. The court shall on application being made to it, grant the appropriate legal aid certificate.

Different kinds of legal aid certificates are contemplated:

legal aid (District Court) certificates
legal aid (preliminary examination) certificate
legal aid (trial on indictment) certificate
legal aid (appeal) certificate
legal aid (case stated) certificate
legal aid (Supreme Court) certificate

Effect of certificate

Where a person has been granted a certificate for free legal aid, he shall be entitled to free legal aid in the preparation and conduct of his case and to have solicitor and counsel (where appropriate) assigned to him.

Statement as to means s. 9(1)

Before a person is granted a legal aid certificate he may be required by the court or judge, as the case may be, granting the certificate to furnish a written statement in such form as may be prescribed by the Minister by regulations under section 10 of this Act about matters relevant for determining whether his means are insufficient to enable him to obtain legal aid.

Penalty for false or misleading statements s. 11(1)

A person who, for the purpose of obtaining free legal aid under this Act, whether for himself or some other person, knowingly makes a false statement or false representation either verbally or in writing or knowingly conceals any material fact shall be guilty of an offence and shall be liable on summary conviction to a £100 fine and or six months imprisonment.

See *Cahill V Reilly & D. P. P. (1992)* later.

Chapter 43

Bail

Bail is a recognizance or bond entered into by an authorised person, who undertakes to ensure that an accused will appear for trial. An accused may be released on his own personal bail, but in serious cases independent bailsmen may be required. A court cannot reject persons as sureties on account of their moral character or political opinion, the chief consideration is that he will have sufficient property in the event of the estreatment of his recognizance. The Criminal Procedure Act, 1967, makes provision with regard to bail.

Sufficiency of bailsmen s. 27

The judge or peace commissioner shall in every case satisfy himself as to the sufficiency of the persons proposed to be accepted to bailsmen.

Provisions as to admission to bail s. 28

(1) A Judge of the District Court or a peace commissioner shall admit to bail a person charged before him with an offence, other than an offence to which section 29 applies, if it appears to him to be a case in which bail ought to be allowed

(2) Refusal of bail at a particular appearance before the District Court shall not prevent a renewal of the application for bail at a subsequent appearance or while the accused is in custody awaiting trial.

(3) Where an application for bail is refused, or where the applicant is dissatisfied with the bail, he may appeal to the High Court.

(4) When a judge or a peace commissioner grants bail to an accused person who is in custody that person, shall on completion of the recognisance, be released if he is in custody for no other cause than the offence in respect of which the bail is granted.

Bail in case of treason, murder and certain other offences s. 29

(1) This section applies to each of the following offences -

(a) treason,

(b) an offence under section 2 or 3 of the Treason Act, 1939,

(c) an offence under section 6, 7 or 8 of the Offences Against the State Act, 1939,

(d) a grave breach such as is referred to in section 3(1)(i) of the Geneva Convention Act, 1962,

(e) an offence under section 9 of the Official Secrets Act, 1963, or an offence under Part II of that Act committed in a manner prejudicial to the safety or preservation of the State,

(f) murder, attempt to murder, conspiracy to murder or piracy, including an accessory before or after the fact.

(2) A person charged with an offence to which this section applies shall not be admitted to bail except by order of the High Court.

Endorsement on warrants as to release on bail s. 30(1)

A judge of the District Court or a peace commissioner on issuing a warrant for the arrest of any person may, if he thinks fit, by endorsement on the warrant, direct that the person named be on arrest released on his entering into such a recognizance, with or without sureties as may be specified in the endorsement,

Release on bail by members of Garda Siochana s. 31

(1) Whenever a person is brought in custody to a Garda Siochana station by a member of the Garda Siochana, the sergeant or other member in charge of the station may, if he considers it prudent to do so and no warrant directing the detention of that person is in force, release him on bail and for that purpose take from him a recognisance, with or without sureties, for his due appearance before the District Court at the appropriate time and place.

(2) The recognisance may be estreated in the like manner as a recognisance entered into before a judge is estreated.

See also rule 39 of the District Court Rules.

Criteria

The Supreme Court has reviewed the law as to the granting of bail.
People (A. G) V O'Callaghan (1966)

The test in deciding whether to allow bail is the probability of the accused evading justice. The Court approved the following which may be taken into consideration with regard to such a probability:

1. seriousness of the offence charged,
2. strength of the evidence,
3. likely sentence to be imposed on conviction,
4. fact that the accused was caught in the Act,
5. accused's failure to answer bail on a previous occasion,
6. possibility of the disposal of illegally obtained property,
7. possibility of interference with witnesses or jurors.

Bail a right

As an accused person is presumed innocent, the granting of bail is a right to which he is entitled. The wrongful refusal or a delay in admitting a person to bail is itself a common law offence.

The Court of Criminal Appeal may admit a convicted person to bail pending the determination of his appeal, if it thinks fit.
Ryan V Director of Public Prosecutions (1989)

It was held by the Supreme Court:

1. It was not within the High Court at common law to refuse an application for bail pending trial if it was satisfied that the applicant if releases on bail would be likely to commit criminal offences before his trial.

2. If the discretion vested in the courts in relation to granting bail were to be exercised in an attempt to prevent the apprehended commission of

crime, it would constitute an abuse of power.

3. Where an application was made by way of appeal to reduce bail pursuant to section 28(3) of the Criminal Procedure Act, 1967, the court was not entitled to make any order other than one reducing or refusing the bail fixed in the District Court.

Per McCarthy J. If an accused person were to be denied his liberty merely because of his accuser's suspicions that if released he might cause grievous harm, this would be far from a balancing of constitutional rights- it would be a recalibration of the scales of justice.

Warrant for arrest

Where a person charged with an offence has been admitted to bail, a Judge of the District Court or a peace commissioner may, on the application of the surety or a member of the Garda Siochana and upon information being made in writing and on oath that the accused is about to abscond for the purpose of evading justice, issue a warrant for the arrest of the accused.

The Criminal Justice Act, 1984 provides:

Offences committed while on bail: consecutive sentences s. 11 (1)

Any sentence of imprisonment passed on a person for an offence committed, while he was on bail shall be consecutive on any sentence passed on him for a previous offence or, if he is sentenced in respect of two or more previous offences, on the sentence last due to expire, so however that, where two or more consecutive sentences as required by this section are passed by the District Court, the aggregate term of imprisonment in respect of those consecutive sentences shall not exceed two years.

People (D. P. P.) V Farrell (1989)

It was held by the Court of Criminal Appeal: By virtue of section 11 it was mandatory on the Court to pass a consecutive sentence in respect of any sentence committed while on bail.

People (D. P. P.) V Dennigan (1989)

It was held by the Court of Criminal Appeal that the court had power under section 11 when imposing a consecutive sentence to suspend that sentence in appropriate circumstances.

Failure to surrender to bail s. 13

(1) If a person who has been released on bail in criminal proceedings fails to appear before a court in accordance with his recognizance, he shall be guilty of an offence and shall be liable on summary conviction to a £1,000 fine and or twelve months imprisonment.

(2) It shall be a defence in any proceeding for an offence under subsection (1) for the accused to show that he had a reasonable excuse for not so appearing.

(3) For the purpose of section 11 an offence under this section shall be treated as an offence committed while on bail.

Chapter 44

Juries

Article 38.5 of the Constitution provides:
Save in the case of the trial of offences under section 2, section 3 or section 4 of this Article no person shall be tried on any criminal charge without a jury.

There is no constitutional definition of what a "jury" is. In a criminal trial matters of law fall to be determined by the judge; matters of fact by the jury.

The Juries Act, 1976, provides:

Qualification and liability for jury service s. 6
Every citizen aged 18 years and upwards and under the age of 70 years, who is entered in a register of Dail electors in a jury district shall be qualified and liable to serve as a juror for the trial of all or any issues which are for the time being triable with a jury drawn from that jury district, unless he is for the time being ineligible or disqualified for jury service.

Ineligibility s. 7
Those declared to be ineligible are specified in Part I of the First Schedule and include the President of Ireland, persons concerned with the administration of justice, members of the Defence Forces, illiterate or deaf persons and mental patients.

Disqualification s. 8
A person shall be disqualified for jury service, if he has been convicted of an offence in any part of Ireland and has at any time been sentenced to imprisonment for a term of five years or more, or has served any part of a sentence of imprisonment in the last ten years.

Excusal from jury service s. 9
Certain persons, who are entitled to serve on a jury if they wish, may be excused. Those excusable as of a right are specified in Part II of the First Schedule and include persons who have recently served as jurors, members of the Oireachtas, members of the religious, registered medical practitioners, nurse, chemists, students, and those aged from 65 to 70 years. Such persons may inform the County Registrar that they wish to be excused. Others in the public service on production of a certificate from their head of department. Others may be excused at the discretion of the County Registrar or the Court.

Challenges without cause shown s. 20

(2) In every trial of a criminal issue which is tried with a jury the prosecution and each accused person may without cause shown challenge seven jurors and no more.

(3) Whenever a juror is lawfully challenged without cause shown, he shall not be included in the jury.

Challenges for cause shown s. 21

(2) In every trial of a criminal issue which is tried with a jury the prosecution and each accused person may challenge for cause shown any number of jurors.

(3) Whenever a juror is challenged for cause shown, such cause shall be shown immediately upon the challenge being mad and the judge shall then allow or disallow the challenge as he shall think proper.

(4) Whenever a juror is challenged for cause shown, and such challenge is allowed by the judge, the juror shall not be included in the jury.

Failure of juror to attend court etc. s. 34

Failing to attend for jury service is an offence for which the penalty on summary conviction is a £50 fine.

False statements by or on behalf of juror s. 35

If any person makes a false representation etc. , it is an offence for which the penalty on summary conviction is a £50 fine.

Service by ineligible or disqualified person s. 36

(1) Any person who serves on a jury knowing that he is ineligible for service shall be guilty of an offence and shall be liable on summary conviction to a £50 fine.

(2) Any person who serves on a jury knowing that he is disqualified shall be guilty of an offence and shall be liable on summary conviction to a £200 fine.

Refusal to be sworn as a juror s. 37

Any person who, on being called upon to be sworn as a juror, refuses to be sworn in a manner authorised by this Act or otherwise by law shall be guilty of an offence and shall be liable on summary conviction to a £50 fine.

Chapter 45

Summons and arrest

The first step in the prosecution of an offence is to secure the appearance of the accused.

This may be affected by:
- (a) summons;
- (b) arrest with a warrant or
- (c) arrest without a warrant.

Summons

A Judge of the District Court may issue a summons in any case where an information or complaint is made before him a Peace Commissioner or a District Court Clerk that any person has committed or is suspected to have committed within his jurisdiction, any offence or act punishable by law.

The District Court Rules 29 to 37 outline the procedure in respect of the issue of summons.

Where there is good grounds for supposing that a summons would not be sufficient to secure the attendance of a person before the Court, he must be arrested.

Arrest

An arrest is the apprehension or restraining of a person in order that he shall be forthcoming to answer according to law to a specific charge. There is no difference in law between arrest and detainer.

Attorney General V Cox (1929)

"This Court does not accept the distinction sought to be made between 'detainer' when a person is not a free agent and no longer the master of his own movements, and 'arrest' as the term is understood in law" per Kennedy C.J.

See also *Dunne V Clinton (1930)*.

A member of the Garda Síochána in making an arrest should touch the body of a person or otherwise restrain his liberty. Provided there is a touching it is not necessary that a person be physically restrained. A person being arrested must be informed of the crime or offence which is alleged against him.

The procedure on arrest is laid down in District Court Rules 38 & 39.

The power of arrest may arise either with or without warrant and either at common law or by statute.

Arrest with a warrant

A warrant to arrest is a written authority usually issued by a Judge of the District Court or a Peace Commissioner having knowledge of the matter, directing the apprehension of a person so that he may be dealt with according to law.

Summons and arrest

State (Rossi and Blythe) V Bell (1957)

Murnaghan J. stated in the High Court that "the purpose of an arrest warrant is twofold: first, to identify to the person charged with the execution thereof the person to be taken into custody, and secondly, to show the latter that he should submit himself to arrest. To effect this twofold purpose, the necessity for the clear identification in the warrant of the person to be arrested is obvious ... the person against whom the warrant is issued must be named in the body of the warrant by his surname and Christian name; and in the very exceptional circumstances where the name is unknown, that fact must be stated, and the person identified by such sufficient description as in the nature of the case leave no reasonable doubt as to his identity:.

O'Brien V Brabner (1885)

It was held that a warrant to arrest should only be sought in a charge of a serious nature when a summons is likely to prove ineffective.

Arrest without a warrant

Considerable powers to arrest without warrant are given at common law any by statute to citizens and the police

A private citizen (including the police) may arrest at common law:

(a) Any person who in his presence commits a felony or gives a dangerous wounding. The law does not merely permit, but requires, the citizen to carry out such an arrest. He may also arrest any person about to commit a felony.

(b) Any person on suspicion of having committed a felony if, and only if, he can show that the particular felony for which he arrested the other was in fact committed and that he had reasonable and probable cause for suspecting the other of having committed it.

(c) Any persons engaged in an affray while it is continuing, or if there is reasonable ground for believing that they mean to renew it.

An error on the part of a private citizen may result in him being sued for damages for false imprisonment.

A private citizen by statute may arrest any person-

(a) Committing an indictable offence in the night (9 pm to 6 am). Prevention of Offences Act, 1851, s. 11.

(b) Committing any offence punishable either upon indictment or upon summary conviction; under the Larceny Act, 1861 (except s. 103); or under the Larceny Act, 1916 (except s. 31);

(c) Offering to him for sale, pledge or delivering any property if he has reasonable cause to suspect that any offence has been committed against the Larceny Act, 1861, or against the Larceny Act, 1916.

(d) Committing any offence punishable upon indictment under the Coinage Offences Act, 1861, s. 31.

(e) Committing any offence punishable under the Vagrancy (Ireland) Act, 1847.

When a private citizen makes an arrest, it is his duty to hand the person arrested over to the Garda Síochána within a reasonable time.

In addition to the foregoing powers which the citizen shares with the them, the Garda Síochána have more extensive powers, both at common law and by statute, to arrest than the citizen.

At common law a member of the Garda Síochána may arrest without warrant:

(a) Any person who commits a felony in his presence.

(b) Where a felony has been committed, upon reasonable suspicion that the person arrested has committed it.

(c) Upon reasonable suspicion that a felony has been committed, though it afterwards transpires no felony has in fact been committed.

(d) For a breach of the peace in his presence, either at the time or immediately afterwards.

The statutory power of a member of the Garda Síochána to arrest are extensive and there is reference throughout the text to such powers.

The use of lethal force by a citizen to resist an unlawful arrest will normally constitute manslaughter, this is so even if the suspect is forearmed with a lethal weapon to resist an attempted unlawful arrest by a Garda.

People (A. G.) V White (1947)

The accused was convicted and sentenced to death by the Special Criminal Court for the murder of a detective garda, while he, with other gardai, was seeking to arrest the accused and another man. Shots were fired between the garda and the accused and another man and the garda was killed. The ground of arrest of the other man without a warrant, was his membership of an illegal organisation, but the garda did not know the identity of the accused and no cause for his arrest was alleged by any witness in the course of the trial. It was held that the Special Criminal Court was entitled to find on the evidence, that the accused fired the fatal shot, but that in the circumstances proved and on the evidence, the offence committed was manslaughter and not murder.

Search Warrants

The Constitution at Article 40.5 provides:

The dwelling of every citizen is inviolable and shall not be forcibly entered save in accordance with law.

Search warrants are normally issued by a Judge of the District Court or Peace Commissioner upon sworn information by a complainant. Before a search warrant may be issued the issuing authority must be satisfied that there are reasonable grounds for suspicion; reliance must not be placed on a mere averment by a member of the Garda Síochána or other person that he has grounds for suspicion.

See, *People (D. P. P.) V Kenny (1990)*, at page 251.

Except in the case of stolen property, there is no power of common law to issue a warrant authorising the search of a house. Provision is made by statute for the issue of search warrants in certain specified cases, and the directions therein must be strictly observed.

The mere fact of an arrest does not justify a general search of the premises where the arrest took place:

Jennings V Quinn (1968)

It was held by the Supreme Court, that the police when effecting a lawful arrest may seize without a search warrant, property in the possession or custody of the arrested person when they believe it is necessary to do so to avoid the abstraction or destruction of that property and when the property is:

(a) evidence in support of the charge upon which the arrest is made, or

(b) evidence in support of any other criminal charge against that person then in contemplation, or

(c) reasonably believed to be stolen property or to be property unlawfully in the possession of that person;

and that they may retain such property for use at the trial of the arrested person, or of any other person or persons.

Search of person in custody

A person in custody may be searched if his conduct is such as to make it prudent and proper to do so. It may be reasonable and necessary for the protection of the police as well as the person in custody.

An arrested person may be searched where it is probable that he has on him-

(a) stolen property,

(b) any instrument of violence, or

(c) any implements connected with the offence charged, or

(d) any articles which may prove useful in evidence.

The right to search does not include the right to examine the private person of a prisoner.

Note the provisions of section 30 of the Offences against the State Act, 1939, at page 315.

Access to a lawyer

The Constitution at Article 40.3.1 provides:

The State guarantees in its laws to respect, and, as far as practicable, by its laws to defend and vindicate the personal rights of the citizen.

Access to a lawyer must be regarded as a personal right.

People (D. P. P.) V Conroy (1986).

Walsh J.: the issue raised by counsel, as to whether the appellant had requested to see his solicitor, fell to be considered in the context of the obligation on the Garda Siochana to observe fair procedure in accordance with Article 40.3 of the Constitution regardless of whether an arrested person has a constitutional right to be asked if he wishes to see a solicitor.

Director of Public Prosecutions V Healy (1990)

It was held by the Supreme Court the right of access to a lawyer when requested by an accused person in custody or his family for and on his behalf must be deemed to be a constitutional right.

The Criminal Justice Act, 1984 (Treatment of Persons in Custody in Garda Siochána Stations) Regulations, 1987 provide:

Information to be given to arrested person R 8(1)
(1) The member in charge shall without delay inform an arrested person or cause him to be informed-

(a) in ordinary language of the offence or other matter in respect of which he has been arrested.

(b) that he is entitled to consult a solicitor, and

(i) in the case of a person not below the age of seventeen years, that he is entitled to have notification of his being in custody in the station concerned sent to another person reasonable named by him, or ...

The information shall be given orally.

Searches R 17
(1) A member conducting a search of a person in custody shall ensure as far as practicable, that the person understands the reason for the search and that it is conducted with due respect for the person being searched.

(2) A person in custody shall not be searched by a person (other than a doctor) of the opposite sex.

Chapter 46

Preliminary examination

The procedure on preliminary examinations is laid down in Part II of the Criminal Procedure Act, 1967, which has been amended by the Criminal Evidence Act, 1992 and the Criminal Justice Act, 1993.

Procedure s. 5

(1) Where an accused person is brought before the District Court charged with an indictable offence, then unless the case is being tried summarily or the accused pleads guilty, the judge shall conduct a preliminary examination of the charge in accordance with the provisions of this part.

(2) References in any enactment to the preliminary investigation of an indictable offence shall be construed as references to the procedures set out in this Part.

A failure to hold a proper preliminary examination means that there has been a failure to afford due process.

Glavin V Governor of Mountjoy Prison (1991)

It was held by Hamilton P. in the High Court; that in the absence of a preliminary examination conducted in the District Court and a valid return for trial, the Circuit Court had no jurisdiction to try a person for a criminal offence.

It was held by the Supreme Court:

2. That the constitutional entitlement of an accused to a trial in due course of law meant a trial in accordance with the law in force at the time when the trial was held.

3. That, although the right to a preliminary examination in the District Court prior to trial on indictment was a legal (as opposed to a constitutional) entitlement, the breach of that legal right meant that the applicant had also been deprived of his entitlement under Article 38.1 of the Constitution to a trial "in due course of law".

The Supreme Court stated that the entitlement of an accused person to a proper valid preliminary examination of an indictable offence is so inexorably bound up with the trial of that person on indictment that a failure to hold a proper preliminary examination means that there has been a failure to afford to the accused the due process that is required by Article 38.1 of the Constitution. Mr. Justice O'Flaherty stated "...Part II of the Criminal Procedure Act, 1967 as amended afforded a valuable protection for an accused person charged with an indictable crime. It meant that he was afforded a full opportunity of considering the case that was to be mounted against him and might in certain circumstances exercise his entitlement to have witnesses make sworn depositions. Before an accused person could be sent forth for trial the Judge of the District Court must decide that there was in fact a sufficient case to put him on trial."

Documents to be served on accused s. 6

(1) The prosecutor shall cause the following documents to be served on the accused -

(a) a statement of the charges,

(b) a copy of any sworn information in writing upon which the proceedings were initiated,

(c) a list of the witnesses whom it is proposed to call at the trial,

(d) a statement of the evidence that is to be given by each of them,

(e) a copy of any document containing information which it is proposed to give in evidence by virtue of Part II of the Criminal Evidence Act, 1992,

(f) where appropriate, a copy of a certificate pursuant to section 6(1) of that Act, and

(g) a list of exhibits (if any).

(2) Copies of the documents shall also be furnished to the Court.

(3) The accused shall have a right to inspect all exhibits.

(4) The prosecutor may cause to be served on the accused and furnished to the Court a further statement of the evidence to be given by any witness a statement of whose evidence has already been supplied.

This service of documents is known as the "book of evidence".

Cowzer V Kirby & D. P. P. (1991)

It was held by Barr J. in the High Court

(1) ... there was no prior authority indicating that in summary proceedings an accused is not in any circumstances entitled to receive, prior to this trial, copies of written statements made by prosecution witnesses.

(2) there was no logic in the proposition that merely because the applicant elected for summary trial he should lose rights which he would have if he had elected for trial on indictment and then would have been served with a book of evidence under section 6; and while the applicant was not entitled to receive a formal book of evidence, the Constitution required that he receive, at the least copies of the statements of all witnesses whose evidence is crucial to the prosecution case against him.

Preliminary examination s. 7

(1) The Judge shall consider the documents and exhibits, any deposition or statement taken in accordance with this section, any evidence given through a live television link and any submissions that may be made by or on behalf of the prosecutor or the accused.

(2) The prosecutor and the accused shall each be entitled to give evidence on sworn deposition and also to require the attendance before the judge of any person, whether included in the supplied list of witnesses or not, and to examine him by way of sworn deposition.

(3) A witness under subsection (2) may be cross-examined and re-examined on his evidence. His deposition shall be taken down in writing, read over to him and signed by him and by the judge.

Preliminary examination

By section 18 of the Criminal Law (Jurisdiction) Act, 1976, there is no entitlement to require the attendance before the Court of a person or to examine him by way of sworn deposition if it appears to the justice that the person is outside the State and that it is not reasonably practicable to secure his attendance before the Court for examination.

By section 11 of the Criminal Justice Act, 1993: The Criminal Procedure Act, 1967, shall, in relation to a person who gives evidence through a live television link at the preliminary examination of an offence to which section 5 of this Act applies, have effect with the following modifications:

(a)(ii) subsection 2 shall not apply in relation to him.

(b) an order maybe made under section 9 requiring him to attend and give evidence before the court to which the accused person concerned has been sent forward for trial and to produce any document or thing specified in the order.

Decision on preliminary examination s. 8

(1) If the judge is of opinion that there is a sufficient case to put the accused on trial for the offence with which he has been charged, he shall send him forward for trial.

(2) If the Judge is of opinion that there is a sufficient case to put the accused on trial for some indictable offence other than that charged, he shall cause him to be charged with that offence, proceed in accordance with section 7(4), which shall have effect with the omission of the words "if he sent forward for trial" in paragraph (a), and, unless section 13 (Procedure where accused pleads guilty in District Court to indictable offence, see chapter X) applies, send him forward for trial.

(3) Subsections (1) and (2) are subject to the provisions of section 2 of the Criminal Justice Act, 1951, which relates to minor offences (see, chapter 4).

(4) If the Judge is of opinion that a summary offence only is disclosed, and the Director of Public Prosecutions consents, he shall cause the accused to be charged with the summary offence and deal with the case accordingly.

(5) If none of the foregoing provisions applies, the judge shall order the accused to be discharged as to the offence under examination.

(6) An order of a judge sending an accused person forward for trial shall be in writing signed by the judge.

A Judge of the District Court may have to decide whether a person is fit to plead or not.

O'Connor V Judges of the Dublin Metropolitan District (1992)

At the hearing of submissions regarding the book of evidence the District Court Judge was informed that the applicant's mental condition was such that his legal representatives were unable to take any proper instructions from him, the preliminary examination then ceased.

It was held by O'Hanlon J. in the High Court:

Preliminary examination

1. That the preliminary examination before the District Court of a charge relating to an indictable offence could not properly continue when the District Court Judge dealing with the matter was not satisfied that the accused person was a person fit to plead.

2. That when the issue of whether an accused person was a person fit to plead arose upon preliminary examination that issue should at that stage be examined and decided by the District Court Judge.

Additional documents s. 11

(1) Where the accused has been sent forward for trial the Director of Public Prosecutions shall cause to be served on him a list of any further witnesses whom he proposes to call at the trial, with a statement of the evidence that is to be given by each of them, a list of any further exhibits, a statement of any further evidence that is to be given by any witness whose name appears on the list of witnesses already supplied, any notice of intention to give information contained in a document in evidence pursuant to section 7(1)(b) of the Criminal Evidence Act, 1992, together with a copy of the document any any certificate pursuant to section 6(1) of that Act, and copies of any statement recorded under section 7 and any deposition taken under that section or under section 14 (Further power to take depositions).

(2) Copies of the document shall also be furnished to the trial court.

Waiver by accused of preliminary examination s. 12

(1) The accused may waive the preliminary examination and elect to be sent forward for trial with a plea of not guilty, unless the prosecutor requires the attendance of a witness under section 7(2).

(2) In the event of such waiver, the judge shall send him forward for trial and the Director of Public Prosecutions shall cause to be served on him any documents required to be supplied to the accused and not already served.

(3) Copies of the document shall also be furnished to the trial court.

(4) A child or young person (within the meaning of the Children Acts, 1908 to 1957) shall not be permitted to exercise a waiver except with the consent of the parent or guardian having the actual possession and control of him.

Chapter 47

The Indictment

When an accused person is sent forward to the Circuit Court or the Central Criminal Court for trial the prosecution must prepare an indictment. This is the formal charge to be preferred by the People of Ireland (acting by or at the suit of the Director of Public Prosecutions or, in the cases reserved for him the Attorney General) against the accused.

Form of indictment

The Criminal Justice (Administration) Act, 1924 determines the form of an indictment, the First Schedule to that Act contains the Indictment Rules and the Appendix to such schedule, contains forms of indictment covering many of the more serious or more common crimes.

An indictment is a written accusation of crime made by "The People at the suit of the Director of Public Prosecutions" against one or more persons and preferred to a jury.

General provisions as to indictments s. 4

(1) Every indictment shall contain, and shall be sufficient if it contains, a statement of the specific offence or offences with which the accused person is charged, together with such particulars as may be necessary for giving reasonable information as to the nature of the charge.

(2) Notwithstanding any rule of law or practice, an indictment shall, subject to the provisions of this Act, not be open to objection in respect of its form or contents if it is framed in accordance with the rules under this Act.

Orders for amendment of indictment s. 6(1)

Where, before trial, or at any stage of a trial, it appears to the court that the indictment is defective, the Court shall make such order for the amendment of the indictment as the court thinks necessary to meet the circumstances of the case, unless the required amendment cannot in the opinion of the court be made without injustice, and may make such order as to the payment of any costs incurred owing to the necessity for amendment as the court thinks fit.

In addition a court may order a separate trial for one or more offences, or it may order the postponement of a trial. Where two or more persons are charged with the same offence, they may be tried together, however if an accused would be prejudiced, separate trials may be ordered.

Example of indictment

The commencement of the indictment is normally as follows:

The People of Ireland
at the suit of the
Director of Public Prosecutions
V
Daniel McLaughlin
The Central Criminal Court.
Charge preferred to the Jury.

Statement of offence

Arson,
contrary to section 2(1) of the Criminal Damage Act, 1991.

Particulars of offence.

You Daniel McLaughlin, on the sixteenth day of April 1993, at Buncrana in the County of Donegal, without lawful excuse, damaged by fire a dwelling-house at Maginn Avenue intending thereby to endanger the life of Donal Quinn, or being reckless as to whether the life of Donal Quinn would be thereby endangered.

Mode in which offences are to be charged R 4

(1) A description of the offence charged in an indictment, or where more than one offence is charged in an indictment, of each offence so charged, shall be set out in the indictment in a separate paragraph called a count.

(2) A count of an indictment shall commence with a statement of the offence charged, called the statement of offence.

(3) The statement of offence shall describe the offence shortly in ordinary language, avoiding as far as possible the use of technical terms, and without necessarily stating all the essential elements of the offence, and if the offence charged is one created by statute, shall contain a reference to the section of the statute creating the offence.

(4) After the statement of the offence, particulars of such offence shall be set out in ordinary language, in which the use of technical terms shall not be necessary:

Provided that where any rule of law or any statute limits the particulars of an offence which are required to be given in an indictment, nothing in this rule shall require any more particulars to be given than those so required.

(5) The forms set out in the appendix to these rules or forms conforming thereto as nearly as may be shall be used in cases to which they are applicable, and in other cases forms to the like effect shall be used, the statement of offence and the particulars of offence being varied according to the circumstances in each case.

(6) Where an indictment contains more than one count, the counts shall be numbered consecutively.

Joinder of charges R 5
Charges for any offences, whether felonies or misdemeanours, may be joined in the same indictment.

Description of property R 6
Description of property shall be in ordinary language and such as to indicate with reasonable clearness the property referred to.

Description of persons R 7
The description of any accused or any person in an indictment, shall be such as is reasonably sufficient to identify him without necessarily being correct and "a person unknown" is sufficient.

Description of documents R 8
It shall be sufficient to describe any document by any name or designation by which it is usually known.

Chapter 48

Arraignment

After an accused person has been sent forward for trial to either the Circuit Court or the Central Criminal Court the next step will normally be the arraignment, this consists of calling the accused to the bar by naming him, reading the indictment to him and asking him whether he pleads guilty or not guilty.

A accused must be present during the course of the trial, unless he so conducts himself as to render a trial in his presence impossible; but he must be present when sentence is passed.

See *People (A. G.) V Messit (1974)*

On arraignment the accused may:
- (a) plead "guilty",
- (b) stand mute,
- (c) take legal objection to the indictment,
- (d) plead "not guilty".

Plea of "guilty"

Where the accused person pleads guilty, the judge will hear the facts of the case from the prosecution, hear evidence of character and any plea in mitigation, before he passes sentence.

Cahill V Reilly & D. P. P. (1992)

It was held by Denham J. in the High Court: Where a custodial sentence becomes probable or likely, after conviction or on a plea of guilty in a situation where it may not have been likely before, the judge of the District Court should inform the accused, if he has not already done so, of his right to be legally represented or his right to apply for legal aid in relation to the sentence.

Stand Mute

If he is found to be "mute of malice", a plea of not guilty will be entered on his behalf. If he is found to be "mute by visitation of God" i.e. deaf and dumb an attempt will be made to make him understand by some means. Otherwise the question must be considered before a jury is sworn whether the accused is unfit to plead.

The test of whether the accused is mentally fit to plead does not appear to be the same as that to be applied on the question of insanity at the date of the alleged offence, but rather, whether the accused is of sufficient intellect to comprehend the course of the proceedings, so as to make a proper defence.

See *O'Connor V Judges of the Dublin ... (1992)* at page 369.

Where a question arises as to the competence of an accused person to plead, the issue must be determined by a jury empanelled for the purpose. See Insanity at page 26.

Legal objection to indictment

If the accused does not stand mute, he may take legal objection to the indictment, and raise them by:

Motion to quash

A motion to quash the indictment may be made where the indictment has a defect which cannot be cured by amendment, or where the court has not cognizance of the offence, or on the ground of want of jurisdiction. It is the duty of a court to quash an indictment that is clearly bad.

Demurrer

A demurrer is a written objection in which the accused admits the truth of all facts alleged in the indictment, but denies that, in point of law that they amount to the crime charged. This plea is obsolete.

Plea Autrefois Acquit or Autrefois Convict;

These pleas are based on the principle that a person cannot be tried for a crime that he has previously been convicted or acquitted off. To succeed in either of these pleas the accused must show that the previous acquittal or conviction was for the offence charged in the present indictment and that it was for the offence of which he could have been convicted on the previous indictment and that in the case of an acquittal it was a valid one after a trial on its merits.

The Criminal Law (Jurisdiction) Act, 1976 at section 15 provides:

It is hereby declared that a person who has been acquitted or convicted of an offence under the laws of Northern Ireland is entitled to plead his acquittal or conviction as a bar to any proceedings in the State for an offence consisting of the acts that constituted the offence of which he has been so acquitted or convicted.

Minister for Supplies V Connor (1945)

It was held by the High Court, that an order made by the District Court to "strike out" a summons constitutes a dismissal of the summons and may not be raised on a plea of *autrefois acquit.*

State (A. G.) V Deale (1973)

It was held by the High Court, that the plea of *autrefois convict* is a matter to be tried by a jury.

Sweeney V Brophy & D. P. P. (1992)

Certiorari is an appropriate remedy to quash a conviction bad on its face or where a court or tribunal acts without or in excess of jurisdiction, but also where it apparently acts within jurisdiction but where proceedings are so fundamentally flawed as to deprive an accused of a trial in due course of law. The Supreme Court so held where the applicant was in peril in the course of a hearing and was entitled to plead *autrefois acquit.*

Plea of "not guilty"

Where an accused pleads not guilty, the case proceeds to trial. An accused person who has signed a plea of guilty in the District Court may, when arraigned plead not guilty.

A plea of not guilty throws on the prosecution the burden of proving every essential ingredient of the offence as stated in the indictment.

Nolle prosequi

The Criminal Justice (Administration) Act, 1924, at section 12 provides that at the trial of a prisoner on indictment, a *nolle prosequi* ("unwilling to prosecute") may be entered after the indictment is preferred to a jury and before a verdict is found.

Chapter 49

Trial

Prosecution case

Counsel for the prosecution normally opens the case, he will outline the matters he intends to prove, will state the facts on which he intends to rely, and the evidence it is proposed to call.

Having opened the case, counsel for the prosecution calls the witness for the prosecution, they are subject to examination-in-chief by him, followed by cross-examination by the defence and re-examination by the prosecution. The defence is entitled to know the case to be answered and matter should not be introduced unless it is contained in the book of evidence.

No case to answer

When council for the prosecution has concluded his case, the defence may ask the judge, or the judge may determine on his own initiative, to direct the jury as a matter of law to find the accused not guilty on the ground that on the evidence the accused has no case to answer. The judge may accept the submission and direct the jury to return a verdict of not guilty.

The judge may on his own initiative, and at any time during the course of the trial, before the summing up, exercise his power to withdraw a case from the jury.

Defence case

Where the judge has not withdrawn the case from the jury, the next stage is the case for the defence. An accused may conduct his own defence. The defence may decide to call no evidence or may only call witnesses as to the good character of the accused.

The procedure will depend on whether or not the accused person is represented by counsel and on whether evidence other than that of the accused himself and witnesses as to character is adduced.

(a) Where evidence is to be adduced other than that of the defendant himself and witnesses only as to character:

(i) The defendant, or his counsel, may if he so wishes, open his defence.

(ii) The defence witnesses (including the defendant, if he wishes to give evidence) will then be examined.

(iii) The prosecuting counsel will sum up the evidence on behalf of the prosecution.

(iv) The defendant, or, where he is represented, counsel, will sum up the evidence for the defence.

(b) Where no evidence is adduced except that of the defendant himself and witnesses as to character, and defendant is not represented by counsel:

(i) The defendant, if he wishes, will give his evidence and witnesses as to character will give their evidence.

(ii) The defendant will address the jury.

(c) Where no evidence is adduced save that of the defendant himself and witnesses as to character, and defendant is represented by counsel:

(i) The defendant gives his evidence, and witnesses as to character will give their evidence.

(ii) Counsel for the prosecution may sum up his case.

(iii) Counsel for the defence will sum up his case.

Absence of jury

All evidence is to be given in the presence of a jury, however they are not concerned with purely legal argument, and are asked by the judge to retire during the course of such an argument.

Summing up

Following the closing speeches, the judge must sum up the case to the jury. His summing up should include: direction on points of law, a review of the evidence, and direction as to burden and standard of proof, see consideration of innocence of an accused at page 13.

Verdict

After the summing up by the judge, the jury retire and consider their verdict. After retirement the verdict of the jury is announced by their foreperson in open court. The jury may add a rider to their verdict, if it does not vary the effect of the verdict. Such as a recommendation to mercy after a verdict of guilty. See *Attorney General V O'Shea (1931)*

Sentence

The imposition of a sentence is a matter for the judge and not for the jury. The accused may be asked by the judge if he wishes to say anything before he is sentenced.

Pleas in mitigation of sentence will then be heard. The "antecedents" of the accused, that is any previous convictions and his character, will be given.

State(O) V O'Brien (1973)

It was held by the Supreme Court that, the selection of punishment and the determination of the length of a sentence are integral parts of the administration of justice in criminal trials, which are exercisable by the courts in accordance with the provisions of the Constitution.

Note the Criminal Justice Act, 1993, at chapter 53.

Chapter 50

Criminal Justice Act, 1984

This Act provides with regard to trial on indictment:

Notice of alibi in trials on indictment s. 20

(1) On a trial on indictment the accused shall not without the leave of the court adduce evidence in support of an alibi unless, he gives notice of particulars of the alibi.

(2) Without prejudice to subsection (1), on any such trial the accused shall not without the leave of the court call any other person to give such evidence unless-

(a) the notice includes the name and address of the witness

(3) The court shall not refuse leave under this section if it appears to the court that the accused was not informed of the requirements of this section.

(4) Any evidence tendered to disprove an alibi may, subject to any directions by the court as to the time it is to be given, be given before or after evidence is given in support of the alibi.

"evidence in support of an alibi" means evidence tending to show that by reason of the presence of the accused at a particular place or in a particular area at a particular time he was not, or was unlikely to have been, at the place where the offence is alleged to have been committed at the time of its alleged commission.

Proof by written statement s. 21

(1) In any proceedings against a person for an offence, a written statement by any person shall, if such of the conditions mentioned below as are applicable are satisfied, be admissible as evidence to the like extent as oral evidence to the like effect by that person.

(2) The said conditions are :

(a) the statement purports to be signed by the person who made it;

(b) the statement contains a declaration by that person to the effect that it is true to the best of his knowledge and belief and that he made the statement knowing that, if it were tendered in evidence, he would be liable to prosecution if he stated in it anything which he knew to be false or did not believe to be true;

(c) a copy of the statement is served, on each of the other parties;

(d) none of the other parties, within twenty-one days, serves on the party so proposing a notice objecting to the statement being tendered in evidence.

Where a statement is tendered in evidence by virtue of this section, and the person by whom the statement was made has stated in it anything which he knew to be false or did not believe to be true, he shall be guilty of an offence and shall be liable on summary conviction to a £1,000 fine and/or twelve months imprisonment, or on conviction on indictment to a

£2,000 fine and/or five years imprisonment.

Proof by formal admission s. 22

Any fact of which oral evidence may be given may be admitted and the admission by any party of any such fact shall as against that party be conclusive evidence.

An admission under this section may with the leave of the court be withdrawn in the proceedings for the purpose of which it is made or any subsequent criminal proceedings relating to the same matter.

Closing speeches s. 24

(a) the prosecution shall have the right to a closing speech in all cases except where the accused is not represented and does not call any witness (other than a witness to character only), and the defence shall have the right to a closing speech in all cases, and

(b) the closing speech for the defence shall be made after that for the prosecution.

Majority verdict s. 25

After the summing up by the judge, the jury retire and consider their verdict. After retirement the verdict of the jury is announced by their foreperson in open court.

(1) The verdict of a jury in a criminal proceeding need not be unanimous in a case where there are not fewer that eleven jurors if ten of them agree on the verdict.

(2) The court shall not accept a verdict of guilty unless the foreman of the jury has stated in open court whether the verdict is unanimous or is by a majority

However such majority verdicts is not accepted unless it appears to the court that the jury have not less than two hours for deliberation.

Director of Public Prosecutions V Kelly (1989)

It was held by the Court of Criminal Appeal, that the minimum period before a majority verdict may be delivered is two hours -

No impairment, however small, of that period may be permitted.

(2) The time spent by a jury back in court listening to the further charge or charges of the trial judge cannot be considered as part of the two hours of deliberation.

Where the facts are clear this leaves no discretionary conclusion for the court of trial.

Section 25 is in accord with the provisions of the Constitution as to a person being tried in due course of law.

O'Callaghan V A. G. & D. P. P. (1992)

It was held by Blaney J. in the High Court:

3. This (constitutional) function was equally well served whether juries were required to act unanimously or whether they were permitted to

convict or acquit by votes of 10 to 2 or 11 to 1.

4. That a person accorded his constitutional right to trial by jury was necessarily tried in due course of law and it followed ... that section 25 did not interfere with the right to trial by jury.

5. That the provision in section 25 requiring a jury to deliberate for at least two hours before a majority verdict could be accepted by a court; did not in any way interfere with the jury reaching. its decision but merely enabled it to reach a decision which otherwise would not have been open to it. The basis for the jury's decision, whether unanimous or by majority, was at all times the evidence given at the trial.

Sections 11 and 13(1) of the Act which deal with bail are at page 359.

Chapter 51

Criminal Justice (Forensic Evidence) Act, 1990

The Criminal Justice (Forensic Evidence) Act, 1990 amends and extends the law to authorise the taking of bodily samples for forensic testing from persons suspected of certain criminal offences.

Power to take bodily samples s. 2
Where a person is in custody under the provisions of section 30 of the Offences against the State Act, 1939, or section 4 of the Criminal Justice Act, 1984, a member of the Garda Síochána may take, or cause to be taken, from that person for the purpose of forensic testing all or any of the following samples :
(a) a sample of -
      (i) blood, *
      (ii) pubic hair, *
      (iii) urine, *
      (iv) saliva, *
      (v) hair other than pubic hair,
      (vi) a nail,
      (vii) any material found under a nail,
(b) a swab from any part of the body other than a body orifice or a genital region,
(c) a swab from a body orifice or a genital region, *
(d) a dental impression, *
(e) a footprint or similar impression of any part of the person's body other than a part of his hand or mouth.
Where a person is in prison, a member of the Garda Síochána may take, or cause to be taken, from that person for the purpose of forensic testing all or any of the samples specified.

Authorisation
A sample may be taken only if -
(a) a member of the Garda Síochána not below the rank of superintendent authorises it to be taken, (this may be given orally but, it shall be confirmed in writing as soon as is practicable) and
(b) in the case of certain samples* , the appropriate consent has been given in writing.
An authorisation shall not be given unless the member of the Garda Síochána giving it has reasonable grounds -
(a) for suspecting the involvement of the person from whom the sample is to be taken -
(i) in a case where the person is in custody, in the offence in respect of which he is in custody, or
(ii) in a case where the person is in prison, in the commission of an offence under the Offence against the State Act, 1939, or an offence

which is for the time being a scheduled offence for the purposes of Part V of that Act or an offence to which section 4 of the Criminal Justice Act, 1984, applies, and

(b) for believing that the sample will tend to confirm or disprove the involvement of the person from whom the sample is to be taken in the said offence.

Consent

Before a member of the Garda Síochána takes, or cause to be taken, a sample, or seeks the consent of the person from whom the sample is required to the taking of such a sample, the member shall inform the person -

(a) of the nature of the offence in which it is suspected that that person has been involved,

(b) that an authorisation has been given and of the grounds on which it has been given, and

(c) that the results of any tests on the samples may be given in evidence in any proceedings.

seeks the consent

"seeks the consent" implies that there is no obligation on a detained person to give such consent. By section 3 below; inferences may be drawn where a consent is refused without good cause. What is meant by "good cause".

Registered medical practitioner

A sample of the kind specified in (a) (i) or (ii), or in (c) may be taken only by a registered medical practitioner and a dental impression may be taken only by a registered dentist or by a registered medical practitioner.

Obstruction

A person who obstruct or attempts to obstruct any member of the Garda Síochána or any other person acting under the powers conferred above shall be guilty of an offence and shall be liable on summary conviction to a fine not exceeding £1,000 or to imprisonment for a term not exceeding 12 months or to both.

Inferences from refusal to consent s. 3

Where a consent is refused without good cause, in any proceeding against a person for the offence -

(a) the court, in determining -

(i) whether to send forward that person for trial, or

(ii) whether there is a case to answer, and

(b) the court, in determining whether that person is guilty of the offence charged, may draw such inferences, if any, from the refusal as appear proper; and the refusal may on the basis of such inferences, be treated as, or as being capable of amounting to, corroboration of any evidence in relation to which the material is material, but a person shall not be convicted of an offence solely on an inference drawn from such refusal.

This section shall not have effect in relation to an accused unless he has been told in ordinary language by a member of the Garda Síochána when seeking his consent that the sample was required for the purpose of forensic testing, that his consent was necessary and, if his consent was not given, what the effect of a refusal by him of such consent could be.

This section shall not apply -

(a) to a person who has not attained the age of 14 years, or

(b) in a case where an appropriate consent has been refused by a parent or guardian.

Destruction of records and samples

By section 4 of the Act provision is made for the destruction of records and samples.

Regulations

By section 5 of the Act provision is made for the Minister for Justice to make regulation regarding the taking of samples.

Chapter 52

Criminal Evidence Act, 1992

Part III Evidence in certain proceedings

Offences to which Part III applies s. 12

This Part applies to-

(a) a sexual offence,

(b) an offence involving violence or the threat of violence to a person, or

(c) an offence consisting of attempting or conspiring to commit, or of aiding, abetting, counselling, procuring or inciting the commission of, an offence mentioned in paragraph (a) or (b).

Evidence through television link s. 13

(1) In any proceedings for an offence to which this Part applies a person other than the accused may give evidence, whether from within or outside the State, through a live television link-

(a) if the person is under 17 years of age, unless the court sees good reason to the contrary,

(b) in any other case, with the leave of the court.

(2) Evidence given under subsection (1) shall be videorecorded.

(3) While evidence is being given through a live television link pursuant to subsection (1) (except through an intermediary pursuant to section 14(1)), neither the judge, nor the barrister or solicitor concerned in the examination of the witness, shall wear a wig or gown.

Evidence through intermediary s. 14

(1) Where-

(a) a person is accused of an offence to which this Part applies, and

(b) a person under 17 years of age is giving, or is to give, evidence through a live television link,

the court may, on the application of the prosecution or the accused, if satisfied that, having regard to the age or mental condition of the witness, the interests of justice require that any questions to be put to the witness be put through an intermediary, direct that any such questions be so put.

(2) Questions put to a witness through an intermediary under this section shall be either in the words used by the questioner or so as to convey to the witness in a way which is appropriate to his age and mental condition the meaning of the questions being asked.

(3) An intermediary referred to in subsection (1) shall be appointed by the court and shall be a person who, in its opinion, is competent to act as such.

Videorecording as evidence at trial s. 16

(1) Subject to subsection (2)

(a) a videorecording of any evidence given by a person under 17 years of age through a live television link at the preliminary examination of an offence to which this part applies, and

(b) a videorecording of any statement made by a person under 14 years of age (being a person in respect of whom such an offence is alleged to have been committed) during an interview with a member of the Garda Siochana or any other person who is competent for the purpose,

shall be admissible at the trial of the offence as evidence of any fact stated therein of which direct oral evidence by him would be admissible:

provided that, in the case of a videorecording mentioned in paragraph (b), either,-

(i) it has been considered in accordance with section 15(2) by the judge of the District Court conducting the preliminary examination of the offence, or

(ii) the person whose statement was videorecorded is available at the trial for cross-examination.

(2)(a) Any such videorecording or any part thereof shall not be admitted in evidence as aforesaid if the court is of opinion that in the interests of justice the videorecording concerned or that part ought not to be so admitted.

(b) In considering whether in the interests of justice such videorecording or any part thereof ought not to be admitted in evidence, the court shall have regard to all the circumstances, including any risk that its admission will result in unfairness to the accused or, if there is more than one, to any one of them.

(3) In estimating the weight, if any, to be attached to any statement contained in such a videorecording regard shall be had to all the circumstances fro which any inference can reasonably be drawn as to its accuracy or otherwise.

(4) In this section "statement" includes any representation of fact, whether in words or otherwise.

Interpretation (general) s. 2

"sexual offence" means rape, buggery, sexual assault (within the meaning of section 2 of the Criminal Law (Rape)(Amendment) Act, 1990), aggravated sexual assault (within the meaning of section 3 of that Act), rape under section 4 of that Act or an offence under-

(i) section 3, 6 or 11 of the Criminal Law Amendment Act, 1885,

(ii) section 1 or 2 of the Punishment of Incest Act, 1980,

(iii) section 17 of the Children Act, 1908, or

(iv) section 1, 2 or 4 of the Criminal Law Amendment Act 1935.

Part IV Competence and compellability of Spouses and former spouses to give evidence

Competence of spouses and former spouses to give evidence s. 21

In any criminal proceedings the spouse or a former spouse of an accused shall be competent to give evidence at the instance-

(a) subject to section 25, of the prosecution, and

(b) of the accused or any person charged with him in the same proceedings.

Compellability to give evidence at instance of prosecution s. 22

(1) In any criminal proceedings the spouse of an accused shall, subject to section 25, be compellable to give evidence at the instance of the prosecution only in the case of an offence which-

(a) involves violence, or the threat of violence, to-

(i) the spouse,

(ii) a child of the spouse or of the accused, or

(iii) any person who was at the material time under age of 17 years,

(b) is a sexual offence alleged to have been committed in relation to a person referred to in subparagraph (ii) or (iii) of paragraph (a), or

(c) consists of attempting or conspiring to commit, or of aiding, abetting, counselling, procuring or inciting the commission of, an offence falling within paragraph (a) or (b).

(2) In any criminal proceedings a former spouse of an accused, shall subject to section 25, be compellable to give evidence at the instance of the prosecution unless-

(a) the offence charged is alleged to have been committed at a time when the marriage was subsisting and no decree of judicial separation or separation agreement was in force, and

(b) it is not an offence mentioned in subsection (1).

Compellability to give evidence at instance of accused s. 24

Subject to section 25, in any criminal proceedings the spouse or a former spouse of an accused shall be compellable to give evidence at the instance of the accused.

Compellability to give evidence at instance of co-accused s. 25

(1) Subject to section 24-

(a) the spouse of an accused shall be compellable to give evidence at the instance of any person charged with the accused in the same proceedings only in the case of an offence mentioned in section 21(1),

(b) a former spouse of an accused shall be compellable to give evidence at the instance of any person charged with the accused in the same proceedings unless-

(i) the offence charged is alleged to have been committed at a time when the marriage was subsisting and no decree of judicial separation was in force, and

(ii) it is not an offence mentioned in section 21(1).

Right to marital privacy s. 26

Nothing in this Part shall affect any right of a spouse or former spouse in respect of marital privacy

Part V

Oath or affirmation not necessary for child etc., witness s. 27

(1) Notwithstanding any enactment, in any criminal proceeding the evidence of a person under 14 years of age may be received otherwise than on oath or affirmation if the court is satisfied that he is capable of giving an intelligible account of events which are relevant to those proceedings.

(2) If any person whose evidence is received as aforesaid makes a statement material in the proceedings concerned which he knows to be false or does not believe to be true, he shall be guilty of an offence and on conviction shall be liable to be dealt with as if he had been guilty of perjury.

(3) Subsection (1) shall apply to a person with mental handicap who has reached the age of 14 years as it applies to a person under that age.

Abolition of requirement of corroboration for unsworn evidence of child, etc. s. 28

(1) The requirement in section 30 of the Children Act, 1908 of corroboration of unsworn evidence of a child given under that section is hereby abolished.

(2) (a) Any requirement that at a trial on indictment the jury be given a warning by the judge about convicting the accused on the uncorroborated evidence of a child is also hereby abolished in relation to cases where such a warning is required by reason only that the evidence is the evidence of a child and it shall be for the judge to decide, in his discretion, having regard to all the evidence given, whether the jury should be given the warning.

(b) If a judge decides, in his discretion, to give such a warning as aforesaid, it shall not be necessary to use any particular form of words to do so.

(3) Unsworn evidence received by virtue of section 27 may corroborate evidence (sworn or unsworn) given by any other person.

Evidence through television link by persons outside the State s. 29

(1) Without prejudice to section 13(1), in any criminal proceedings a person other than the accused who is outside the State may, with the leave of the court, give evidence through a live television link.

(2) Evidence given under subsection (1) shall be videorecorded.

(3) Any person who while giving evidence pursuant to subsection (1) makes a statement material in the proceedings which he knows to be

false or does not believe to be true, shall whatever his nationality be guilty of perjury.

(4) Proceedings for an offence under section 5(3) may be taken and the offence for all incidental purposes be treated as having been committed, in any place in the State.

Copies of documents in evidence s. 30

(1) Where information contained in a document is admissible in evidence in criminal proceedings, the information may be given in evidence, whether or not the document is still in existence, by producing a copy of the document, or the material part of it, authenticated in such manner as the court may approve.

(2) It is immaterial for the purposes of subsection (1) how many removes there are between the copy an the original, or by what means (which may include facsimile transmission) the copy produced or any intermediate copy was made..

(3) In subsection (1) "document" includes a film, sound recording or videorecording.

Chapter 52

Criminal Justice Act, 1993

The Act provides:

Review of certain sentences s. 2

(1) If it appears to the Director of Public Prosecutions that a sentence imposed by a court on conviction of a person on indictment was unduly lenient, he may apply to the Court of Criminal Appeal to review the sentence.

(2) An application under this section shall be made, on notice given to the convicted person, within 28 days from the day on which the sentence was imposed.

(3) On such application, the Court may either -

(a) quash the sentence and in place of it impose on the convicted person such sentence as it considers appropriate, being a sentence which could have been imposed on him by the sentencing court concerned, or

(b) refuse the application.

(4) Section 6 of the Prosecution of Offences Act, 1974 (which prohibits certain communications in relation to criminal proceedings), shall apply with any necessary modifications, to communications made to the persons mentioned in that section for the purpose of influencing the making of a decision in relation to an application under this section as it applies to such communications made for the purpose of making a decision to withdraw or not to initiate criminal proceedings or any particular charge in criminal proceedings.

Appeal on point of law to the Supreme Court s. 3

(1) An appeal shall lie to the Supreme Court by the convicted person or the Director of Public Prosecutions from the determination of the Court of Criminal Appeal of an application under section 2 if that Court, the Attorney General or the Director of Public Prosecutions certifies that the determination involves a point of law of exceptional public importances and that it is desirable in the public interest that an appeal should be taken to the Supreme Court.

(2) The Supreme Court may, for the purposes of its decision on such an appeal, either -

(a) remit the case to the Court of Criminal Appeal to deal with, or

(b) deal with it itself and for that purpose exercise any powers of that Court,

and that Court and the Supreme Court, as may be appropriate, may if necessary, quash any sentence imposed by the Court of Criminal Appeal and in place of it impose on the convicted person such sentence as it considers appropriate, being a sentence which could have been imposed on him by the sentencing court concerned.

Effect of certain offences on persons in respect of whom committed s. 5

(1) In determining the sentence to be imposed on a person for an offence to which this section applies, a court shall take into account, and may, where necessary, receive evidence or submissions concerning, any effect (whether long-term or otherwise) of the offence on the person in respect of whom the offence was committed.

(2) This section applies to -

(a) a sexual offence within the meaning of the Criminal Evidence Act, 1992,

(b) an offence involving violence or the threat of violence to a person, and

(c) an offence consisting of attempting or conspiring to commit, or aiding, abetting, counselling, procuring or inciting the commission of, an offence mentioned in paragraph (a) or (b).

Compensation orders

Sections 6, 7, 8 and 9 of the Act make provision for compensation orders, whereby offenders are required by a court to pay compensation to the victim for any resulting personal injury or loss.

This power is to be exercised unless the court sees reason to the contrary.

Index

Index

Statutes Revised
on Commercial Law

1695 - 1913

Statutes of Frauds, 1695
Life Assurance Act, 1774
Statute of Frauds Amendment Act, 1828
Bills of Exchange (Ireland) Act, 1828
Infants Property Act, 1830
Carriers Act, 1830
Railway and Canal Traffic Act, 1854
Bills of Lading Act, 1855
Bills of Exchange (Ireland) Act, 1864
Promissory Notes (Ireland) Act, 1864
Life Insurance (Ireland) Act, 1866
Policies of Assurance Act, 1867
Infants Relief Act, 1874
Bills of Sale (Ireland) Act, 1879
Bankers' Books Evidence Act, 1879
Bills of Exchange Act, 1882
Bills of Sale (Ireland) Act, (1879) Amendment Act, 1883
Merchandise Marks Act, 1887
Factors Act, 1889
Partnership Act, 1890
Merchandise Marks Act, 1891
Industrial and Provident Societies Act, 1893
Trustee Act, 1893
Sale of Goods Act, 1893
Trustee Act, 1893 (Amendment) Act, 1894
Industrial and Provident Societies (Amendment) Act, 1895
Life Assurance Companies (Payments into Court) Act, 1896
Friendly Societies Act, 1896
Money-lenders Act, 1900
Limited Partnership Act, 1907
Friendly Societies Act, 1908
Assurance Companies Act, 1909
Merchandise Marks Act, 1911
Industrial and Provident Societies (Amendment) Act, 1913

£49.95 post free

ISBN 1 871509 07 6

Available from: Sean E. Quinn, 15 Rathclaren, Bray, Co. Wicklow

Criminal Law

in

Ireland

Second Edition

£45

post free

Is available from:
Sean E. Quinn, 15 Rathclaren, Bray, Co. Wicklow, Ireland.

Telephone : -353-1-286 7206

Criminal Law in Ireland

Supplement 1995

Irish Law Publishing

Published in 1995 by Irish Law Publishing,
15 Rathclaren, Killarney, Bray, Co. Wicklow, Ireland

First Edition	1988
Paperback Edition (with Supplement)	1991
Second Edition	1993
Second Paperback Edition (with Supplement)	1995

Quinn, Sean Eugene

Criminal Law in Ireland

ISBN 1 871509 14 9 Pck.

Contents

Criminal Law (Sexual Offences) Act, 1993 (No. 20)

The primary purpose of the Act was to decriminalise buggery between adult persons. It does this by repealing the existing law prohibiting buggery between persons and proposing new provisions prohibiting that conduct with mentally impaired persons and with persons under 17 years of age.

It also repeals the law that makes gross indecency between men an offence and proposes new prohibitions on that conduct with mentally impaired males and with males under 17 years of age. In addition, consequential changes are made to the law on prostitution and new provisions to strengthen that law are included.

Interpretation   s. 1.

(1) In this Act—

"motor vehicle" means a mechanically propelled vehicle; intended or adapted for use on roads;

"public place" means any place to which the public have access whether as of right or by permission and whether subject to or free of charge;

"solicits or importunes" includes soliciting or importuning from or in a motor vehicle, and cognate words shall be construed accordingly;

"street" includes any road, bridge, lane, footway, subway, square, court, alley or passage, whether a thoroughfare or not, which is for the time being open to the public; and the doorways, entrances and gardens abutting on a street and any ground or car-park adjoining and open to a street, shall be treated as forming part of a street.

The definitions of "public place", "street" and "motor vehicle" are intended to save repetition in the main body of the Act. The expression "solicits or importunes" is defined as including soliciting or importuning from or in a motor vehicle, i.e. kerb-crawling.

(2) In this Act a person solicits or importunes for the purposes of prostitution where the person—

(a) offers his or her services as a prostitute to another person,

(b) solicits or importunes another person for the purpose of obtaining that other person's services as a prostitute, or

(c) solicits or importunes another person on behalf of a person for the purposes of prostitution.

(3) In this Act references to sexual intercourse shall be construed as references to carnal knowledge as defined in section 63 of the Offences against the Person Act, 1861.

(4) In this Act and in any other enactment, whether passed before or after this Act, a reference to a prostitute includes a reference to a male person who is a prostitute and a reference to prostitution shall be

397

construed accordingly.

(5) In this Act a reference to a subsection is a reference to the subsection of the provision in which the reference occurs unless it is indicated that reference to some other provision is intended.

Abolition of offence of buggery between persons s. 2

Subject to sections 3 and 5 of this Act, any rule of law by virtue of which buggery between persons is an offence is hereby abolished.

Buggery is a common law offence; section 61 of the Offences against the Person Act, 1861 merely provides the penalty, it does not create the offence. Section 2 abolishes any such rule of law that makes buggery between persons an offence. It does not affect the law on buggery between persons and animals (bestiality) which continues to be an offence. The section is subject to sections 3 and 5 below which protect persons under 17 years of age and persons who are mentally impaired, respectively.

Buggery of person under 17 years of age s. 3

A person who commits or attempts to commit an act of buggery with a person under the age of 17 years (other than a person to whom he is married or to whom he believes with reasonable cause he is married) shall be guilty of an offence and shall be liable on conviction on indictment to—

(a) in the case of an act of buggery with a person under the age of 15 years, imprisonment for life,

(b) in the case of an attempt to commit an act of buggery with a person under the age of 15 years, imprisonment for a term not exceeding 5 years in the case of a first conviction, and in the case of a second or any subsequent conviction imprisonment for a term not exceeding 10 years,

(c) in the case of an act of buggery with a person of or over the age of 15 years and under the age of 17 years, imprisonment for a term not exceeding 5 years in the case of a first conviction, and in the case of a second or any subsequent conviction imprisonment for a term not exceeding 10 years, and

(d) in the case of an attempt to commit an act of buggery with a person of or over the age of 15 years and under the age of 17 years, imprisonment for a term not exceeding 2 years in the case of a first conviction, and in the case of a second or any subsequent conviction imprisonment for a term not exceeding 5 years.

This section protects persons under 17 years of age from buggery or attempted buggery (the same age under which girls are protected against persons having unlawful carnal knowledge of them). The penalties on indictment are the same as for having unlawful carnal knowledge or attempted unlawful carnal knowledge of a girl under 15 years of age or between 15 and 17 years of age as provided at sections 1 and 2 of the Criminal Law Amendment Act, 1935.

Gross indecency with male under 17 years of age s. 4.

A male person who commits or attempts to commit an act of gross indecency with another male person under the age of 17 years shall be guilty of an offence and shall be liable on conviction on indictment to imprisonment for a term not exceeding 2 years.

Section 11 of the Criminal Law Amendment Act, 1885 proscribes acts of gross indecency between men with a maximum penalty on conviction of 2 years imprisonment. Section 11 is being repealed and is being replaced by this section which will make it an offence for a male person to commit an act of gross indecency with another male person who is under 17 years of age. The penalty on conviction on indictment will remain a maximum of 2 years imprisonment.

Protection of mentally impaired persons s. 5

(1) A person who—

(a) has or attempts to have sexual intercourse, or

(b) commits or attempts to commit an act of buggery, with a person who is mentally impaired (other than a person to whom he is married or to whom he believes with reasonable cause he is married) shall be guilty of an offence and shall be liable on conviction on indictment to

(i) in the case of having sexual intercourse or committing an act of buggery, imprisonment for a term not exceeding 10 years, and

(ii) in the case of an attempt to have sexual intercourse or an attempt to commit an act of buggery, imprisonment for a term not exceeding 3 years in the case of a first conviction, and in the case of a second or any subsequent conviction imprisonment for a term not exceeding 5 years

(2) A male person who commits or attempts to commit an act of gross indecency with another male person who is mentally impaired shall be guilty of an offence and shall be liable on conviction on indictment for a term not exceeding 2 years.

(3) In any proceedings under this section it shall be a defence for the accused to show that at the time of the alleged commission of the offence he did not know and had no reason to suspect that the person in respect of whom he is charged was mentally impaired.

(4) Proceedings against a person charged with an offence under this section shall not be taken except by or with the consent of the Director of Public Prosecutions.

(5) In this section "mentally impaired" means suffering from a

disorder of the mind, whether through mental handicap or mental illness, which is of such a nature or degree as to render a person incapable of living an independent life or of guarding against serious exploitation.

This section will protect mentally impaired women from persons who attempt to have or have sexual intercourse with them or who attempt to commit or commit buggery with them. It will also protect mentally impaired men from buggery or an attempt to commit buggery, or gross indecency, with them. The previous law, at section 4 of the 1935 Act, protecting women who, in the words of the section are idiots, imbeciles or feebleminded, has been repealed and replaced by the sexual intercourse provisions of this section.

Subsection (1) creates the offence of having, or attempting to have, sexual intercourse or committing, or attempting to commit, an act of buggery, with a mentally impaired person. The penalties on conviction are up to ten years imprisonment in the case of having sexual intercourse or committing an act of buggery and up to three years for a first conviction in the case of an attempt and up to five years in the case of a second or any subsequent attempt. The previous penalty under section 4 of the 1935 Act was imprisonment for not more than two years.

Subsection (2) provides the same protection to mentally impaired males against gross indecency as section 4 provides for persons under 17 years of age.

Soliciting or importuning for purposes of commission of sexual offence   s. 6.

A person who solicits or importunes another person for the purposes of the commission of an act which would constitute an offence under section 3, 4 or 5 of this Act or section 1 or 2 of the Criminal Law Amendment Act, 1935, shall be guilty of an offence and shall be liable on summary conviction to a fine not exceeding £1,000 or to imprisonment for a term not exceeding 12 months or to both.

This section creates a new offence of soliciting or importuning another person for the commission of an act which would constitute an offence under specified sections as well as section 1 or 2 of the Criminal Law Amendment Act, 1935. Under this section, it is be an offence to so solicit or importune a girl under 17 years of age or a mentally impaired woman to commit buggery or to have sexual intercourse or a boy under 17 years or a mentally impaired man to commit buggery or for the purposes of gross indecency. It replaces a provision at section 1(1) of the Vagrancy Act, 1898 which made it an offence for a male person to, in a public place, persistently solicit or importune for immoral purposes.

Soliciting/importuning for purposes of prostitution   s. 7.

A person who in a street or public place solicits or importunes another person or other persons for the purposes of prostitution shall be guilty of an offence and shall be liable on summary conviction to a fine not exceeding

(a) £250, in the case of a first conviction,

(b) £500, in the case of a second conviction, or

(c) £500 or to imprisonment for a term not exceeding 4 weeks or to both, in the case of a third or any subsequent conviction.

This section makes it an offence to solicit or importune another person or other persons for the purposes of prostitution. It replaces the previous laws on soliciting or importuning for the purposes of prostitution which have been rendered inoperable, by the courts, due to the use of the term "common prostitute" in the present law and the general requirement that there be evidence of annoyance to passers-by.

The penalty on summary conviction has been increased, the previous fine was £2. The offence will apply to soliciting or importuning by a prostitute, by a client or by a third party (e.g. tout) on behalf of a prostitute or client, and will apply whether the prostitute, the client or the third party is male or female. The soliciting or importuning can take place in or from a motor vehicle (section 1(1)).

In this connection see also section 23 of the Criminal Justice (Public Order) Act, 1994 below, which deals with the prohibition of advertising of brothels and prostitution.

Loitering for purposes of prostitution s. 8.

(1) A member of the Garda Siochana who has reasonable cause to suspect that a person is loitering in a street or public place in order to solicit or importune another person or other persons for the purposes of prostitution may direct that person to leave immediately that street or public place.

(2) A person who without reasonable cause fails to comply with a direction under subsection (1) shall be guilty of an offence and shall be liable on summary conviction to a fine not exceeding

(a) £250, in the case of a first conviction,

(b) £500, in the case of a second conviction, or

(c) £500 or to imprisonment for a term not exceeding 4 weeks or to both, in the case of a third or any subsequent conviction.

(3) In this section "loitering" includes loitering in a motor vehicle.

The previous laws which made loitering for the purposes of prostitution or solicitation an offence which were also rendered inoperable by the courts are repealed. Section 8 does not reintroduce the offence of loitering. Instead, it gives a Garda power to direct a person to leave a street or public place where he has reason to suspect that the person is loitering in that street or public place in order to solicit or importune another person or other persons for the purposes of prostitution. The section applies to prostitutes, clients and third parties and includes loitering in a motor vehicle. An offence will only be committed where a person fails, without reasonable cause, to comply with a direction from a Garda.

Organisation of prostitution   s. 9

A person who for gain-

(a) controls or directs the activities of a prostitute in respect of prostitution,

(b) organises prostitution by controlling or directing the activities of more than one prostitute for that purpose, or

(c) compels or coerces a person to be a prostitute, shall be guilty of an offence and shall be liable—

(i) on summary conviction to a fine not exceeding £1,000 or to imprisonment for a term not exceeding 6 months or to both, or

(ii) on conviction on indictment to a fine not exceeding £10,000 or to imprisonment for a term not exceeding 5 years or to both.

This section provides for three new offences. They replace the previous law which made it an offence for a woman to exercise control over prostitutes for gain. The new offences are gender neutral. An offence can be committed through the control or direction of one prostitute or of more than one prostitute or by coercing or compelling a person to be a prostitute. The penalties are a fine of up to £10,000 or up to 5 years imprisonment where the conviction is on indictment. The penalty for the previous offence of a woman exercising control over a prostitute was a maximum of 2 years imprisonment.

Living on earnings of prostitution   s. 10.

(1) A person who knowingly lives in whole or in part on the earnings of the prostitution of another person and aids and abets that prostitution shall be guilty of an offence and shall be liable on summary conviction to a fine not exceeding £1,000 or to imprisonment for a term not exceeding 6 months or to both.

(2) If a judge of the District Court is satisfied on the sworn information of a member of the Garda Siochana not below the rank of sergeant that there are reasonable grounds for suspecting that any premises or any part of a premises is used by a person for the purposes of prostitution, and that any person residing in or frequenting the premises or part of the premises is living in whole or in part on the earnings of the prostitution of another person, he may issue a warrant under his hand authorising any member of the Garda Siochana, accompanied by other members of the Garda Siochana, at any time or times within one month from the date of issue of the warrant, on production if so requested of the warrant, to enter, if need be by force,

and search the premises and arrest that person.

(3) A person who obstructs or interferes with a member of the Garda Siochana acting under the authority of a warrant under subsection (2) shall be guilty of an offence and shall be liable on summary conviction to a fine not exceeding £1,000 or to imprisonment for a term not exceeding 6 months or to both.

This section replaces the previous provision at section 1(1)(a) of the Vagrancy Act, 1898 which had a penalty on conviction of up to 2 years imprisonment. In order to protect persons such as dependent children or parents of a prostitute, the new offence can only be committed where the person living on the earnings of prostitution also aids and abets that prostitution.

Subsection (1) creates the offence with a penalty on summary conviction of a maximum fine of £1,000 or imprisonment for a term not exceeding 6 months, or both.

Subsection (2) updates section 1(2) of the Vagrancy Act, 1898. Under it, a member of the Garda Siochana not below the rank of sergeant can apply to a District Court judge for a search warrant for a premises where it is suspected that the premises is used by a person for the purpose of prostitution and that a person residing in or frequenting the premises is living in whole or in part on the earnings of prostitution.

Brothel keeping s. 11 .

A person who-

(a) keeps or manages or acts or assists in the management of a brothel,

(b) being the tenant, lessee, occupier or person in charge of a premises, knowingly permits such premises or any part thereof to be used as a brothel or for the purposes of habitual prostitution, or

(c) being the lessor or landlord of any premises or the agent of such lessor or landlord, lets such premises or some part thereof are or is to be used as a brothel, or is wilfully a party to the continued use of such premises or any part thereof as a brothel,

shall be guilty of an offence and shall be liable -

(i) on summary conviction to a fine not exceeding £1,000 or to imprisonment for a term not exceeding 6 months or to both, or

(ii) on conviction on indictment to a fine not exceeding £10,000 or to imprisonment for a term not exceeding 5 years or to both.

This section repeats section 13(1) of the Criminal Law Amendment Act, 1935, but with increased fines. Previously, a person found guilty of brothel keeping was liable on first conviction to a fine not exceeding £100 or up to 6 months imprisonment or to both and, for a subsequent conviction, the maximum fine was £250 and up to 5 years imprisonment. Under this section, the fine on summary conviction is up to £1,000 or up to 6 months imprisonment or both, and on conviction on indictment the maximum fine is now £10,000 or up to 5 years imprisonment, or both.

Amendment of section 19 of 1935 Act   s. 12.

Section 19 of the Criminal Law Amendment Act, 1935, is hereby amended by -

(a) the substitution of "sergeant" for "inspector" in each place it occurs, and

(b) the substitution in subsection (4) of "£500" for "five pounds".

Section 19 of the 1935 Act is concerned with the issue of search warrants in respect of premises suspected of being brothels. During a search the Gardai may demand the name and address of every person found on the premises and any person refusing to comply with such a demand or who gives a false name or address is guilty of an offence and liable on summary conviction to a fine not exceeding £5. This section increases the fine to a maximum of £500. Also for conformity with section 10 the duties of a member of the Garda Siochana of at least inspector rank under section 19 of the 1935 Act will now be performed by a member not below the rank of sergeant. Those duties include satisfying a District Court judge, when applying for a search warrant, that there are reasonable grounds for suspecting that a premises is a brothel.

Powers of arrest   s. 13

(1) If a member of the Garda Siochana reasonably suspects that a person has committed an offence under section 4, 6, 7, 8(2) or 10(3) of this Act he may—

(a) arrest that person without warrant, or

(b) require him to give his name and address and, if the person fails or refuses to do so or gives a name or address that the member reasonably suspects to be false or misleading, the member may arrest that person without warrant.

(2) A person who fails or refuses to give his name or address when required under subsection (1), or gives a name or address which is false or misleading, shall be guilty of an offence and shall be liable on summary conviction to a fine not exceeding £500.

This section gives the Gardai power to arrest without warrant anyone they reasonably suspect of having committed an offence under section 4, 6, 7, 8(2) or 10(4) of this Act. Alternatively, they can demand the name and address of such person or persons and failure to give a name or address, or giving a false name or address, will be an offence for which the Gardai can arrest without warrant.

Repeals s. 14.

The enactments specified in column (2) of the Schedule to this Act are hereby repealed to the extent specified in column (3) of that Schedule.

Section 14 deals with repeals (most of these have been referred to at the appropriate paragraphs above relating to the substantive provisions of the Act to which the repeals relate). It also repeals sections 61 and 62 of the Offences against the Person Act, 1861 (except in so far as they apply to buggery or attempted buggery with animals).

Short title and collective citation s. 15.

(1) This Act may be cited as the Criminal Law (Sexual and Offences) Act, 1993.

(2) The Criminal Law Amendment Acts, 1885 to 1935, and this Act may be cited together as the Criminal Law (Sexual Offences) Acts, 1885 to 1993.

Schedule

Enactments repealed extent of repeal

Dublin Police Act, 1842: Section 14, paragraph 11.

Town Police Clauses Act, 1847: Section 28, the words "Every common Prostitute or Nightwalker loitering and importuning Passengers for the Purpose of Prostitution:".

Towns Improvement (Ireland) Act, 1854: Section 72, the words "Every common Prostitute or Nightwalker loitering and importuning Passengers for the Purpose of Prostitution, or being otherwise offensive, shall be liable to a fine not exceeding Forty Shillings:".

Offences against the Person Act, 1861: Section 61 and 62 (save in so far as they apply to buggery or attempted buggery with animals).

Criminal Law Amendment Act, 1885: Section 11.

Criminal Law Amendment Act, 1912: Sections 3 and 7.

Criminal Law Amendment Act, 1935: Sections 4, 13 and 16.

Criminal Procedure Act, 1993 (No. 40)

The purpose of the Act is to provide:

- a means whereby a person who alleges that a miscarriage of justice has occurred and who has exhausted the normal appeal procedure can appeal again to the Court of Criminal Appeal (section 2);

- a restatement and extension of the powers of the Court of Criminal Appeal (section 3), to allow for this section 34 of the Courts of Justice Act, 1924 and section 5 of the Courts of Justice Act, 1928 are being repealed;

-a procedure where a convicted person, who alleges that a new or newly discovered fact shows that a miscarriage of justice has occurred, petitions the minister for justice in relation to the grant of a pardon by the President under Article 13.6 of the Constitution (section 7);

- for the establishment of a committee to inquire into an allegation that a miscarriage of justice has occurred (section 8);

-that compensation will be payable by the State where a miscarriage of justice is established (section 9);

-that a judge will advise the jury to have due regard to the lack of corroboration in any case where the sole evidence against an accused is his own confession (section 10).

The provisions of the Act arise in part from the recommendations made in part I of the Report of the Committee to enquire into certain Aspects of Criminal Procedure.

Interpretation. s. 1

(1) In this Act—

"the Court" means the Court of Criminal Appeal but, in sections 2 to 5 and 7, as modified by section 6, also includes the Courts-Martial Appeal Court;

"legal aid certificate" means a certificate granted under the appropriate provision of the Criminal Justice (Legal Aid) Act, 1962.

(2) In this Act—

(a) a reference to a section is to a section of this Act, unless it is indicated that reference to some other enactment is intended,

(b) a reference to a subsection or paragraph is to the subsection or paragraph of the provision in which the reference occurs, unless it is indicated that reference to some other provision is intended.

(3) A reference in this Act to any enactment shall be construed as a reference to that enactment as amended or adapted by or under any subsequent enactment.

Criminal Procedure Act, 1993

Review by Court of Criminal Appeal of alleged miscarriage of justice or excessive sentence. s. 2.

(1) A person—

(a) who has been convicted of an offence either—

(i) on indictment, or

(ii) after signing a plea of guilty and being sent forward for sentence under section 13(2)(b) of the Criminal Procedure Act, 1967, and

who, after appeal to the Court including an application for leave to appeal, and any subsequent re-trial, stands convicted of an offence to which this paragraph applies, and

(b) who alleges that a new or newly-discovered fact shows that there has been a miscarriage of justice in relation to the conviction or that the sentence imposed is excessive,

may, if no further proceedings are pending in relation to the appeal, apply to the Court for an order quashing the conviction or reviewing the sentence.

(2) An application under subsection (1) shall be treated for all purposes as an appeal to the Court against the conviction or sentence.

(3) In subsection (1)(b) the reference to a new fact is to a fact known to the convicted person at the time of the trial or appeal proceedings the significance of which was appreciated by him, where he alleges that there is a reasonable explanation for his failure to adduce evidence of that fact.

(4) The reference in subsection (1)(b) to a newly-discovered fact is to a fact discovered by or coming to the notice of the convicted person after the relevant appeal proceedings have been finally determined or a fact the significance of which was not appreciated by the convicted person or his advisers during the trial or appeal proceedings.

(5) Where—

(a) after an application by a convicted person under subsection (1) and any subsequent re-trial the person stands convicted of an offence, and

(b) the person alleges that a fact discovered by him or coming to his notice after the hearing of the application and any subsequent re-trial or a fact the significance of which was not appreciated by him or his advisers during the hearing of the application and any subsequent re-trial shows that there has been a miscarriage of justice in relation to the conviction, or that the sentence was excessive,

he may apply to the Court for an order quashing the conviction or reviewing the sentence and his application shall be treated as if it were an application under that subsection.

Jurisdiction of Court of Criminal Appeal in relation to appeals.   s. 3.

(1) On the hearing of an appeal against conviction of an offence the Court may—

(a) affirm the conviction (and may do so, notwithstanding that it is of opinion that a point raised in the appeal might be decided in favour of the appellant, if it considers that no miscarriage of justice has actually occurred), or

(b) quash the conviction and make no further order, or

(c) quash the conviction and order the applicant to be re-tried for the offence, or

(d) quash the conviction and, if it appears to the Court that the appellant could have been found guilty of some other offence and that the jury must have been satisfied of facts which proved him guilty of the other offence—

(i) substitute for the verdict a verdict of guilty of the other offence, and

(ii) impose such sentence in substitution for the sentence imposed at the trial as may be authorised by law for the other offence, not being a sentence of greater severity.

(2) On the hearing of an appeal against sentence for an offence the Court may quash the sentence and in place of it impose such sentence or make such order as it considers appropriate, being a sentence or order which could have been imposed on the convicted person for the offence at the court of trial.

(3) The Court, on the hearing of an appeal or, as the case may be, of an application for leave to appeal, against a conviction or sentence may—

(a) where the appeal is based on new or additional evidence, direct the Commissioner of the Garda Siochana to have such inquiries carried out as the Court considers necessary or expedient for the purpose of determining whether further evidence ought to be adduced;

(b) order the production of any document, exhibit or other thing connected with the proceedings;

(c) order any person who would have been a compellable witness in the proceedings from which the appeal lies to attend for examination and be examined before the Court, whether or not he was called in those proceedings;

(d) receive the evidence, if tendered, of any witness;

(e) generally make such order as may be necessary for the purpose of doing justice in the case before the Court.

(4) For the purposes of this section, the Court may order the

examination of any witness whose attendance might be required under this section to be conducted, in a manner provided by rules of court, before any judge or officer of the Court or other person appointed by the Court for the purpose, and allow the admission of any depositions so taken as evidence before the Court.

(5) The reference in subsection (1)(d) to a jury shall, where the trial was before a court sitting without a jury, be construed as a reference to that court.

(6) Section 32 of the Courts of Justice Act, 1924, is hereby amended by the addition after "pending the determination of his appeal" of "or application for leave to appeal".

(7) A legal aid certificate which was granted in relation to the trial of an accused person who has been ordered by the Court under this section to be re-tried shall have effect as if it had been granted also in relation to his re-trial.

(8) The references in section 44(2) of the Offences Against the State Act, 1939, to section 34 of the Criminal Justice Act, 1924, and section 5 of the Criminal Justice Act, 1928, shall be construed as references to this section.

Re-trial. s. 4.

(1) Where a person is ordered under this Act to be re-tried for an offence he may, notwithstanding any rule of law, be again indicted and tried and, if found guilty, sentenced for that offence.

(2) In a case to which subsection (1) relates the Court may—

(a) where a legal aid certificate does not apply in respect thereof, order that the costs of the appeal and of the new trial, in whole or in part, be paid by the State, unless the Court is of opinion that the necessity for the appeal and the new trial has been contributed to by the defence,

(b) order that the accused be detained in custody or be admitted to bail pending the re-trial on such terms as the Court thinks proper,

(c) order that any property or money forfeited, restored or paid by virtue of the conviction or of any order made on the conviction be retained pending the re-trial.

Summary determination. s. 5.

(1) If it appears to the registrar of the Court that a notice of an application for leave to appeal does not show any substantial ground of appeal or, in the case of an application under section 2, that the application does not disclose a *prima facie* case that a miscarriage of justice has occurred in relation to the conviction or that the sentence is

excessive, he may, without calling for the report of the official stenographer, refer the application to the Court for summary determination; and where the case is so referred the Court may, if it considers that the application is frivolous or vexatious and can be determined without adjourning it for a full hearing, dismiss it summarily, without calling on anyone to attend the hearing or to appear on behalf of the prosecution.

(2) The jurisdiction of the Court under subsection (1) may be exercised by a single judge of the Court and an appeal may be made to the Court by the convicted person against the summary determination of an application.

Application to Courts-Martial Appeal Court. s. 6.

(1) References in sections 2 to 5 and 7 to the Court shall include references to the Courts-Martial Appeal Court, and those provisions shall have effect in relation to that court with the necessary modifications.

(2) For the purposes of subsection (1)—

(a) the references in section 2 to a conviction or sentence shall be construed as references to a conviction or sentence of a court-martial;

(b) the reference in section 3 to the jury shall be construed as a reference to the court-martial;

(c) the references in section 3 to the trial shall be construed as references to the court-martial;

(d) the reference in section 3(3) to the Commissioner of the Garda Siochana shall be construed as a reference to the Adjutant-General of the Defence Forces;

(e) the reference in section 4(1) to any rule of law shall include a reference to anything in the Defence Act, 1954.

(3) The Superior Courts Rules Committee may, with the concurrence of the Minister for Justice, make rules of court for the purposes of this section.

Petition for grant of pardon. s. 7.

(1) If a person-

(a) who has been convicted of an offence,

(b) who after appeal against the conviction stands convicted of an offence, and

(c) who alleges that a new or newly-discovered fact shows that a miscarriage of justice has occurred in relation to the conviction, petitions the Minister for Justice with a view to the Government advising the President to grant a pardon under Article 13.6 of the

Constitution and no further proceedings are pending in relation to the appeal, the following provisions of this section shall apply.

(2) The Minister for Justice shall make or cause to be made such inquiries as he considers necessary and—

(a) if he is of opinion either

(i) that the matters dealt with in the petition could appropriately be dealt with by way of an application to the Court pursuant to section 2, or

(ii) that a case has not been made out that a miscarriage of justice has occurred and that no useful purpose would be served by further investigation, shall inform the petitioner accordingly and take no further action, and

(b) in any other case, shall recommend to the Government either—

(i) that it should advise the President to grant a pardon in respect of the offence of which the applicant was convicted, or

(ii) that it should appoint a committee pursuant to section 8 to inquire into and report on the case.

(3) In subsection (1)(c) the reference to a new fact is to a fact known to the convicted person at the time of the trial or appeal proceedings the significance of which was appreciated by him, where he alleges that there is a reasonable explanation for his failure to adduce evidence of that fact.

(4) The reference in subsection (1)(c) to a newly-discovered fact is to a fact discovered by or coming to the notice of the convicted person after the relevant appeal proceedings have been finally determined or a fact the significance of which was not appreciated by the convicted person or his advisers during the trial or appeal proceedings.

(5) References in subsections (1) and (2) to the Minister for Justice shall, in relation to a conviction by court-martial, be construed as references to the Minister for Defence.

(6) Nothing in this section shall affect any functions of the Minister for Justice in relation to a petition to him from a person other than a person mentioned in subsection (1) with a view to the Government advising the President to grant a pardon under Article 13.6 of the Constitution.

Committee to inquire into alleged miscarriages ...   s. 8

(1) The Government, for the purpose of enabling it to decide whether or not to advise the President to exercise the right of pardon conferred by Article 13.6 of the Constitution, may establish a committee to inquire into any or all of the matters dealt with in a petition for the grant of a pardon by the President and to report whether, in the opinion of

the committee, the President should be so advised.

(2) The committee shall be a tribunal within the meaning of the Tribunals of Inquiry (Evidence) Acts, 1921 and 1979.

(3) Where a committee consists of more than one member, the Government shall designate one of the members to be its chairman.

(4) The person constituting the committee (or, where the committee consists of more than one member, its chairman) shall be either a judge or former judge or a practising barrister or solicitor of not less than ten years standing.

5) A committee may receive such evidence and other information as it sees fit, whether or not that evidence or information is or would be admissible in a court of law.

Compensation for miscarriage of justice. s. 9.

(1) Where a person has been convicted of an offence and either—

(a) (i) his conviction has been quashed by the Court on an application under section 2 or on appeal, or he has been acquitted in any re-trial, and

(ii) the Court or the court of re-trial, as the case may be, has certified that a newly-discovered fact shows that there has been a miscarriage of justice, or

(b) (i) he has been pardoned as a result of a petition under section 7, and

(ii) the Minister for Justice is of opinion that a newly-discovered fact shows that there has been a miscarriage of justice,

the Minister shall, subject to subsections (2) and (3), pay compensation to the convicted person or, if he is dead, to his legal personal representatives unless the non-disclosure of the fact in time is wholly or partly attributable to the convicted person.

(2) A person to whom subsection (1) relates shall have the option of applying for compensation or of instituting an action for damages arising out of the conviction.

(3) No payment of compensation under this section shall be made unless an application for such compensation has been made to the Minister for Justice.

(4) The compensation shall be of such amount as may be determined by the Minister for Justice.

(5) Any person who is dissatisfied with the amount of compensation determined by the Minister may apply to the High Court to determine the amount which the Minister shall pay under this section and the award of the High Court shall be final.

(6) In subsection (1) "newly-discovered fact" means—

(a) where a conviction was quashed by the Court on an application under section 2 or a convicted person was pardoned as a result of a petition under section 7, or has been acquitted in any re-trial, a fact which was discovered by him or came to his notice after the relevant appeal proceedings had been finally determined or a fact the significance of which was not appreciated by the convicted person or his advisers during the trial or appeal proceedings, and

(b) where a conviction was quashed by that Court on appeal, a fact which was discovered by the convicted person or came to his notice after the conviction to which the appeal relates or a fact the significance of which was not appreciated by the convicted person or his advisers during the trial.

Uncorroborated confession. s. 10

(1) Where at a trial of a person on indictment evidence is given of a confession made by that person and that evidence is not corroborated, the judge shall advise the jury to have due regard to the absence of corroboration.

(2) It shall not be necessary for a judge to use any particular form of words under this section.

Appeal from Central Criminal Court. s. 11.

(1) The right of appeal to the Supreme Court, other than an appeal under section 34 of the Criminal Procedure Act, 1967, from a decision of the Central Criminal Court is hereby abolished.

(2) This section shall not apply to a decision of the Central Criminal Court in so far as it relates to the validity of any law having regard to the provisions of the Constitution.

Expenses. s. 12

The expenses incurred in the administration of this Act shall, to such extent as may be sanctioned by the Minister for Finance, be paid out of moneys provided by the Oireachtas.

Repeals. s. 13

The enactments referred to in column (2) of the Schedule to this Act are hereby repealed to the extent mentioned in column (3) of the Schedule.

Short title. s. 14

This Act may be cited as the Criminal Procedure Act, 1993.

Schedule

Enactments repealed extent of repeal
Court of Justice Act, 1924, Section 34;
Court of Justice Act, 1928, Section 5;
Courts-Martial Appeals Act, 1983, Section 18.

Criminal Justice (Public Order) Act, 1994 (No. 2) -

The purpose of the Act is three-fold: firstly it updates the law in relation to public order offences; secondly, it provides for an offence specifically aimed at racketeering and thirdly, it provides for the implementation of Certain recommendations made by the Committee on Public Safety and Crowd Control.

Part I Preliminary and General

Short title   s. 1.

(1) This Act may be cited as the Criminal Justice (Public Order) Act, 1994.

(2) The Vagrancy Acts, 1824 and 1988, and section 13 may be cited together as the Vagrancy Acts, 1824 to 1993.

(3) This Act shall come into operation one months after its passing.

Interpretation (General)   s. 2.

(1) A reference in this Act to a Part or to a section is a reference to a Part or section of this Act unless it is indicated that a reference to some other Act is intended.

(2) A reference in this Act to a subsection or to a paragraph is to the subsection or paragraph of the provision in which the reference occurs unless it is indicated that a reference to some other provision is intended.

Part II Offences Relating to Public Order

The provisions in this Part arise in part from recommendations made by the Law Reform Commission in two reports: their Report on Offences under the Dublin Police Acts and Related Offences and their Report on Vagrancy and Related Offences. The previous provisions were based on nineteenth century legislation; were not geared to modern realities and provided out-dated and inadequate penalties.

The law has been restated and modernise in relation to the major public order offences. As a consequence the common law offences of riot, rout, unlawful assembly and affray are abolished.

Interpretation (Part II)   s. 3.

(1) In this Part, except where the context otherwise requires—
"dwelling" means a building, vehicle or vessel ordinarily used for habitation;
"private place" means a place that is not a public place;
"public place" includes-

(a) any highway,

(b) any outdoor area to which at the material time members of the public have or are permitted access, whether as of right or as a trespasser or otherwise, and which is used for public recreational purposes,

(c) any cemetery or churchyard,

(d) any premises or other place to which at the material time members of the public have or are permitted to have access, whether as of right or by express or implied permission, or whether on payment or otherwise, and

(e) any train, vessel or vehicle used for the carriage of persons for reward.

Intoxication in public places s. 4.

(1) It shall be an offence for any person to be present in any public place while intoxicated to such an extent as would give rise to a reasonable apprehension that he might endanger himself or any other person in his vicinity.

(2) A person who is guilty of an offence under this section shall be liable on summary conviction to a fine not exceeding £100.

(3) Where a member of the Garda Siochana suspects, with reasonable cause, that an offence under this section or under section 5 or 6 is being committed, the member concerned may seize, obtain or remove, without warrant, any bottle or container, together with its contents, which—

(a) is in the possession, in a place other than a place used as a dwelling, of a person by whom such member suspects the offence to have been committed, and

(b) such member suspects, with reasonable cause, contains an intoxicating substance.

Provided that in the application of this subsection to section 5 or 6, any such bottle or container, together with its contents, may only be so seized, obtained or removed where the member of the Garda Siochana suspects, with reasonable cause, that the bottle or container or its contents, is relevant to the offence under section 5 or 6 which the member suspects is being committed.

(4) In this section—

"bottle or container" does not include a bottle or container for a substance which is in the possession of the person concerned for a purpose other than the intoxication of that or any other person;

"intoxicated" means under the intoxicating influence of any alcoholic drink, drug, solvent or other substance or a combination of substances and cognate words shall be construed accordingly.

Disorderly conduct in public place   s. 5.
(1) It shall be an offence for any person in a public place to engage in offensive conduct
(a) between the hours of 12 o'clock midnight and 7 o'clock in the morning next following, or
(b) at any other time, after having been requested by a member of the Garda Siochana to desist.
(2) A person who is guilty of an offence under this section shall be liable on summary conviction to a fine not exceeding £500.
(3) In this section "offensive conduct" means any unreasonable behaviour which, having regard to all the circumstances, is likely to cause serious offence or serious annoyance to any person who is, or might reasonably be expected to be, aware of such behaviour.

Threatening, abusive or insulting behaviour in public place.   s. 6.
(1) It shall be an offence for any person in a public place to use or engage in any threatening, abusive or insulting words or behaviour with intent to provoke a breach of the peace or being reckless as to whether a breach of the peace may be occasioned.
(2) A person who is guilty of an offence under this section shall be liable on summary conviction to a fine not exceeding £500 or to imprisonment for a term not exceeding 3 months or to both.

Distribution or display in public place of material which is threatening, abusive, insulting or obscene.   s. 7.
(1) It shall be an offence for any person in a public place to distribute or display any writing, sign or visible representation which is threatening, abusive, insulting or obscene with intent to provoke a breach of the peace or being reckless as to whether a breach of the peace may be occasioned.
(2) A person who is guilty of an offence under this section shall be liable on summary conviction to a fine not exceeding £500 or to imprisonment for a term not exceeding months or to both.
(3) In this section "public meeting" means any meeting to which members of the public have access, whether on payment or otherwise.

Failure to comply with directions of Garda Siochana.   s. 8
(1) Where a member of the Garda Siochana finds a person in a public place and suspects, with reasonable cause, that such person—

(a) is or has been acting in a manner contrary to the provisions of section 4, 5, 6, 7, or 9, or

(b) without lawful authority or reasonable excuse, is acting in a manner which consists of loitering in a public place in circumstances, which may include the company of other persons, that give rise to a reasonable apprehension for the safety of persons or the safety of property or for the maintenance of the public peace, the member may direct the person so suspected to do either or both of the following, that is to say:

(i) desist from acting in such a manner, and

(ii) leave immediately the vicinity of the place concerned in a peaceable or orderly manner.

(2) It shall be an offence for any person, without lawful authority or reasonable excuse, to fail to comply with a direction given by a member of the Garda Siochana under this section.

(3) A person who is guilty of an offence under this section shall be liable on summary conviction to a fine not exceeding £500 or to imprisonment for a term not exceeding 6 months or to both.

Wilful obstruction   s. 9

Any person who shall in any manner wilfully prevent or interrupt the free passage of any person or vehicle in any public place shall be liable on summary conviction to a fine not exceeding £200.

Section 13(3) of the Summary Jurisdiction (Ireland) Act, 1851 (which has been repealed) specified a fine of not more than £1 for this offence.

Increase in penalty for common assault etc.   s. 10

The Criminal Justice Act, 1951, is hereby amended by the substitution for subsection (2) of section 11 of the following:

"(2) A person convicted of common assault or battery shall be liable to a fine not exceeding £1,000 or, at the discretion of the Court, imprisonment for a term not exceeding twelve months or to both such fine and imprisonment.".

The previous provision provided for a £50 fine and or six months imprisonment.

Entering buildings, etc. with intent   ...   s. 11

(1) It shall be an offence for a person-

(a) to enter any building or the curtilage of any building or any part of such building or curtilage as a trespasser, or

(b) to be within the vicinity of any such building or curtilage or part of such building or curtilage for the purpose of trespassing thereon,

in circumstances giving rise to the reasonable inference that such entry or presence was with intent to commit an offence or with intent to unlawfully interfere with any property situate therein.

(2) A person who is guilty of an offence under this section shall be liable on summary conviction to a fine not exceeding £1,000 or to imprisonment for a term not exceeding 6 months or to both.

Amendment of Vagrancy Act, 1824, s. 12

Section 4 (as applied to Ireland by the Prevention of Crimes Act, 1871) of the Vagrancy Act, 1824, is hereby amended by the deletion of "every person being found in or upon any dwelling house, warehouse, coach-house, stable, or outhouse, or in any enclosed yard, garden or area, for any unlawful purpose;".

Trespass on building. s. 13

(1) It shall be an offence for a person, without reasonable excuse, to trespass on any building or the curtilage thereof in such a manner as causes or is likely to cause fear in another person.

(2)(a) Where a member of the Garda Siochana finds a person in a place to which subsection (1) relates and suspects, with reasonable cause, that such person is or has been acting in a manner contrary to the provisions of that subsection, then the member may direct the person so suspected to do either or both of the following, that is to say:

(i) desist from acting in such a manner, and

(ii) leave immediately the vicinity of the place concerned in a peaceful or orderly manner.

(b) It shall be an offence for any person, without lawful authority or reasonable excuse, to fail to comply with a direction given by a member of the Garda Siochana under this section.

(3)(a) A person who is guilty of an offence under subsection (1) shall be liable on summary conviction to a fine not exceeding £1,000 or to imprisonment for a term not exceeding 12 months or to both.

(b) A person who is guilty of an offence under subsection (2) shall be liable on summary conviction to a fine not exceeding £500 or to imprisonment for a term not exceeding 6 months or to both.

Riot s. 14

(1) Where—

(a) 12 or more persons who are present together at any place (whether that place is a public place or a private place or both) use or threaten to use unlawful violence for a common purpose, and

(b) the conduct of those persons, taken together, is such as would cause a person of reasonable firmness present at that place to fear for his or another person's safety, then, each of the persons using unlawful violence for the common purpose shall commit the offence of riot.

(2) For the purposes of this section—

(a) it shall be immaterial whether or not the 12 or more persons use or threaten to use unlawful violence simultaneously at any place;

(b) the common purpose may be inferred from conduct;

(c) no person of reasonable firmness need actually be, or be likely to be, present at that place.

(3) A person guilty of an offence of riot shall be liable on conviction on indictment to a fine or to imprisonment for a term not exceeding 10 years or to both.

(4) The common law offence of riot is hereby abolished.

Violent disorder   s. 15

(1) Where—

(a) three or more persons who are present together at any place (whether that place is a public place or a private place or both) use or threaten to use unlawful violence, and

(b) the conduct of those persons, taken together, is such as would cause a person of reasonable firmness present at that place to fear for his or another person's safety,

then, each of the persons using or threatening to use unlawful violence shall be guilty of the offence of violent disorder.

(2) For the purposes of this section—

(a) it shall be immaterial whether or not the three or more persons use or threaten to use unlawful violence simultaneously;

(b) no person of reasonable firmness need actually be, or be likely to be, present at that place.

(3) A person shall not be convicted of the offence of violent disorder unless the person intends to use or threaten to use violence or is aware that his conduct may be violent or threaten violence.

(4) A person guilty of an offence of violent disorder shall be liable on conviction on indictment to a fine or to imprisonment for a term not exceeding 10 years or to both.

(5) A reference, however expressed, in any enactment passed before the commencement of this Act—

(a) to the common law offence of riot, or

(b) to the common law offence of riot and to tumult,

shall be construed as a reference to the offence of violent disorder.

(6) The common law offence of rout and the common law offence of unlawful assembly are hereby abolished.

Affray   s. 16

(1) Where—

(a) two or more persons at any place (whether that place is a public place or a private place or both) use or threaten to use violence towards each other, and

(b) the violence so used or threatened by one of those persons is unlawful, and

(c) the conduct of those persons taken together is such as would cause a person of reasonable firmness present at that place to fear for his or another person's safety, then, each such person who uses or threatens to use unlawful violence shall commit the offence of affray.

(2) For the purposes of this section:

(a) a threat cannot be made by words alone;

(b) no person of reasonable firmness need actually be, or be likely to be, present at the place where the use or threat of violence occurred.

(3) A person shall not be convicted of the offence of affray unless the person intends to use or threaten to use violence or is aware that his conduct may be violent or threaten violence.

(4) A person guilty of an offence of affray shall be liable—

(a) on summary conviction to a fine not exceeding £500 or to imprisonment for a term not exceeding 12 months or to both,

(b) on conviction on indictment to a fine or to imprisonment for a term not exceeding 5 years or to both.

(5) The common law offence of affray is hereby abolished.

Blackmail, extortion and demanding money with   ...   s. 17

(1) It shall be an offence for any person who, with a view gain for himself or another or with intent to cause loss to another, makes.makes any unwarranted demand with menaces.

(2) For the purposes of this section—

(a) a demand with menaces shall be unwarranted unless the person making it does so in the belief—

(i) that he has reasonable grounds for making the demand, and

(ii) that the use of the menaces is a proper means of reinforcing the demand;

(b) the nature of the act or omission demanded shall be immaterial and it shall also be immaterial whether or not the menaces relate to action to be taken by the person making the demand.

(3) A person guilty of an offence under this section shall be liable—

(a) on summary conviction to a fine not exceeding £1,000 or to imprisonment for a term not exceeding 12 months or to both,

(b) on conviction on indictment to a fine or to imprisonment for a term not exceeding 14 years or to both.

This is a provision specifically tailored to deal with the problem of racketeering. There is existing law which can be used to deal with this type of offence, the main provisions are contained in section 30 of the Larceny Act, 1916 and section 3 of the Criminal Damage Act, 1991.

Assault with intent to cause bodily harm or commit indictable offence. s. 18

(1) Any person who assaults any person with intent to cause bodily harm or to commit an indictable offence shall be guilty of an offence.

(2) A person guilty of an offence under this section shall be liable—

(a) on summary conviction, to a fine not exceeding £1,000 or to imprisonment for a term not exceeding 12 months or to both,

(b) on conviction on indictment, to a fine or to imprisonment for a term not exceeding 5 years or to both.

Assault or obstruction of peace officer s. 19

(1) Any person who—

(a) assaults a peace officer acting in the execution of the peace officer's duty, knowing that he is, or being reckless as to whether he is, a peace officer acting in the execution of his duty, or

(b) assaults any other person acting in the aid of a peace officer, or

(c) assaults any other person with intent to resist or prevent the lawful apprehension or detention of himself or any other person for any offence,

shall be guilty of an offence.

(2) A person guilty of an offence under subsection (1) shall be liable -

(a) having elected for summary disposal of the offence, on summary conviction, to a fine not exceeding £1,000 or to imprisonment for a term not exceeding 12 months, or to both,

(b) on conviction on indictment, to a fine or to imprisonment for a term not exceeding 5 years or to both.

(3) Any person who resists or wilfully obstructs a peace officer acting in the execution of his duty or a person assisting a peace officer in the execution of his duty, knowing that he is or being reckless as to whether he is, a peace officer acting in the execution of his duty, shall be guilty of an offence.

(4) A person guilty of an offence under subsection (3) shall be liable on summary conviction to a fine not exceeding £500 or to imprisonment for a term not exceeding 6 months or to both.

(5) The provisions of this section are in addition to and not in substitution of any provision in any other enactment relating to assault

or obstruction of a peace officer.

(6) In this section—

"peace officer" means a member of the Garda Siochana, a prison officer, a member of the Defence Forces;

"prison" means any place for which rules or regulations may be made under the Prisons Acts, 1826 to 1980, section 7 of the Offences against the State (Amendment) Act, 1940, section 233 of the Defence Act, 1954, section 2 of the Prisoners of War and Enemy Aliens Act, 1956, or section 13 of the Criminal Justice Act, 1960;

"prison officer" includes any member of the staff of a prison and any person having the custody of, or having duties in relation to the custody of, a person detained in prison.

This section restates in modern form section 38 of the Offences Against the Person Act, 1861 (which is repealed); the penalty is increased from 2 to 5 years imprisonment and a peace officer now includes a prison officer or a member of the Defence Forces.

Part III Crowd Control at Public Events

This Part deals with crowd control at public events, the provisions are along the lines of recommendations made by the Committee on Public Safety and Crowd Control which was chaired by Mr. Justice Liam Hamilton. It gives the Gardai a comprehensive and clear statutory basis with which they can deal with crowd control rather than rely, on common law powers.

Interpretation s. 20

In this Part—

"container" does not include a container for any medicinal product;

"disposable container" includes—

(a) any bottle, can or other portable container or any part thereof (including any crushed or broken portable container or part thereof) for holding any drink which, when empty, is of a kind normally discarded or returned to, or left to be recovered by, the supplier, and

(b) any crate or packaging designed to hold more than one such bottle, can or other portable container;

"event" has the meaning assigned to it by section 21(1);

"intoxicating liquor" includes any container containing intoxicating liquor, whether or not a disposable container.

Control of access to certain events, etc. s. 21

(1) If it appears to a member of the Garda Siochana not below the rank of superintendent that it is necessary in the interests of safety or

for the purpose of preserving order to restrict the access of persons to a place where an event is taking or is about to take place which attracts, or is likely to attract, a large assembly of persons (in this Part referred to as the "event"), he may authorise any member of the Garda Siochana to erect or cause to be erected a barrier or a series of barriers on any road, street, lane, alley or other means of access to such a place in a position not more than one mile therefrom for the purpose of regulating the access of persons or vehicles thereto.

(2) Where a barrier has been erected in accordance with subsection (1), a member of the Garda Siochana in uniform may by oral or manual direction or by the exhibition of any notice or sign, or any combination thereof

(a) divert persons generally or particularly and whether in or on vehicles or on foot to another means of access to the event, including a means of access to that event on foot only, or

(b) where possession of a ticket is required for entrance to the event, prohibit a person whether in or on vehicles or on foot from crossing or passing the barrier towards the event where the person has no such ticket, or

(c) indicate that to proceed beyond the barrier while in possession of any intoxicating liquor, disposable drinks container or offensive article will render such liquor, container or article liable to confiscation.

(3) A member of the Garda Siochana shall not prohibit a person from crossing or passing a barrier erected under this section save for the purpose of diverting the person to another means of access to the event, if it appears to the member that the person is seeking do so for the purpose only of—

(a) going to his dwelling or place of business or work in the vicinity of the event, or

(b) going for any other lawful purpose to any place in the vicinity of the event other than the place where the event is taking place or is about to take place.

(4) A person who—

(a) fails to obey a direction given by a member of the Garda Siochana under subsection (2) for the purposes of paragraph (a) or (b) thereof, or

(b) fails to comply with the terms of a notice or sign exhibited under subsection (2) for the purposes of paragraph (a) or (b) thereof,

shall be guilty of an offence.

(5) A person guilty of an offence under this section shall be liable on summary conviction to a fine not exceeding £500.

Criminal Justice (Public Order) Act, 1994

Surrender and seizure of intoxicating liquor etc., s. 22

(1) Where in relation to an event—

(a) a barrier has been erected under section 23 and it appears to a member of the Garda Siochana that a person on foot or in a vehicle is seeking to cross or pass the barrier, or has crossed or passed the barrier, for the purpose of going to the place where the event is taking place or is about to take place, or

(b) it appears to a member of the Garda Siochana that a person is about to enter, or has entered, the place where the event is taking place or is about to take place, and the person has, or the member of the Garda Siochana suspects with reasonable cause that the person has, in his possession—

(i) any intoxicating liquor, or

(ii) any disposable container, or

(iii) any other article which, having regard to the circumstances or the nature of the event, could be used to cause injury,

the member may exercise any one or more of the following powers—

(I) search or cause to be searched that person or any vehicle in or on which he may be in order to ascertain whether he has with him any such liquor, container or other article,

(II) refuse to allow that person to proceed to the event or to proceed further, as the case may be, unless that person surrenders permanently to a member of the Garda Siochana as directed by the member such liquor, container or other article.

(2) Where a member of the Garda Siochana refuses to allow a person to proceed to the event or to proceed further by virtue of subsection (1)(II) and the person does not surrender the alcoholic liquor, disposable container or other article concerned, the member may require the person to leave the vicinity in an orderly and peaceful manner as directed by the member.

(3) A person who, without lawful authority or reasonable excuse, fails to comply with a requirement under subsection (2) shall be guilty of an offence.

(4) A person guilty of an offence under this section shall be liable on summary conviction to a fine not exceeding £500.

Part IV Miscellaneous and Repeals

Prohibition of advertising of brothels / prostitution. s. 23

(1) A person who publishes or causes to be published or distributes or causes to be distributed an advertisement which advertises a brothel or the services of a prostitute in the State or any premises or services in

the State in terms, circumstances or manner which gives rise to the reasonable inference that the premises is a brothel or that the service is one of prostitution shall be guilty of an offence

(2) A person who is guilty of an offence under subsection (1) shall be liable-

(a) on summary conviction to a fine not exceeding £1,000,

(b) on conviction on indictment to a fine not exceeding £10,000.

(3) In any proceeding for an offence under subsection (1) it shall be a defence for the accused to show that he is a person whose business is to publish or distribute or to arrange for the publication or distribution of advertisements and that he received the advertisement in question for publication or distribution in the ordinary course of business and did not know and had no reason to suspect that the advertisement related to a brothel or to the services of a prostitute.

(4) Where an offence under subsection (1) is committed by a body corporate or by a person purporting to act on behalf of a body corporate or an unincorporated body of persons and is proved to have been attributable to any neglect on the part of, any person who, when the offence was committed, was a director, member of the committee of management or other controlling authority of the body concerned, or the manager, secretary or other officer of the body, or who was purporting to act in any such capacity, that person, as well as the body, shall be guilty of an offence and shall be liable to be proceeded against and punished as if that person were guilty of the first-mentioned offence.

(5) In this section-

"advertisement" includes every form of advertising or promotion, whether in a publication or by the display of notices or posters or by the means of circulars, leaflets, pamphlets or cards or other documents or by way of radio, television, computer monitor, telephone, facsimile transmission, photography or cinematography or other like means of communication;

"distribute" means distribute to the public or a section of the public and cognate words shall be construed accordingly;

"publish" means publish to the public or a section of the public and cognate words shall be construed accordingly.

This section was proposed at committee stage by the Minister for Justice.

Arrest without warrant s. 24

(1) Where a member of the Garda Siochana finds any person committing an offence under a relevant provision, the member may arrest such person without warrant.

(2) Where a member of the Garda Siochana is of the opinion that an offence has been committed under a relevant provision, the member may —

(a) demand the name and address of any person who the member suspects, with reasonable cause, has committed, or who the member finds committing, such an offence, and

(b) arrest without warrant any such person who fails or refuses to give his name and address when demanded, or gives a name or address which the member has reasonable grounds for believing is false or misleading.

(3) Any person who fails or refuses to give his name and address when demanded by virtue of subsection (2), or gives a name or address when so demanded which is false or misleading, shall be guilty of an offence.

(4) A person guilty of an offence under subsection (3) shall be liable on summary conviction to a fine not exceeding £500 or to a term of imprisonment not exceeding 6 months or to both.

(5) In this section "relevant provision" means section 4, 6, 7, 8, 11, 13, 14, 15, 16, 17, 18, or 19.

Continuance of existing powers of Garda Siochana   s. 25

Any power conferred on a member of the Garda Siochana by this Act is without prejudice to any other power exercisable by such a member.

Repeals   s. 26

The Acts specified in the Schedule to this Act are hereby repealed to the extent specified in the third column of that Schedule.

Schedule

Enactments repealed   Extent of Repeal

Dublin Police Act, 1836, (6 & 7 Will. 4, c. 29), Section 9.
Dublin Police Act, 1842, (5 & 6 Vict., c. 24), Para. 13, Section 14.
Summary Jurisdiction (Ireland) Act, 1851, (13 & 14 Vict., c. 92), Para. 3, Section 13.
Offences against the Person Act, 1861, (24 & 25 Vict., c. 100), Section 38.
Prevention of Crimes Act, 1871, (34 & 35 Vict., c. 112), Section 12.
Larceny Act, 1916, (6 & 7 Geo. 5, c. 50), Sections 29 to 31.

Road Traffic Act, 1994 (No. 7)

The Act: (a) restates and strengthen the law relating to drink driving, (b) introduces new measures to secure better enforcement of the Road Traffic Acts, (c) introduces new arrangements for making traffic regulations, (d) devolves certain functions to local authorities.

Part I of the Act deals with preliminary and general matters such as definitions, power to make regulations and repeal of provisions which are replaced.

Part 11 re-enacts, in an amended form, those provisions of the Road Traffic (Amendment) Act, 1978 which relate to the functions and duties of the Medical Bureau of Road Safety and its Director.

Part III Driving Offences

This Part restates and amends existing law in relation to drink driving.

The main items of significance are:

—a reduction in the maximum permissible alcohol levels for drivers of vehicles,

—provisions governing evidential breath analysis, including a maximum permissible breath alcohol level equating with the blood and urine levels,

—power to vary the maximum level of alcohol permissible for drivers and to set different limits for different classes of drivers,

—power to detain intoxicated drivers where the release of the drivers could be a threat to the safety of themselves or other persons,

—power to enter a hospital to take a blood or urine specimen from a driver involved in a traffic accident,

—amendments to existing drink driving provisions to close loopholes shown up by Court cases.

Interpretation of Part III   s. 9.

(1) In this Part—

"analysis" includes any operation used in determining the concentration of alcohol in a specimen of breath, blood or urine, and any operation used in determining the presence (if any) of a drug or drugs in a specimen of blood or urine, and cognate words shall be construed accordingly;

"Bureau" has the meaning assigned to it by section 37(1) of the Act of 1968;

"designated" means designated by a member of the Garda Siochana;

"doctor" means a person registered in the General Register of Medical Practitioners established under section 26 of the Medical Practitioners Act, 1978;

"intoxicant" includes alcohol and drugs and any combination of drugs

427

or of drugs and alcohol.

(2) A reference in this Part (other than sections 10 and 11) to section 49 or 50 of the Principal Act is to the section inserted by this Part.

This section re-enacts, with modifications, section 9 (the interpretation section of Part III of the Act of 1973. The proposed changes are as follows:

—the definition of analysis has been extended to include the testing of blood for the presence of drugs,

—the term "doctor" replaces the term "registered medical practitioner"; it is defined as a person registered in the General Register of Medical Practitioners,

—the inclusion of a definition of "intoxicant" for the purpose of Part III, the same definition is also included in the amended sections 49 and 50 of the Road Traffic Act, 1961 for the purposes of those sections.

Prohibition on driving vehicle while under influence of intoxicant. s. 10

The following section is inserted in the Principal Act in substitution for section 49 of that Act:

49 (1)(a) A person shall not drive or attempt to drive a mechanically propelled vehicle in a public place while he is under the influence of an intoxicant to such an extent as to be incapable of having proper control of the vehicle.

(b) In this subsection 'intoxicant' includes alcohol and drugs and any combination of drugs or of drugs and alcohol.

(2) A person shall not drive or attempt to drive a mechanically propelled vehicle in a public place while there is present in his body a quantity of alcohol such that, within 3 hours after so driving or attempting to drive, the concentration of alcohol in his blood will exceed a concentration of 80 milligrammes of alcohol per 100 millilitres of blood.

(3) A person shall not drive a mechanically propelled vehicle in a public place while there is present in his body a quantity of alcohol such that, within 3 hours after so driving or attempting to drive, the concentration of alcohol in his urine will exceed a concentration of 107 milligrammes of alcohol per 100 millilitres of urine.

(4) A person shall not drive or attempt to drive a mechanically propelled vehicle in a public place while there is present in his body a quantity of alcohol such that, within 3 hours after so driving or attempting to drive, the concentration of alcohol in his breath will exceed a concentration of 35 microgrammes of alcohol per 100 millilitres of breath.

(5) (a) The Minister may, by regulations made by him, vary the concentration of alcohol for the time being standing specified in

subsection (2), (3) or (4) of this section, whether generally or in respect of a particular class of person, and the said subsection shall have effect in accordance with any such regulations for the time being in force.

(b) A draft of every regulation proposed to be made under this subsection shall be laid before each House of the Oireachtas and the regulation shall not be made until a resolution approving of the draft has been passed by each such House and section 5(2) of this Act shall not apply to a regulation made under this subsection.

(6) (a) A person who contravenes subsection (1), (2), (3) or (4) of this section shall be guilty of an offence and shall be liable on summary conviction to a fine not exceeding £1,000 or to imprisonment for a term not exceeding 6 months or to both.

(b) A person charged with an offence under this section may, in lieu of being found guilty of that offence, be found guilty of an offence under section 50 of this Act.

(7) Section 1(1) of the Probation of Offenders Act, 1907, shall not apply to an offence under this section.

(8) A member of the Garda Siochana may arrest without warrant a person who in the member's opinion is committing or has committed an offence under this section.".

This section re-enacts, with amendments and additions, section 49 of the Road Traffic Act, 1961 as inserted by section 10 of the Act of 1978 and contains certain new provisions. The section deals with the offence of driving or attempting to drive a mechanically propelled vehicle in a public place while under the influence of an intoxicant. The principal amendment is a reduction in the maximum permissible alcohol level at which a person is permitted to drive, or attempt to drive, a vehicle from 100 to 80 milligrammes of alcohol per 100 millilitres of blood and from 135 to 107 milligrammes of alcohol per 100 millilitres of urine.

The new provisions are as follows:

—a maximum permissible alcohol level of 35 microgrammes of alcohol per 100 millilitres of breath, equating with the blood and urine levels,

—the Minister may by regulations (subject to prior approval by both Houses of the Oireachtas) vary the levels of alcohol permissible in a person's blood, urine or breath and set different limits for different classes of drivers,

—a power for a member of the Garda Siochana to enter on private property to secure an arrest for an offence under the section.

The maximum penalty provided in the section remains unchanged i.e. a maximum fine of £1000 and/or a maximum of 6 months imprisonment .

Road Traffic Act, 1994

Prohibition on being in charge of vehicle while under influence of intoxicant. s. 11 .

The following section is inserted in the Principal Act in substitution for section 50 of that Act:

"50.(1) (a) A person shall be guilty of an offence if, when in charge of a mechanically propelled vehicle in a public place with intent to drive or attempt to drive the vehicle (but not driving or attempting to drive it), he is under the influence of an intoxicant to such an extent as to be incapable of having proper control of the vehicle.

(b) In this subsection 'intoxicant' includes alcohol and drugs and any combination of drugs or of drugs and alcohol.

(2) A person shall be guilty of an offence if, when in charge of a mechanically propelled vehicle in a public place with intent to drive or attempt to drive the vehicle (but not driving or attempting to drive it), there is present in his body a quantity of alcohol such that, within 3 hours after so being in charge, the concentration of alcohol in his blood will exceed a concentration of 80 milligrammes of alcohol per 100 millilitres of blood.

(3) A person shall be guilty of an offence if, when in charge of a mechanically propelled vehicle in a public place with intent to drive or attempt to drive the vehicle (but not driving or attempting to drive it), there is present in his body a quantity of alcohol such that, within 3 hours after so being in charge, the concentration of alcohol in his urine will exceed a concentration of 107 milligrammes of alcohol per 100 millilitres of urine.

(4) A person shall be guilty of an offence if, when in charge of a mechanically propelled vehicle in a public place with intent to drive or attempt to drive the vehicle (but not driving or attempting to drive it), there is present in his body a quantity of alcohol such that, within 3 hours after so being in charge, the concentration of alcohol in his breath will exceed a concentration of 35 microgrammes of alcohol per 100 millilitres of breath.

(5) (a) The Minister may, by regulations made by him, vary the concentration of alcohol for the time being standing specified in subsection (2), (3) or (4) of this section, whether generally or in respect of a particular class of person, and the said subsection shall have effect in accordance with any such regulations for the time being in force.

(b) A draft of every regulation proposed to be made under this subsection shall be laid before each House of the Oireachtas and the regulation shall not be made until a resolution approving of the draft has been passed by each such House and section 5(2) of this Act shall not apply to a regulation made under this subsection.

(6) (a) A person guilty of an offence under this section shall be liable on summary conviction to a fine not exceeding £1,000 or to imprisonment for a term not exceeding 6 months or to both.

(b) A person charged with an offence under this section may, in lieu of being found guilty of that offence, be found guilty of an offence under section 49 of this Act.

(7) Section 1(1) of the Probation of Offenders Act, 1907, shall not apply to an offence under this section.

(8) In a prosecution for an offence under this section it shall be presumed that the defendant intended to drive or attempt to drive the vehicle concerned until he shows the contrary.

(9) A person liable to be charged with an offence under this section shall not, by reference to the same occurrence, be liable to be charged under section 12 of the Licensing Act, 1872, with the offence of being drunk while in charge, on a highway or other public place, of a carriage.

(10) A member of the Garda Siochana may arrest without warrant a person who in the member's opinion is committing or has committed an offence under this section.".

This section re-enacts, with amendments and additions, section 50 of the Road Traffic Act, 1961 as inserted by section 11 of the Act of 1978. It relates to the offence of being in charge of a mechanically propelled vehicle in a public place while under the influence of an intoxicant and contains provisions corresponding to those in section 10. The section also provides for increased penalties i.e. a maximum fine of £1,000 and/or a maximum of 6 months imprisonment. This is the same maximum penalty which applies under the preceding provision.

Obligation to provide preliminary breath specimen. s. 12.

(1) Whenever a member of the Garda Siochana is of opinion that a person in charge of a mechanically propelled vehicle in a public place has consumed intoxicating liquor, he may require the person-

(a) to provide, by exhaling into an apparatus for indicating the presence of alcohol in the breath, a specimen of his breath and may indicate the manner in which he is to comply with the requirement;

(b) to accompany him to a place (including a vehicle) at or in the vicinity of that public place and there require him to provide, by exhaling into such an apparatus, a specimen of his breath and may indicate the manner in which he is to comply with the requirement;

(c) where he does not have such an apparatus with him, to remain at that place in his presence or in the presence of another member of the Garda Siochana until such an apparatus becomes available to him (but he shall not require him to so remain for more than one hour) and he may then require the person to provide, by exhaling into such an apparatus, a specimen of his breath and may indicate the manner in which he is to comply with the requirement.

(2) A person who refuses or fails to comply forthwith with a requirement under this section, or to comply forthwith with such a requirement in a manner indicated by a member of the Garda Siochana, shall be guilty of an offence and shall be liable on summary conviction to a fine not exceeding £1,000 or to imprisonment for a term not exceeding 6 months or to both.

(3) A member of the Garda Siochana may arrest without warrant a person who in the member's opinion is committing or has committed an offence under this section.

(4) In a prosecution for an offence under this Part or under section 49 or 50 of the Principal Act it shall be presumed, until the contrary is shown, that an apparatus provided by a member of the Garda Siochana for the purpose of enabling a person to provide a specimen of breath pursuant to this section is an apparatus for indicating the presence of alcohol in the breath.

Section 12 re-enacts, with modifications, section 12 of the Act of 1978 obliging a person to provide a preliminary breath specimen if requested by a member of the Garda Siochana (i.e. a screening breath test). New subsections provide that a member of the Garda Siochana may require a driver to accompany him to a nearby place, including a vehicle, to provide a breath specimen and may require the driver to remain at that place in his presence or in the presence of another member of the Garda Siochana for up to one hour until a breath testing apparatus becomes available. The penalty for refusing or failing to provide a preliminary breath specimen remains unchanged i.e. a maximum fine of £1000 and/or a maximum of 6 months imprisonment.

Obligation to provide specimen following arrest   s. 13.

(1) Where a person is arrested under section 49(8) or 50(10) of the Principal Act or section 12(3), or where a person is arrested under section 53(6), 106(3A) or 112(6) of the Principal Act and a member of the Garda Siochana is of opinion that the person has consumed an intoxicant, a member of the Garda Siochana may, at a Garda Siochana station, at his discretion, do either or both of the following—

(a) require the person to provide, by exhaling into an apparatus for determining the concentration of alcohol in the breath 2 specimens of his breath and may indicate the manner in which he is to comply with the requirement,

(b) require the person either—

(i) to permit a designated doctor to take from the person a specimen of his blood, or,

(ii) at the option of the person to provide for the designated doctor a specimen of his urine,

and if the doctor states in writing that he is unwilling, on medical grounds, to take from the person or be provided by him with the specimen to which the requirement in either of the foregoing subparagraphs related, the member may make a requirement of the person under this paragraph in relation to the specimen other than that to which the first requirement related.

(2) Subject to section 23, a person who refuses or fails to comply forthwith with a requirement under subsection (1)(a) shall be guilty of an offence and shall be liable on summary conviction to a fine not exceeding £1,000 or to imprisonment for a term not exceeding 6 months or to both.

(3) Subject to section 23, a person who, following a requirement under subsection (1)(b) —

(a) refuses or fails to comply with the requirement, or

(b) refuses or fails to comply with a requirement of a designated doctor in relation to the taking under that subsection of a specimen of blood or the provision under that subsection of a specimen of urine,

shall be guilty of an offence and shall be liable on summary conviction to a fine not exceeding £1,000 or to imprisonment for a term not exceeding 6 months or to both.

(4) In a prosecution for an offence under this Part or under section 49 or 50 of the Principal Act it shall be presumed, until the contrary is shown, that an apparatus provided by a member of the Garda Siochana for the purpose of enabling a person to provide 2 specimens of breath pursuant to this section is an apparatus for determining the concentration of alcohol in the breath.

(5) Section 1(1) of the Probation of Offenders Act, 1907, shall not apply to an offence under this section.

This section replaces sections 13 and 14 of the Act of 1978 and obliges certain persons to provide a breath, blood or urine specimen following arrest. It extends the requirement in those sections of the 1978 Act to give a breath/blood/urine specimen following arrest for driving and/or being in charge of a vehicle while under the influence of an intoxicant to the offences of dangerous driving and taking a vehicle without authority. The requirement to provide a specimen of breath has been extended to a requirement to provide two specimens of breath for evidential purposes. This is necessary to comply with new procedures outlined in section 17. The section also provides that the member of the Garda Siochana will decide the form of the specimen to be provided. The penalty for refusing or failing to provide a specimen remains unchanged i.e. a maximum fine of £1,000 and/or a maximum of 6 months imprisonment.

Obligation to accompany member to Garda Siochana station, not under arrest, to provide blood or urine specimen. s. 14.

(1) Whenever a member of the Garda Siochana is of opinion that a person in charge of a mechanically propelled vehicle in a public place is under the influence of a drug or drugs to such an extent as to be incapable of having proper control of the vehicle, he may require the person to accompany him to a Garda Siochana station.

(2) A person who refuses or fails to comply with a requirement under subsection (1) shall be guilty of an offence and shall be liable on summary conviction to a fine not exceeding £1,000 or to imprisonment for a term not exceeding 6 months or to both.

(3) A member of the Garda Siochana may arrest without warrant a person who in the member's opinion is committing or has committed an offence under subsection (2).

(4) Where a person is at a Garda Siochana station either pursuant to subsection (1) or having been arrested under subsection (3), a member of the Garda Siochana may there require the person either —

(a) to permit a designated doctor to take from the person a specimen of his blood, or

(b) at the option of the person, to provide for the designated doctor a specimen of his urine,

and if the doctor states in writing that he is unwilling, on medical grounds, to take from the person or be provided by him with the specimen to which the requirement in either of the foregoing paragraphs related, the member may make a requirement of the person under this subsection in relation to the specimen other than that to which the first requirement related.

(5) Subject to section 23, a person who, following a requirement under subsection (4)—

(a) refuses or fails to comply with the requirement, or

(b) refuses or fails to comply with a requirement of a designated doctor in relation to the taking under that subsection of a specimen of blood or the provision under that subsection of a specimen of urine,

shall be guilty of an offence and shall be liable on summary conviction to a fine not exceeding £1,000 or to imprisonment for a term not exceeding 6 months or to both.

(6) Section 1(1) of the Probation of Offenders Act, 1907, shall not apply to an offence under this section.

This section re-enacts section 17 of the Act of 1978 with minor amendments. It empowers a member of the Garda Siochana to require a blood or urine specimen to be provided by a person in charge of a mechanically propelled vehicle where the member is of the opinion that the person is under the influence of drugs. The penalty for refusing or failing to provide a specimen remains unchanged i.e. a maximum fine of £1,000 and/or a maximum of 6 months imprisonment.

Obligation to provide blood or urine specimen while in hospital   s. 15.

(1) Where, in a public place, an event occurs in relation to a mechanically propelled vehicle in consequence of which a person is injured, or claims or appears to have been injured, and is admitted to, or attends at, a hospital and a member of the Garda Siochana is of opinion that, at the time of the event,—

(a) the person was driving or attempting to drive, or in charge of with intent to drive or attempt to drive (but not driving or attempting to drive), the mechanically propelled vehicle, and

(b) the person had consumed an intoxicant,

then such member may, in the hospital, require the person either —

(i) to permit a designated doctor to take from the person a specimen of his blood, or

(ii) at the option of the person, to provide for the designated doctor a specimen of his urine, and if the doctor states in writing that he is unwilling, on medical grounds, to take from the person or be provided by him with the specimen to which the requirement in either of the foregoing subparagraphs related, the member may make a requirement of the person under this subsection in relation to the specimen other than that to which the first requirement related.

(2) Subject to section 23, a person who, following a requirement under subsection (1) —

(a) refuses or fails to comply with the requirement, or

(b) refuses or fails to comply with a requirement of a designated doctor in relation to the taking under that subsection of a specimen of blood or the provisions under that subsection of a specimen of urine,

shall be guilty of an offence and shall be liable on summary conviction to a fine not exceeding £1,000 or to imprisonment for a term not exceeding 6 months or to both.

(3) Notwithstanding subsection (2), it shall not be an offence for a person to refuse or fail to comply with a requirement under subsection (1) where, following his admission to, or attendance at, a hospital, the person comes under the care of a doctor and the doctor refuses, on medical grounds, to permit the taking or provision of the specimen

concerned.

(4) Section 1(1) of the Probation of Offenders Act, 1907, shall not apply to an offence under this section.

This section provides a new power for both a member of the Garda Sfochana and a designated doctor to enter a hospital to take a blood or urine specimen from a driver suspected of being involved in a traffic accident. It provides that it is an offence for such a person to refuse or fail to provide a specimen unless the doctor in the hospital in charge of the person refuses to permit the taking of the specimen on medical grounds. The penalty for refusing or failing to provide a specimen is a maximum fine of £1,000 and/or a maximum of 6 months imprisonment.

Detention of intoxicated drivers where a danger to selves or others. s. 16

(1) Where a person is—

(a) at a Garda Siochana station having been arrested under section 49(8) or 50(10) of the Principal Act or section 12(3) or 14(3), or

(b) required under section 14(1) to accompany a member of the Garda Siochana to a Garda Siochana station and complies with the requirement,

he may, at the Garda Siochana station, if the member of the Garda Siochana for the time being in charge of the station is of opinion that the person is under the influence of an intoxicant to such an extent as to be a threat to the safety of himself or others, be detained in custody for such period (not exceeding 6 hours from the time of his arrest or, as the case may be, from the time he was required to accompany a member to the station) as the member of the Garda Siochana so in charge considers necessary.

(2) Where a person is detained under subsection (1), the member of the Garda Siochana for the time being in charge of the Garda Siochana station shall—

(a) in case the person detained is or the said member is of opinion that he is 18 years of age or more, as soon as is practicable, if it is reasonably possible to do so, inform a relative of the person or such other person as the person so detained may specify of the detention, unless the person so detained does not wish any person to be so informed, and

(b) in case the person detained is or the said member is of opinion that he is under the age of 18 years, as soon as is practicable, if it is reasonably possible to do so, inform a relative of the person or such other person as the person so detained may specify of the detention.

(3) A person detained under subsection (1) shall—

(a) in case he is or the member of the Garda Siochana for the time being in charge of the Garda Siochana station is of opinion that he is 18 years of age or more, upon the attendance at the station of a person being either a relative of, or a person specified pursuant to subsection (2) by, the person so detained, be released by the said member into the custody of that person, unless—

(i) the latter person is or the said member is of opinion that he is under the age of 18 years,

(ii) the person so detained does not wish to be released into the custody of the latter person, or

(iii) the member aforesaid is of opinion that the person so detained continues to be under the influence of an intoxicant to such an extent that, if he is then released into the custody of the latter person, he will continue to be a threat to the safety of himself or others,

and shall, if not so released, be released at the expiration of the period of detention authorised by subsection (1), and

(b) in case he is or the member of the Garda Siochana for the time being in charge of the Garda Siochana station is of opinion that he is under the age of 18 years, upon the attendance at the station of a person being either a relative of, or a person specified pursuant to subsection (2) by, the person so detained, be released by the said member into the custody of that person, unless the latter person is or the said member is of opinion that he is under the age of 18 years, and shall, if not so released, be released at the expiration of the period of detention authorised by subsection (1).

This section provides a new power for a member of the Garda Síochana to detain an intoxicated driver who has been arrested where the release of the driver could be a threat to the safety of themselves or of other persons. The section contains a number of safeguards to protect the rights of a driver detained and specifies a maximum period of detention of 8 hours.

Procedure following provision of breath specimen .. s.17.

(1) Where, consequent on a requirement under section 13(1)(a) of him, a person provides 2 specimens of his breath and the apparatus referred to in that section determines the concentration of alcohol in each specimen—

(a) in case the apparatus determines that each specimen has the same concentration of alcohol, either specimen, and

(b) in case the apparatus determines that each specimen has a different concentration of alcohol, the specimen with the lower concentration of alcohol,

shall be taken into account for the purposes of sections 49(4) and 50(4) of the Principal Act and the other specimen shall be disregarded.

(2) Where the apparatus referred to in section 13(1) determines that in respect of the specimen of breath to be taken into account as aforesaid the person may have contravened section 49(4) or 50(4) of the Principal Act, he shall be supplied forthwith by a member of the Garda Siochana with 2 identical statements, automatically produced by the said apparatus in the prescribed form and duly completed by the member in the prescribed manner, stating the concentration of alcohol in the said specimen determined by the said apparatus.

(3) On receipt of the statements aforesaid, the person shall on being requested so to do by the member aforesaid—

(a) forthwith acknowledge such receipt by placing his signature on each statement, and

(b) thereupon return either of the statements to the member.

(4) A person who refuses or fails to comply with subsection (3) shall be guilty of an offence and shall be liable on summary to a fine not exceeding £500 or to imprisonment for a term not exceeding 3 months or to both.

(5) Section 21(1) shall apply to a statement under this section as respects which there has been a failure to comply with subsection (3)(a) as it applies to a duly completed statement under this section.

This section provides for the procedures following the taking of a breath specimen under section 13. Where a person has provided two specimens of breath under that section, the specimen with the higher reading will be disregarded. The statement of the concentration of alcohol in the person's breath to be used in evidence will be the printout from the breath testing apparatus and the person concerned will be supplied with a copy of the statement.

Procedure regarding taking of specimens of blood and provision of specimens of urine. s. 18.

(1) Where under this Part a designated doctor has taken a specimen of blood from a person or has been provided by the person with a specimen of his urine, the doctor shall divide the specimen into 2 parts, place each part in a container which he shall forthwith seal and complete the form prescribed for the purposes of this section.

(2) Where a specimen of blood or urine of a person has been divided into 2 parts pursuant to subsection (1), a member of the Garda Siochana shall offer to the person one of the sealed containers together with a statement in writing indicating that he may retain either of the containers.

(3) As soon as practicable after subsection (2) has been complied with, a member of the Garda Siochana shall cause to be forwarded to the Bureau the completed form referred to in subsection (1), together

Road Traffic Act, 1994

with the relevant sealed container or, where the person has declined to retain one of the sealed containers, both relevant sealed containers.

(4) In a prosecution for an offence under this Part or under section 49 or 50 of the Principal Act, it shall be presumed until the contrary is shown that subsections (1) to (3) have been complied with.

This section re-enacts, with minor modifications, section 21 of the Act of 1978 detailing the procedures to be adopted following the taking and provision of specimens of blood or urine.

Procedure at bureau regarding specimens. s. 19.

(1) As soon as practicable after it has received a specimen forwarded to it under section 18, the Bureau shall analyse the specimen and determine the concentration of alcohol or (as may be appropriate) the presence of a drug or drugs in the specimen.

(2) Where the Bureau receives 2 specimens of blood so forwarded together in relation to the same person or 2 specimens of urine so forwarded together in relation to the same person, it shall be sufficient compliance with subsection (1) for the Bureau to make an analysis of and determination in relation to one of the 2 specimens of blood or (as may be appropriate) one of the 2 specimens of urine.

(3) As soon as practicable after compliance with subsection (1), the Bureau shall forward to the Garda Siochana station from which the specimen analysed was forwarded a completed certificate in the form prescribed for the purpose of this section and shall forward a copy of the completed certificate to the person who is named on the relevant form under section 18 as the person from whom the specimen was taken or who provided it.

(4) In a prosecution for an offence under this Part or under section 49 or 50 of the Principal Act, it shall be presumed until the contrary is shown that subsections (1) to (3) have been complied with.

This section re-enacts, with minor modifications and additions section 22 of the Act of 1978 detailing the procedure to be followed by the Medical Bureau of Road Safety regarding specimens.

Provisions regarding certain evidence in prosecutions under sections 49 and 50 of Principal Act. s. 20.

(1) On the hearing of a charge for an offence under section 49 or 50 of the Principal Act, it shall not be necessary to show that the defendant had not consumed intoxicating liquor after the time when the offence is alleged to have been committed but before the taking or provision of a specimen under section 13, 14 or 15.

(2) Where, on the hearing of a charge for an offence under section 49

or 50 of the Principal Act, evidence is given by or on behalf of the defendant that, after the time when the offence is alleged to have been committed but before the taking or provision of a specimen under section 13, 14 or 15, he had consumed intoxicating liquor, the court shall disregard the evidence unless satisfied by or on behalf of the defendant—

(a) that, but for that consumption, the concentration of alcohol in the defendant's blood (as specified in a certificate under section 19) would not have exceeded the concentration of alcohol for the time being standing specified in subsection (2) of the said section 49 or 50, as may be appropriate, whether generally or in respect of the class of person of which the defendant is a member,

(b) that, but for that consumption, the concentration of alcohol in the defendant's urine (as specified in a certificate under section 19) would not have exceeded the concentration of alcohol for the time being standing specified in subsection 30(3) of the said section 49 or 50, as may be appropriate, whether generally or in respect of the class of person of which the defendant is a member, or

(c) that, but for that consumption, the concentration of alcohol in the defendant's breath (as specified in a statement under section 17) would not have exceeded the concentration of alcohol for the time being standing specified in subsection (4) of the said section 49 or 50, as may be appropriate, whether generally or in respect of the class of person of which the defendant is a member.

(3) (a) A person shall not take or attempt to take any action (including consumption of alcohol but excluding a refusal or failure to provide a specimen of his breath or urine or to permit the taking of a specimen of his blood) with the intention of frustrating a prosecution under section 49 or 50 of the Principal Act.

(b) A person who contravenes this subsection shall be guilty of an offence and shall be liable on summary conviction to a fine not exceeding £1,000 or to imprisonment for a term not exceeding 6 months or to both.

(4) Where, on the hearing of a charge for an offence under section 49 or 50 of the Principal Act, the court is satisfied that any action taken by the defendant (including consumption of alcohol but excluding a refusal or failure to provide a specimen of his breath or urine or to permit the taking of a specimen of his blood) was so taken with the intention of frustrating a prosecution under either of those sections, the court may find him guilty of an offence under subsection (3).

This section re-enacts, with minor modifications, section 18 of the Act of 1978. This section provides that it is an offence to take alcohol with a view to frustrating a prosecution under section 49 or section 50 of the 1961 Act as amended and provides that the Court will disregard any evidence of having consumed intoxicating liquor between the time of the alleged offence and the giving of a specimen. Minor amendments are consequential on the reduction of the maximum permissible blood and urine alcohol levels, the introduction of a new maximum permissible breath alcohol level and the power of the Minister to vary the levels by regulations. The maximum penalty provided in the section remains unchanged i.e. a maximum fine of £1,000 and/or a maximum of 6 months imprisonment.

Provisions regarding certain evidence in proceedings under Road Traffic Acts 1961 to 1994. s. 21.

(1) A duly completed statement purporting to have been supplied under section 17 shall, until the contrary is shown, be sufficient evidence in any proceedings under the Road Traffic Acts, 1961 to 1994, of the facts stated therein, without proof of any signature on it or that the signatory was the proper person to sign it, and shall, until the contrary is shown, be sufficient evidence of compliance by the member of the Garda Siochana concerned with the requirements imposed on him by or under this Part prior to and in connection with the supply by him pursuant to section 17 (2) of such statement.

(2) A duly completed form under section 18 shall, until the contrary is shown, be sufficient evidence in any proceedings under the Road Traffic Acts, 1961 to 1994, of the facts stated therein, without proof of any signature on it or that the signatory was the proper person to sign it, and shall, until the contrary is shown, be sufficient evidence of compliance by the designated doctor concerned with the requirements imposed on him by or under this Part.

(3) A certificate expressed to have been issued under section 19 shall, until the contrary is shown, be sufficient evidence in any proceedings under the Road Traffic Acts, 1961 to 1994, of the facts stated therein, without proof of any signature on it or that the signatory was the proper person to sign it, and shall, until the contrary is shown, be sufficient evidence of compliance by the Bureau with the requirements imposed on it by or under this Part or Part V of the Act of 1968.

(4) In a prosecution for an offence under section 49 or 50 of the Principal Act or section 13, 14 or 15 it shall be presumed until the contrary is shown that each of the following persons is a designated doctor—

(a) a person who by virtue of powers conferred on him by this Part took from another person a specimen of that other person's blood or was provided by another person with a specimen of that other person's urine,

(b) a person for whom, following a requirement under section 13(1), 14(4) or 1(1) to permit the taking by him of a specimen of blood, there was a refusal or failure to give such permission or to comply with a requirement of his in relation to the taking of such a specimen,

(c) a person for whom, following a requirement under section 13(1), 14(4) or 15(1) to provide for him a specimen of urine, there was a refusal or failure to provide such a specimen or to comply with a requirement of his in relation to the provision of such a specimen

(5) Where, pursuant to section 13, 14 or 15, a designated doctor states in writing that he is unwilling, on medical grounds, to take from a person a specimen of his blood or be provided by him with a specimen of his urine, the statement signed by the doctor shall, in any proceedings under the Road Traffic Acts, 1961 to 1994, be sufficient evidence, until the contrary is shown, of the facts stated therein, without proof of any signature on it or that the signatory was the proper person to sign it.

This section re-enacts section 23 of the Act of 1978 with amendments. The section gives evidential value to the statement, form and certificate provided for in sections 17,18 and 19 respectively. The section also provides a presumption that certain persons are "doctors" for the purposes of prosecutions.

Costs of prosecutions under sections 49 and 50 of Principal Act and Part III. s. 22.

(1) Where a person is convicted of an offence under section 49 or 50 of the Principal Act or section 13, 14 or 15, committed after the commencement of this section, the court shall, unless it is satisfied that there are special and substantial reasons for not so doing, order the person to pay to the court a contribution towards the costs and expenses incurred by the Bureau in the performance of its functions not exceeding such amount as may, for the time being, stand prescribed.

(2) Payments under subsection (1) shall be disposed of in such manner as may be prescribed.

This section provides that in addition to any fine, term of imprisonment or disqualification, a person found guilty of a drink driving offence will be ordered by the Court to pay a contribution towards costs incurred in the detection and prosecution of the offence subject to a maximum amount to be prescribed in regulations made by the Minister.

Defence to refusal to permit taking of specimen of blood or to provide 2 specimens of breath. s. 23.

(1) In a prosecution of a person under section 13 for refusing or

failing to comply with a requirement to provide 2 specimens of his breath, it shall be a defence for the defendant to satisfy the court that there was a special and substantial reason for his refusal or failure and that, as soon as practicable after the refusal or failure concerned, he complied (or offered, but was not called upon to comply) with a requirement under the section concerned in relation to the taking of a specimen of blood or the provision of a specimen of urine.

(2) In a prosecution of a person for an offence under section 13, 14 or 15 for refusing or failing to comply with a requirement to permit a designated doctor to take a specimen of blood or for refusing or failing to comply with a requirement of a designated doctor in relation to the taking of a specimen of blood, it shall be a defence for the defendant to satisfy the court that there was a special and substantial reason for his refusal or failure and that, as soon as practicable after he refusal or failure concerned, he complied (or offered, but was not called upon, to comply) with a requirement under the section concerned in relation to the provision of a specimen of urine.

(3) Notwithstanding subsections (1) and (2), evidence may be given at the hearing of a charge of an offence under section 49 or 50 of the Principal Act that the defendant refused or failed to comply with a requirement to provide 2 specimens of his breath, or that the defendant refused or failed to comply with a requirement to permit the taking of a specimen of his blood or to comply with a requirement of designated doctor in relation to the taking of a specimen of blood, as the case may be.

This section re-enacts, in an amended and more comprehensive manner, section 19 of the Act of 1978 which provides a defence for the refusal or failure to permit the taking of a blood specimen. The section extends the defence clause to the taking of breath specimens. However, in all cases, the defence that there was a special and substantial reason for the refusal or failure is conditional on the person providing a specimen in an alternative form.

Bar to certain defence to charges under sections 49 and 50 of the Principal Act. s. 24.

It shall not be a defence for a person charged with an offence under section 49(1) or 50(1) of the Principal Act to show that, in relation to the facts alleged to constitute the offence, an analysis or determination under the Road Traffic Acts, 1961 to 1994, has not been carried out or that he has not been requested under section 12 to provide a specimen of his breath.

This section re-enacts section 20 of the Act of 1978 and provides that it is not a defence for a person charged under section 49(1) or 50(1) of the 1961 Act to show that an analysis or determination had not been carried out.

Part IV Driving Licences

This Part deals with driving licences and disqualification orders.

The principal provisions in this Part are: (a) a requirement to carry a driving licence at all times when driving, (b) increases in mandatory disqualification periods for certain offences and a requirement to pass a driving test and obtain a certificate of competency following conviction for drink driving offences and for dangerous driving.

Requirement to carry driving licence ... s. 25.

The following section is inserted in the Principal Act in substitution for section 40 of that Act:

40 (1)(a) A member of the Garda Siochana may demand, of a person driving in a public place a mechanically propelled vehicle or accompanying pursuant to regulations under this Act the holder of a provisional licence while such holder is driving in a public place a mechanically propelled vehicle, the production to him of a driving licence then having effect and licensing the said person to drive the vehicle, and if the person refuses or fails so to produce the licence there and then, he shall be guilty of an offence.

(b) Where a person of whom the production of a driving licence is demanded under this section refuses or fails to produce the licence there and then, a member of the Garda Siochana may require the person to produce within 10 days after the date of the said requirement the licence in person to a member of the Garda Siochana at a Garda Siochana station to be named by the person at the time of the requirement and, if the person refuses or fails so to produce the licence, he shall be guilty of an offence.

(c) In any proceedings a certificate, purporting to be signed by the member in charge of the Garda Siochana station at which the defendant concerned was required, pursuant to paragraph (b), to produce the driving licence, stating that the defendant did not, within 10 days after the day on which the production was required, produce a driving licence in accordance with the said paragraph (b) shall, without proof of the signature of the person purporting to sign the certificate or that he was the member in charge of the Garda Siochana station, be evidence, until the contrary is shown, of the facts stated in the certificate.

(d) Where any person is required to produce a driving licence at a Garda Siochana station and the person produces the licence within 10 days after the day on which the production was required, the member in charge of the Garda Siochana station shall issue a certificate stating that the licence was so produced and such certificate shall be evidence of the facts stated in the certificate.

(2) Where a person of whom the production of a driving licence is demanded or required under this section produces the licence in accordance with the demand or requirement, but refuses or fails to permit the member of the Garda Siochana to whom it is produced to read the licence, he shall be guilty of an offence.

(3) Where a person of whom the production of a driving licence is demanded or required under this section refuses or fails so to produce the licence or produces the licence but refuses or fails to permit the member of the Garda Siochana to whom it is produced to read the licence, the member may demand of the person his name and address and, if the person refuses or fails to give to the member his name and address or gives to the member a name or address which is false or misleading, he shall be guilty of an offence.

(4) A member of the Garda Siochana may arrest without warrant —

(a) a person who pursuant to this section produces a driving licence to the member but refuses or fails to permit the member to read it, or

(b) a person who, when his name and address is lawfully demanded of him by the member under this section, refuses or fails to give to the member his name and address or gives to the member a name or address which the member reasonably believes to be false.

(5) A person who, when the production of a driving licence is demanded or required of him under this section, does not produce the licence because he is not the holder of a driving licence shall be deemed to fail to produce his driving licence within the meaning of subsection (1) of this section.".

This section replaces section 40 of the Road Traffic Act, 1961 which requires a person to produce a driving licence if demanded by a member of the Garda Siochana. Under the existing section 40, a person is allowed a period of 10 days within which to produce a driving licence at a nominated Garda Station. The new section provides that a driving licence must be produced immediately and effectively requires a driver to carry a driving licence at all times when driving a vehicle. The new section retains the option for a member of the Garda Siochana to require production of a driving licence within ten days.

Consequential disqualification orders. s. 26.

The following section shall be substituted for section 26 of the Principal Act:

"26 (1) Subject to subsection (5)(b) of this section, where a person is convicted of an offence specified in the Second Schedule to this Act, the court shall make an order (in this Act referred to as a consequential disqualification order) declaring him to be disqualified for holding a driving licence.

(2) Subject to subsection (3) of this section, a consequential disqualification order shall operate to disqualify the person to whom the order relates for holding any driving licence whatsoever during a specified period or during a specified period and thereafter until he has produced to the appropriate licensing authority, as may be specified in the order, a certificate of competency or a certificate of fitness or both.

(3) A consequential disqualification order resulting from a conviction for an offence under section 49 or 50 or section 53, where the contravention involved the driving of a mechanically propelled vehicle or section 106, when the contravention involved non-compliance with paragraph (a) or (b) of subsection (1) of that section, injury was caused to person, a mechanically propelled vehicle was involved in the occurrence of the injury and the convicted person was the driver of the vehicle concerned, section 13, 14 or 15 of the Road Traffic Act, 1994 shall operate to disqualify the person to whom the order relates for holding any driving licence whatsoever during a specified period and, unless the court is satisfied that a special reason (which it shall specify when making its order) has been proved by the convicted person to exist in his particular case such that it should not so operate, thereafter until he has produced to the appropriate licensing authority, as may be specified in the order, a certificate of competency or both a certificate of competency and a certificate of fitness.

(4) (a) Subject to paragraph (b) of this subsection, the period of disqualification specified in a consequential disqualification order shall, where the person to whom the order relates is convicted of an offence under—

(i) section 49 or 50 of this Act,

(ii) section 53 of this Act tried on indictment,

(iii) section 106 of this Act, where the contravention involved non-compliance with paragraph (a) or (b) of subsection (1) of that section, injury was caused to person, a mechanically propelled vehicle was involved in the occurrence of the injury and the convicted person was the driver of the vehicle concerned, or

(iv) section 13, 14 or 15 of the Road Traffic Act, 1994, be not less than 2 years in the case of a first offence under the section concerned and not less than 4 years in the case of a second or any subsequent conviction for an offence under the same section

(b) The period of disqualification specified in a consequential disqualification order shall, where the person to whom the order relates is convicted of an offence under—

(i) section 49 or 50 of this Act, or

(ii) section 13, 14 or 15 of the Road Traffic Act, 1994,

and the court is satisfied that a special reason (which it shall specify when making its order) has been proved by the convicted person to exist in his particular case to justify such a period, be less than 2 years but not less than 1 year in the case of a first offence under the section concerned.

(5) (a) Subject to paragraph (b) of this subsection, the period of disqualification specified in a consequential disqualification order shall, where the person to whom the order relates is convicted of an offence under—

(i) section 53 of this Act tried summarily, or

(ii) section 56 of this Act,

be not less than 1 year in the case of a first offence under the section concerned and not less than 2 years in the case of a second or any subsequent offence under the same section committed within the period of 3 years from the date of the commission of the previous offence or, in the case of more than one such offence, the last such offence.

(b) Where a person is convicted of an offence under—

(i) section 53 of this Act tried summarily, or

(ii) section 56 of this Act,

the court may, in the case of a first offence under the section concerned, where it is satisfied that a special reason (which it shall specify when making its order) has been proved by the convicted person to exist in his particular case to justify such a course—

(I) decline to make a consequential disqualification order, or

(II) specify a period of disqualification in the consequential disqualification order of less than 1 year.

(6) Where a person is convicted of an offence under section 49 or 50 of this Act (whether before or after the commencement of sections 10 and 11 of the Road Traffic Act, 1994) or section 13, 14 or 17 of the Road Traffic (Amendment) Act, 1978, or section 13, 14 or 15 of the Road Traffic Act, 1994 ('the former section') and is subsequently convicted of one or more offences under another of those sections ('the latter section') the conviction under the latter section shall, for the purposes of this section, be regarded as a second or, as the case may be, a subsequent conviction for an offence under the latter section.

(7) The period of disqualification specified in a consequential disqualification order shall, in a case not coming within subsection (4) or (5) of this section, be not less than 6 months.

Road Traffic Act, 1994

(8) Where a person is convicted of an offence ('the later conviction') under section 49 or 50 of this Act (whether before or after the commencement of sections 10 and 11 of the Road Traffic Act, 1994) or section 13, 14 or 17 of the Road Traffic (Amendment) Act, 1978, or section 13, 14 or 15 of the Road Traffic Act, 1994, and—

(a) the conviction is, or is by virtue of subsection (6) of this section to be regarded as, a second or subsequent conviction for an offence under the same section, and

(b) a period of 4 years or more during which such person was not disqualified for holding a driving licence has elapsed since the previous conviction of the person by reference to which the later conviction is, or is by virtue of the said subsection (6) to be regarded as, a second or subsequent conviction,

the court may, for the purposes of this section, deal with the later conviction as a first conviction.

(9) Subject to subsections (10) and (11) of this section, in every case in which an appeal may be brought in respect of a conviction for an offence on conviction of which a consequential disqualification order may be made, jurisdiction to make, confirm, annul or vary a consequential disqualification order is hereby conferred on the appellate court unless it otherwise has that jurisdiction or the conferring of that jurisdiction is unnecessary because the appeal is by way of rehearing.

(10) A consequential disqualification order shall not be annulled on appeal unless—

(a) the conviction by reference to which it was imposed is reversed, or

(b) the provisions of subsection (5)(b) of this section apply.

(11) Where a consequential disqualification order is, on an appeal, made or varied, the requirements of subsections (2) to (7) of this section shall be complied with and the provisions of subsection (8) of this section, where relevant, shall also apply.".

This section replaces section 26 of the Road Traffic Act, 1961 and sets out the disqualification periods to apply for drink driving and other road traffic offences. The section provides that a person found guilty of an offence listed in the Second Schedule to the 1961 Act (as inserted by this Act) will be automatically disqualified from holding a driving licence and gives the Court the option to impose a disqualification until a certificate of competency (driving test) or a certificate of fitness is obtained. Subsection (3) introduces a new requirement to the effect that a person found guilty of an offence of driving while under the influence of an intoxicant (section 49 of the 1961 Act) or being in charge of a mechanically propelled vehicle while under the influence of an intoxicant (section 50 of the 1961 Act) or dangerous driving (section 53 of the 1961 Act) or any of the "refusal" offences in section 13, 14 or 15 will, in addition to the minimum period of disqualification, be automatically disqualified until the person passes a driving test and produces a certificate of competency. The mandatory disqualification periods on conviction for the following offences are also increased to two years in the case of a first offence and to four years in the case of a second or any subsequent offence:

—driving while under the influence of an intoxicant,

—being in charge of a vehicle while under the influence of an intoxicant,

—dangerous driving where the contravention caused death or serious bodily harm to another person,

—refusing or failing to provide a specimen.

A mandatory disqualification period of one year is introduced for a first offence of dangerous driving (where the contravention did not cause death or serious bodily harm to another person) and uninsured driving. For these offences a mandatory disqualification period of two years will apply in the case of a second or any subsequent offence. The remaining offences listed in the Second Schedule are subject to a mandatory six month disqualification period. The section also restates existing provisions which provide that an appeal court will have the same power of dealing with disqualification as the lower court, including the power to increase the period or reduce it to the minimum as laid down.

Amendment of provisions relating to removal of consequential disqualification orders. s. 27.

Section 29 of the Principal Act is hereby amended by the insertion of the following subsection after subsection (1):

"(1A) Notwithstanding the provisions of subsection (1)(a)

(a) a person in respect of whom a consequential disqualification order has been made on conviction for an offence to which subsection (4) or (5) of section 26 (as inserted by section 26 of the Road Traffic Act, 1994) of this Act applies, and in respect of which the period of disqualification specified in the order is required by the said subsection (4) or (5), as the case may be, to be not less than 2 years, may at any time and (save as hereinafter mentioned) after the expiration of 9 months from the beginning of the period of disqualification and before the expiration of that period, apply to the court which made the order, for the removal of the disqualification, and that court, if it considers that circumstances exist which justify such a course, may by order remove the disqualification as from a specified date not earlier than 1 year after the beginning of the period of disqualification but, if it does so, shall order the person to comply with any requirement contained in the disqualification order that the person produce to the appropriate licensing authority the certificate or certificates therein specified;

(b) a person in respect of whom a consequential disqualification order has been made on conviction for an offence to which subsection (4) of section 26 (as so inserted) of this Act applies, and in respect of which the period of disqualification specified in the order is required by the said subsection (4) to be not less than 4 years, may at any time and (save as hereinafter mentioned) from time to time after the expiration of 21 months from the beginning of the period of disqualification and before the expiration of that period, apply to the court which made the order, for the removal of the disqualification, and that court, if it considers that circumstances exist which justify such a course, may by order remove the disqualification as from a specified date not earlier than 2 years after the beginning of the period of disqualification but, if it does so, shall order the person to comply with any requirement contained in the disqualification order that the person produce to the appropriate licensing authority the certificate or certificates therein specified,

and the references in the other provisions of this section to subsection (1) of this section shall be construed as including references to this subsection.".

This section inserts a new subsection into section 29 of the Road Traffic Act, 1961 detailing the provisions relating to the removal of consequential disqualification orders. The new subsection extends the minimum period which must pass before an application may be made to the Court for a review of disqualification orders and for the removal of such orders where they apply for a period of two years or more.

Provision of particulars of disqualifications to certain persons.   s. 28.

The following is substituted for section 42(4)(d) of the Principal Act:

"(d) the notification to licensing authorities and such other (if any) persons as may be prescribed of the making, confirming, annulling, varying or removal of a consequential, ancillary or special disqualification order or the making, confirming or annulling of endorsements ordered under section 36 of this Act. ".

This section restates section 42 (4) (d) of the Road Traffic Act, 1961 which provides for licensing authorities to be notified of disqualifications or endorsements and extends it to include other prescribed persons.

Application of provisions of Principal Act to provisional licences   s. 29.

(1) Sections 22(2), (4) and (5), 26, 27, 28(1), (3), (4) and (5), 29, 30, 31, 32, 34, 36, 37, 39 and 41 of the Principal Act shall be deemed

to apply to provisional licences as they apply to driving licences except that—

(a) where a person has been disqualified under section 26 or 27 of the Principal Act for holding a driving licence during a specified period and thereafter until he has produced to the appropriate licensing authority a certificate of competency, the person may, at the end of the specified period, apply for and be granted a provisional licence in accordance with the provisions of section 35 of the Principal Act;

(b) where a person has been disqualified under section 28(2) of the Principal Act for holding a driving licence, he may apply for and be granted a provisional licence in accordance with the provisions of the said section 35; and

(c) where a holder of a provisional licence in respect of vehicles of any class for a period has been granted a certificate of competency in respect of such class he shall not, by virtue of the application of section 22 (5) of the Principal Act to provisional licences, be disqualified for applying for a driving licence in respect of vehicles of that class for any period which or part of which is within that period.

(2) Section 35 of the Principal Act is hereby amended by the substitution in paragraph (c) of subsection (3) for "defendant" of "person driving the vehicle".

This section provides that certain provisions of the Road Traffic Act, 1961 will apply to provisional licences as well as to driving licences. The sections concerned are mainly those relating to disqualifications and endorsements.

Part V deals with speed limits and includes:
—a new statutory motorway speed limit,
—devolution of power to county councils and county borough corporations to apply speed limits to roads in their areas.

Part VI contains provisions governing regulation of traffic, including parking controls. The main items of significance are:
—the transfer of functions of the Garda Commissioner in relation to the making of traffic and parking bye-laws to the Minister,
—devolution of power to local authorities in relation to the introduction and management of paid parking controls in their areas,
—greater autonomy for local authorities in the implementation of traffic management measures in their areas.

Part VII Miscellaneous

This Part contains miscellaneous provisions including a new power for members of the Garda Siochana to detain and impound vehicles for motor tax or motor insurance offences or where the driver is too young to hold a driving licence

Powers of Entry   s. 39.

(1) A member of the Garda Siochana may for the purpose of arresting a person under section 106 (3A) (inserted by this Act) of the Principal Act, enter without warrant (if need be by use of reasonable force) any place (including a dwelling) where the person is or where the member, with reasonable cause, suspects him to be and, in case the place is a dwelling, the member shall not so enter unless he or another such member has observed the person enter the dwelling concerned.

(2) A member of the Garda Siochana may for the purpose of arresting a person under section 49(8) or 50(10) of the Principal Act. enter without warrant (if need be by use of reasonable force) any place (including the curtilage of a dwelling but not including a dwelling) where the person is or where the member, with reasonable cause, suspects him to be.

(3) A member of the Garda Siochana may, for the purpose of making a requirement of a person under subsection (1) of section 15, enter without warrant any hospital where the person is or where the member, with reasonable cause, suspects him to be.

(4) A designated doctor may, for the purpose of taking from a person a specimen of his blood or being provided by a person with a specimen of his urine under subsection (1) of section 15, enter any hospital where the person is or where the doctor is informed by a member of the Garda Siochana that the person is.

Amendment of section 106 of Principal Act   s. 45.

Section 106 of the Principal Act is hereby amended by the insertion after subsection (3) of the following new subsection:

"(3A) A member of the Garda Siochana may arrest without warrant a person who in the member's opinion is committing or has committed an offence under subsection (3) of this section where the contravention involves or, as may be appropriate, involved non-compliance with paragraph (a) or (b) of subsection (1) of this section, injury was caused to person, a mechanically propelled vehicle was involved in the occurrence of the injury and the first-mentioned person is, or as may be appropriate, was in the member's opinion the driver of the vehicle concerned.".

Amendment of section 107 of Principal Act.   s. 46.

Section 107 of the Principal Act is hereby amended by the insertion after subsection (4) of the following new subsection:

"(4A) (a) A requirement under subsection (4) of this section may be made of a person either personally or in a notice in writing served upon him by registered post.

(b) Notwithstanding the said subsection (4), where a requirement under that subsection is made of a person in a notice served upon him by registered post the person shall not be guilty of an offence unless he fails to comply with the requirement within the time (being not less than 14 days from the date on which the notice was posted) specified in the notice.".

Summary proceedings   s. 48.

(1) Notwithstanding section 10(4) of the Petty Sessions (Ireland) Act, 1851, and subject to subsection (2), summary proceedings for an offence under section 64 or 115 of the Principal Act may be instituted—

(a) at any time within 6 months from the date on which the offence was committed, or

(b) at any time within 3 months from the date on which evidence sufficient, in the opinion of the person by whom the proceedings are instituted, to justify proceedings comes to such person's knowledge,
   whichever is the later.

(2) Summary proceedings mentioned in subsection (1) of this section shall not be instituted later than 3 years from the date on which the offence was committed.

(3) For the purposes of this section, a certificate signed by the person instituting the proceedings or on his behalf by a person authorised by him to sign such a certificate on his behalf stating the date on which evidence described in subsection (1)(b) of this section came to the knowledge of the first mentioned person shall, until the contrary is shown, be sufficient evidence in any proceedings under section 64 or 115 of the Principal Act of the facts stated therein, without proof of any signature on it or that the signatory was the proper person to sign it, and shall, until the contrary is shown, be sufficient evidence of compliance by the first mentioned person with the requirements imposed on him by this section.

Minor and consequential amendments.   s. 49(1)(a)

(iv) by the substitution for the definition of "public place" of the following definition:

"'public place' means—

(a) any public road, and

(b) any street, road or other place to which the public have access with vehicles whether as of right or by permission and whether subject to or free of charge;";

Summary of maximum penalties

Fines and imprisonment:
A maximum fine of £1,000 and/or a maximum of six months imprisonment applies to the following:

—section 10 (section 49 of Road Traffic Act, 1961): driving while under the influence of an intoxicant (no change);

—section 11 (section 50 of Road Traffic Act, 1961): being in charge of a mechanically propelled vehicle while under the influence of an intoxicant (increased—previous penalty for a first offence was a maximum fine of £350 and/or a maximum of three months imprisonment: no change in the case of a second or subsequent offence);

—section 12: refusal or failure to provide a preliminary breath specimen (no change);

—section 13: refusal or failure to provide a breath, blood or urine specimen following arrest or to comply with a requirement of a designated doctor (no change);

—section 14: refusal to accompany a member of the Garda Siochana to a Garda station when suspected of being under the influence of drugs or subsequent refusal or failure to provide a blood or urine specimen or to comply with a requirement of a designated doctor (no change);

—section 15: refusal or failure to provide a blood or urine specimen in a hospital or to comply with a requirement of a designated doctor (new offence);

—section 20: take action (excluding a refusal or failure to provide a specimen) with the intention of frustrating a prosecution (no change).

A maximum fine of £500 and/or a maximum of three months imprisonment will apply to an offence under section 17 of refusing to sign a statement to acknowledge details of the result of a breath test (fine increased from £350).

Consequential Disqualifications (section 26):
Not less than two years for a first offence and not less than four years for a second or subsequent offence within any period of four years* will apply to the following offences:

*The maximum four year period for calculating whether an offence is a first or subsequent offence does not apply to dangerous driving causing death or serious bodily harm .

*—dangerous driving of a mechanically propelled vehicle causing death or serious bodily harm: (increased from one and three years respectively);

—section 10 (section 49 of Road Traffic Act 1961): (increased from one and three

454

years respectively);

—section 11 (section 50 of Road Traffic Act 1961): (increased from nil and six months respectively);

—section 13: (increased — This section replaces the separate "refusal" offences in sections 13 and 14 of the Road Traffic (Amendment) Act, 1978. Different periods currently apply depending upon the section under which the specimen was requested);

—section 14 involving refusal or failure to provide a blood or urine specimen or to comply with a requirement of a designated doctor: (increased from six months);

—section 15: (new offence).

Not less than one year for a first offence and not less than two years for a second or subsequent offence within any period of three years will apply to the following offences:

—dangerous driving of a mechanically propelled vehicle not causing death or serious bodily harm: (increased from nil and 6 months respectively);

—uninsured driving: (increased from nil and 1 year respectively).

Not less than six months will apply to the remaining offences listed in the Second Schedule.

Requirement to obtain a certificate of competency (section 26):

A new requirement to pass a driving test, and obtain a certificate of competency, following consequential disqualification, will apply to the following offences:

—sections 10 and 11 (sections 49 and 50 of Road Traffic Act, 1961);

—sections 13, 14 or 15 involving refusal or failure to provide a specimen or to comply with a requirement of a designated doctor;

—dangerous driving of a mechanically propelled vehicle.